Forces in Modern British Literature

Forces in Modern British Literature

1885—1946

WILLIAM YORK TINDALL

Essay Index Reprint Series

BOOKS FOR LIBRARIES PRESS
FREEPORT, NEW YORK

Reprinted 1970 by arrangement with Alfred A. Knopf, Inc.

STANDARD BOOK NUMBER:
8369-1730-8

LIBRARY OF CONGRESS CATALOG CARD NUMBER:
79-117857

PRINTED IN THE UNITED STATES OF AMERICA

To

ERNEST HUNTER WRIGHT

PREFACE

CONTEMPORARY literature, says T. S. Eliot, "tends to be degrading." However this may be, contemporary British literature is important, better at its best than Victorian literature, which tends so little to be degrading. No Victorian novelist is as good as Joyce, and no Victorian poet as good as Yeats.

This book, an exploration of contemporary British literature, is intended for the reader who knows something about it and wants to know more. Selection was necessary, but I have included many minor writers who are interesting for one reason or another. The arrangement is planned to show the character of contemporary literature as a whole and to emphasize books rather than authors. The year 1885 seemed a good beginning because at that time naturalism and symbolism began to shape British literature; around that time Yeats, Shaw, and Moore commenced their work, and Hopkins was in full career; and shortly after that time Joyce and Virginia Woolf were born. Since almost everything in the literature of the 1940's is implicit in the literature of the 1880's, I have treated the intervening period as a unit. Developments within its complexity determine my chapters. Their patterns are various, at their simplest chronological, suggesting causes and effects; but such patterns are conveniences. My concern has been with meanings and values.

The labyrinth of contemporary British literature is part of a greater design that involves the literatures of America and the Continent. It is foolish to isolate part of this whole, yet impossible in a book of this size to do justice to the whole. By way of compromise I have tried, while considering the part, to preserve a sense of the whole by pointing to connections between British and other literatures, especially French, and between British literature and foreign ideas. Hence the brief accounts of Baudelaire, Zola, Henry James, Bergson, Freud, Kafka, the surrealists, and many others. The footnotes, chiefly bibliographical, will guide those who care to follow additional clues.

Although literature since 1885 constitutes a whole, there is little reason but convenience for separating it from earlier literature. The literature of our time belongs to the great romantic movement with which we associate Wordsworth and Rousseau. Labels like "romantic," at once tiresome and useful, help us to understand the character of a period and of its individual works. But when one says "romantic," one must define, for nothing is more confusing than romanticism and nothing more complex. Because of this complexity the many definers of romanticism, missing the whole, identify one or more of its parts. Like my predecessors, I shall content myself with isolating what I consider some of the principal qualities of romanticism: the transcendental, the exploratory, and the bourgeois.

Since the Renaissance, humanism and science have conspired to make received religion an unsatisfactory vehicle for man's constant aspiration. To satisfy that aspiration some tried to make religion suitable again. Wesleyanism, the Oxford Movement, and synthetic Orientalism are typical results. Others tried to find religious satisfaction in secular objects—in flowers, mountains, ruins, savages, heroes, and the past. Shelley, Thoreau, Carlyle, Rimbaud, Dostoyevsky, Shaw, and D. H. Lawrence come easily to mind. For the eighteenth-century conviction that churches were churches and flowers flowers, these transcendentalists substituted wonder.

Classicism is making the most of limitations. The eighteenth century, having fixed the limits of reality, achieved perfection within them. In poetry the couplet was the type and symbol of limitation and perfection. Jane Austen, perfect in her province, chose to ignore what lay beyond it. But some of her contemporaries, impatient with limits, began to explore regions above, behind, and below her reality. For later artists reality included all nature from the material to the immaterial, all kinds and classes of men, all levels of consciousness. With the aid of science, symbol, and myth these explorers continually penetrated new areas of experience and, at whatever cost to perfection, enriched the arts.

Such enrichment coincided with the emergence of the present ruling class. Limitation was aristocratic. As capital succeeded to land, the revolt against limits became bourgeois. Rapid technical change, so characteristic of bourgeois industry, became characteristic of bourgeois art. Romanticism, becoming an expression of the middle class, became the triumph of middle-class taste. That many romantic artists have been enemies of the middle class is unimportant; for, since a ruling class determines its enemies, our artists and their arts are unmistakably bourgeois. Whether or not we like romanticism and the middle class, we too are middle-class romantics. Contemporary literature excites us not only because it is important, wonderful, expansive, and degrading perhaps, but because it is our expression.

Parts of this book that appeared in *Accent* and the *American Scholar* are reprinted by kind permission of the editors. The librarians of the Columbia University Library were unfailingly helpful. To these, particularly Jean Macalister, Charles Claar, and Jane Davies, I give my warmest thanks. I am no less grateful to James Gilvarry, who lent me many books from his excellent library and shared with me his knowledge of the Irish and English literature in which he is curiously strong. For their learned contributions I thank Edward LeComte, Jean Spaulding, and Ruth Temple. My students, who teach me more than I teach them, have been generous with their aid, especially Bosley Brotman, Edward Easton, Elizabeth Isaacs, Allen Mandelbaum, Irving Massey, Thomas Merton, Rosemary Neiswender, Julia Peebles, Morton Seiden, Grover Smith, Lavita Weissman, A. M. Williams, Arthur Zeiger, and all those who, sitting around tables, explicated texts. For reading what I wrote and for offering suggestions (which, I am glad to say, I took) I owe a great debt to William Bridgwater, Milton Rugoff, Herbert Weinstock, and Cecilia, my wife.

Columbia University
October 15, 1946

W. Y. T.

ACKNOWLEDGMENTS

I am indebted to Dodd, Mead & Company for permission to quote from *The Simpleton of the Unexpected Isles* by Bernard Shaw, copyright, 1936, by Bernard Shaw; to Harcourt, Brace and Company, Inc., for permission to quote from *Mrs. Dalloway, To the Lighthouse,* and *The Common Reader* by Virginia Woolf; to Henry Holt and Company, Inc., for a passage reprinted from "The Listeners" included in *Collected Poems* by Walter de la Mare, copyright, 1920, by Henry Holt and Company; to Alfred A. Knopf, Inc., for permission to quote from *Look at All Those Roses* by Elizabeth Bowen, from *The Plumed Serpent* by D. H. Lawrence, and from *Collected Poems* by Henry Treece; to Brandt & Brandt for permission to quote from Max Beerbohm's *Seven Men,* published by Alfred A. Knopf, Inc., copyright, 1920, by Max Beerbohm; to The Macmillan Company for permission to quote from *The Dynasts* by Thomas Hardy and from *Autobiography, Essays,* and *Collected Poems* by W. B. Yeats; to New Directions for permission to quote from *The World I Breathe* by Dylan Thomas; to Charles Scribner's Sons for permission to quote from *Plays* by August Strindberg; to The Viking Press for permission to quote from *A Portrait of the Artist as a Young Man* by James Joyce; to the family of Gerard Manley Hopkins and to the Oxford University Press for permission to quote from *The Letters of Gerard Manley Hopkins to Robert Bridges.*

I am indebted to Dylan Thomas for permission to quote from a letter printed in *New Verse.*

CONTENTS

Forces in Modern British Literature

CHAPTER I

Exile

THE artist's exile from middle-class society accounts in part for the character of our literature. Causes, if not effects, of this exile are easy to understand. More people than ever before could read, but, while literacy spread, its level fell and fewer could follow what they read. Moral and utilitarian, the ruling class had little tolerance for beauty, which, at best, seemed useless or disreputable. In effect, readers and the ruling class, like republican Plato before them, led the artist to the gates of the city and sent him along.

Accustomed to expressing feelings and ideas shared with a literate audience, poets slowly realized their disinclination or inability to express feelings so much coarser than their own or to celebrate the growing ugliness around them. Byron and Shelley abandoned England, while Carlyle and Arnold scolded on the shore. And on the French coast, looking out of his window, Baudelaire was filled with the "immense nausea of billboards."

Poets occupied their exile with poems and with theories about them. By example and reason they announced the independence of art, its freedom not only from society and moral convention but from nature itself. Some were content to shock the Philistines. Others, retreating into ivory towers, privately pursued naked beauty up the stairs. Pure literature became impure and, after a while, difficult. The enemies of the people, satisfying themselves, left the satisfaction of common taste to journalists and commercial artists.

This situation is the subject of George Gissing's *New Grub Street* (1891). Edwin Reardon, the hero, and to some extent a self-portrait, is kept by refinement, neurosis, and poverty from supplying "good, coarse, marketable stuff for the world's vulgar." By temperament he is unable to curry favor with editors, reviewers, and the literary gang, who, praising friends, damning enemies, tell the ignorant what is what. Jasper Milvain, however, knowing literature a trade, reasonably maintains that "we people of brains are justified in supplying the mob with the food it likes." As his field he takes the "upper middle-class of intellect, the people who like to feel that what they are reading has some special cleverness, but who can't distinguish between stones and paste." Whelpdale descends further than this middle-brow, planning a paper for "the quarter-educated; that is to say, the great new generation that is being turned out by the Board Schools." Adapting themselves to reality, Milvain and Whelpdale are suitably rewarded, but Reardon miserably expires. This novel, Gissing's best, is the best picture of audience and writer in our time. It is bitter, moving, and filled with honest observation; but Gissing weakened the effect by taking extreme examples as types and by mixing self-pity with satire. Self-pity, however, is an emotion of exiles.

As if to prove the soundness of Gissing, Arnold Bennett confessed with disconcerting honesty in *The Truth about an Author* (1903) to sentiments identical with Milvain's; and in his *Journals* (1932) he called himself an artist "with strong mercantile interests." Seeing the nature of his audience, he indefatigably supplied it with trash:

sensational novels, absurd plays, "pocket philosophies," books on how to do this or that. With consequent wealth he bought a yacht, supported a mistress, and expired amidst comforts. But Bennett was an artist as well as a commercial artist. To satisfy himself he sometimes wrote a "serious" work for which he expected no reward. That these works, surprisingly, were as acceptable as the trash he wrote is to be explained perhaps by his acceptance of the world. No artist of our time was less an exile.[1]

I

About the middle of the last century the doctrine of art for art's sake began to encourage the exiled. Affirming the separation of art from middle-class society, art for art's sake implies the autonomy of art and artist, the rejection of didactic aim, and the refusal to subject art to moral or social judgments.[2] A work of art, the exiles said, must be judged by beauty alone. This doctrine, said Tennyson, is "the way to Hell."

An art remote from common life, intolerably pursuing ideals opposite to those of society, may seem evasive. But ivory towers in suburbs are commentaries upon them. Given ugliness and limited morality, and the pursuit of beauty becomes as inevitable and useful as the antimacassar. If this art is to be justified by beauty alone, its position becomes less sure. But many of the works produced in the name of beauty are equal in beauty to those of Tennyson.

Art for the sake of art, which flowered during the eighties and nineties in the work of Wilde, Moore, and

[1] *A Great Man* (1904), is a cynical picture of the popular novelist and his public. Cf. Virginia Woolf on the "Middlebrow," *The Death of the Moth* (1942).

[2] Albert J. Farmer: *Le Mouvement esthétique et "décadent" en Angleterre* (1931). Louise Rosenblatt: *L'Idée de l'art pour l'art dans la littérature anglaise pendant la période victorienne* (1931). William Gaunt: *The Aesthetic Adventure* (1945).

Symons and later in the work of Joyce, had many roots in the past. Its ultimate origins were in the German romantic philosophers and in Keats and Poe. Rossetti, isolated from society, revived Keats and offered an art without moral or social purpose. Morris, desolated by the ugliness around him, tried to restore beauty to useful things. Gautier in *Mademoiselle de Maupin* (1834), Baudelaire in his poems and in his preface to Poe, and Flaubert in his novels illustrated or recommended art for art's sake. Getting the doctrine from them, Whistler brought it to Swinburne, whose essays pugnaciously defended *Poems and Ballads* (1866) from his middle-class critics. While Swinburne inflamed the young, Walter Pater seduced them. In the famous conclusion to his *Renaissance* (1873), where gemlike flames consumed them as they discriminated moments for the moments' sake, Pater summarized his German, French, and English predecessors in a prose that was itself the best argument for the cause of art. *Marius the Epicurean* (1885), tempered by Pater's almost religious asceticism, proved almost as seductive. Young men read these books, exaggerated what they read, and painted the nineties yellow.

Young Oscar Wilde discovered beauty at Oxford, where amid his fabulous blue china he read Swinburne, Rossetti, Baudelaire, and Pater, whose *Renaissance* became his "golden book."[3] Upon his graduation Wilde became apostle of beauty to the Philistines. Basing his conduct upon that of Swinburne and Baudelaire, his beautiful costume of velveteen shorts and silk stockings upon what he

[3] Hesketh Pearson: *The Life of Oscar Wilde* (1946). Arthur Ransome: *Oscar Wilde* (1912). André Gide: *Si le grain ne meurt* (1920). Vincent O'Sullivan: *Aspects of Wilde* (1936). Frank Harris: *Oscar Wilde* (1916). Robert Sherard: *Bernard Shaw, Frank Harris and Oscar Wilde* (1936).

In *De Profundis* Wilde refers to *The Renaissance* as "that book which has had such strange influence over my life." See T. S. Eliot's attack on Pater in *The Eighteen-eighties* (1930), edited by Walter de la Mare.

thought Rossetti meant, Wilde astounded Piccadilly. He was extravagant but shrewd. His shocking presence was designed not only to dramatize the ideas of the æsthetic philosophers but to make himself known. It did. Consequently his *Poems* (1881) went through five editions. In these mediocre verses, which, anticipating Eliot's, summarize the past by theft and allusion, Wilde urged the Spirit of Beauty to elevate the "cheating merchants." Seeing little harm as yet in this eccentric, they caricatured his poppy and his lily in *Punch.* In *Patience* (1881) W. S. Gilbert, cleverly reflecting popular judgment, presented Wilde as an æsthetic sham, whose anti-Philistine excesses might be attributed to Rossetti and Swinburne. But America had never heard of Wilde. That *Patience* might have point, D'Oyly Carte, the producer, hired Wilde in 1882 to make a lecture tour of the States. He consented to this Philistine plan because it gave him further publicity and the chance to spread his gospel. A cartoon by Max Beerbohm shows the apostle of beauty confronting bearded farmers. He exhorted them to abandon morality for beauty, to liberate art from didactic purpose, to beautify dress, furniture, and pots.[4] He told them of Rossetti, Swinburne, and Whistler. Of the sunflower and the lily he observed: "We love these flowers in spite of what Mr. Gilbert may tell you, not for any vegetable fashion at all, but because they are elegant in design."

Whistler, who had brought the word to Swinburne, now brought it in his Chelsea studio to Wilde and sharpened his wit. Annoyed with Wilde's vulgarization of beauty, Whistler said in *Ten O'clock* (1885) that art is so far beyond the understanding of the public, who judge it by its subject and its morality, that the attempt of ama-

[4] In America Wilde delivered lectures on "The English Renaissance" and "Decorative Art in America." Lloyd Lewis and Henry Smith: *Oscar Wilde Discovers America* (1936).

teur æsthetes to make it popular is absurd. Art is superior not only to Wilde and the public, but to nature. This brilliant statement of art for the artist's sake annoyed Wilde, who, defending the æsthetic movement in the *Pall Mall Gazette,* affirmed that poets, not painters, were the proper judges of art. The controversy continued in the *World.* Whistler called Wilde a simple sunflower, and Wilde him a butterfly. Whistler, wittier than Wilde, won.

> What has Oscar in common with Art? except that he dines at our tables and picks from our platters the plums for the pudding he peddles in the provinces. Oscar—the amiable, irresponsible, esurient Oscar—with no more sense of a picture than of the fit of a coat, has the courage of the opinions . . . of others.[5]

Wilde appears to have been moved. Abandoning his æsthetic costume and his attempt to vulgarize beauty, he adopted, like Whistler, the deportment of the dandy and proceeded to justify Whistler's charge of unoriginality by using *Intentions* (1891) to make Whistler's extreme position more extreme. Art, says Wilde in these essays, is so independent of common morality that it is immoral, so superior to nature that it is artificial, so remote from subject matter that it expresses nothing but itself. The names of Gautier, Baudelaire, Pater, and Swinburne, cited to support this extravagance, reveal his other sources. His originality is his style, which with paradox, reversal of popular saying, and epigram gave new point to old doctrine. "Nothing," he said, "succeeds like excess."

This manifesto was only the beginning. Wilde shocked the public more with immoral, witty art. In *The Picture of Dorian Gray* (1891) Lord Henry, a dandy who despises the ugly middle class, expounds to innocent Dorian the

[5] For the controversy, see Whistler: *The Gentle Art of Making Enemies* (1890). "The Soul of Man under Socialism," Wilde's plea for anarchism, is his most comprehensive statement of the conflict of artist and public.

New Hedonism, a mixture of Huysmans and Pater. The search for new experiences, each more exquisite than the last, leads Dorian, like a depraved Marius, to varieties of sin; for like the middle class he confuses vice with art and vice versa. Cautiously reviewing this story in the *Bookman,* Pater called Dorian's career "an unsuccessful experiment in Epicureanism, in life as a fine art." The public was less moderate. Angry journalists found Wilde intolerable. In his prefatory epigrams Wilde told these moralists that "all art is quite useless"; in letters to the press he found his book too moral to be good; and in private he called it "vicious but perfect."

Although Wilde amused and flattered them in his harmless plays, respectable men, seeing him as their enemy, bided their time. His strange amours, which proved that artists as well as art are above received morality, gave the respectable their chance. Wilde's imprisonment in 1895 was a penalty more severe perhaps than one deserved whose principal, if not his capital, sin was imprudence. But his punishment was less the punishment of particular misdemeanors than the symbolic revenge of a class upon artists and their arts.

George Moore's amours were prudent or fictive. Hence his safety among Philistines; but Moore incurred, if not the penalty of their laws, their censure. They blamed him for seeing life whole in novels he wrote according to the methods of Zola and Flaubert. The circulating libraries, which could make or break an author, banned his books. In *Confessions of a Young Man* (1888) Moore attacks those who would subject all literature to the requirements of young ladies. Using the arguments of Swinburne and Gautier, he proclaims the freedom of the artist and of art, which he illustrates as shockingly as possible. He would gladly sacrifice the virtue of innumerable models, he boasts, for one glorious picture. A pagan in evening dress, he describes his horrid pleasures. In *Modern Painting* (1893), essays on the French, he repeats Whistler's views on the unimportance of subject and morality.

But Pater was Moore's principal model and his philosopher. In 1885 he read *Marius* and found that English, no less than French, was capable of style. This book became his "Bible"; he praised Pater in his *Confessions* and sent him a copy. In 1889 he met Pater, whose British reserve, tried by Moore's Irish impulsiveness, sought refuge in Oxford. But Moore persisted in his devotion and under Pater's spell discovered the sentence, the paragraph, and finally, to Wilde's amusement, style.

To Moore, literature, already separated from society, became style, separated from substance. Decreasingly interested in what he said and increasingly in how he said it, he experimented in memoir and novel with pure, then purer style. The full effects of this development were not obvious until *The Brook Kerith* (1916) and *Héloïse and Abélard* (1921), which may be read for style alone, but if read for substance are less readable. In *Pure Poetry* (1924), an anthology, inspired by Abbé Brémond, of poetry separated from intellectual, social, or moral substance, Moore applied to poetry the principles he had applied so well to prose. Art for art's sake and the school of Pater and Flaubert could expect no further triumph.[6]

Pure poetry and the cult of Pater were also the ideals of the Rhymers' Club, founded in 1891 by William Butler Yeats, Ernest Rhys, and T. W. Rolleston. Of the ten or twelve members Arthur Symons, Ernest Dowson, and Lionel Johnson, besides the founders, were the chief. At the Cheshire Cheese they read to one another the poems they published in two anthologies. They considered Dow-

[6] See Moore's remarks on style in *Avowals* (1919), and *Conversations in Ebury Street* (1924). Charles Morgan: *Epitaph on George Moore* (1935), analyzes the style.

son the best poet, Johnson, the second, and Yeats the third. Apart from society in the Cheshire Cheese, their Latin Quarter, they pursued beauty as far as decorum allowed. In this refuge from confusion and the times, they breathed the atmosphere of Pater, which was too thin for life. Yeats and Rhys adapted themselves to external reality; the others succumbed, falling off stools in pubs, collapsing in gutters, jumping off cliffs, or going mad. Their lives, according to Yeats, reflect the disparity between world and ideal, their verses all that is opposite to their lives.[7]

The poems of Dowson fix fine sensations and moods, finding in purity of form a vehicle that is its own end. Fastidious in diction, deliberate in craft, they celebrate the fleeting moment. Perfect, minor, "Neobule" and "Villanelle of Sunset" attenuate the tradition of Swinburne, Poe, and Flaubert. Dowson's most famous poem, "*Non sum qualis eram bonæ sub regno Cynaræ*," symbolizes the conflict between Pater's ideal and reality. Flinging roses, crying for madder music, stronger wine, Dowson follows the course of Dorian Gray and all the students of sensation.[8]

Johnson wrote ascetic, marmoreal verse, says Yeats, to subdue disorder, his age's and his own. A traditionalist like Dowson, he sought refuge in the manner of Dryden and Gray. Yet this all but classical verse reflects the other

[7] The best accounts of the group are in Yeats: *Autobiography*, Ernest Rhys: *Everyman Remembers* (1931), John Davidson: *Earl Lavender* (1895). Anthologies: *The Book of the Rhymers' Club* (1892), *The Second Book of the Rhymers' Club* (1894).

For the æsthetic nineties see Holbrook Jackson: *The Eighteen Nineties* (1913), Osbert Burdett: *The Beardsley Period* (1925), William Rothenstein: *Men and Memories* (Vol. I, 1931), B. I. Evans: *English Poetry in the Later Nineteenth Century* (1933). Anthologies: A. J. A. Symons: *An Anthology of Nineties Verse* (1929); Donald Davidson: *British Poetry of the Eighteen-nineties* (1937).

[8] *The Poetical Works of Dowson* (1934), edited by Desmond Flower. *Verses* (1896). *Decorations* (1899). Mark Longaker: *Ernest Dowson* (1944).

side of Pater, his religious austerity. In an essay on Pater, Johnson, who had been Pater's student at Oxford, condemns those who, misinterpreting the master, "live for a succession of exquisite emotions, the gifts of beauty in nature and in art." Pater, his true follower proclaims, had no followers; and reading Johnson's excellent, cold poem "By the Statue of King Charles at Charing Cross," one finds it hard to disagree.[9]

The verses of Arthur Symons, devoted to exquisite emotions, each more exquisite, owe almost as much to Pater as to Baudelaire. From the *Renaissance* and from a visit to the master, Symons learned that life and prose could be fine arts. Burning with a hard gemlike flame must have held for adolescent Welsh Methodists like Symons an attractiveness that staggers the imagination.[10]

Contemplating his contemporaries in *The Works of Max Beerbohm* (1896), Max Beerbohm devoted one essay to Wilde and the cult of Rossetti, another to Pater. These essays constitute the obituary of æstheticism by an aloof, eminently reasonable young man on whom, Wilde said, the gods had bestowed the gift of perpetual old age. Of the year 1880 Beerbohm observes: "To give an accurate and exhaustive account of that period would need a far less brilliant pen than mine." Although when at school, he says in "Diminuendo," he read Pater in bed by the light of a dark lantern, he was disappointed, upon coming to Oxford, by Pater's military demeanor and bright dogskin gloves. The cult of the moment was too arduous in any case; for to be at the focus of all experience, as Pater advised, one would have to be the Prince of Wales.

[9] *Poetical Works* (1915), edited by Ezra Pound; *Poems* (1895). *Ireland* (1897). *Post Liminium* (1912), essays. Arthur Patrick: *Lionel Johnson* (1939).

[10] *Collected Poems* (1902); *Days and Nights* (1889); *Silhouettes* (1892); *Images of Good and Evil* (1899). Symons wrote two essays and a book on Pater.

"I belong," sighed Beerbohm, announcing its end, "to the Beardsley period."

Yeats too belonged. He was the friend of Wilde and Symons and all the Rhymers. His poetry and more especially his prose of the nineties reveal the cult of Morris and Rossetti. Like Swinburne before him, Yeats based his æsthetics largely upon Blake's and conformed to the laws, not of society, but of the imagination. Looking back in his introduction to *The Oxford Book of Modern Verse* (1936) at the poets of his group, Yeats saw Pater behind their abandonment of "moral earnestness" and their attempt to "purify poetry of all that is not poetry." The style of "Rosa Alchemica," a story Yeats published in the *Savoy,* shows this influence. So does the increasing richness of his expository prose, which began simply enough and ended by almost defeating its purpose. The trouble with the splendid prose, so rhythmic, suggestive, and metaphorical, of his collected essays is that it does not say what it means; and that is the trouble with *A Vision* (1925), which the clearest style might leave unclear.

But communication was of small concern to an enemy of the people. Yeats's father, an artist without commercial talents, had taught his son to despise getting ahead and to hold in contempt those who had got ahead. That contempt embraced the middle-class world. Yeats addressed his writings to men outside this world, to poets, peasants, and aristocrats, who would know by instinct and tradition what he meant. In his essay "What is Popular Poetry?" (1901) he glances with disdain at those who, conforming to the requirements of the middle class, have written abstract, didactic verse. "The triviality of emotion, the poverty of ideas, the imperfect sense of Beauty" of Longfellow, for example, or Mrs. Hemans or even Burns, show their remoteness from the great tradition.[11]

[11] J. B. Yeats: *Letters to his Son* (1944). W. B. Yeats: *Essays* (1924).

When Yeats set out to reform Ireland and liberate her, he found himself in a quandary. The situation demanded didactic, patriotic poetry and propaganda in prose; the Irish middle class cried for this poetry and this prose. But, refusing to compromise with his ideal of art for art's sake, he set about the work of reform with a difficult poetry of music and suggestion and the prose of Walter Pater. He would enchant them with beauty. His defeat was inevitable, and, on the whole, good for his poetry, which got from it the loftiness it lacked.

The other master of English in our time, James Joyce, was no less indebted to the æstheticism of the nineties, but he hid it like a Jesuit. Refusing to accept the "tyranny of the mediocre," young Stephen Daedalus of *Stephen Hero* (1944) calls himself an "outlaw" and makes a philosophy of self-expression.[12] The æsthetic theory that he expounds here and in *A Portrait of the Artist* (1916), though based upon sentences from Aquinas, has no place in it for religious, moral, or social purpose. Art, says Stephen, is the "human disposition of sensible or intelligible matter for an esthetic end," and beauty, which resides in the most pleasing relations of part to part, has three qualities: "wholeness, harmony, radiance." Good art is static, above desire or loathing; bad is kinetic, either pornographic or didactic. "That," says Lynch, "has the true scholastic stink." The president of the Jesuit college with whom Stephen debates this theory in *Stephen Hero* is even more penetrating. To use Aquinas in order to justify art for art's sake, he moderately observes, is paradoxical.

It took a Jesuit to see what Jesuitical Joyce had done. Reared during the nineties by Yeats and the Jesuits, Joyce had combined his two traditions. He admired the Paterite

[12] *Stephen Hero* is part of an early version of *A Portrait.* The spelling is Daedalus in the first, Dedalus in the second.

prose of Yeats so much that he committed the stories to memory and imitated their rhythms in his own essay on Mangan. Echoes of Yeats's poetry fill Joyce's prose. The delicate, pseudo-Elizabethan verses of *Chamber Music* (1907) strain memories of Ben Jonson through the tradition of Dowson and Yeats.[13] That, perhaps, is why Arthur Symons found them good. "The good," says Stephen, echoing the nineties, "is the beautiful." But Joyce was to pursue unsocial beauty into obscurities beyond the lights of the English nineties. The prose that he developed for these further excursions was not in the tradition of Pater or Yeats but in that of Flaubert and the symbolists, and, like Flaubert's, Joyce's prose does its work with precision.

The critical habit of the æsthetes was generally impressionistic. For this Pater was also responsible; but he had examples in Hazlitt and Baudelaire. A skeptic, disillusioned about all certainties but his senses and perceptions, Pater also followed Kant. The æsthetic critic, Pater says in the preface to *The Renaissance,* looks for pleasurable sensations, each unique, in the fairer forms of art. His aim is to know his "impression" as it really is. What the book or picture is hardly matters. What, Pater asks, is it "to *me*?" After determining the unique impression, the critic may support his feeling by analysis or find its causes in history. In his criticism of La Gioconda, Pater does not tell us about the picture but about his feeling about it.

In "The Critic as Artist," a dialogue in *Intentions,* Wilde repeats Pater's ideas with some exaggeration. The æsthetic critic, he says, does not analyze or tell the history of an object, but on the basis of his impression, exploiting his personality, creates a new work of art, often better than the object. Only a poet, he continues, can be a critic. In practice, however, he criticized by epigram.

George Moore, who called Pater the "president of the

[13] Joyce's later poems are in *Pomes Penyeach* (1927).

high court of criticism," says in *Impressions and Opinions* (1891): "I understand criticism more as the story of the critic's soul than as an exact science." Of Rimbaud he says: "My object is . . . to convey a sensation of this strange boy." Moore's criticism of literature in this book and in his *Confessions* is impressionistic; but in *Modern Painting* (1893), on a subject of which he had some technical knowledge, he is often analytic and controversial.

Under Pater's personal direction, Symons most closely approximated the method of the master. "On Criticism" in *Dramatis Personæ* (1923) and the essay on Pater in *Studies in Prose and Verse* (1904) praise Pater for making criticism a fine art. Fixing the peculiar quality of each work, determining its effect upon his soul, extracting the essence of beautiful moments, noting nuances, the critic, says Symons, appreciates the good and ignores the bad. Good critics, like the Goncourts, aim to "give sensation, to flash the impression of the moment." From the eighties to recent times Pater's method commonly appealed to those who, revolting against the external world, whether of science or society, wanted a congenial refuge.

The criticism of Virginia Woolf is the climax of this romantic tradition. Her *Common Reader* (1925) and its sequel, showing the familiar prejudice against analysis, history, and scholarship, reflect her anti-intellectual position and the delicacy of her feelings. An essay on Hazlitt gives her principles. This critic, she says, "builds up with the freest use of imagery and colour the brilliant ghost that the book has left glimmering in his mind. The poem is re-created in glowing phrases. . . . He singles out the peculiar quality of his author." In the essay on Christina Rossetti, Virginia Woolf restates the critic's aim: "to expose the mind bare to the poem and transcribe in all its haste and imperfection whatever may be the result of the impact." Haste and imperfection, however, are no part of her work. She was as meticulous as Pater, whom she echoed, and the most benign and generous of critics.

Recent critics of impressionism have been less generous. In *Principles of Literary Criticism* (1924) I. A. Richards attacks it as inexact, and art for art's sake as mistaken. Rebelling against the moralists, the æsthetes, thinking art different in kind from other experiences, fell into worse error. For art, says Richards, differs from other experiences only in higher organization; and form, despite Whistler and Clive Bell, cannot be separated from substance. Although crude, moralists are nearer than æsthetes to the truth. Moral, utilitarian, pragmatic, Richards proposes in place of impressionism a method based upon pseudo-science. The critic, unconcerned with moving the reader, must determine meaning by semantic analysis, and value by behavioristic psychology.[14]

T. S. Eliot, who classes Richards among bad critics, also rebelled against the school of Pater and Symons. In the essays on criticism in *The Sacred Wood* (1920) and in *The Use of Poetry and the Use of Criticism* (1933) he says that criticism must be objective, impersonal, cold, making use of comparison and analysis to support the sensibility. To the impressionists, criticism was a kind of poetry, but poetry misdirected; for although criticism enters poetry, poetry must not enter criticism. The unpoetical critic, Aristotle, Dryden or Gourmont, displaying universal intelligence, avoids the condition of Symons. Eliot's criticism, as one might suppose, is dogmatic and austere; and its tone, as he confesses, is one of "pontifical solemnity." Its happiest effects are those of tone, taste, and poetry. The value lies in those poetic penetrations (of intellects at the tips of senses or of Marvell's identity with Laforgue) which have served to misguide a generation

[14] In *Coleridge on Imagination* (1934), condemning Pater as meaningless, Richards renews his plea for scientific criticism.

through the past. It is difficult, however, to see how these happy conceits differ from the impressions of Pater or Symons except in greater brilliance.

Although condemned as "emotive," impressionism or the sensitive reader's response to a book, which after all is what concerns other readers next to their own response, is as valuable as analysis or dogma, and perhaps their basis. Impressionism differs in manner and tone from the methods of Richards and Eliot, but it also fixes fine shades and the quintessence of things.

"To fix the last fine shade, the quintessence of things," says Arthur Symons in "The Decadent Movement in Literature,"[15] is the "ideal of the Decadence." Decadent, an epithet applied by Philistine malice to impressionists and æsthetes, was received by them as a badge of distinction. Symons, Wilde, and, in France, the generation of Laforgue were called and called themselves decadent. The word, however, does not imply value, but rather a difference in character due to time. A decadent work may be good or bad, better or worse than nondecadent works; but it differs in nature from those of an earlier period as Camembert differs from Gruyère. Both are good; but Camembert has a past.

A literary tradition, having exhausted its normal possibilities, invites three courses. The poet may imitate the perfect expression of his predecessors, in which case he is dead. He may start a new tradition, but this is permitted to few and only with the help, apparently, of social change. Or, keeping within the limits of the old tradition, he may make it extraordinary. This poet is decadent.

Pope and Swift perfectly expressed the Augustan tra-

[15] Published 1893, reprinted in *Dramatis Personæ* (1923). This manifesto is an answer to an essay against decadence by Richard Le Gallienne (1892), reprinted in *Retrospective Reviews* (1896). Cf. Le Gallienne's "Decadent to His Soul," *English Poems* (1892).

dition, Erasmus Darwin and Gibbon its decadence. Darwin is inferior in value to Pope, but it cannot be said that Gibbon is remarkably inferior to Swift. With the help of the French Revolution, Wordsworth started a new tradition, which expressed itself in the work of his contemporaries and the early Victorians. After such perfection nothing was left for Wilde and his contemporaries but imitation, the course of William Watson, or extraordinary variation, the course of all artists with life in them. Although Wilde is inferior to Wordsworth, Yeats is not.

There is reason to call contemporary literature the literature of romantic decadence. This does not mean that all our works are decadent, for some are imitative and dead. The good alone are decadent. The allusiveness of Eliot, the artificiality of Edith Sitwell, the transcendentalism of Huxley, the complexity of Joyce and Dylan Thomas, the deliquescence of Virginia Woolf, are not only romantic but, compared with customary strangeness, strange. "Strangeness added to beauty," which Pater, defining his quality, called the quality of romanticism, better defines its decadence.

The decadents of the nineties differ from their successors in being aware of their condition and proud of it. Symons was an ostentatious decadent. In "The Decadent Movement in Literature" he finds the younger generation enjoying the "*maladie de fin de siècle,*" that "new and beautiful and interesting disease." Artificial, morbid, without simplicity or sanity, he and his companions, refining upon refinement, seek the exceptional and the remote. As might be expected, the verses that Symons composed before and after this manifesto are decadent, especially the hothouse verses on the hothouse.[16]

Oscar's garden must have supplied it. A carnation, like a primrose, is Wordsworthian; but a green carnation,

[16] "Violet," in *London Nights* (1895).

though of the family, is abnormal. Although a lily is romantic, a gilded lily is decadent.[17] As Wilde observes in "The Critic as Artist":

> The subject-matter at the disposal of creation becomes every day more limited in extent and variety. Providence and Mr. Walter Besant have exhausted the obvious. . . . The old roads and dusty highways have been traversed too often. Their charm has been worn away . . . and they have lost that element of novelty or surprise which is so essential for romance.

Under these circumstances, he continues, the artist must seek out fine moods, exquisite moments, curious new sensations. No better definition of decadence has been framed. Nor has decadence been more obviously illustrated, as Symons said, than by *Dorian Gray,* "The Sphinx," or *Salomé.* Cyril in "The Decay of Lying" belongs to the Tired Hedonists' Club, whose members, adoring Domitian, wear faded roses. But "the very flower of decadence," said Wilde, is Pater's *Renaissance,* which should have provoked the last trump. The decorative elegance of Beardsley, the exquisite refinement of Dowson, and the depravity of John Gray are no less extraordinary than Oscar's garden. But these are products of the declining century, and since the disgrace of Wilde, decadence, displaying itself in private, has become obscure.

II

Of the difficult writers in our time, some are exiles from middle-class society, others followers of these exiles. The

[17] In *The Green Carnation* (1894), Robert Hichens burlesqued the enormities of Wilde and his followers. In *Degeneration* (translated 1895), Max Nordau mistook decadence for disease. However foolish his conclusions, his analysis is almost as sound as that of Mario Praz, whose *Romantic Agony* (1933) traces the decadence to its romantic roots.

French symbolists have been perhaps the most influential of the exiles and the most obscure. It is among the followers of the symbolists that one finds in its perfection the obscurity nowadays so characteristic of polite letters. Some of these followers themselves are exiled, others fashionable, some both.

Baudelaire was an exile; his poetry, in a sense, was private. But he never had recourse to that obscurity which later on became the response of those in his position. The French classical tradition of clarity and craftsmanship remained too strong for him to break, and he translated his hallucinations into the clear, impeccable, and final terms of his tradition. Whatever his implications, he drew his images from familiar reality and maintained coherence on the manifest level where he might outrage the reader without confusion. "I have cultivated my hysteria," he remarked; but he cultivated it in the manner of a formal gardener.

Before glancing at his informal successors it might be well to consider the case of another early exile who went further toward predestined obscurity. Gerard Manley Hopkins, a spiritual exile from the heretics of his time, was a literary exile from them and from the Jesuits to whom he had fled. Isolation and faithfulness to his own nature produced those maddening ellipses, those distortions of common usage, those syntactical innovations which even today keep his poetry from common readers. The knowledge that he had no audience but Robert Bridges exempted him from the obligation to temper his honesty. "I do not write for the public," he said, and added: "No doubt my poetry errs on the side of singularity," but "indeed I was not over-desirous that the meaning of all should be quite clear." He confessed he was dismayed that Bridges found him unintelligible; but it was his aim, said Hopkins, to express, not to communicate:

> If it is possible to express a subtle and recondite thought on a subtle and recondite subject in a subtle and recondite way and with great felicity and perfection, in the end, something must be sacrificed, with so trying a task, in the process, and this may be the being at once, nay perhaps even the being without explanation at all, intelligible.[18]

They disorder these things better in France. Exile, which permitted Hopkins to cultivate his honesty, drove the followers of Baudelaire to extremes of privacy that make Hopkins seem almost social. Since Hopkins remained unpublished until 1918, it was permitted the French to teach future exiles a becoming obscurity.

Rimbaud was a better teacher than Scotus. This genius of fifteen emerged from a middle-class home, looked at the world, and found it "full of grocers." Following Baudelaire, he proceeded first to shock and confound them, and then, leaving grocers to their grocery, he tried to penetrate the unknown. The defeat of this endeavor caused him to abandon poetry and to become, like his grocer, a man of substance. That gun-running in Abyssinia which has been considered his exile from society was not an exile, however, but rather, like the top hat he purchased in London, a symbolic, bitter, and self-mortifying acceptance of things as they are. The exile of Rimbaud was his life in France while still a poet. "One is an exile," he exclaimed, "in one's own country."

Exile brought privacy and obscurity with it. He did not write for grocers, but for himself. He made no attempt to make his poems comprehensible or, indeed, to publish them. Turning what Verlaine called the "face of an exiled angel" inside out, he embarked upon an exploration of his unconscious. Logic and the categories of reason were discarded. He suppressed the interference of his conscious

[18] Quotations are from *The Letters of Gerard Manley Hopkins to Robert Bridges* (1935).

mind by drugs, fatigue, and depravity, and penetrated beyond his deranged senses to the domain of dream and madness where few could follow him. In *Illuminations*, that great, strange, and very private book, he made words express vision and, using them as a means of discovery rather than of expression, compelled them to do what they cannot do. "I noted the inexpressible," he said. Had Dr. Johnson been around, that sociable man might have observed of Rimbaud as he once observed of some obscure eighteenth-century predecessor: "Sir, if Mr. X has experienced the unutterable, Mr. X should not attempt to utter it."

Observing the manners of Rimbaud, Mallarmé, and the other exiles, Jean Moréas in 1886 decided to assert their patterns as principles, to make obscurity, if not an end, an estimable means, and to declare the poet's independence of the common reader. Once established, the pattern would serve as a guide for younger exiles; and even for those who were as yet indifferent to exile it would be a badge of unfashionable fashion. Moréas made it clear that the symbolist poem, avoiding description, statement, logic, and references to matters external to itself, was a complex structure of overtones, indirections, and private images.

The labyrinth of obscurity had been established, and poets great and small, exiled and fashionable, honest and knavish, followed its conventions as the only normal course for men so abnormal as they. By the time of the surrealists Rimbaud was not the only guide to the country he explored, for by this time Freud and Jung had come to his assistance. Reason and common sense, the hope of classicist and bourgeois alike, had ceased to please. The increasing disorder of society had turned the eyes of artists within and above themselves. The new physics, displacing old dogmas of matter and continuity, now permitted truths of equal validity to exist on several levels, and, seeming to affirm the unimportance of cause and effect, reinvited the metaphysical and the irrational.

The symbolist tradition from Baudelaire to surrealism produced much of the greatest poetry of our time. It is a pity that this poetry should remain unintelligible to the society that unintentionally produced it. The decay of logical structure, its replacement by free association and the unconscious, the conception by poets of the poem as a self-contained organism with internal but without clear external references, the natural desire to baffle the vulgar, the emphasis upon expression rather than communication—all these, while improving poetry, have placed it beyond the common understanding. The separation of poet from audience, which gave poetry its present character, must be deplored even by its readers as socially unhealthy. But the blame for this separation falls more perhaps upon society than upon the poet; for society exiled the poet before he exiled himself. And popular education, confirming exile, continues to prepare the reader for Tennyson.

In England the French symbolist tradition did not produce significant obscurities until around 1910. For the æsthetes of the nineties the strangeness of Baudelaire was enough. They knew of Mallarmé and Rimbaud, but their obscurity was too advanced perhaps to suit the purposes of more backward exiles. With the appearance of T. S. Eliot, however, French obscurity found British tongue.

Eliot was an exile in a society composed of Sweeney, Bleistein, Krumpacker, Klipstein, and of Burbank and Prufrock at its best. "I have never," Eliot once said in an address to Americans, "I have never met Sweeney on a footing of social equality." Men of such sensibility are among our principal exports.

As he got the word "sensibility" from the French critics,

so from Laforgue he got the idea of incoherence, of free association, and of poetry as a drama of suggestive images and overtones. To this he and Pound added the allusiveness of disappointed professors. Although Eliot's difficulty comes largely from his careful suppression of intellect, for a long time it was customary to call him an intellectual poet. His pedantry, his ceaseless praise of the marriage of feeling and intellect, and his denial of emotion obscured the fact that he is a very emotional poet.

Eliot has used his rational prose to explain the irrationality of his verse. His essays, better as manifesto than criticism, compose the best rationalization of obscurity. The seasoned reader, he says, does not bother to understand poetry. He just enjoys it. He himself, confesses Eliot, enjoyed the French long before he could understand them. They had omitted transitions, statements, logical framework, and other things of low intensity. They were complex; for the complexity of our civilization, playing on a refined sensibility, trying to be true to thought and feeling at once, must produce complexity. Moreover, poetry is as unintellectual as a secretion. The meaning or prose sense of a poem is superfluous, and if there at all, is there to keep the mind of the reader diverted while the poem does its work. The work of the poem is not communication. Standing alone between poet and reader, the poem corresponds to the feeling of the poet and may excite a feeling in the reader, but the poet may feel pink, the reader blue. These essays are of social significance; for through them Eliot has tempered the loneliness of recent poets, who, thanks to him, enjoy a considerable audience. They are read by other poets and by his readers.

Joyce's exile was darker than Eliot's and more genuine. In *The Day of the Rabblement* (1901), a two-page pamphlet directed against the Irish Literary Theatre for coming to terms with the public, Joyce says: "No man can be a lover of the true or the good unless he abhors the multitude; and the artist, though he may employ the crowd, is very careful to isolate himself." Employing the crowd, Joyce maintained this isolation, increased it by physical exile, and created characters to illustrate the exile of their creator. Stephen Dedalus, whose name implies the artist martyred by society, deliberately severed his connections with mother, church, and country. "I will not serve that in which I no longer believe," he says, "whether it call itself my home, my fatherland or my church: and I will try to express myself in some mode of life or art as freely as I can and as wholly as I can, using for my defence the only arms I allow myself to use, silence, exile and cunning." Mr. Bloom and H. C. Earwicker are outlanders and symbolic exiles. And by its title and implications the play *Exiles* reveals Joyce's preoccupation with his state. Although he felt that art can exist today only in isolation from society, Joyce suffered from a sense of guilt over his own exile. Stephen's hunt for a father, his brooding over his mother, and his almost unwholesome concern with country and church show Joyce's longing, never to be gratified, to recover what he had renounced.

The early works are simple enough. But as Joyce's exile deepened he became more and more deeply involved with himself. His mind, lost in the labyrinth of its own being, turned in upon itself, and to express what it found there, turned naturally to the French tradition. In *Finnegans Wake* Joyce surpassed Rimbaud in creating a self-contained private universe into which he might retire to deepen his exile and his sense of guilt. Exile and guilt are among the recurring themes of *Finnegans Wake*. Both are expressed in the fragmentary and distorted allusions to St. Augustine's phrase "*securus iudicat orbis terrarum.*"[19] The passage to which this phrase belongs is significant:

[19] *Finnegans Wake,* pp. 76, 96, 263, 513, 593.

"The calm judgment of the world is that those men cannot be good who in any part of the world cut themselves off from the rest of the world."

Since Joyce never expected to find the "ideal reader with an ideal insomnia" who could read his book, it is not clear why he bothered to publish it unless even the exiled ego requires this social support. But the few imperfect readers he has secured are as grateful to him for this inconsistency as the commoner reader is indifferent. True to the policy of silence, exile, and cunning, Joyce issued no explanations. But his fellow exiles in Paris, Stuart Gilbert, Eugene Jolas, and Elliot Paul, published a manifesto that, since it seems not to refer to their work, may refer to his.[20] Proclaiming the end of grammar and communication, the autonomy of the imagination in search of a fabulous world, the litany and hallucination of the word, and the triumph of Rimbaud, they stated what the tradition of exile implied: "the plain reader be damned."

The course of Henry James had been similar to that of Joyce. From Flaubert, James received that conception of the novel as art which he announced in *Partial Portraits* (1888). Although his ideas resembled those of Swinburne and Pater, James never came into conflict with the middle class; for his treatment of their depravity as a psychological problem of the most delicate sort and as the only surviving tradition in a disordered world was too subtle to offend. Since it was his misfortune, however, to be a little repelled by what he adored, he was forced to save elegance by indirection. As he saved it he became more and more complicated until he lost his audience and wrote for himself and a few friends. The need for communication no longer impeded the development of a style which, expanding in qualifications, hints, self-conscious colloquialisms, and tropical metaphors, became almost impenetra-

[20] *transition,* June 1929.

ble. He occupied a labyrinth of his own design. The decadence of his manner suited his subject. He was, he said, in a letter of 1914, a student of the greatest drama in history, the decline of the British Empire. But the exiled observer was deceived by appearances.

Lamenting the separation of artist and audience, poets of the early thirties in *New Signatures* (1932) promised clearer poetry when the audience for poetry was greater. The generation of Auden was clearer than the generation of Eliot, but not clear enough to be commonly read. The next generation relapsed into privacy. Dylan Thomas's excellent poems are as decadent and obscure as *Finnegans Wake*.

Thomas is best when most obscure. This is not easy to explain, but it is possible that, divorced not only from society but, because of society, from the world, the poet finds it difficult to write about things as they are. Disgusted or unexcited by his world, he is compelled to treat it indirectly, and, translating it into private imagery, to pass it through dream. So processed, things as they are become other things, exciting to poets if not to readers.

Meanwhile readers complain about darkness for which they are responsible, and through their more literate agents call for meaning.[21] Reviewers for the larger periodicals refuse to admit the importance of Joyce, and, celebrating popular fiction or middle-brow essay, make short work of the younger poets. Respectable periodicals refuse to accept the poetry of exile. Through editors and the laws of commerce the middle class punishes its exiles by denying them a hearing. Hence "little magazines" where, unpopular and strange, exiles may display their isolation.[22]

These magazines, contemporaries of the *Daily Mail*,

[21] E.g., John Sparrow: *Sense and Poetry* (1934).

[22] Frederick Hoffman, Charles Allen, and Carolyn Ulrich: *The Little Magazine, a History and a Bibliography* (1946).

are almost peculiar to our times. Rossetti's *Germ* and the innumerable magazines of the French symbolists started the current tradition. The first little magazine of importance in England was the *Yellow Book* (April 1894–April 1897). Published by John Lane, who published Wilde, edited by Henry Harland and Aubrey Beardsley, this quarterly was intended to organize the decadence.[23] Prose and poetry by Moore, James, Beerbohm, Symons, pictures by Beardsley and Nettleship, proclaimed art for art's sake and offended the public with their wickedness, realism, or beauty. But John Lane, astutely tempering the effect, also printed "Reticence in Literature," by Arthur Waugh, Evelyn's father, who expressed the moral position of the Philistines. The fourth issue, January 1895, is the last good one; for in April, Wilde was tried and the celebration of beauty became dangerous. To save himself Lane purged the *Yellow Book*. Subsequent issues are dull except for a story by young Enoch Arnold Bennett and another by H. G. Wells.

The decay of decadence made Symons grieve. With Beardsley and Leonard Smithers, a publisher more daring than Lane, Symons started the *Savoy* to succeed and surpass the *Yellow Book*. In this periodical, which survived public displeasure for eight issues (January to December 1896), Symons published æsthetes, naturalists, and intellectuals, and wrote the last issue himself. Outraged by Beardsley's drawings and his prose, booksellers refused to sell the abominable magazine.

The *Egoist* (1914–19), founded as a feminist periodical, turned under the influence of Ezra Pound to the advancement of imagism and French literature. Dora Marsden and Harriet Weaver, who was to become Joyce's patron, were editors, Richard Aldington and T. S. Eliot assistant editors. This radical magazine published the prose of

[23] J. Lewis May: *John Lane and the Nineties* (1936).

Wyndham Lewis, eccentric poetry in free verse, Joyce's *Portrait of the Artist,* and parts of *Ulysses.* More splendid than this, Eliot's *Criterion* (1922–39) and Cyril Connolly's *Horizon* (1940–) became almost respectable.

During the thirties little magazines abounded. *New Verse* (1933–9), edited by Geoffrey Grigson, expressed the generations of Auden and Dylan Thomas. *Twentieth Century Verse* (1937–9), edited by Julian Symons, and *Poetry* (*London*) (1939–), edited by Tambimuttu, gave tongue to gangs into which exiles divided as they became more numerous, each hostile to others and to the world.

Of the editors, aside from Eliot, Cyril Connolly, critic and novelist, is the most fascinating. In the guise of Palinurus, the submerged pilot, Connolly devotes *The Unquiet Grave* (1945) to *maximes* and *pensées* that fix a mental climate, not his alone but his world's. These exquisite mutterings of anxiety, petulance, and guilt, so civilized and yet so confidential, are nothing like the sounds from *The Condemned Playground* (1945), a miscellany of reviews, essays, and wicked parodies that prove him the exile's spokesman. Destroying novels of the middle class, anticipating the fashions that move the exiled (although he seems immune as yet to Kierkegaard and the existentialists), he praises James and Forster. In "Writers and Society," which distinguishes between entertainer and artist, he laments the artist, free alone in middle-class society, but barely tolerated where free and condemned by indifference or hostility to his solitude.[24]

While poets admired or loathed one another in their magazines, while Eliot, defining poetry as poetry, justified it as independent organism, while other critics said a poem does not say but is, I. A. Richards and William Empson provided a method for bringing poet and reader together again. Poetry, says Richards in *Principles of Literary*

[24] Cf. *Enemies of Promise* (1939), criticism and autobiography.

Criticism (1924), is communication. This shocking idea had consequences. It follows, he continues, that reader and critic must determine the meaning of a poem. Since the ambiguity of words is profound and emotive words are easily confused with references, the reader must be aware of the doubleness of talk and of the semantic scale along which words slide from meaning to meaning.[25] The reader of a poem must know that meaning is not sense alone, but also feeling, tone, intention. To miss one of these is to fail. At Cambridge, Richards made his students read poems. The results as analyzed in *Practical Criticism* (1929) were deplorable. Missing one meaning or more, these students showed that they could not read. Richards blames the state of society for their inability. Taste, he says, has declined, democracy has lowered the level of culture, traditions have died. As cure he proposes semantics. The possibilities of the new science are explored in *Coleridge on Imagination* (1934), where, sliding the words of Coleridge along the scale, Richards shows that idealistic Coleridge meant what materialistic Richards means. After this triumph he spent the next few years promoting Basic English, a limited speech, which, if foreigners spoke it, would improve their communication with the English.

Of recent poetry and its critics Richards continually speaks in these three books. He attacks those who complain that poetry is unintelligible, those who think the whole meaning of a poem is its prose sense, and those emancipated men who claim that prose sense has no place in poetry. From their ignorance of fourfold meaning he defends Hopkins, Auden, Empson, and Eliot, whose allu-

[25] Cf. *Mencius on the Mind* (1932), *The Philosophy of Rhetoric* (1936), and his earlier, more difficult study (with C. K. Ogden), *The Meaning of Meaning* (1923). *Science and Poetry* (1926), defines poetry as pseudo-statement that organizes impulses and attitudes.

siveness and ambiguity are products of the time, whose sense is subordinated to feeling and tone. Some modern poetry, he admits, is truly private, failing in communication; but failure in communication is commonly the fault of reader, not of poet. Aided by the science of meaning, Richards analyzes *The Waste Land* to show that if readers read Richards, poems would please. If he wrote better, more readers might read. His ugly use of the language he analyzes so well is his best argument for Basic English.

The prose of Richards's disciple William Empson is as unattractive and, proving that readers are subtler and hardier than Richards supposed, as influential. Elaborating ideas from Richards and Robert Graves in *Seven Types of Ambiguity* (1931), Empson makes of them an instrument for penetrating obscurities. Since words of poetry are ambiguous and ambiguity is multiplied by context, the proper approach is analytic. His method, which amounts to careful reading or *explication de textes,* is excellent when applied by a reader of Empson's acuteness to metaphysical poetry of the seventeenth century and to difficult poetry of our time.[26] Although his division of ambiguity into seven types is unnecessary and pretentious, his exemplary analyses are exemplary. The meanings he attempts are at once the meaning of the poem to the poet and the meanings to its readers. Empson's virtue is to have adapted criticism to exiled poetry. His faith that darkest poetry yields to analysis seems justified by the successful application of his method to Dylan Thomas.

[26] *Some Versions of Pastoral* (1938) (with the title *English Pastoral Poetry* in the United States) is remarkable for an explication of Marvell's "Garden." Empson confesses a debt to the analysis of a Shakespearian sonnet by Robert Graves in *A Survey of Modernist Poetry* (1928). Empson's method was also anticipated by Graves in *Poetic Unreason* (1925).

As puzzles for explicators Empson composed the excellent, compressed, ambiguous poems of *Poems* (1935), and *The Gathering Storm* (1940). The method is metaphysical. See essays on Empson by Cleanth Brooks and Richard Eberhart in *Accent,* Summer 1944.

CHAPTER II
Left

CRITICS of the middle class have been less radical on the whole than moderate. From the eighties, however, writers occupying positions somewhat to the left of center have expressed in novel, tract, play, or poem their impatience with convention or economy. The works of Bernard Shaw and of the Auden generation excellently illustrate this literature in all its varieties.

I

Around 1880 Shaw showed his contempt of bourgeois morality by becoming an anarchist. But after reading a French translation of *Das Kapital,* he became a socialist, at first a member of the Social Democratic Federation, a Marxist society, then in 1884 a member of the Fabian Society. Finding his spiritual home among the "gas and water socialists," he managed to combine more effectively than William Morris the traditions of socialism and art.[1]

[1] For social background see Helen Lynd: *England in the Eighteen-eighties* (1945); Esme Wingfield-Stratford: *The Victorian Sunset* (1932), *The Victorian Aftermath* (1934); Edward Pease: *The History of the Fabian Society* (1916); Sidney Webb: *Socialism in England* (1889).

Archibald Henderson: *Bernard Shaw, Playboy and Prophet* (1932); Hesketh Pearson: *G.B.S., a Full Length Portrait* (1942).

Shaw: *A Manifesto* (1884), *Fabian Essays in Socialism* (1889), *Wil-*

From 1879 he had occupied his leisure with the composition of five edifying novels, unpublishable except in socialist magazines. Of these novels *An Unsocial Socialist,* written in 1883, is best. Trefusis, the wealthy hero, turning against his caste, expresses his contempt of Philistine society, its economic foundations, its virtues, and its sentiments. Leaving his lovely wife because love interferes with duty, he retires to a young ladies' seminary, where he works for his living disguised as a lawn-mower. In this capacity he ceaselessly repeats the ideas of Marx to all who will listen. This eloquent egoist, enemy of capitalists, clergymen, physicians, and wives, set the pattern for the Shavian hero. Although the novel abounds in outrageous paradoxes and, except for the interminable orations of its hero, is lively enough and gay, the characters are less convincing than what they represent. The rational and the preposterous deserved, and later got, a better vehicle. But William Morris read the novel, liked the ideas, and became Shaw's friend.

The hero of *The Irrational Knot* is rational to the point of inhumanity. This novel, written in 1880 before Shaw's conversion, deals with the effect of caste upon marriage. Edward Conolly, the Irish-American engineer, is far from respectable; for he has neither an unearned income nor a public-school education. The creature dares marry a lady despite the apoplectic disapproval of her father. Unable to endure the rational and the infra dig, she sensibly elopes with one of her own class, an Eton man, who abandons her with illegitimate child. The deserted engineer, applauding her superiority to convention, offers in vain to take her back. In the 1905 preface to this shocking, second-rate

liam Morris as I Knew Him (1936). *Anarchism versus State Socialism* (1889), Shaw's tract in favor of anarchism, was reprinted, to Shaw's embarrassment, from the *Anarchist,* the magazine where it originally appeared.

novel, Shaw finds his fault to have been ignorance of money, the moral basis of that cultured class which will murder or steal "in the name of law and order." But his own original morality, he says, makes this novel one "of the first order." Such morality is almost the only value of his other early novels.[2]

Knowledge of money at last forced upon Shaw the desirability of making some. He saw his chance in the "new journalism," the attempt to adapt journalism to the needs of an expanding, newly literate public. The headline, the interview, and other seductions made their appearance during the eighties. By its sensational character W. T. Stead's *Pall Mall Gazette*, one of the most fascinating products of the new journalism, earned for its proprietor the name of Bed Stead. To please the unaccustomed eye, journalists adopted a colloquial style, filled at its best with wit and color, and descending at its worst, as Shaw confesses in *Dramatic Opinions*, to the split infinitive. The brilliant styles of Wilde, Henley, Chesterton, and Shaw were formed in this cynical school. Writing in his direct, easy manner for many journals, Shaw discovered in himself a commercial shrewdness far from socialistic, and he enjoyed a calculated success. The music criticism in which by praising Wagner he puzzled the Philistine is filled with harmless irreverence and common sense.[3]

As Shaw continued to please, astonish, and displease, he discovered in the "new drama" of Ibsen another vehicle for his talents. Shaw had ignored the English theater of the eighties, which specialized in melodramas, sentimental farces, and adaptations of the well-made play of Scribe, Sardou, and Dumas the younger. None of these had in-

[2] *Immaturity*, written in 1879; *Love among the Artists*, written in 1881; and that eugenic romance *Cashel Byron's Profession* (1886).

[3] His columns are reprinted in *Music in London, 1890–94* (1932), and *London Music in 1888–1889* (1937).

tellectual or æsthetic interest, none was realistic in dialogue, character, or action, and none gave any sign of the social and domestic problems attending the advance of the middle class. The artificial excitement of melodrama stopped short of sex and other natural endeavors. Plots of well-made plays were so well made that, as John Mason Brown has observed, if a character was to get tuberculosis in the last act, in the first he must have had at least catarrh.

Changing all that, Ibsen adapted the stage to modern conditions. Like Lillo and Heywood before him, he wrote bourgeois and domestic tragedy, in which, surpassing his early predecessors, he revealed by conflict of character and idea the depths of human nature and of society. His frankness in exposing domestic and social troubles and all the horrors of the suburb lifted the protective convention by which they had been concealed. In *A Doll's House* (1879) he presented the nature of middle-class marriage, in *Ghosts* (1881), his masterpiece, he exposed respectable hypocrisy, and in *An Enemy of the People* (1882) he showed a humanitarian at war with middle-class interests. These and other problem plays were followed by the enigmatic *Hedda Gabler* (1890), a character study that elevated the stage to the level of the novel. Technique was as revolutionary as substance. Ibsen established the convention of the stage as a four-walled room, in which, while the audience peered through an imaginary wall, the characters spoke and acted as if the imaginary wall were real and the room their own. Soliloquies disappeared with asides. Plots, depending now upon character and situation, became unmechanical. Symbols of duck and tower presented a reality beyond the limits of such realism. And from these northern austerities arose what Yeats considered an odor of spilled poetry. Edmund Gosse was the first Englishman to discover Ibsen. His propaganda and that of William Archer made Ibsen known in England during the eighties, and their translations made him available to readers. With this preparation *A Doll's House* was produced in London, to the displeasure of the middle class, in 1889.

A Doll's House contains little that Shaw had not said in *The Irrational Knot.* It was for this reason that he remained unexcited when during the middle eighties he, Eleanor Marx, and other Fabians took part in a private performance of the play. Later, however, converted by his friend William Archer, Shaw realized that Ibsen's value for him was a form for the ideas he shared with the master.

Dazzled with the possibilities of the theater, Shaw became an Ibsenite. In July 1890 he lectured the Fabians on the new drama of ideas, and, expanding this lecture, published in 1891 *The Quintessence of Ibsenism.* By this time Florence Farr had appeared in *Rosmersholm* and J. T. Grein had produced *Ghosts* at the Independent Theatre, founded in 1891 on the model of Antoine's Théâtre Libre. Shaw took occasion in his tract to defend these productions against Clement Shorter and the other Philistine critics who found Ibsen long, nasty, and brutish. Far from being an enemy of virtue, says Shaw, Ibsen is the first moralist of Europe, the enemy of conventional virtue. His plays show that middle-class ideals of marriage, family, and love disguise a shocking reality, especially the ideal of the womanly woman, Ibsen's doll, which makes her her husband's slave. Although his interest in Ibsen seems no more than moral, social, and domestic, Shaw must have seen beyond the didactic moralist to the artist and technician; for what he learned from Ibsen was not morality, of which he had enough, but how to write a play. In the light of the plays he wrote this tract appears less tract than manifesto.

Widowers' Houses, his first play and the first of the "new" or "higher" dramas, was written for Grein and produced by him in 1892 at the Independent Theatre. At each of the two performances socialists applauded what others hissed. Both were right; for the play is a socialist attack on landlords of slum property, who, while oppressing the poor, profess philanthropic ideals and maintain respectable demeanors. The plot involves municipal fraud and the defeat of an idealist by landlord and womanly woman. Although the idea is important and the technique up to date, the dialogue is too clever for orthodox Ibsenism and the play too poor.

Shaw's next two plays could not be produced, the first because no producer would produce it, the second because the official censor, true to his class, found it immoral. *The Philanderer,* written in 1893, produced at last in 1907, deals with the womanly woman and the "new woman," with marriage as slavery to a middle-class ideal, and with the vogue, displeasing to Shaw, that Ibsen was enjoying among the unworthy. The characters, members of an Ibsen club, talk about woman's freedom to smoke, use roller skates, or leave the home; yet all but two of them are imperfect Ibsenites, Philistines in disguise. Charteris, "an Ibsenist philosopher," is the real thing. He despises marriage, ideals, and respectability, and he trifles with virtue. It is his fate to be pursued by womanly women, whose disguise as Ibsenites he easily penetrates. But Sylvia, who smokes, dresses like a man, and derides marriage, is a comfort. In this fantastic play Shaw discovered his destined mixture of frivolity and Ibsenism, of the real and the unreal. *Mrs. Warren's Profession,* written the same year, is more of the same and somewhat better. Against the clergymen, capitalists, and men of leisure who form the detestable background stand Vivie Warren, a new woman, and her mother, who manages a chain of brothels for Sir George. Vivie, a formidable creature, has been to Girton

College. She smokes, of course, dresses sensibly, and is devoid of attractiveness. This new woman, reared in ignorance of her mother's profession, is attracted, when she discovers it, by its unsentimental character, but on second thought rejects it as respectable and capitalistic. She also rejects her suitor and his unearned income, and leaves her home to earn her living. When Ibsen's Nora slammed that Norwegian door, the noise went farther than could have been predicted. Vivie Warren is an Ibsen girl.

Mrs. Warren's Profession, whose virtues are its dialogue and idea, not its realism or character, was timely. It reflects the feminist movement, which since the time of John Stuart Mill had proposed a distinction between women and property, and now, abetted by Ibsen, rocked the pillars of society. Fabians were feminists. Shaw's friend Annie Besant had left her husband. Everywhere new women ascended bicycles and were off to college or to work. Shaw, reflecting upon these things, was but one of many, of whom Grant Allen was easily the most notorious. In *The Woman Who Did* (1895), a novel, Allen tells of Herminia, another Girton girl, whose rejection of marriage surprises her conventional suitor. "Surely, surely," he exclaims, "you won't carry your ideas of freedom to such an extreme, such a dangerous conclusion!" She did.[4]

Finding no stage for these "unpleasant" plays, Shaw finally published them in 1898, providing them with preface and elaborate stage directions in order to help the reader of novels to visualize the action and understand its meaning. The thwarted dramatist had learned, however, that attacks upon middle-class society were unprofitable un-

[4] The later developments of feminism are illustrated by H. G. Wells's *Ann Veronica* (1909), and by Virginia Woolf's *A Room of One's Own* (1929) and *Three Guineas* (1938). To illustrate a feminist point, Orlando of *Orlando* (1928), changing sex, remains the same.

less tempered to the capacity of the middle class. The "pleasant" plays that followed represent a prudent compromise between his ideals and his needs.

The best of these, *Candida,* written in 1894, is an Ibsenite problem play, still too shocking for immediate production. It concerns the intrusion into a middle-class home of a poet who asks the woman of the house to choose between her husband and himself. Marchbanks, the poet, is a fluttering, ambiguous creature, calculated to annoy the manly man. Morell, the clerical husband, instead of kicking Shaw's idea of a poet downstairs, abides his wife's decision. Clear-eyed Candida decides to remain at home on the ground that her husband, more childish than Marchbanks, needs her more. These decisions provide the dated shocks. Morell's decision, rising above the rights of property, admits the independence of his wife, and her decision reflects an unconventional superiority to duty. For the first time Shaw's characters and their psychology are almost human, and for the first time he approximated Ibsen.

In 1895 Shaw became drama-critic for the *Saturday Review.* The selections from this column printed in *Dramatic Opinions and Essays* (1906) are among his most readable writings. As Wagner served as criterion in Shaw's music criticism, so Ibsen served in this. Shaw condemned pre-Ibsenite and pseudo-Ibsenite drama. Shakespeare wrote well before the time of Ibsen. Blaming the bard for intellectual and moral sterility, Shaw called attention to himself. This campaign against Shakespeare, which horrified the respectable, was designed to advance the cause of Ibsen and, by breaking the grip upon the stage of established actors who found in Shakespeare their best vehicle, to clear the way for new drama with new actors and new conventions. Shaw destroyed the well-made play, his chief rivals, and Mrs. Pat Campbell, who acted in their plays.

His cruel brilliance was made bearable by the extravagance of the new journalism and by the extremity of his judgments. Having established his reputation and the new drama, Shaw yielded his chair in 1898 to Beerbohm, the "incomparable Max," whose urbane columns were reprinted in *Around Theatres* (1924).

The London Stage Society, founded in 1899 to produce Shaw and Ibsen, staged *Candida* in 1900 and *Mrs. Warren's Profession* in 1902. When Granville-Barker began to produce Shaw and other new dramatists at the Court Theatre in 1904, Shaw found in the noncommercial theater the commercial success of his dreams. His socialism naturally declined, his religious inclination increased, and the plays he wrote for the next few years, when of social significance, concern marriage and caste, softened for middle-class consumption by farce and sometimes comedy. His prefaces of this period often concern the virtue of money, an idea of his own corroborated by Samuel Butler. This idea was shocking only because it was so implicit in the middle-class mind that few had mentioned it.

Getting Married (1908) is announced as an attack upon those who regard an attack upon marriage as an attack upon property. The daring preface on sex and society suggests easy, cheap divorce and economic independence for wives. Under present laws, says Shaw, the home, regarded as the holy of holies, is little better than a stable. But the inaction of the play that follows takes place in a kitchen where all sit around and talk about the preface upon which the play depends. Shaw had discovered the secret of sedentary farce as had Ibsen that of static tragedy. The clever lines and fantastic characters make good theater, and the harmless conclusion, avoiding the issues dangerously approached, is less illustrative of the new drama than of a new prudence. The setting of *Misalliance* (1910), another farce, is the house of a rich manufacturer of underwear. But the social meaning, if any, is diffused by conversations among new women, superwomen, and miseducated men, whose words and characters are innocuously grotesque.

Fanny of *Fanny's First Play* (1911) is a Fabian and a suffragette. The critics of her indecorous play within a play think Shaw wrote it because of the tedious speeches and the author's "physiological incapacity for passion." They are not so far wrong, however, as he thought. For years he had called himself better than Shakespeare. But Shaw's inhumanity, whether physiological or psychological in origin, his prosaic mind, his growing dependence upon preface and round-table discussion, and his reluctance to dramatize his ideas made Shaw Shakespeare's opposite. One night Yeats dreamed of Shaw as a "smiling sewing machine." The portrait is excellent. But Shaw had all the virtues of his defects. His passionless intellect gave intellectual vigor to a stage that wanted it. His strange characters and their lines proved capital vehicles for actors. And his plays, good theater even at their least dramatic, combine at their best some merits of Ibsen, Wycherley, and Bunyan. This original confusion, working by its assumptions and its tone, amused and taught its audience. And Shaw wickedly announced to enemies of didactic art that "art should never be anything else."

He described *Pygmalion* (1914) as "intensely and deliberately didactic." That is one of his jokes, as the play, confounding his critics, was one of his surprises. Whatever didactic element it contains is so well dramatized that, remaining unstated, it insinuates itself through art. The creation of the artificial duchess suggests that accent, the artificial mark and instrument of caste, is the only difference except wealth between the classes. The inhumanity of Higgins, based upon subtle observation, is thoroughly human. These subtleties, however, do not injure social point.

In 1911 Shaw abandoned the conservative Fabians. But the war or the boredom of prosperity turned him again to social and political problems and to the composition of longer manifestoes, talkier plays. *The Intelligent Woman's Guide to Socialism and Capitalism* (1928) presents his post-Fabian position. Like the Fabians he abhors Marx, class war, class dictatorship, and revolutionary violence. But he condemns trade unions and democracy, preferring dictatorships. After their fashion, he says, all men must be forcibly fed, clothed, lodged, taught, employed, and, if reluctant, "executed in a kindly manner." *Everybody's Political What's What* (1944) need not detain the intelligent woman. Somewhat rambling in structure but brisk in style, this product of what he calls his "second childhood" recommends equal income for all except Shaw and the selection of rulers by competitive examination. These repeated ideas emerge with difficulty from long attacks on vaccination, Cæsarian operations, tonsillectomy, disinfection, Pavlov, and orthodox religion which make it plain that the ancient journalist, as a wit remarked, had outlived the time for which he was born too soon.

Before we glance at the political plays of Shaw's senility, *Heartbreak House* (1921) demands notice. In this house and its occupants Shaw symbolized "cultured, leisured Europe before the war" as Chekhov, his model, had before him. The tragedy of England, says Shaw in the excellent preface to this excellent play, is the refusal of the best part of the ruling class to rule, the separation of culture from power, and the resulting government by business men seeking private gain. In the first two acts of the play Shaw introduces a group of eccentrics, who gradually harden into types: the practical business man, the

burglar, the colonial official, the horsy woman, the futile socialist, and the enjoyer of unearned income who has read Shaw, understands all things, and does nothing about them. Through these two acts these morally emancipated, cultured, foolish, or reactionary people move about the parlor of superior light comedy; and the spectator thinks this their element until the last act, when what seemed domestic comedy, expanding now on the terrace, becomes far larger than the limits of the original parlor and much more sinister. In the last act, lest his moral miss its point, the anxious author made the play a conversation piece. But even this return to habitual explicitness is not without drama. Hardly has Hector Hushabye condemned his class as useless, dangerous, and—for leaving government to business men—responsible for what is coming, when a bomber drops a bomb on them, as one of them observes, to keep the home fires burning. This play, tracing the collapse of civilization to the irresponsibility of the civilized, the "blunders of boobies," and "the cupidity of capitalists," could not be produced while hostilities continued.

The depression sent Shaw back to the social and political play. *The Apple Cart* (1929) is trivial. But the preface neatly restates Shaw's objections to irresponsible plutocracy. *Too True to Be Good* (1932) concerns the misery of riches. What seems at first a Shavian paradox seems next the work of a tractarian for Sunday schools, and finally seems a more or less serious treatment of labor and leisure and their distribution. In the play the wealthy heroine, having eloped with a clerical burglar to enjoy the leisure of theft, asks, in her boredom and spiritual starvation, freedom for what? As the curtain descends she finds a purpose of a sort, and the burglar preaches as if words were still effectual. The characters are authentically Shavian; the play, a farce, is bright, witty, and full of the old extravagance; but, wanting unity of theme and action, it remains as ineffectual as the burglar's words. As the curtain falls on the first act, Shaw observes: "The play is now virtually over; but the characters will discuss it at great length for two acts more." The reference of "it" is unclear, for the characters proceed to discuss not only freedom but Freud, the quantum theory, the ending of certainties, relations of parents and children, disease and medicine, cocktails, cuddling, and the younger generation. Shaw's trouble was not so much his disregard of Aristotelian unity as his attempt to compress the chaos of the thirties into a form suitable for the neater problems of the nineties. The preface of *On the Rocks* (1933) commends the liquidation of incorrigibles for the public good, as practiced by Stalin and Pontius Pilate. But Shaw's approval of this end is contingent upon the means since he dislikes cruelty, he says, "even cruelty to other people." The play that is appended to this preface proposes a ready and easy way to establish a new commonwealth. Painless liquidation is also the theme of *The Simpleton of the Unexpected Isles* (1935), a fantasy. The angels who perform the social task of Ogpu attend to stockbrokers, medical men, and other parasites. An attempt by capitalistic police to arrest an angel in Leicester Square fails to arrest the Last Judgment. *The Millionairess* (1935) establishes the need of controlling those whose talent is money-making, and, in the person of Epifania, presents a plutocrat whose unscrupulousness and indifference to social good are exemplary. The English bishop of *Geneva* (1938) is such another. Embodying the prejudices of the middle class, he faints when confronted with a commissar and, upon resuscitation, dies. In these ultimate farces Shaw speaks almost as kindly of Stalin as of Mussolini.

Shaw had outlasted the new drama. When it began, however, he was but one, though easily the first, of many. During the eighties Arthur Wing Pinero wrote well-made sentimental comedies in the manner of the French or dramas remotely in the manner of T. W. Robertson, author of *Caste*. Brought face to face with reality by Ibsen, Pinero rapidly reformed. *The Second Mrs. Tanqueray* (1893) is his first good play and the first good play of the new drama. The problem is that of a woman with a past, who, upon her marriage to a respectable widower, is compelled to endure social ostracism, her husband's effort to shield his daughter from contamination, and his daughter's coldness. When her cold stepdaughter is about to marry an old lover of Mrs. Tanqueray's, Mrs. Tanqueray solves her problem by suicide. This pathetic play, which misses tragedy, takes its well-made plot from France but its natural dialogue and action from Ibsen. *The Notorious Mrs. Ebbsmith* (1895) presents a new woman, hostile, of course, to marriage. The attempt of this sensible, dowdy, socialist agitator to brave opinion and live in sin with Lucas Cleeve is defeated by his conventionality and the worldliness of the Duke (played by George Arliss), who thinks women toys. An attractive dress symbolizes the victory of convention, and the rescue of the Bible from the stove the defeat of emancipation.

To Shaw, reviewing for the *Saturday Review*, this Ibsenite play was pseudo-Ibsenite, and, since it showed the defeat of the new woman by Philistine society, almost immoral. There may have been something to these charges, for Pinero's plays found ready acceptance in the commercial theater. Unable to find even a little theater for most of his, Shaw could find no merit in his fortunate rival.

The hand of the established craftsman, too apparent in the tooled perfection of Pinero's plays, and an emphasis greater upon character than upon problem, though not unlike that of *Hedda Gabler*, displeased didactic Shaw. It was clear to others, however, that Pinero had more power than Shaw to create human beings and display their discomforts in middle-class society. But Pinero proved unable to develop, and, like Ibsen and Dumas *fils,* his masters, he wanted wit.[5]

Henry Arthur Jones, whom Shaw admired, evolved into a social playwright by way of melodrama. *The Silver King* (1882), a melodrama as splendid in its kind as *Sweeney Todd, the Demon Barber of Fleet Street,* was financially the most successful play of the eighties. It is still of interest not only for its soliloquies, asides, sentiment, and violence but for the villain's justification of middle-class villainy by Darwin's survival of the fittest. Although melodramatic, *The Middleman* (1889) concerns social problems, the exploitation, for instance, of worker by capitalist and the hypocrisy of the respectable; for under Robertson's influence Jones was turning to the realities around him. In 1884 Jones adapted Ibsen's *Doll's House* for popular consumption, giving it a happy ending and *Breaking a Butterfly* for title; but he admitted later that he had been unaware of Ibsen's value. Realizing this value in the nineties, he studied Ibsen to some purpose, but never to such purpose as Pinero or Shaw.

The Case of Rebellious Susan (1894) is the first of the comedies under which Jones concealed the aim of the social critic. Like Nora, Susan walks out of the middle-class home, but here the resemblance ceases. Susan matches her husband's infidelity by her own, but, advised by cynical Sir Richard Kato, preserves appearances. This

[5] Of Pinero's later plays, three are conspicuous: *Iris* (1901), *The Thunderbolt* (1908), and *Mid-Channel* (1909).

Granville-Barker, who became the chief producer of new dramatists, wrote competent plays according to their patterns: *The Voysey Inheritance* (1905), *Waste* (1907), and *The Madras House* (1910), his most Shavian. St. John Hankin's plays are distinguished by their cynicism: *The Return of the Prodigal* (1905), *The Cassilis Engagement* (1907). St. John Ervine specialized in strong, austere characters: *Jane Clegg* (1913), *John Ferguson* (1915). The best short survey of the new drama is the last part of Allardyce Nicoll's *British Drama* (1925).

cynical conformity carries Jones's criticism of Mrs. Grundy, to whom he addressed, with the published play, an epistle. *Michael and His Lost Angel* (1896), his favorite, though primarily a study of character, bears in its treatment of the cleric and his fallen woman a social burden. After the financial failure of this strange, dark play, one of the most powerful of the nineties, Jones returned to the social comedy at which he excelled. *The Liars* (1897) and *The Hypocrites* (1906) deal, as their titles suggest, with the "organized hypocrisy" forced upon the governing class by its moral code. The first of these is among the most smoothly contrived of well-made plays; the second with its squires, vicars, and ladies is a gallery of detestable middle-class portraits, relieved by that of the curate, an honest, unsuccessful man. *Mrs. Dane's Defence* (1900) is Jones's closest approach to Ibsen, but the problem is too unreal to support the elaborate apparatus of detection with which society surrounds it. Although the cruelty of respectable people has never been more faithfully presented, the play loses its force in melodrama and sentimentality.

Jones shared the views of Shaw and Ibsen, but in the person of the *raisonneur,* borrowed from Dumas *fils,* upheld the hypocrisy each play attacked. This worldliness strangely invited the critical applause of Shaw, who seems to have been able to pass beneath surfaces to the didactic intention they conceal. It is likely, moreover, that Pinero's enemy saw less of a rival in Jones.

In 1900 James Joyce's essay "Ibsen's New Drama" appeared in the *Fortnightly Review.* Joyce, who had learned Norwegian to read the master, praised him not for action or character but for the perception of naked truth. Ibsen, pleased, wrote to Archer, who wrote to Joyce, and Joyce to Ibsen in Norwegian. Admiration of Ibsen's static quality and his "lofty impersonal power" seems to have assisted

Joyce in achieving these qualities in *Ulysses*, but before this he had written *Exiles*, published in 1918, an Ibsenite triangle involving that change in family relationship which became Joyce's constant theme. Although it is one of the best of the Ibsen tradition, this play, overshadowed by Joyce's greater works, is prized mostly for what light it sheds on his mind and his development as an artist.[6]

From among these good, small, higher dramatists one emerged higher than they and more thoroughly representative of their kind. In the hierarchy they compose, John Galsworthy[7] stands below Shaw alone and somewhat to his right. Legal Galsworthy began with *The Silver Box*, discovered and produced in 1906 by Granville-Barker. This play involves the difference between the justice accorded by the middle class to its own members and that to workers and the unemployed. Through his austerities of plot and dialogue Galsworthy presents a problem not for solution but for contemplation. He seems dispassionate, but as the children cry without and as the innocent are rejected or led away, his sentiments project a slight mist from the wings. There are no villains around, nor heroes, but only commonplace men, little victims of social pressures larger than their comprehension, which make them irresponsible and pitiable. Galsworthy is concerned less with his people than with the ponderous forces of middle-class society.

This admirably constructed play, in which nothing is irrelevant or weak, was followed by another better and no less severe. *Strife* (1909) presents the problem of worker, union, and boss. The unauthorized strike of tinplate workers proves as wasteful as it is inevitable. Only

[6] Vivienne Koch Macleod: "The Influence of Ibsen on Joyce," *Publication of the Modern Language Association*, LX (September 1945); Bernard Bandler, "Joyce's *Exiles*," *Hound and Horn*, VI (January-March 1933).

[7] H. V. Marrot: *The Life and Letters of John Galsworthy* (1936).

the death of a woman is accomplished and the breaking of two emergent men, stronger than most of Galsworthy's characters: Roberts, the symbolic worker, and Anthony, the capitalist. *Justice* (1910) concerns the injustice of the criminal code. More complicated than the usual Galsworthy play, which achieves its end by monolithic simplicity, this one appears scattered. In *The Fugitive* (1913) sentiment triumphs. Fleeing the middle-class home, the heroine receives the weight of the social displeasure poised over Nora's door. Bourgeois marriage is bad; prostitution, to which she is driven by her nurtured incapacity, worse. These two comparative failures were atoned for by *The Skin Game* (1920), which reveals the hidden conflict within the middle class between landlord and capitalist, and by *Loyalties* (1922), among the finest studies of caste. Into a country house, swarming with products of the public school, comes De Levis, a Jew, an outsider, and a cad, of course, but suffered for his riches. Ignorant of the code, he breaks it. Loyalties, torn between truth and playing the game, generally incline toward the latter, except the loyalty of the lawyer, which, transcending caste, inclines toward law. This is a good play, differing from some of Shaw's in dramatizing the problem. In *Old English* (1924), Galsworthy's last important play, sentiment emerges from the wings to moisten an ancient capitalist, who nevertheless remained an adequate vehicle for George Arliss.

By the time of *Old English* the social-problem play, except for vestigial Shaw's, was all but extinct. His preface to *Heartbreak House* tells of the war's effect. Never financially profitable, the new drama was driven from even the littlest theater during the war by rising rents, which, permitting nothing less entertaining than whimsy or musical comedy, made the stage respectable again. For a time the serious drama found refuge in the suburbs, then in the provinces, but pursued by rents, against which it had once exclaimed, it gradually tired or, what was worse, moved on to Dublin or New York. After the war the situation proved little better. The war created new problems, but these problems were unsuitable for Ibsen's parlor. Three walls and a fictive fourth, admirably designed for domestic problems and for limited intrusions by labor, finance, or caste, were insufficiently elastic for problems now international or all but universal in their dimensions. What the theater needed was a new stage, one adapted, for example, to the production of Hardy's *Dynasts*, a stage, as Allardyce Nicoll has suggested, something like a three-ring circus. In the absence of this improvement, the theater, always dependent upon its stage, lost touch with current reality, which was now and again attended to by the movies. Maugham, Coward, and Milne, however, continued to fill what once was Ibsen's stage with charming plays.

J. B. Priestley, who shared the stage of the thirties with James Bridie, started as a novelist. *The Good Companions* (1929) is a hearty picaresque novel of escape from social pressures. This comfortable entertainment was followed by *Angel Pavement* (1930), depression-born and realistic. Here, facing what his good companions had avoided, Priestley commenced his criticism of a "rotten system." The greedy, the frustrated, and the unemployed, victims or creators of society, fill his panorama. Its survey is accompanied by something of the gusto of Wells or Dickens and by something of their attitudes. The first plays of Priestley, excellently made, more subtly continue his exposure of middle-class unscrupulousness. *Dangerous Corner* (1932), a play of mounting tension, showing what happened and by double exposure what might have happened, reveals concealed enormities. Under the disarming surprises of what seems good commercial comedy *Labur-*

num Grove (1933) makes an exposure of respectability the more devastating for its brightness of tone. Experimental plays in which the problems of time and the unconscious temporarily took the place of society were succeeded by a flood of social tracts, novels, and plays released by appeasement and the war. In these hasty condemnations of the "unteachables" Priestley predicted the abolishment of greed and caste, and fixing his hopes of real democracy not upon the Communist Party but, at the suggestion of Mr. Churchill's government, upon the common people, he planned foundations for a rational society. This propaganda is successfully dramatized in *They Came to a City* (1942), a Shavian fantasy of the New Jerusalem. Having made expressionism popular, Priestley became, upon the re-emergence of the Labour Party in 1945, its most popular advocate.

Although technically less adventurous than Priestley, James Bridie is a playwright of somewhat greater distinction. *The Last Trump* (1938) is remarkable for the dour portrait of a capitalist, and *The King of Nowhere* (1938) suggests an alliance among wealth, fascism, and lunacy. Only a few of his plays, however, and these not his best, have such social bearing. Of his best plays *A Sleeping Clergyman* (1933) is a many-scened cavalcade of heredity and medicine, and *Tobias and the Angel* (1930), of course, is myth. Bridie is as various as he is copious. He has written historical fantasies, melodramas, and comedies that manage to combine the manners of Barrie and Shaw, all of them competently made and all superior entertainments.[8]

[8] The plays of James Bridie (Dr. Osborne Mavor) have been collected in several volumes with explanatory prefaces. The most Shavian of his plays are *What Say They?* (published 1940) and *The Golden Legend of Shults* (1939), fantastic comedies. The latter, more daring than most, uses the techniques of cinema and revue, symbolic scenery, and a chorus to destroy the middle class.

II

Once thought red, writers of Auden's generation were little more than pink. Now that the excitement is over, certain things besides this color emerge: some of the poems of Auden, some of MacDiarmid's and Cornford's, the criticism of Caudwell and of Orwell, and the novels of Isherwood. These have value for our time and perhaps beyond it; but the value of this impractical generation may have been practical. The victory of Labour in the election of 1945, which seemed as significant to Harold Laski as the victory of the middle class in 1832, may have been made easier by poets clamoring for blood.

In the early thirties things looked more hopeful for the left. The depression, proving again the failure of capitalist economy, had shown the young the need of a new position. The failure of the general strike of 1926 and the greater failure of the Labour government of 1929–31 had destroyed for most the hope of social democracy. For the young and the depressed the only recourse seemed the Communist Party, which, after years of obscure bickering with Labour, now enjoyed a boom. As antidote to dying capitalism this party offered a classless society, production not for profit but for use, and the right to work. After the violence of the inevitable revolution, society would submit to the dictatorship of the proletariat until society and proletariat were one. In this classless condition human nature, expanding, could realize its possibilities, and culture, no longer confined to a leisure class or menaced by profit, would be universal. Consisting of a few intellectuals and workers, the party was as exclusive and enigmatic as the Society of Jesus. But it welcomed the aid of those middle-class men who, realizing the necessity of necessity, walked leftward and within their bourgeois limitations were proletarian in tendency. Writers of this kind (and few were of any other) were known as fellow travelers.

John Strachey, Etonian and ex-Labourite, was the party's first important apologist. In *The Coming Struggle for Power* (1933) he proves by Marx and Lenin that capitalism is destroying itself through monopoly and imperialism, that Shaw and Wells are thoroughly bourgeois, and that communism, which he describes with sober lucidity, is the only hope for Britain. His literary criticism was moderate. *Literature and Dialectical Materialism* (1934), though partly devoted to exposing the "fascist unconscious" in D. H. Lawrence and others, maintains that literature is literature. We do not pretend, says Strachey, that a poet is good because he is a Marxist or bad because he is not, nor are we too hard on fellow travelers. Such moderation was peculiar.

According to many writers for *Left Review,* a critical journal that flourished from 1934 to 1938 under the editorship of Edgell Rickword, art is propaganda. This orthodox opinion, which replaces æsthetic value with political expediency, was held by Anthony Blunt, for example, and Edward Upward. The latter's essay in *The Mind in Chains* (1937), a leftist symposium edited by C. Day Lewis, proclaims that no book at the present time can be good "unless it is written from a Marxist or near Marxist viewpoint." Applying this standard, Upward finds Joyce and Proust to be without value; for talent without dialectical materialism is helpless before reality. Other essays of this volume urge artists to embrace the proletariat and be free.

In *Illusion and Reality* (1937) Christopher Caudwell, the ablest and most philosophical of Marxist critics, rejects this notion of art as propaganda. Art, he says, is the product of society and performs a social function; its purpose is to adapt responses to economic co-operation by adjusting conflicts of individual, society, and nature. This theory, which combines the anthropologists with I. A.

Richards and Marx, permits a criticism at once orthodox and reasonable. Although Caudwell finds Shakespeare bourgeois, he does not find him bad. The trouble with recent poetry, he says, is the isolation of poet from society; but this isolation, as illusory as the bourgeois idea of freedom, merely reflects the individualism of the poet's class.[9]

While critics theorized, poets were adjusting their responses to the proletariat and to bloody revolution. Of these poets Hugh MacDiarmid was first and, by proletarian standards, best. His "First Hymn to Lenin" is good by any standard. Written in Scots dialect, this muscular prayer, which uses the language of daily speech, heightened by feeling and given finality, captures something of the grandeur of Yeats. MacDiarmid's other poems show that his proletarian façade conceals the bourgeois technician who knows and profits by the work of Rilke, Joyce, and Eliot. Exercises in erudite verbalism and lovely ambiguous lyrics like "O wha's been here afore me, lass," are commoner than Marxist poems. Although Burns's successor writes too much indifferent verse, he is memorable for having made poetry out of the "Cheka's necessary murders."[10]

Following MacDiarmid's lead came younger poets—Auden, Day Lewis, Spender, and their chums—constituting the main literary current of the early thirties. All were products of public school and university, but all had ostensibly abandoned their class for the proletariat, which could not understand them. Some of them appear to have become members of the Communist Party for a time, but,

[9] In *Studies in a Dying Culture* (1938) Caudwell (Christopher Sprigg) detects the bourgeois illusion of freedom in Shaw, Wells, and Lawrence. Cf. Alick West: *Crisis and Criticism* (1937); Philip Henderson: *The Poet and Society* (1939).

[10] MacDiarmid (Christopher Grieve): *First Hymn to Lenin* (1931), *Second Hymn to Lenin* (1933), *Selected Poems* (1944); *Lucky Poet* (1943), autobiography.

whether members or not, all were fellow travelers. According to Caudwell, this group consisted of bourgeois anarchists, destructive of their own class but incapable of joining its successor. Socialists in economics, these "romantic revolutionaries" remained individualists in art. The party welcomed their aid while rebuking their limitations. Events have proved the accuracy of Caudwell's analysis.

This group announced itself in two anthologies, *New Signatures* (1932) and *New Country* (1933), both edited by Michael Roberts, who saw the end of isolated, erudite poetry and the achievement by his contributors of new proletarian attitudes toward life. Both are represented by William Plomer's "Epitaph for a Contemporary" who was shot by the proletariat for remaining a gentleman. But on the whole the volumes are less revolutionary than their prefaces announce them to be and far less exciting. Auden, Day Lewis, and Spender were the most hopeful signs. These anthologies were succeeded by *New Writing* (1936–9), a semiannual of poetry and prose edited by John Lehmann and revived by him now and again under various titles.[11] Here the original group was augmented by John Cornford, whose poems in the fourth volume seemed to Lehmann the only successful poems produced on "hard-thinking Marxist lines" by an English writer—and perhaps they are.

The best poet of the Auden generation is Auden. His *Poems* (1930) reveal a new social consciousness in original rhythms, conversational or jazz techniques, and unlimited sensitivity. By these rhythms, and by suitable images of deserted factories, frontiers, invalid chairs, glaciers, and schoolboy games, Auden suggests the death

[11] See Lehmann: "Without My Files," *Penguin New Writing* (1944), for a survey of the periodical and its contributors.

of his class. Ideas for improvement, resembling those of D. H. Lawrence, stop short of Marx, who had little use for the individual change of heart that Auden prescribed. "No ruffian badge" of party membership nor "bombs of conspiracy" spoiled an energetic preoccupation with death. *The Orators* (1932), with its schoolboy pranks and technical improvisations, conceals what Strachey called the fascist unconscious. Here the death of society is celebrated again, and again in *The Dance of Death* (1933), a masque and Auden's most Marxist poem. Its music-hall techniques lead to the entrance of Karl Marx, muttering about liquidation as he brings the curtain down. Even this burlesque of their convictions was gratefully received by waiting multitudes. Auden's later poems, those of *Look, Stranger!* (1936), for example, if at all Marxist, are so by indirection. "Fish in the unruffled lakes" and "Lay your sleeping head, my love," illustrate nothing but his excellence and his protean variety. The three poetic plays he wrote with Christopher Isherwood concern the decay of the present world in fascism, imperialism, and war, not an inevitable future. Of these *The Ascent of F6*, produced in 1937, is the most remarkable. The theme of this political allegory is the plight of the intellectual, torn between the pulls of left and right, disloyal to both and therefore to himself. While flat characters occupy the mountain scenery, Mr. and Mrs. A. provide a suburban chorus from their boxes; and while devices from cinema and radio speed or interrupt the action, the Announcer announces. Rhythms of Sweeney and of middle-class rhetoric supply immediacy and despair. The climax, where allegory yields to expressionism, advances above, below, and beyond the limits that confined the commercial stage. It is not surprising that Auden's hero, like the hero of Eliot's *Family Reunion*, should assume the postures of Œdipus and Telemachus:

for ours is a time of hunting mothers and hunted fathers.[12]

Of these fashionable poets Stephen Spender is next best and somewhat more orthodox. Toward the end of *Poems* (1933) are several revolutionary lyrics, threatening death to exploiters, pitying the unemployed, and, in their imagery of aerodromes and railways, looking to a Wellsian future. Advising "young comrades" to forsake their fathers' houses, Spender points to dawns "exploding like a shell" and to new roots seeking water. These poems, mostly in free verse, show lyric intelligence and Spender's admiration of Whitman and Lawrence. Aside from "Pylons," "The Funeral" is worthiest of notice and most original. Here Russian workers carry to a grave (while red flags wave) a dead worker, "one cog in a golden and singing hive." Revolutionary enthusiasm may excuse the presence of cogs in the hive and explain the general looseness of these poems, which were, however, a welcome change from Eliot. But *Vienna* (1934) is imitation Eliot and imitation Auden. Technically derivative as it is, this promising poem is the first celebration of a revolutionary theme by one of the group. Spender's waste land is Vienna, where, in January 1934, rebellious socialists and workers were destroyed by capitalists. In the fourth and best section, which is interrupted by echoes of the first three, Spender's private world responds to intrusive reality. The doors of this world gradually closed. Although his essays on literature and communism seem Marxist enough to an outsider; Spender's defense of the artist's individuality and his right to choose theme and treatment displeased Caud-

[12] *Collected Poetry* (1945). Auden and Isherwood: *Journey to a War* (1939), on the "fascist" invasion of China, is notable for impartiality and a noble sonnet on a dead Chinese soldier. *On the Frontier* (published 1938), the third of their poetic plays, has a fine opening chorus of workers. See Auden Number of *New Verse* (November 1937), and Empson's "Just a Smack at Auden," *The Gathering Storm* (1940). Isherwood's *Lions and Shadows* (1938) concerns the Auden group.

well.[13] And as John Lehmann sadly observed, Spender increasingly deserved liquidation with E. M. Forster and other liberals. Other severer critics began to call Spender the Rupert Brooke of the depression, but it would have been better to call him the Shelley.

The early and best verses of C. Day Lewis use the metaphysical manner of the seventeenth century and the erudite manner of Eliot to celebrate the individual and his troubles. Social conscience stirred in *The Magnetic Mountain* (1933), where the manners of Auden and Hopkins conspire over a dying society, indicated by rusting factories and the other machinery of Auden's world. Some of the poems are revolutionary in theme. In *A Hope for Poetry* (1934), a group manifesto and an explanation of technical ancestry, Day Lewis praises Auden and Spender in return for their praise, as if taking in one another's washing could make it red.

Revolution in Writing (1935) is Day Lewis's defense of poetry and of the individual's rights against bourgeois society and demanding Marxists. Rejecting propaganda, he calls, while trying to be true to Marx, for liberal æsthetics. The position of Day Lewis and the other fellow travelers was a difficult one. Bourgeois by nature, proletarian by sympathy, they found themselves neither here nor there. Many of Day Lewis's poems concern internal conflict. "I look to the left, comrades," he exclaims while looking to the right. *Noah and the Waters* (1936), a morality play in the Auden-Eliot manner, though provided with an epigraph from the *Communist Manifesto*, shows Noah in the posture of Day Lewis, tempted by burgesses on one hand and on the other by the proletarian flood.[14]

[13] *The Destructive Element* (1935), *Forward from Liberalism* (1937). *Trial of a Judge* (1938), a poetic play, is anti-fascist.

[14] *Transitional Poem* (1929), *From Feathers to Iron* (1931). His most revolutionary poems are 34 and 36, Part IV of *The Magnetic Mountain*.

Louis MacNeice, of the Auden group, a better poet than Spender or

The menace of fascism did more than the unaided Communist Party could to provide a credible cause. In the later thirties when the People's Front, under party control, embraced all leftist groups but Labour, leftist literature became anti-fascist literature. Franco's Spain provided from 1936 to 1938 the emotional center. Finding at last a clear position, poets abandoned pacifism, visited Spain, wrote poems about it, or enlisted in the International Brigade. Tom Wintringham, small poet and political commissar in the brigade, fell wounded. Christopher Caudwell died manning his machine gun; John Cornford, Julian Bell, and Ralph Fox died manning theirs. To celebrate these heroes and symbolic Spain, Spender and Lehmann edited *Poems for Spain* (1939), to which Spender, Wintringham, Cornford, Auden, and others contributed. Spender's poems, descriptive and pathetic, want revolutionary conviction. Auden's "Spain," previously published in 1937, is better as poetry than as propaganda. By "poets exploding like bombs" Auden ambiguously intends his more desperate comrades and by "the flat ephemeral pamphlet and the boring meeting" the life of the party.[15]

Spain was what English poetry needed. But Spain was not enough to inspire the proletarian novel, which, defeated by orthodoxy, perhaps, continued to languish. Ralph Bates, who worked and fought in Spain, devoted one of the best of these, *The Olive Field* (1936), to Spanish workers and landlords and the insurrection of 1934. His individuals according to Marx are less alive than the

Day Lewis, did not share their revolutionary enthusiasm; but his poems are filled with conviction of impending disaster: *Poems* (1935), *Plant and Phantom* (1941). With Auden he wrote *Letters from Iceland* (1937). *Modern Poetry* (1938).

[15] John Lehmann's *Noise of History* (1934), contains good prose poems on the workers of Berlin and Vienna. The most detached critic of the group, Lehmann made the best survey of it: *International Literature*, No. 4 (1936). *In Letters of Red* (1938), edited by E. A. Osborne, is the penultimate anthology.

group and its relation to the symbolic trees. Although not proletarian, the fantasies of Rex Warner and the Berlin and Vienna novels of Christopher Isherwood are anti-fascist and not unreadable.[16]

Loyalist politics and Stalin's pact with Hitler in 1939 finally diverted the fellow travelers. A sudden shift of party line, which made of England's war against fascism an imperialistic adventure, enabled poets to see the value of what they had surrendered for something thought better. They saw the party plain, no longer as guide to the world's proletariat, but as the instrument of Russian policy. Deferring their quarrel with their class, fellow travelers discovered they were British, wrote poems about air raids, became air-raid wardens, or attacked the Russians.

The betrayal of the left caused John Strachey to relapse into the Labour Party and after its victory to accept a post in the cabinet.[17] The relapse of George Orwell, though less dramatic, is more typical. Disillusioned in Spain, he devoted the principal essay of *Inside the Whale* (1940) to the innocence of fellow travelers. Communism, he concludes, makes intellectual honesty impossible. It is intellectual honesty that distinguishes the essays known in America as *Dickens, Dali and Others* and in England as *Critical Essays* (1946). Remarkable as well for their easy directness, these examinations of popular literature are

[16] Bates: *The Fields of Paradise* (1940). Isherwood's *Prater Violet* (1945), on the Vienna rebellion and the menace of Hitler, symbolizes England's attitude by umbrella and irrelevant movie. Isherwood admits his generation consisted of "parlor socialists." Arthur Calder-Marshall: *Pie in the Sky* (1937). John Sommerfield: *May Day* (1936). *Europa in Limbo* (1937) and *Fandango* (1940), by Robert Briffault, are poor but orthodox.

[17] The disillusionment of Strachey, Laski, and Victor Gollancz of the Left Book Club is recorded in their *Betrayal of the Left* (1941), to which Orwell contributed. Herbert Read, who had called himself a communist, proclaimed himself an anarchist in *Poetry and Anarchism* (1938) and other tracts. His position, not unlike that of the other poets, is more precisely defined.

sociological criticism of the first order. *Animal Farm* (1945), the most brilliant political satire since Swift's, is directed against Stalin and his commissars. As the pigs betray the barnyard revolution, they change its slogans. All animals are equal, to be sure, but some "are more equal than others."

Backsliding in *The New Realism* (1939), where he defends the artist's integrity, Spender reveals his complete relapse into liberalism in the poems of *Ruins and Visions* (1942), where, looking within himself, he becomes, as he says, involved in his own entrails.[18] Day Lewis's *Word over All* (1943), praised by Spender as the best of the year, is resigned and defeated verse. As air-raid warden he helped England "defend the bad against the worse" while recapturing infant memories or, forgetting his class, was nice to a working man. To Lehmann's sorrow, Auden, Isherwood, and Bates departed for capitalistic America, Isherwood to become a yogi, Auden, to all appearances, a Christian, and Bates a book-reviewer. But while Louis MacNeice, whose interests were less political than those of his friends, was composing his "Epitaph for Liberal Poets,"[19] illiberal MacDiarmid, still a party member, was founding a quarterly to maintain the heat of dialectical materialism or to reheat it. And Sean O'Casey, who had once been secretary to James Connolly's militant workers in Ireland, produced in 1940 *The Star Turns Red*, the ideal Marxist melodrama. With these loyal Celts to his left and the Labour Party to his right, moderate Laski surveyed the empty field.

[18] Spender was also involved in the translation of Lorca and of Rilke, who, along with Kierkegaard, had become the darlings of the liberal. The vogue of Kierkegaard, an individualist, followed disillusionment with communism. Complicated by Germans, Kierkegaard's philosophy resulted in the existentialism of Sartre, which on the political plane appears to be another expression of bourgeois anarchism.

[19] *Springboard* (1944). Cf. "To a Communist," *Poems* (1935).

CHAPTER III

Right

THIS chapter deals less with reactionary philosophies than with their effects, direct, peripheral, and indirect. Nationalism, imperialism, fascism, and neoclassicism produced propaganda, of course, and with it much of greater excellence: poems by Yeats, prose by Kipling and Eliot, and—far from these on the periphery—some novels of Conrad.

I

"Imperialism," said Lenin—and it is foolish to quarrel with him—"is the monopoly stage of capitalism." Faced at last with the failure of *laissez faire*, capitalists turned to monopoly, state control imposed from above, and the geographical extension of monopoly. Colonies gave them the markets and materials they needed and the chance to export their capital. In the late nineteenth century, trusts and the great powers representing them extended monopolies to empty places. Rival monopolies, established by small wars, led to greater wars, which threatened to destroy what they were designed to protect.

British imperialism of this time was the attempt of the middle class to prevent its decline. This attempt, inspired by growing German and American competition, was supported by doctrines of racial supremacy, formulated by

Houston Chamberlain and others, by a theory of state supremacy, expounded by Bernard Bosanquet, and by Darwin's ideas of fitness. The *Daily Mail* was founded in 1896. Here and elsewhere journalists and poets made empire glamorous enough to serve as a substitute for religion. Fear and hate, the principal sentiments, accompanied thoughts of righteousness. The Liberal Party, representing an earlier stage of capitalism, declined and fell, to be succeeded in 1895 by the Tory government of Lord Salisbury, of which Joseph Chamberlain was the significant member. Under him British imperialism attained its perfection. Rudyard Kipling was its simple-minded singer.[1]

It would be simplest to dismiss Kipling's verse as doggerel. But the verses he wrote, from *Departmental Ditties* (1886) to those which interrupted his last collections of prose, are often more than that. Some are ballads suitable for baritones in parlors, some are hymns suitable for Anglicans at worship, and some, like "If—," are suitable for framing on walls. A master of thumping, splendid rhythms, of the language of daily speech, and of rhyming abstractions, he generally wrote what Yeats called popular poetry, verse that pleases a class commonly indifferent to literature. The sensitivity is limited, the response to reality is crude, the whole escapes becoming poetry because it is conscious and contrived. But in this kind, a kind in which Longfellow excelled, Kipling's verse is good. Good journalism, metrical talent, and simple morality never produced anything more haunting than "Mandalay" or "Gentlemen-Rankers" or "Gunga Din." Sometimes Kipling rose above this kind to poetry: "Recessional," a triumph of tone, "Cities and Thrones and Powers," and a translation

[1] See Élie Halévy: *A History of the English People, 1895–1905* (1926). Rudyard Kipling: *Something of Myself* (1937). Edward Shanks: *Rudyard Kipling* (1940). Hilton Brown: *Rudyard Kipling* (1946). Edmund Wilson: *The Wound and the Bow* (1941). George Orwell: *Critical Essays* (1946).

from Horace. In "The Way through the Woods" he approached the Georgians.

A poet with such gifts was fitted to become the laureate of Joseph Chamberlain's designs. Although Kipling rejected Tory honors, and thought himself independent, he was among the last of public poets. While others, expressing themselves alone, exiled themselves from the middle class, Kipling, sharing its sentiments, expressed it. That he was unconscious of doing this made his conscious verses better and assured their sale.

His idea of empire may be deduced from "Recessional," "The White Man's Burden," and "Loot." It was the duty of the chosen race to bring order to "lesser breeds without the Law." These unfortunates, all right when servile, consisted of Irishmen, Indians, Russians, Burmese, and Americans. The Law, the middle-class Englishman's idea of what was what, was enforced by a thin red line, keeping the borders against unarmed outsiders. The ascetics who administered the Law were gentlemen trained for the purpose by playing games at public schools. No profit or reward softened their Indian discomforts save their sense of work well done. They were aided by common men, soldiers of the line, fine fellows, respectful of their betters. Kipling was so far from knowing what his sahibs were about that he despised business men and members of Parliament. Unaware that imperialism was capitalism and that democracy was their necessary condition, the confused, angry man allied himself with feudal aristocracy, which, though dead, was their disguise. He consorted when he could with Cecil Rhodes and the Viceroy.

But Kipling had started as a common journalist. His earliest stories, unlike the verse of his imperial days, are filled with sympathy for all the swarming humanity about him. *Plain Tales from the Hills* (1888) presents the follies and wisdom of Anglo-Indian society at Simla, especially those of "wonderful" Mrs. Hauksbee. At the other end of the social scale are a native girl who loses the hands that embraced a sahib, and three soldiers, Mulvaney and his chums. The prose, swift and sure, and the impeccable craft suggest long study of Maupassant and Stevenson. Slight characters are supported by local-colored places. *Soldiers Three* (1888) invites comparison with Dumas. Mulvaney, a fabulous creature, fills myths whose only flaw is the dialect with which Kipling tried in vain to make himself unreadable. Exploiting India as artist, not as sahib, he pleased by his sharp, exotic flavor. It took barbarous Vermont to make a sahib of him.

Having tired of India, Kipling tried to become an American, but, defeated by Vermont, became an imperial Englishman instead and spent his time abusing Americans. His excuse is that one of his American relatives was almost as unbearable as he. Even in his hate he was fortunate, for the middle class of England, fearing American machines, found his hate their own and paid him well for it. Expanding from Vermont to include the non-English world, his hate provided protective shells into which he could withdraw to shield his wounded sensitivity and limit it. Upon the reality that he had warmly welcomed he began to impose middle-class patterns. These emotional and moral limitations and the growing technical proficiency that made his stories a little slick made him the symbol as well as the prophet of his class.

The success of the American stories is their British tone. "An Error in the Fourth Dimension" shows an irresponsible American capitalist breaking the British code and, rejected by responsible British capitalists, fleeing to the "unkempt" banks of the Hudson. "An Habitation Enforced," no less condescending, shows good rich Americans in England. Having learned that in England only Englishmen may speak, these boobies are grateful when spoken to. The squire's lady accepts them, they attend the established church, and are happy ever after. Kipling, who simplified all, had succeeded in simplifying Henry James. "The Captive," a story of the Boer War, presents Laughton O. Zigler, an Ohio capitalist, who, unfaithful to the breed, has been "fighting for niggers, as the North did." He sees his error, becomes an acceptable subject, and in "The Edge of the Evening" breaks the law with impunity as a sahib may. In "Sea Constables," a story of 1915, British brokers and bankers, suspecting a Yankee of being pro-German, let him die without medical attention because he is "altogether outside the game." Similar treatment is accorded a dying "Hun," representing another rival empire, in "Mary Postgate."

Stories of triumphant empire accompany these. In "The Devil and the Deep Sea" English pearl-poachers poach pearls in waters of one of the "lesser law-breaking Powers." The moral is that England protects her pirates and that Englishmen can repair machinery. An English gunboat in "Judson and the Empire" subdues a Brazilian democratic revolution that threatens to interrupt the exploitation of Brazil by the General Development Company. Such stories are too numerous to list, but it is impossible altogether to ignore those which attack democracy in favor of government by sahibs. In "A Walking Delegate," conservative, perhaps Republican, horses on a Vermont farm trample a social-democratic yellow horse who advises revolt against oppression. "With the Night Mail" and "As Easy as A.B.C," Wellsian dreams of mechanical Utopia, reveal a time when government by self-appointed experts has succeeded the "rule of the mob." With intolerable machines these specialists come from London to subdue a democratic rebellion in Illinois. Other stories praise machines, which by their order, co-operation, and discipline symbolized the Empire. As Romance brought up the 9.15, the simplest reader could feel its splendid inhumanity.

Mechanical perfection of plot and efficiency of prose, however admirable, were not enough to make Kipling a novelist; for a novelist must have greater understanding of people than Kipling's self-imposed limitations generally allowed. *The Light that Failed* (1890) failed; and *Captains Courageous* (1897), however salty, is flawed by the sudden reformation of the hero. But in *Kim* (1901) Kipling triumphed. This great nostalgic novel, recapturing his earlier delight in the multitudes of India, presents with sympathetic tolerance not only sahibs but men of lesser breed, the excellent Lama, the horse-trader, and the lady of the litter. The Grand Trunk Road symbolizes the essential theme, the color, confusion, and humanity of India. The manifest theme is a double quest, that of the Lama to escape the Wheel of Things and that of Kim to find the Red Bull in a Green Field. After picaresque adventures each finds satisfaction, but, as Edmund Wilson points out in his acute essay, these satisfactions are on separate planes, which it was the duty of the novelist to reveal in conflict or to reconcile. Kipling failed to do justice to the demands of his theme, but he did succeed in creating a work at once imperialistic and good. What he called his "Daemon," that part of his nature which was uncommercial, must have had a hand in *Kim*.

In *Stalky and Co.* (1899) Kipling made his semi-public school more public by introducing the practical jokes, vengeances, and small cruelties that were his obsession. *The Jungle Book* (1894) is loved by every child, but even here that didactic nature inherited from many Methodists made his jungle an allegory of empire. The Bander-logs, democratic outsiders, are destroyed by the Law of the Jungle. If, like a child, one can ignore their imperial function, Kaa and the other animals are fine people. "How the

Rhinoceros Got His Skin," the best of the *Just So Stories* (1902), is one of the best of Kipling's stories. *Puck of Pook's Hill* (1906), inferior to these, celebrates imperial virtues in the Roman defense of the wall, but is generally concerned with the glories of little England and "all her thousand years."

It was the Boer War that made a Little Englander and an introvert of imperial Kipling. Disillusioned by the hollowness disclosed, he never fully recovered. "Recessional" had warned against boastfulness and pride, and "The Lesson," written at the end of the war, is filled with apprehension. Although he returned again and again to his earlier themes, he became increasingly introspective. Cancer, shades, and strange obsessions surrounded old, suffering Kipling, a great master of prose who had kept himself from other greatness.

W. E. Henley, small poet, critic, and editor, patron of Kipling, Shaw, and Wells, was a lesser poet than Kipling but of the same breed. He admired piracy, served Stevenson as the model for John Silver, and preached the cult of virility. His early *Poems* (1888), some of them composed in primitive free verse, deal for the most part with his experiences in hospital where he lost a leg. "Invictus" with its courageous platitudes belongs with "If—" among poems of middle-class philosophy. During the Boer War, Henley wrote jingoistic verses, popular, obvious, and hysterical. These imperial sentiments had been expressed somewhat better in 1890 in his "Song of the Sword," a celebration in free verse of military violence and survival of the fittest. With Kipling he shared the dream of unending progress through empire and machine. This dream is the subject of "A Song of Speed," his last poem. In mechanical free verse he tells how Alfred Harmsworth, proprietor of the *Daily Mail*, took him for a ride in a 1901 Mercédès. As he handled her pipes and her cylinders

Henley succumbed to religious awe.[2] There were other poets of that kidney—Henry Newbolt, for instance, an even more nautical Kipling, and, later, Rupert Brooke, whose patriotic sonnets, agreeable to patriots, are of less importance than his poems of fish.

The parents of W. H. Hudson were North Americans, he was Argentinian, but, disregarding these accidents, he remained an Englishman. Fascinated by the British ranchers of the pampas, he regarded himself as one of them, though he differed from his neighbors in being interested more in the birds and flowers than in the other natural resources of the pampas. In *The Purple Land that England Lost* (1885) the British hero regrets that England did not seize Uruguay in 1807 when it had the chance. England would have introduced system and cleanliness into a lawless dirty land. But faced there with nature's noblemen, he reconsidered the point, confessing a British readiness to regard people of other nationalities with a certain amount of contempt. "With us, perhaps, the feeling is stronger than with others, or else expressed with less reserve."[3]

As Hudson occupies a thin red circle somewhat more remote from the center than Kipling's, Charles M. Doughty and T. E. Lawrence occupy circles still more remote but in the same system. More or less unintentionally these two great men assisted imperial designs upon Arabia. England needed control of Arabia, as of Egypt and the Sudan, in order to protect the flow of wealth from India. In 1875 England acquired the necessary shares in the Suez Canal. It was not accidental that Doughty's exploration of Arabia commenced in 1876. Unconscious of his function, however, he resembled those

[2] Jerome Hamilton Buckley: *William Ernest Henley* (1946).

[3] Hudson's excellent autobiography, *Far Away and Long Ago* (1918), is his best work. Morley Roberts: *W. H. Hudson* (1924).

explorers and missionaries who commonly preceded the flag. *Travels in Arabia Deserta* (1888), the great sprawling story of his adventures, is no less peculiar for its matter than for its style, which fits the matter like a blanket. Crabbed, cantankerous, and archaic, formidable in diction, original in syntax, this wonderful style, repelling all but the hardiest reader, succeeds in exposing the author and itself. Emergent Doughty is of the rough-hewn tribe of Hardy, Hopkins, and the author of *Beowulf*. T. E. Lawrence's *Seven Pillars of Wisdom* (1926) is equally singular.[4] Starting as archæologist in Mesopotamia, and as spy disguised as archæologist in the region of Sinai, Lawrence became in 1916 the organizer of the Arab revolt against the Turks. He was a British agent, but his independence and whimsicality and the original character of his strategy and tactics incurred official displeasure while ensuring his success. Far from being a conscious imperialist, he promised the Arabs freedom from "colonial schemes of exploitation," allayed their natural fears of England, and did what he could to foil the French. But the promises upon which he relied did not survive Versailles and its mandates. French Syria and British Iraq took the place of an Arab state. Troubled by thoughts of England's dishonor and his own, Lawrence retired monastically to the air force, where, as private, he found comfort in speed and in the friendship of Winston Churchill. Lawrence's book, recounting his Arabian exploits, tells of exploding trains and of politicians and camels. Written in the most familiar of grand manners, pungent and clear, this book approaches the epic as Lawrence the heroic.

Concerning thin red circles: some, epicycles on the system, were occupied by other writers. The commercial

[4] *Revolt in the Desert* (1927) is an abridgment of *The Seven Pillars*. *The Mint*, an account of his experiences in the air force, is still in manuscript. Liddell Hart: *Colonel Lawrence* (1934).

exploitation of inferiors had opened up new territories for literary exploitation, producing many novels and stories that without being imperialistic are colonial. Of these, those of Joseph Conrad are important.

Conrad spoke of himself as "a Polish nobleman, cased in British tar," and his political conservatism is what one might expect. During his nautical career he was gun-runner for a royalist faction. In a letter of 1886 he condemned socialism as a doctrine born in Continental slums and socialists as unscrupulous rascals. The socialists, anarchists, and nihilists of *The Secret Agent* (1907) and *Under Western Eyes* (1911) are vain and foolish, though presented with exemplary detachment. Ever puncturing the illusions of his friend Cunninghame Graham, socialist and adventurer, Conrad was cynical, yet enamored of British law.

Although Conrad favored the extension of British law to less fortunate countries, he was not an imperialist. He sometimes sneered at Kipling, even at his "Recessional," found Henley "a horrible bourgeois," disapproved of the Boer War and the Spanish-American War, which inspired "The White Man's Burden." But while ironic or indignant about the pretensions of American, Belgian, Dutch, French, and German imperialism and convinced that taking the earth away from defenseless people is "not a pretty thing," he saw little but good in British imperialism. In "The Heart of Darkness" Marlow finds the red patches on the map of Africa good "because one knows that some real work is done in there." Although most imperialism is "robbery with violence," British imperialism is redeemed by efficiency, "idea," and conscience. In his colonial stories Conrad generally avoided British colonies, preferring instead those of the Belgians and the Dutch.

Taking empire as his frame and traders as his people, Conrad pondered what man and nature do to man within this frame. *Almayer's Folly* (1895), his first novel, is a story of Dutch and English traders, half-castes, and natives in Borneo. The incursion of Dutch empire is part of the plot, but the emphasis falls upon the minds of Almayer, his native wife, and his daughter. Dealing with some of the same people in similar contact, *An Outcast of the Islands* (1896) makes tragedy of misalliances that Kipling would have treated within the categories of caste. Trade, empire, and the indignation of natives form the background for a slow-motion adventure story in which introverts, clogged with their dream, move about like sleep-walkers. Pages of brooding or analysis separate the question from its answer and the gesture from its object. Even the semicolons are a little sleepy. British progress in the Malay States and German competition frame "The End of the Tether" (1902), much livelier and more readable, a story of conflict between love and duty. These heavy studies of the soul in trouble are involved in their exotic places; but no ideas emerge, for Conrad had little use for them. They are implicit, however, in his two accounts of the Belgian Congo, which, though further studies of human suffering, are almost attacks upon colonial policy. "An Outpost of Progress" (1898) is an ironic picture of ineffectuals in a Congo trading post. After reading an article on "Our Colonial Expansion," these bringers of light feel for a time an almost British sense of mission, and question the exchange of ivory and slaves. "The Heart of Darkness" (1902), Conrad's most powerful and enigmatic story, is another nightmare. The discovery by Marlow and Kurtz of the nature of things and Kurtz's dying exclamation are the theme for which the forest provides intrusive darkness. But on the edge of darkness the "imbecile rapacity" of the Belgians is exposed to British contempt.

In Patusan, Lord Jim's racket shows British imperialism

at its best, but in the composite South American republic of *Nostromo* (1904) Mr. Gould's silver shows it to less advantage. Mr. Gould and other British capitalists, who control silver mine and railroad, control that country's politics, backing a reactionary dictator in the interests of order. Mr. Gould's integrity is British, but his American backer, a capitalist without ideals, is unredeemed. Emerging from political chaos, the mine absorbs the country, exploited natives resent it, and Mr. Gould loses his soul. Nostromo, that vain, simple man, loses his life for silver, which has become symbolic. Only Mrs. Gould and Decoud, the detached cynic, remain above materialism. Almost a sermon, this slow, descriptive novel, with its sleepy power, remains, like all of Conrad's art, essentially ambiguous.[5]

Darkest Africa provided W. Somerset Maugham with the scene for *The Explorer* (1907), a novel in which an Etonian explores, subdues wicked slave-traders, establishes a virtuous British trading company, and enables England to claim a territory larger than herself. Maugham matured; and the short stories he wrote in the 1920's, though imperial in setting, are far from imperialistic in aim. His places are Samoa, Malaya, and Borneo, his people sahibs; but his themes are the effect upon them of lonely places and colored people. Mixed marriage, caste, infidelity, and tropical anxieties are presented with the detachment, lucidity, and form of Maupassant. "Rain" and "The Letter" are the most famous and the most cynical. In "Before the Party" the wife of a drunken Resident in Borneo cuts his throat in a crisis of disapproval, which her British relatives consider "frightfully bad form." In

[5] G. Jean-Aubry: *Joseph Conrad, Life and Letters* (1927). Conrad: *Tales of Unrest* (1898). H. M. Tomlinson is one of Conrad's most devoted followers. *Gallions Reach* (1927), elaborately introspective, concerns adventure at sea and in the Malay jungle. Cf. *The Sea and the Jungle* (1912).

"The Outstation" a lonely outpost in Borneo or Malaya is the scene of conflict between a snob from Eton and a cad from the colonies. As Maugham says of himself, he is "competent" and "readable." His most readable stories are those of *Ashenden or the British Agent* (1928), where want of substance permitted triumph of style. No writer of our time commands an easier elegance or shows to better advantage the effect of the eighteenth century. *The Moon and Sixpence* (1919) is colonial in part; but this embellishment of the life of Gauguin is important for presenting the artistic morality of the nineties with the kind of wisdom that ensures popularity. Maugham is among the most excellent of commercial artists. But more than that, he is remarkable among Englishmen of his generation and class for treating outsiders, even colonials, without arrogance. Though he loves his country, he cannot stand it, and lives elsewhere.[6]

The skeptical twenties, looking wickedly at things, looked wickedly at empire. Maugham's stories have the detachment and cynicism of that happy time. But E. M. Forster's *Passage to India* (1924), having irony, is even more typical. Here Forster, a Little Englander in other novels, displays sahibs and natives, the first maintaining white supremacy with the emotions of Southern colonels, the second, insulted and injured, nursing hysteria upon despair. He impartially exposes the injustice of officials, the shoddiness of educated natives, and, in the diminishing coda, the Anglo-Indian dilemma. But the troubles of empire are the lesser theme. What seems greater, though less clear, is the echo in the Marabar caves, reducing all to nothing, introducing ancient night. This noise gives

[6] The short stories are collected in *Altogether* (1934) (in the United States entitled *East and West*). *The Gentlemen in the Parlour* (1930), travelogue, and *The Narrow Corner* (1932), novel, concern the Orient. *The Summing Up* (1938), autobiography.

Miss Quested her hallucination, Dr. Aziz his trial, and Mrs. Moore her horror. The central enigma is Mrs. Moore. What does she signify? What is her power? She does little, says less, yet deeply stirs the native heart. Her caves invite Freudian or anthropological tickets; but, evading such devices, she sinks below them. Upon such depths the white man and his burden seem negligible. This irony was part of Forster's plan. His distinction is to have suggested more than he said and, exceeding the lateral extensions of Kipling, to have made the Empire bottomless.

The responsible thirties, Christian or socialist, sometimes failed to include empire among their responsibilities. Azania of Evelyn Waugh's *Black Mischief* (1932) is Abyssinia, which civilized powers long to civilize. Sharing this longing, Seth, the Emperor, introduces boots, contraceptives, and other signs of progress and culture. His subjects eat them. European fools or knaves increase the turbulence, which brings a Franco-British mandate. At once horrible and funny, Waugh's satire, not unlike Voltaire's, is impartial. If native disorder is hopeless, British order is suburban or stupid. If Basil Seal eats his mistress at a cannibal banquet, it is no worse than might occur under more civil auspices. Mandoa of Winifred Holtby's *Mandoa, Mandoa!* (1933) is Waugh's Abyssinia revisited; and some of her visitors are his.[7] Her novel attempts too many things, but succeeds among them at satire upon "policy, profit, and reform." Her imperialists, victorious in the elections of 1931, are decorous. But the slave trading of Mandoa to which they object is no worse in her eyes than the employment or unemployment of British workers or of natives in Kenya. That Waugh and Holtby, though obsessed with the barbarous, the civilized, and

[7] The humanity of *South Riding* (1936), Miss Holtby's other important book, makes it far more than local government fictionized. For Miss Holtby's life see Vera Brittain: *Testament of Friendship* (1940).

the bizarre, were unrepresentative of their class was proved a few years later by the words of Mr. Churchill. Kipling, turning in his grave, paused at those words.

II

Reaction invites equal and opposite or sometimes greater reaction. British imperialism produced Irish nationalism, no less reactionary on the whole, and with it a literature better at its best than that of contemporary England. The westward course of empire was not extraordinary. Civilized by British garrison, police, landlords, and business men, the population of Ireland declined from eight million in 1841 to four million in 1911. Some starved while landlords exported food, some emigrated, and some survived. The remnant became impatient, destroying Englishmen in alleys now and then or in Phoenix Park, and even the Anglo-Irish complained a little and celebrated Ireland in poetry or in prose. Since education was a monopoly of the ruling class and since the Irish Church, unlike the French, was inimical to intellect or imagination, the literature of Irish nationalism was generally Anglo-Irish. Ornaments of the renaissance were Yeats and Joyce, the one Anglo-Irish, the other Irish. A third was Anglo-Irish Synge.[8]

This quickening, in which oppression, the compactness of Dublin, and genius conspired, began in the eighties. When it began, Parnell was giving hope of independence by parliamentary action. His Land League was helping peasants against landlords, to the displeasure of George Moore, landlord, who expressed it in *Parnell and His Island* (1887). The failure of Gladstone's Home Rule bill in 1886, the death of Parnell in 1891, and the return of Tories to power brought promise of more coercion and for most an end to hope of constitutional remedies. Par-

[8] Dorothy Macardle: *The Irish Republic* (1937). Ernest Boyd: *Ireland's Literary Renaissance* (1922).

nell's fall and death split Irish patriots into factions. Fenians of the Irish Republican Brotherhood constructed bombs. Maud Gonne carried them about or planted them in likely places; and G Men stirred about her when she stirred.[9] Sublimating poets, disgusted by the betrayal of Parnell, turned from politics and found happiness in a heroic past which, by enlarging the soul, might ensure a future.

Standish O'Grady's *History of Ireland* appeared in 1878 and 1880. Before this, Sir Samuel Ferguson had made poems of Ireland's heroic past, but it was O'Grady who fathered the renaissance by disclosing in his imaginative, unorthodox history the glories of Finn MacCool and Cuchulain.[10] Here was the matter that James Clarence Mangan, no scholar, had wanted to make his patriotic verse better. After O'Grady came George Sigerson, translating Gaelic poems, and Douglas Hyde, founder of the Gaelic League, who restored the forgotten language and by his *Love Songs of Connacht* (1893) and other translations provided an English style, Irish in rhythm, extravagance, and idiom, for Lady Gregory and Synge. Folklorists went about interrupting peasants. T. W. Rolleston and John Todhunter, inspired by these labors, commenced as Irish poets; and Katharine Tynan tuned her small Catholic instrument to pagan song. Anthologies announcing these and other poets confirmed the revival.[11]

[9] Maud Gonne MacBride: *A Servant of the Queen* (1938). British agents in Ireland were called G Men.

[10] The Celtic revival extended to Scotland and Wales under Fiona Macleod (William Sharp) and Ernest Rhys, both followers of Yeats. See Elizabeth Sharp: *William Sharp* (1912), and Ernest Rhys: *Wales England Wed* (1940). In the 1930's Welsh and Scottish nationalism revived. Keidrych Rhys: *Modern Welsh Poetry* (1944). Maurice Lindsay: *Modern Scottish Poetry* (1946). Magazines: *Wales, Scottish Art and Letters, Poetry Scotland.*

[11] *Poems and Ballads of Young Ireland* (1888), *A Treasury of Irish Poetry in the English Tongue* (1900).

To the first of these anthologies W. B. Yeats contributed "The Madness of King Goll" and "The Stolen Child," folk and legendary poems. When he commenced as poet in 1885, he had used the techniques of Spenser and the English romantics for Arcadian and Hindu themes, but now, instructed by O'Grady and the folklorists, he began to write ballads about priest and peasant and songs about the little people. From the legendary cycles he took Cuchulain, Fergus, and Tir-nan-og or the Land of Youth. Distorting his materials to fit his problems, he used Fergus as his symbol and became obsessed with Cuchulain's fights with son and wave. The most ambitious of these legendary poems is "The Wanderings of Oisin" (1889), in which by inventing much and by covering the severe original with ornament he made it nineteenth-century rococo. Adjectives like "pearl-pale" and "glimmering" try to anticipate effects and to create a twilight atmosphere, which, a product of the English romantic movement, is no more Celtic than a London fog. In this diffuse, dreamy narrative Yeats debated facing reality or escaping it.[12]

Yeats collected folk tales from the peasants or from the collections of earlier folklorists. When Lady Gregory became his patron, they visited her tenants and published the result of their inquiries in 1920 as *Visions and Beliefs in the West of Ireland.* For her excellent versions of the two epic cycles, written in peasant-flavored prose, he provided enthusiastic introductions. Her prose taught him much and he rewrote his own collections in it. Surveying the work of Irish folklorist and poet, he observed that there is no fine literature without nationality, and, pronouncing England dead, claimed a place near Davis, Mangan, Ferguson.[13]

[12] Yeats: *Collected Poems* (1933). Joseph Hone: *W. B. Yeats* (1943).

[13] Yeats: *Fairy and Folk Tales of the Irish Peasantry* (1888), *The Celtic Twilight* (1893), *Stories of Red Hanrahan* (1904). *Letters to the*

Yeats did not thoroughly approve, however, of the abstract and sometimes jingoistic verses of Thomas Davis and his school; nor did he thoroughly approve of the Irish Republican Brotherhood, of which for a time he was a member. His adoration of Maud Gonne was tempered by dismay at her conspiracies and her eloquence. Like his friend John O'Leary, the old Fenian, Yeats followed a more pacific ideal. He proposed to liberate the Irish by symbolic poetry and poetic drama, by the examples of Cuchulain and Oisin, by swooning diction and suitable rhythms. For a while Yeats remained true to this ideal, but his patriotism, never free from thoughts of Lady Gregory and Maud Gonne, was complicated by prudence and love.

The Irish Literary Theatre provided further complication. Founded in 1899 by Yeats, George Moore, and Edward Martyn, its financial backer, this uncommercial theater endured for three bad seasons. Their venture was doomed from the start by disagreement about ends, Moore and Martyn wanting Ibsen, and Yeats poetry and legend. His *Land of Heart's Desire,* a mild poetic play on fairies, had been produced in London by Florence Farr in 1894. *The Countess Cathleen,* far greater, was the first choice of the Literary Theatre for the season of 1899. At the first performance the lovely lines and sleepy atmosphere failed to prevent a riot (described by Joyce in *A Portrait of the Artist*) of Catholics injured by theological irregularity. The doubts of Martyn, a pious man, had been quieted by theologians he consulted, but the doubts of the audience, wanting such assurance, were expressed by shrill cries. Undiscouraged, Yeats continued to think he could elevate

New Island, 1934, edited by Horace Reynolds, contains essays written between 1888 and 1892.

Augusta Gregory: *Cuchulain of Muirthemne* (1902), *Gods and Fighting Men* (1904).

that audience by the power of poetry and by the nobility of an aristocrat selling her immortal soul for potatoes. Martyn's *Heather Field*, produced the following night, was quietly received. This well-constructed play about the defeat of a landlord by wife, weeds, and madness reflects Martyn's admiration for *The Master Builder* and *The Wild Duck*. Pulled in two directions, the theater collapsed, but it had shown the possibility of a national drama and had introduced Yeats to Lady Gregory. Under their management an Irish theater, avoiding Ibsen, was to become bucolic and great.[14]

This theater, later known as the Abbey or the National Theatre Society, was established by Frank and William Fay in 1901 for native actors acting native matters, heroic or peasant, especially the latter. They replaced Anglo-Saxon attitudes with those of Irishmen and the idiom of London with that of the Western World. Distinguished actors—the Fays, Sara Allgood, Dudley Digges, and others—attracted distinguished dramatists, whose plays are among the best of our time. A. E. composed for them his twilit *Deirdre*, a prose play in three acts, remarkable for an invocation of Mananaun MacLir. This tentative play was produced in 1902 with Yeats's *Cathleen Ni Houlihan*, written for and acted by Maud Gonne. The success of these plays assured a native drama.[15]

Pursuing his ideal, Yeats had seen possibilities in this company. *Cathleen Ni Houlihan*, first of many folk dramas it produced, was his only popular play. In the symbolic

[14] A. E. Malone: *The Irish Theatre* (1929). Una Ellis-Fermor: *The Irish Dramatic Movement* (1939). Moore's *Hail and Farewell* contains a hilarious account of the Literary Theatre. Denis Gwynn: *Edward Martyn and the Irish Revival* (1930). Moore's *Strike at Arlingford* (1893), a mediocre play produced in London, and *The Bending of the Bough* (1900), by Moore and Martyn, are Ibsenite. Martyn's *Maeve* (1900) is legendary.

[15] W. G. Fay and Catherine Carswell: *The Fays of the Abbey Theatre* (1935).

figure of the Poor Old Woman who had "the walk of a queen" he embodied Ireland's wrongs and her desire to rid the house of strangers. By verse no longer lyric but dramatic he centered Irish feelings and pleased his girl. Bred to a harder thing than triumph, he and Lady Gregory quickly assumed control of the theater and perfected its policies. In *Samhain,* its publication, he dissociated the company from Martyn's middle-class drawing-room, announced a return to the people, and promised a poetical drama "which tries to keep at a distance from daily life." For ten years plays and controversies constituted his daily life.[16]

The Pot of Broth, a slight prose comedy, was produced in 1902. Written in collaboration with Lady Gregory, and in her peasant idiom, the play is more hers than his. More typical of Yeats, *The King's Threshold,* played in 1903, symbolizes in the poet's hunger strike his fight for recognition by a world hostile to poetry. This theme from the Finn cycle served of course to express Yeats's own position and his desire. The procession of tempters and the variety of the verse make his poem dramatic. *On Baile's Strand* (1904), another one-act poetic play, reveals again his obsession with Cuchulain and elevates a familiar theme by majestical verse. The austerities of Yeats's *Deirdre* (1906) renew this favorite. Condensation, the chorus of musicians, and the subtlety of his heroine combine to make this version greater than A. E.'s if less than Synge's. Of the many plays Yeats wrote for the Abbey, these are representative and best. He had dreamed of a theater for verse plays remote from nature and society, but defeated by society, which, clamoring for pedestrian comedy, displayed indifference to his beautiful verse and to the symbols he substituted for characters, Yeats retired

[16] Yeats: *Plays in Prose and Verse* (1922), *Plays and Controversies* (1923), *Collected Plays* (1934); *Autobiography* (1938).

to his parlor, where with plays for dancers he pleased fit audience though few.[17] He was not a great dramatist but a great poet. Starting with the desire to hear his verses spoken, he wrote fine poems, like *The Shadowy Waters,* disguised as plays; but he gradually adapted himself to the theater, learned its craft, and achieved dramatic poetry. Its value perhaps was to give his lyric poetry hardness and power. But to the theater the poet's value was practical. In the capacity of director he served as Synge's bulldog.

Having found J. M. Synge trying to be Arthur Symons in Paris, Yeats persuaded the mistaken man to try the Aran Islands.[18] There he learned the rhythms and idioms that became his instrument and he learned there about the people in whose passions he found what was hidden in himself. On his return to Dublin, in love with life and art, he wrote those plays that assured his place as one of the two principal dramatists in English in his time.

The Shadow of the Glen, a one-act comedy produced in 1903, is an old wives' tale of husband pretending death to test his wife's fidelity. He is old, the place is lonesome, and she is bored. What might have been problem play or cynical farce rises to the plane of myth. Synge turned in 1904 to high tragedy. *Riders to the Sea* reveals in the death of Maurya's sons the death of all men and the sorrow of women. The sea is fate's agent and its symbol, the keening a chorus. Nothing greater, starker, or less restrained had appeared on the contemporary stage, and

[17] In 1916 Yeats began to write plays for dancers, inspired by the Japanese Noh plays. E.g., *The Only Jealousy of Emer,* a symbolist play for maskers, accompanied by zither, drum, and flute. See "Certain Noble Plays of Japan" and his other essays on the poetic play in *Essays* (1924). Ezra Pound introduced him to the Noh play.

[18] *The Aran Islands* (1907) is the journal of his visit. Maurice Bourgeois: *John Millington Synge and the Irish Theatre* (1913). Daniel Corkery: *Synge and Anglo-Irish Literature* (1931), a plea for intolerant nationalism.

nothing, though the medium is prose, so poetic. *The Well of the Saints* (1905) is strange, bitter comedy, no less universal. The conflict of dream and reality, Yeats's theme, is also Synge's. Martin and Mary Doul, blind beggars, think each other beautiful. A Saint, coming with his can of holy water, restores their sight. Examining the world, they do not like the look of it. She finds him a horror, he her a hag. Blind again, they refuse another cure. *The Tinker's Wedding*, published in 1908 but never played at the Abbey for fear of Irishmen, is a Chaucerian fabliau of covetous priest and blasphemous peasants. Wanting message, it is less irreverent than indifferent.

The Playboy of the Western World (1907), Synge's greatest comedy, work of a poet and a craftsman, triumphs by abundant, laughing speech and by what Yeats called "astringent joy and hardness." A delight to read, the play is a greater delight to see and hear. But the extravagant characters, their confusion of the heroic with the eloquent, their freedom from common things, displeased. Patriots hissed, and puritans, purer than elsewhere, booed. Their riots lasted all that week. Yeats, Synge's champion, offending nation, defended art.

It was the word "shifts" that bothered some who did not understand the shifts of Synge. For these Wicklow and the Aran Islands had provided patterns to be improved by imagination. For the speech Hyde and Lady Gregory had provided patterns; but such speech as Synge's had not been heard. Such people as his had not been seen. Patriots, however, wanted in place of the stage Irishman of tradition, not Synge's invention, but an impeccable dummy, suitably speaking. Maud Gonne resigned in anger from the National Theatre Society.

Deirdre of the Sorrows, left unfinished, was posthumously produced in 1910. Done in Synge's language, this three-act tragedy makes folk tale of legend, and heroic peasants of heroes. His Deirdre, more conscious than most of his characters, knows lovers age, and this knowledge makes her welcome doom. His other characters, uncircumscribed by logic, are generally careless of reasons for what they do. They are fabulous, acting less than existing, and existing through their speech. For his craft Synge found hints in Maeterlinck, Loti, and even Zola, but, changing what he took from them as he changed all, he remained singular.

Lady Augusta Gregory, who patronized Synge at Coole along with Yeats, Hyde, and others, was greater as patron, manager, and translator than as playwright. But not the least of her services to the Anglo-Irish renaissance are the one-act comedies she wrote to provide the Abbey with relief from the intolerable greatness of Synge. These comedies, written in her peasant idiom and dependent upon the mugging of her players, display a landlord's tolerance for the humors of tenants and for the complications of their simplicity. Her achievement is *The Gaol Gate* (1906), a one-act piece approaching tragedy and the gruesome humor of Synge.[19]

Lennox Robinson, who followed Synge among the Abbey's directors, wrote several fine plays of which *The Whiteheaded Boy* (1916), a comedy, is the most important. Unlike many good plays, this one is good reading not only for its dialogue but for the stage directions in Irish idiom and the author's asides, which, destroying his characters' characters, are as queer as Irish humor itself. An earlier play, *The Cross-Roads* (1909), in which nationalistic aspiration is defeated by a return to the land, shows that harrowing combination of darkness and auster-

[19] Gregory: *Our Irish Theatre* (1913), *Lady Gregory's Journals* (1946), *Seven Short Plays* (1908).

For the Abbey, Padraic Colum wrote his excellent peasant plays, *The Fiddler's House* (1907), and *Thomas Muskerry* (1910). Cf. T. C. Murray: *Maurice Harte* (1912).

ity which distinguished the Cork realists, those gloomy men who had learned from Ibsen and Turgenyev ways of dissecting suffering peasants.[20]

Under Robinson's management the Abbey produced the best plays since Synge's, those of Sean O'Casey, Dubliner. His characters are Dubliners the bleakness and violence of whose lives, though proper to a slum, reflect the tradition of Zola. *The Shadow of a Gunman* (1923) concerns poets, gunmen, and the Black and Tans. Comic at first, the tone changes and the tension rises until the appalling climax. Nationalism, ceasing to be ideal and implicit, openly occupies the turbulent center. *Juno and the Paycock* (1924), one of O'Casey's best plays, creates against the background of civil war the character of Captain Jack Boyle, the paycock. Made for the use of Barry Fitzgerald, the paycock displays himself while his wife scolds, his daughter loses her virtue, and his son, crippled by a bomb, is carried away by Irregulars. The screaming violence of the climax yields in memory, however, to the humors of Boyle, who is less comic relief than comic triumph set off by surrounding tragedy. *The Plough and the Stars* (1926) is an excellent loosely constructed tragedy, not unlike the histories of Shakespeare in design and, not unlike them, better seen than read. Without outstanding characters, the play deals with the tenants of a single house, communist, republican, Orangeman, together with consumptives, wives, and whores. Their individual tragedies during Easter Week stand for Ireland's troubles, but the play, far from propaganda, is a dramatist's job. Not that delight in language by which O'Casey resembles Synge, but that similar delight in people which moved O'Casey to create imperfect patriots caused the audience

[20] Robinson: *The Clancy Name* (1908), *Plays* (1928), *More Plays* (1935), *Curtain Up* (1942), autobiography. *The Irish Theatre* (1939), edited by Robinson.

to riot, though soothed once more from the stage by Yeats, O'Casey's discoverer. Whether the reception of *The Plough and the Stars* or the Abbey's prudent rejection of his next play was the immediate cause of his departure for London, where his subsequent plays were produced, is debatable. The rejected play, *The Silver Tassie* (1929), starting realistically enough in a Dublin kitchen, becomes symbolic fantasy and war's indictment. The scenes at the front or in the hospital, where people bound about and break into bad verse at the drop of a hat, are less effective, though sufficiently nightmarish, than the domestic scenes at which O'Casey excelled. But distracted by Eugene O'Neill and the Continental expressionists, O'Casey turned his back on realism and slum. *Within the Gates* (1934) is a symbolic play of a London park in which a kind of rhythm takes the place of plot and significant creatures appear, reappear, and mysteriously declaim. The point, unclear as in many symbolic plays, appears to be the disorder of the world. As the gramophone announces the fall of London Bridge, as the man in plus-fours pursues his girl, as the chorus of down-and-outs goes down and out, the park appears another waste land, depression-born and portentous. Attempting too much, the play achieves too little.

The proletarian sympathies evident in these plays developed into melodrama with *The Star Turns Red* (1940), a play whose revolutionary violence makes English fellow-traveling seem pale. "Militant workers," waving red flags, conquering policemen and fascists, convert the soldiers sent against them. Fascist and liberal priests take sides as the Red Star supplants the Cross. But O'Casey's later plays, *Purple Dust*, published in 1940, and *Red Roses for Me*, in 1942, are remarkable neither for communism nor for success. The first of these is a preposterous comedy of rich Englishmen who, trying to settle in an Irish house, have trouble with Irishmen, telephones, cows, and flood. The second is a symbolic fantasy of Dublin Catholics, Protestants, strikers, and police, written in language of such richness that the point is obscured and one is left only with the conviction that, as a flower girl says, "It's a bleak, black an' bitther city."[21]

Increasingly neither here nor there, O'Casey dissipated that realistic gift which had helped save the Abbey, weakened by the troubles and almost destroyed by the curfew. The financial backing of Miss A. E. F. Horniman, an Englishwoman, had been withdrawn, the audience declined, and unpaid actors left the scene. But a subsidy from the Free State, new actors, such as Barry Fitzgerald, and the appearance of new dramatists restored the Abbey's fortunes. Besides O'Casey there were George Shiels, harmless and popular, and Teresa Deevy.[22] Most notable of the newcomers were Denis Johnston and Paul Vincent Carroll, who demand the space the others deserve.

Rejected at first by Lady Gregory, Johnston got his start at the Gate Theatre, where in 1929 Michael MacLiammoir and Hilton Edwards, the managers, produced *The Old Lady Says 'No'!* Commonly supposed to allude to Lady Gregory, but actually alluding to the Poor Old Woman, or Ireland herself, this brilliant nightmare shows Robert Emmet wandering in search of his love through the streets and homes of modern Dublin, meeting flappers, Trinity students, animate statues, and bohemians. As the discouraged patriot wanders, talking in tags from Pearse

[21] Autobiographies: *I Knock at the Door* (1939), *Pictures in the Hallway* (1942), *Drums under the Windows* (1946). *The Story of the Irish Citizen Army* (1919). *The Flying Wasp* (1937), his reply to the critics.

[22] For these and other dramatists see Curtis Canfield: *Plays of Changing Ireland* (1936). Lord Dunsany's fantasies are somewhat apart from the Irish movement: *The Glittering Gate* (1909), *A Night at an Inn* (1916).

and Parnell, the fluid scenery shifts and those he meets talk in tags from Swift, Thomas Moore, Yeats, O'Casey, and Joyce. These memories and the conflict of ideal and real constitute a commentary upon Ireland past and present and upon the sentimental tradition of the Poor Old Woman. Most of what occurs on the stage occurs in the hero's head, whence, after the expressionistic manners of Strindberg and Joyce, it is projected and given substance. *The Moon in the Yellow River*, produced at the Abbey in 1931, is almost equally sardonic. This grotesque, witty play of the Shannon River project and the conflict between Republic and Free State, between Ireland and her idealists, is the kind of play Shaw might have written. That zeal for experiment which is Johnston's distinction and the Gate's was never more admirably illustrated than by *A Bride for the Unicorn*, written for the revolving stage and produced without it at the Gate in 1933. Not expressionistic by the author's own assurance, this queer play, symbolist at least, pursues ideas of love, time, and death. Doing this, it creates a myth by the aid of myths. Public schoolboys, a drunken bust, a masked lady, and other portents confront clocks with or without hands and, speaking melodious prose or verse, assume the attitudes of politics, finance, law, and war. Nothing could be less Irish and nothing a clearer anticipation of Auden and Isherwood.

As the intolerance of Eire increased so did the critical spirit, commoner among exiles than among those successful at home. The plays of Paul Vincent Carroll, as severe as Johnston's, are anticlerical and hostile to insularity. *Shadow and Substance*, produced at the Abbey in 1937, owes much of its excellence to Canon Skeritt, an actor's delight, whose austere conception of Catholicism quarrels with the vulgarity and emotionalism of his curates. His priggishness and inhumanity, expressed in some of the finest lines of the modern drama, yield to the simple-minded saintliness of Brigid, his servant. This play could be produced in Eire because criticism is subordinated to character. But the bitterness of *The White Steed* (1939) proved more suitable for New York. In this play Carroll's usual conflict between schoolmaster and cleric serves as a center for a secular rebellion against a book-burning priest whose "clerical fascism" threatens the state. This intolerant man and the judge, a Gaelic snob, are opposed by a policeman, a saloon-keeper, the old canon, and Nora, who, calling upon the spirits of Niamh and Oisin, gallops off on the pagan steed.

To understand these Irish dramatists and the poets, the course of politics or something of it must be known. During the early years of the Abbey three political factions quarreled with England and each other, John Redmond's Parliamentary party, Arthur Griffith's Sinn Fein, and James Connolly's organized workers. Griffith's plan to destroy the English by nonrecognition, which attracted Edward Martyn and Maud Gonne, seemed bourgeois to Connolly, who desired class war. Padraic Pearse and Thomas MacDonagh, poets and critics, and Constance Markiewicz, daughter of Lord Gore-Booth, supporting independence, favored all radicals. The Boy Scouts, for example, received from Constance Markiewicz heroic tales and directions for using bombs. In August and September 1913 the strike of Connolly's workers was punished by a general lock-out and consequent famine. Defeated, Connolly and Larkin organized the Irish Citizen Army to rival and finally to aid the I.R.B. Volunteers,[23] who drilled incessantly and conspired. Constance Markiewicz and Sean O'Casey, conspirators, drilled with the Citizens; Pearse, de Valera, Joseph Plunkett, and Roger Casement with the Volunteers. Despairing of pacific rem-

[23] Irish Republican Brotherhood.

edy and encouraged by England's preoccupation with Germany, Padraic Pearse proclaimed the Irish Republic on Easter Monday 1916 and led both armies into action. Constance Markiewicz led her battalion, the Boy Scouts charged the magazine in vain, and near the Post Office the O'Rahilly fell. The British, victorious by artillery, executed sixteen leaders, Pearse, MacBride, Connolly, MacDonagh, Plunkett, and Casement among them, and imprisoned Constance Markiewicz. The surviving Boy Scouts were ignored.

Griffith's Sinn Fein was dead, but taking its name, republicans maintained under the I.R.B. a campaign of peaceful, then violent resistance. In 1918 Constance Markiewicz, at large, was imprisoned again. Discouraged Englishmen, borrowing from Germans the policy of frightfulness, invented the Black and Tans, and by 1921 besides ambush and murder there was open war. The treaty ending this war split the Irish into two factions, those who tolerated British Home Rule and those of the I.R.B. and the I.R.A., who wanted independence. In 1922 these factions engaged in civil war, out of which, exhausted and dismembered, de Valera's nation slowly emerged. Set free at last, Cathleen Ni Houlihan found herself in chains—of reaction now and piety. She sent her sons to help the fascists of Spain, and, as if to show the persistence of memory, though giving little comfort to Hitler, gave less to eloquent Churchill. Purer than other girls, she abhorred *Ulysses* and when she could find a copy burned it.

These matters appear not only in the plays of O'Casey and Carroll but in the political poems of Yeats. Standing somewhat above action like old O'Leary, Yeats used events to enlarge imagination and elevate it. During the lock-out of September 1913, while A. E. wrote passionate letters to the press in defense of Connolly's workers, Yeats wrote "September 1913," a lofty poem attacking employers who, "born to pray and save," were faithless to "romantic Ireland." Rooted hostility to the middle class gave Yeats a clear position on Connolly's side, but the Easter rising found him on the fence. Curiously, it is to this ambiguous position that "Easter, 1916" owes its force. The great bare poem is less concerned with the rising than with the conflicts it produced in the poet, compelled by love of country to praise those whom he despised or despised and loved. His allusions are to Constance Markiewicz, Pearse, MacDonagh, and MacBride. Pearse and MacDonagh were bad poets, and MacBride, that "vainglorious lout," had married Maud Gonne. By surprise and disharmony of sense and tone Yeats makes them fools and heroes at once. In the last part, asking if their excess was vain, he approaches the position of Lady Gregory. Too close to landlords to be undivided, the poet was none the less aroused, and in "Sixteen Dead Men" and "The Rose Tree," poems on the executions, excitement conquers division. As for Constance Markiewicz, the poet's feelings were mixed. Yeats had known her in Sligo when, young, she rode to hounds from Lissadell, her father's house. That this aristocratic deportment, this elegance and grace, should have yielded to politics seemed a pity to be lamented in song. "On a Political Prisoner" records her transformation into something "bitter and abstract." "In Memory of Eva Gore-Booth and Con Markiewicz" is her elegy and her sister's. Taught by Maud Gonne to dread what makes women windy, unlovable, and plain, Yeats used perfection of rhythm and tone to condemn not only politics but time itself. The ending, obscure because compressed, grandly proposes the destruction of time by fire and escape to that Georgian gazebo, fireproof and timeless, beyond all common folly. This fine poem shows

Yeats a reluctant republican if a republican at all.[24] "Nineteen Hundred and Nineteen" and "Meditations in Time of Civil War," poems occasioned by the troubles, reveal Yeats a sorrowing spectator of violence, called from his tower by Irregulars or hiding the sight of them by philosophy. In these poems there is little to choose between the mother-murdering Black and Tans and the "leveling" Irish.

Surpassing most of the earlier poems in excellence, these poems differ in kind. The rhythms, no longer relaxing, are firm, the surfaces hard, the words general; and the phrasing is sometimes colloquial. That mixture of "passion and precision" which Yeats had noticed in great houses was his. These poems, "cold and passionate as the dawn," though no less personal than the earlier poems, seem by their austerity impersonal and dramatic. The themes are new. Instead of dream and legend these poems handle life. Half are occasional, some are bitter epigrams upon the Abbey's audience or the middle class, and some, as we have seen, are political. These poems approach the classical state of charged emotion, of surface impassibility, and, within tight limits, of perfection.

This finality has many causes. To replace the pre-Raphaelites Yeats had turned to cleaner models—Landor, Ben Jonson, Donne, and classical Blake. Practice in dramatic verse had given Yeats impersonality, and the bitterness of conflict with the Abbey's pit had made his softness hard. Defeated in his hope of a theater remote from life, he had retired to a "place of stone" whence, facing the world, he could defy it. Defeat and defiance

[24] "Coole Park, 1929" expresses fear that agrarian policy threatened great houses. The fear was justified. The Irish government, instead of making a national monument of Coole, razed the house with all its memories of Yeats and Synge, and shared the Seven Woods.

are suitably expressed in "To a Friend Whose Work Has Come to Nothing," "Lines Written in Dejection," and "The Fisherman." Their tone, born in part of drama and defeat, owes as much to aristocracy. At Coole, Lady Gregory had shown him spaciousness. When he went with her to Italy, he discovered Ferrara and Urbino, and on his return, in the pages of Symonds's *Renaissance,* the culture of their courts. With patrons like the good dukes, whom Lady Gregory distantly approximated, a poet could be free from mob and middle class. Later at the court of Sweden, walking backward down the stairs after receiving the Nobel prize from a royal hand, Yeats felt his convictions fortified. For him the ideal society, banishing the middle class, consisted of noble patrons and their retainers, poets and peasants, each happy in their degree.[25] Understandable and foolish alike, this ideal, a product of the middle class, gave theme, form, and tone to many of his finest poems, among them "To a Wealthy Man Who Promised a Second Subscription . . ." and "Sailing to Byzantium." In the latter poem Byzantium, replacing as symbol the Land of Youth, gave Yeats as the mechanical bird of the Emperor Theophilus freedom from time and nature and the opportunity to sing of both to lords and ladies there.[26] Expressing world and self by their opposites, Yeats had found adjustment and a kind of ease.

To secure or perhaps to rationalize this success, Yeats had invented the doctrine of the mask. Torn between the pulls of abstraction and lushness, dream and reality, circumstance and self, trying to be true to one or another, he had made poems that seemed to him too full of feeling

[25] His last years were enlarged by the company of Lady Dorothy Wellesley, poet, to whom Yeats gave more space in the *Oxford Book of Modern Verse* than he gave to Eliot. See *Letters on Poetry from W. B. Yeats to Dorothy Wellesley* (1940).

[26] Yeats's probable source for the golden bird is George Finlay's *History of the Byzantine Empire* (1906).

or too empty. Intellectual and emotional by turns, he needed a device to make him both at once and to unite reality with dream. His mask, the necessary device, is his attempt to be his opposite. However hopeless this attempt may seem, it had practical value. Placing his conflicts upon a stage, the mask dramatized them, enabling him to regard them coldly with an artist's eye. Art is not self-expression, he announced, but what is most unlike it. This useful fiction, persuading romantic Yeats that he was classical, enabled him to be impersonal and personal at once, dramatic and lyric, and to write better than he could. In a romantic time when direct expression of the self is easy and often fatal to perfection, the classical ideal of impersonality, as Eliot was also to decide, is an instrument for romantic success. His mask upon him, Yeats wrote the noble poems of his middle and later periods, and by being untrue to self became most true to it. Many of his earlier poems, now sentimental in his eyes, passed through the mask and emerged in grandeur.

We may follow this process by comparing the last stanza of "The Sorrow of Love" (1892):

> And now the sparrows warring in the eaves,
> The curd-pale moon, the white stars in the sky,
> And the loud chaunting of the unquiet leaves,
> Are shaken with earth's old and weary cry,

with the final version:

> . . . and on the instant clamorous eaves,
> A climbing moon upon an empty sky,
> And all that lamentation of the leaves,
> Could but compose man's image and his cry.[27]

Archaic, particular, and descriptive diction has been replaced by general terms of Latin origin, yet their colorless

[27] *Collected Poems*, p. 46.

restraint is charged with a new intensity and greater humanity. By his classical tone Yeats increased the energy of romantic feeling, and by their discord created a kind of conceit.

His "humanistic" position is shown again in the preface to *Fighting the Waves,* a poetic play for maskers, produced by the Abbey and published in *Wheels and Butterflies* (1934), where Cuchulain's fight, like Irving Babbitt's, represents hostility alike to science and to flux. Some years earlier, after considering Catholicism, Yeats had bade Von Hügel, the theologian, good-by, but this passing interest is significant. In tradition Yeats was seeking an antidote to Cosgrave's or de Valera's Eire and the world itself. For a time he thought he had found what he wanted in General Eoin O'Duffy, who led his blue-shirted Irish Brigade in Franco's cause, but after writing "Three Marching Songs" for Irish fascists, Yeats repented and revised.[28]

In old age Yeats returned to the romantic Ireland of his youth. The *Last Poems* (1940), mostly of politics and love, attack Eire for failing to live up to his ideal, condemn Cromwell, and praise Ireland's heroes. These nostalgic, lusty poems, different from anything Yeats had written, owe form and spirit to translations from the Gaelic by F. R. Higgins and Frank O'Connor.[29] In the heartiness of Higgins and in Egan O'Rahilly's laments for vanished aristocracy, translated by O'Connor, Yeats found himself expressed. He assisted O'Connor with these poems

[28] Their first state, with his political commentary, may be found in *The King of the Great Clock Tower* (1934), their second in *Last Poems* (1940). Cf. *On the Boiler* (*c.* 1939).

[29] Higgins: *The Gap of Brightness* (1940). O'Connor: *The Fountain of Magic* (1939). Daniel Corkery's *The Hidden Ireland* (1925), a survey of Gaelic poetry of the eighteenth century, opened up this field for O'Connor and Yeats. Yeats's growing interest in eighteenth-century Ireland also included Swift and Berkeley: *Words upon the Window Pane* (1930), *Essays* (1937).

before going home to imitate and improve them. That Yeats should have been attracted by O'Rahilly's aristocratic yearning needs no explanation, but that he should have been attracted by the lustiness of other eighteenth-century Gaels would be astonishing in one so old were it not known that he had submitted to an operation for restoring youth. It is to this perhaps that we owe the songs of the chambermaid and that which begins "Come swish around, my pretty punk."

Of other Irish poets, those who wrote before 1920 may be classed with the Georgians. In *New Songs* (1904) A. E. presented the work of several young poets, among them Seumas O'Sullivan, Padraic Colum, Susan Mitchell, Eva Gore-Booth, and Ella Young. Colum's *Wild Earth* (1909) is the poetic equivalent of his earthy plays. Seumas O'Sullivan, inspired by A. E. and the softer Yeats, lost himself in Celtic twilight. James Stephens, also A. E.'s disciple but odder than these, combined the fantastic and sometimes the divine with urban and pastoral reality. Some poems of *Insurrections* (1909) and *Songs from the Clay* (1915) achieve the quality of his better novels. But words like "thrill," "rapture," and "robed in flame" indicate the conservatism with which he and A. E.'s other poets sang the rustic, the urban, or the imaginative. From the ordinary productions of the group one brilliant book emerges, Susan Mitchell's *Aids to the Immortality of Certain Persons in Ireland* (1908). Her witty preface and wittier verses parody or caricature George Moore, the principal victim, Yeats, Martyn, and all the politicians. "Ode to the British Empire," a parody of "Recessional," is the final word on the subject.[30]

[30] Oliver St. John Gogarty, Joyce's Mulligan, wrote one fine poem, "Begone, Sweet Ghost," *Selected Poems* (1933). *As I Was Going down Sackville Street* (1937), his capricious memoir of Ireland's great, is worth reading. Of later poets Denis Devlin is most interesting: *Intercessions* (1938), *Lough Derg* (1945).

The novels of James Stephens are better on the whole than his poems. His best work, uniting as works of Irishmen are supposed to do the fantastic and the real, is *The Crock of Gold* (1912), and of this the best part is the first chapter, on philosophers and wives. Although policemen and leprechauns are a good mixture, the intrusion of Pan is a mistake, and the book declines into an allegory of intellect and intuition, each modified by the other and saved in the nick of time by the Hosting of the Shee from the middle class of Dublin. Stephens's humor, his gift of simple statement, and his unfortunate love of philosophizing about men and women are again displayed in *The Demi-Gods* (1914), the story of Patsy MacCann, the guardian angels, and Brien O'Brien. As might be expected of A. E.'s disciple who read Blavatsky on Easter Monday 1916, the machinery he used is Theosophical or incorrect. Not malice surely, but innocence made him place archangel above seraph and cherub. But their earthly deportment and the conversation of MacCann redeem this book from cosmical extravagance. In *Irish Fairy Tales* (1920) Stephens retold legendary matters in admirable prose, some pages of which are as good as his best.[31] But *The Charwoman's Daughter* (1912), a story of the Dublin slums inspired by Barrie perhaps, is sweet and sentimental.

Liam O'Flaherty's slum is closer to Zola's, and its creatures, by Dostoyevsky's aid, are more appropriate than Stephens's Mary Makebelieve. A political melodrama of extreme violence, *The Informer* (1925) deals with communistic opposition to the middle-class Free State during the twenties. Monstrous Gypo, his liquidators, emerging from their cellars to advance the Workers' Republic,

[31] *Deirdre* (1923) and *In the Land of Youth* (1924) are excellent prose versions of the epic materials.

fanatics, neurotics, and whores frame or serve a psychological study of great penetration. *The Martyr* (1933) is a melodrama of 1922. The Irregulars are internally divided, some Catholics, some communists, and some, like Angela Fitzgibbon (Con Markiewicz?), habitual agitators. The Free Staters, aided by British arms, use thugs to support the middle class. Scenes of violence and of love are contrived in the manner of a popular magazine of the second class. These crude novels and his others owe their power to O'Flaherty's experiences with Connolly's workers in 1913, with the British army during the war, and with the Irish communists in the troubles. After *I Went to Russia* (1931) his political position was neither left nor right, but betwixt and between. And his intentions as artist were frankly commercial.

Two Cork realists, Frank O'Connor and Sean O'Faolain, are the most considerable of Eire's remaining writers. While others prefer exile, these two persist out of that sense of national duty which kept Yeats at his post, though many of O'Faolain's works are banned or hissed and O'Connor's might be but for his record during the troubles.

Frank O'Connor, known for poetic translations from the Gaelic, is better known for short stories which, like most in our time, follow Maupassant's pattern or Chekhov's mood, generally the latter. In *Guests of the Nation* (1931) brief episodes from the English troubles or the civil war, suggesting more than they say, reveal character and establish tone. "Guests of the Nation," a dark powerful story of the shooting of English hostages, is less reminiscent of Chekhov, however, than of O'Flaherty. "Nightpiece with Figures" is more typical: men of the I.R.A. talking to the nuns feel better for the talk though little has been said and nothing tangible has occurred.

Bones of Contention (1936) employs bare lucid prose, and *Crab Apple Jelly* (1944), somewhat tarter, the rhythms and syntax of Cork, for local ironies. Schoolteachers, peasants, priests, shopkeepers, lady doctors, and small officials compose a cross-section of Cork and its county. The implications of discouragement and decay that fill these stories become explicit in *Dutch Interior* (1940), a novel built of short stories, each complete and incomplete. Apparently incoherent at first, the episodes, cohering at last, become symphonic. The title implies the kind of reality through which obscure people move in the rain (for it is always raining), hiding their hopelessness under buffoonery or wit. It cannot be supposed that the resemblance between Joyce's Dubliners and O'Connor's Corkers is altogether casual.

Decay, irrelevant violence, and the lovable dampness of Cork fill the stories of Sean O'Faolain, whose work, relatively free from plot, resembles that of O'Connor and the Russians. The decline of big houses, the fanaticism of the I.R.A. and Black and Tan, the tragedies of people trapped in the pitiful struggle, are the themes of "Midsummer Night Madness" and "The Small Lady," the outstanding stories of *Midsummer Night Madness* (1932). Nowhere has the spirit of place been caught more happily than in this excellent book. His best novel, *A Nest of Simple Folk* (1933), an epic of rebellion's birth from provincial decay, follows the misfortunes of Leo Donnell through Fenianism to the rising of 1916. The dull man, wasting his inheritance, repeatedly jailed for simple-minded outrage, rises through persistence to heroic stature and becomes a symbol of Ireland's cause. His opposite is Hussey, the policeman, a spy upon his kind. More than patriotic, this novel is a gallery of living creatures with windows through which Cork, its vicinity, and its times appear with solidity and brilliance. The effect of Turgenyev, O'Faolain's master, is plain, and, to a lesser degree, that of Maupassant and of Balzac.[32]

O'Faolain's quarrel with Eire, whose soil and people he loves, is shown in *She Had to Do Something,* a bitter comedy hissed at the Abbey in 1937. This slight Chekhovian play concerns the efforts of a puritanical canon to suppress a ballet, immoral because inadequately clothed. The angry audience of the Abbey is rebuked by O'Faolain in the preface to the printed text. More bitter than the play itself, this document is his declaration of war against the mob, sterilized by patriotic and religious fervor, which, imposing vulgarity upon the artist, demands not national but nationalistic literature, not life but piety. O'Faolain quotes with approval from *The Day of the Rabblement* (1901), that arrogant pamphlet in which Joyce had denounced the mob and the conforming theater. Harried by mob and middle class, against whom Yeats had fought in vain, and silenced by censorship, the remaining artists of Eire, says O'Faolain, are strangers at home. The nation that hooted Synge and exiled Joyce was less inimical to art than this bourgeois theocracy.

III

Meanwhile British reaction took a parallel course. But while Eire herself embraced reaction and Irish writers became her protestants, some English writers became more reactionary than their government. Among older writers Shaw, and among younger Lawrence, Hulme, Wyndham Lewis, and Eliot represent reaction in all its kinds. No longer imperialist, it turned toward fascism, classicism, or religion. From right as well as left, artists, seeking order, kicked at the decaying body of liberalism.

That Shaw's socialism was skin-deep in spots was shown in the late nineties by his passion for Nietzsche's super-

[32] *Bird Alone* (1936), *Come Back to Erin* (1940), novels.

man, more congenial to his somewhat sadistic temper [33] than the undifferentiated man of Sidney Webb. The appearance of amoral supermen in *Cæsar and Cleopatra* (1907), *Man and Superman* (1905), and *Major Barbara* (1905), his growing distaste for democracy, and his later admiration of dictators indicate the shape of his thought.[34] Perhaps its most curious expression is *On the Rocks* (1933), to all appearances a fascist play with a socialist preface. In this fantastic diversion—fantastic because each expresses what he thinks—order, agreeable to financiers, landlords, and business men, is imposed from above by a minister encouraged by a charlatan's advice. It is true, of course, that fascism is sometimes difficult to distinguish from socialism. But if socialism at all, the socialism of *On the Rocks* is national socialism. Liquidation, discussed in the preface, increasingly appealed to Shaw. Sometimes, as here, he condemned Hitler's abuse of this instrument. Sometimes he damned the Jews or praised the Russians. But this ambiguous evidence is less difficult than it seems. The great eclectic was neither socialist nor fascist but Shavian, and his varieties of doctrine were good business.

Bucolic theocracy was D. H. Lawrence's remedy for confusion. Seeing money and machines as enemies of soul, Lawrence prophesied doom to money-changers and mechanics. He did not take his stand with the workers from whom he had sprung, however, or with the aristocrats

[33] Although Shaw's preference for effeminate or supermanly heroes and for supermanly heroines may be explained by his desire to be outrageous, it fits the pattern of sadism traced through nineteenth-century literature by Mario Praz in *The Romantic Agony* (1933).

[34] The superman is also celebrated in *The Devil's Disciple* (1899) and *The Doctor's Dilemma* (1906). *Geneva* (1938) ambiguously presents Hitler, Mussolini, and Franco. See Shaw: *Bernard Shaw & Fascism* (1927).

with whom, like Yeats, he snobbishly consorted, but somewhat apart from them. To destroy democratic liberalism he proposed dictatorship by a hero, descended on one side from Nietzsche and Wagner and on the other from Mme Blavatsky and the noble savage. Under this great pious man natural aristocrats would replace the middle-class world with another, better and more natural. Lawrence's novels and stories describe the emergence of this savior, and two novels describe his political career. Bidding good-by to socialists and Jewish financiers, Somers of *Kangaroo* (1923) finds suitable refuge in the semi-fascistic cult of Kangaroo, whose plan, however, turns out to be too tentative and imperfect for devotion. But Don Ramon of *The Plumed Serpent* (1926) is the ideal dictator. Convinced that Mexicans are oppressed by socialists, Catholics, and international financiers, this great man founds a fascist organization, primitive and religious in character, and by a coup imposes theocracy upon Mexico. Destroying machines or thinking with the blood, Mexicans find their peace in his will and, when unoccupied by love, dance beneath the vital sun. This partial anticipation of Hitler's Germany owes its resemblance to similar causes. It might be supposed that, had he lived, Lawrence would have become a Nazi; but although he liked the German youth movement, he was too much of an individual to follow the leader. What Lawrence wanted was to become dictator himself. He had a few followers. By some of the British fascists of the thirties *The Plumed Serpent* was taken as text and Don Ramon as pattern. But this enormous novel is so seductive with its hypnotic rhythms, its barbaric splendor, its characters on the border of trance, that these thoughtless men can hardly be blamed. Rolf Gardiner adored Lawrence and Hitler while Oswald Mosley marched his shirty men around. But although in other respects Lawrence's disciple, Aldous Huxley satirized the British fascists, and so did P. G. Wodehouse.[35]

Similar reaction in politics accompanied the rise of classicism. This chaste development, so exotic in our age as to seem more romantic than our other excesses, generally comes from France. But Robert Bridges, the earliest of contemporary classicists, no less indifferent to France than to politics, expressed his traditionalism by tone, rhythm, and diction. Experiments with these and a comfortable income produced poems of almost incredible emptiness. Yeats admired their grandeur and Hopkins their technique.[36]

A distaste for romantic extravagance and for the abundant but somewhat vulgar language of Shakespeare, whose impropriety revolted Bridges, caused that fastidious man to adopt the general diction of the eighteenth century. In his lyrics the Thames is "silver," the verdure of its banks "declines" while zephyrs cool the "sweltering pasturage" and "fleecy clouds disport." Forgetting Wordsworth, the idle reader awaits the reappearance of the finny tribe and, with Dr. Johnson, dismisses the streaks of the tulip. Lest such neoclassicism seem worthless, the reader, recalling the severities of Lionel Johnson or of the later Yeats, should remember that general diction, which turns the bird-infested, individual tree into something

[35] Huxley: *Point Counter Point* (1928). Wodehouse: *The Code of the Woosters* (1938).

[36] Bridges: *Poetical Works* (1914), *Milton's Prosody* (1921), *Collected Essays* (1927–36). Albert Guerard: *Robert Bridges, a Study of Traditionalism in Poetry* (1942).

Like Bridges, Sacheverell Sitwell wrote splendid, empty poems that exist by surface tension: *Collected Poems* (1936). His sister, Edith, who considers him the greatest modern poet, holds the texture of his o's and a's incomparable. His stanzas on swans and the passage on Agamemnon's tomb are musical; but *Canons of Giant Art* (1933), has more than music, for here the poet takes his stand with the Italian fascists. Cf. *All Summer in a Day, an Autobiographical Fantasia* (1926).

regular like an artichoke, has virtues for evil times, as Grant Wood, in another medium, discovered. The "Ode to Spring," as classical as lawns, is representative. And for examples of more experimental prosody "Wintry Delights," in classical hexameters, and "A Passer-by," that splendid poem in sprung rhythm, will serve.

In phonetic spelling and loose Alexandrines *The Testament of Beauty* (1929) expresses the philosophy behind experiment and decorum. It was neo-Platonism that allowed Bridges, ascending from beauty to beauty, to ignore evil as irrelevant. The happy philosopher turned aside from war and poverty and walked alone with the Muse in her garden. Lest this reaction to our times seem extraordinary, the reader should remember that Eliot's Tiresias turned his back upon the waste land and went fishing off the edge of it. Given a waste land, some will contemplate tin cans and rusty springs, others lawns or, like Chirico, corridors. Although as up to date as *The Waste Land, The Testament of Beauty* is less exciting and, like most didactic verse since Pope, lacks his virtue. But not even Eliot has given a more suitable expression to the humanism of the middle class.

In France classicism, also a memory of past grandeur, was a tool in the service of religion or politics, and a cry against Rousseau, Bergson, and the symbolists. French classicists were of several varieties, each professing love for Racine. There was Charles Maurras, editor of the *Action française,* who progressed from literature to politics, first royalist, then fascist. As fascist he was sentenced by angry Frenchmen in 1945 to life imprisonment. Jacques Maritain progressed from secular literature to Thomas Aquinas, under whose austere auspices he gave Christians again the illusion of being rational. Julien Benda, immune to politics and religion, upheld the claims of pure reason and the Latin tradition against Bergson and his followers.

These intolerant men, whose existence would be enough to establish the romantic character of our age, were matched in America by Irving Babbitt and Paul Elmer More, who, trying to dam romantic flux by taste, culture, and traditional wisdom, announced balance as cure for the unbalanced. In England the principal classicists, disciples of these, were T. E. Hulme, Wyndham Lewis, and T. S. Eliot.[37]

T. E. Hulme, the most thoughtful, was their leader. Alone of classicists a follower of Bergson, he atoned for an inconsistency no Frenchman could allow by approximating the neo-Thomist position. In "Humanism and the Religious Attitude" he condemns the relative values of recent times and praises the absolute values of the Middle Ages. Absolute or religious values are based upon the acceptance of original sin, relative or humanist values upon its rejection. Art based upon humanist values, the art of Zola, for example, or Shelley, is realistic, subjective, and unlimited. Art based upon religious values, the art of Byzantium or Chartres, is unnatural and limited. In "Romanticism and Classicism," Hulme's other important essay, he enters the humanist field, previously condemned, and divides it into two parts, good and bad. Classical art, crowding man's limits, is good; romantic, overflowing them, bad. He foresees the end of romanticism and a period of dry hard verse, descriptive in character, adorned by fancy, lit by common day. The new classicism will not be a return to Alexander Pope, but, different as a result of the emotional metaphysics we have had to endure, will be original though spare. These manifestoes, representing

[37] For classicism see P. M. Jones: *Tradition and Barbarism, a Survey of Anti-Romanticism in France* (1930); Régis Michaud: *Modern Thought and Literature in France* (1934). Benda: *Belphégor* (1918). Michael Roberts: *T. E. Hulme* (1938).

what his disciples heard, may owe their inconsistencies to developing thought or to the fact that *Speculations* (1924), the volume in which his classical papers posthumously appeared, was edited by romantic Herbert Read.

Shortly before Hulme was killed in the war, his classical disciples began to repeat or to illustrate his teaching. Vorticism, in part a hoax, was its most violent application. To *Blast, Review of the Great English Vortex,* an outrageous magazine, two issues of which appeared, one in 1914, the other in 1915, Wyndham Lewis and Ezra Pound together with Gaudier-Brzeska and Eliot contributed manifestoes, pictures, or poems. Demanding classicism, Lewis, the editor, praised castor oil, machines, and hairdressers as violations of nature. In painting and sculpture vorticism was the cubistic abstraction Hulme recommended. In poetry it was a more violent kind of imagism. Hulme's invention, imagism had grown too soft and ladylike. Vorticism was the attempt of his followers to rescue it from Amy Lowell and recapture his ideal of dry, hard, classical verse. Pound and Eliot were the vorticist poets. Abandoning petals, turning to satire, Pound composed verses, still imagistic, but harsher now and dry. His models were the classical epigram and the chiseled verses of Gautier. "The Bath Tub" and "Mœurs Contemporains," epigrams, were followed by the Mauberley poems, Pound's best. His companion simultaneously composed the Sweeney poems, his happiest. These elegant quatrains mix Gautier with the symbolists according to Hulme's prescription.

Hulme's disciples were extravagant: Pound became a fascist and Eliot a royalist, but even among these right-thinking men Wyndham Lewis seems extravagant. Starting as cubist painter, but soon defeated by public indifference, he turned to propaganda and satire in the attempt to defend art and destroy stupidity with "laughter like bombs." *The Art of Being Ruled* (1926), his manifesto, is a declaration of war against Bergson. Against flux and time Lewis upholds the static, the spacial, the intellectual. Classing himself in all but theology (an important exception) with the neo-Thomists, he takes his stand with Benda and with Hulme. Art, he says, is menaced by the democratic mob and by a conspiracy among capitalists trying, by debasing taste, to assure their gains. To this end these wicked men encourage the cults of childishness, feminism, savagery, and anti-intellectualism, all traceable to Bergson's flux, and all inimical to proper art. In a series of angry books, of which *Time and Western Man* (1927) is first and most notable, the "enemy," as he called himself, attacked each of these cults and their literary adherents. He attacked Joyce for his fluid relativity, Lawrence for his primitivism, the surrealists for their unconsciousness. African music, sun-bathing, and feminine sensibility, he said, further ensure the doom of white, adult, Western civilization.[38] It was his tragedy that in defense of reason he seemed hysterical and that in defense of plastic austerity he became loose and colorful. Fighting disorder with chaos, he bored.

When propaganda bored Lewis, he found relief in satire. In *Tarr* (1918) and *The Wild Body* (1928), Rabelaisian experiments in the gigantic and the grotesque, he laughed at man, that mechanical animal, particularly at man in his bohemian character. *The Apes of God* (1932), his most considerable satire, is modeled upon

[38] *Paleface* (1929), *The Diabolical Principle* (1931), *The Doom of Youth* (1932), *Men without Art* (1934). *One-Way Song* (1933), verse. *The Enemy* (1927), a magazine. *Blasting and Bombardiering* (1937), autobiography. Terence Armstrong: *Apes, Japes, and Hitlerism, a Study and Bibliography of Wyndham Lewis* (1932). Cecil Melville: *The Truth about the New Party* (1931).

Voltaire and Swift, whom Lewis would resemble more closely if he were a better writer. This attack upon Bloomsbury bohemians, especially the three Sitwells, whose cult of childishness affronted him, is a fictional version of his tracts. Its merit is gusto, its defect diffuseness. In this long novel the hero behind the scenes is Pierpont, a fascist, who directs the half-wits toward Lewis's ends.

As early as 1926 Lewis had seen Italian fascism as a cure for romantic disorder. His increasing distaste for capitalism and communism led him to Hitler, in whose praise he wrote a book called *Hitler* (1931). Here Lewis sees that man defending the Aryan West against Jews, blacks, Bergsonists, and other exotics. Interested in what is under his nose, Hitler is classical.

Roy Campbell, the South African poet, was another, lesser Lewis, and his disciple. Having produced gorgeous dithyrambs and pseudo-classical satires upon Bloomsbury bohemians, especially Lesbians, he wrote *Broken Record* (1934), an autobiography, to explain his position. Like Lewis an enemy of Jews, communists, and softies, he sees fascism, Italian and German, as the only hope for the Western tradition. He salutes Maurras and Léon Daudet as masters, attacks Hugh MacDiarmid, and expresses devotion to bull-throwing, shark-catching, and pugilism. This furious convert to Catholicism made Franco's cause his own. In *Mithraic Emblems* (1936), singing the Spanish civil war, he sees fascists as "Christs in uniform." As full of ornament as a Victorian parlor, but more violent, his verses unite modern fury with nineteenth-century technique. In *Flowering Rifle* (1939), a long satiric poem in suitable couplets, he celebrates Franco's victory, applauds Chamberlain's umbrella, and condemns those misguided Englishmen who had sided in humanitarian and liberal zeal with Jew against Christian, black against white. The final scene discloses the Blessed Virgin smiling upon her triumphant fascists.[39]

Similar in tendency, T. S. Eliot differs from Campbell and Lewis as does his prim lucidity from their colorful violence. To counteract romantic confusion, Eliot, demanding impersonality, assumed at first the position of the secular traditionalist. In "Tradition and the Individual Talent" and "The Function of Criticism," essays written in 1917 and 1923, he professes allegiance to something outside himself, at this period the great tradition of European letters. During the twenties his sensibility, requiring stimulation, turned to politics. In the *Criterion,* which he was devoting to the advancement of classicism, he expressed contempt of democracy and a guarded affection for fascism. Indecorous Mussolini, like the Church of Rome, seemed too foreign to the ideals of the public school. It was a pity, said Eliot, surveying the British fascists, that these almost wholly admirable men should go to Italy for name and symbol. How much better and more British to go to Charles Maurras and the *Action française.*[40] Inflamed by Maurras, whom he published and lauded, Eliot, once unitarian, found classicism a trinity. In *For Lancelot Andrewes* (1928) he proclaimed himself

[39] *The Flaming Terrapin* (1924), *Adamastor* (1930), *The Georgiad* (1931), *Wyndham Lewis* (1932), *Flowering Reeds* (1933), *Talking Bronco* (1946).

Evelyn Waugh, another convert, expressed admiration of Italian fascism in *Waugh in Abyssinia* (1936), the companion volume to *Scoop* (1938), his hilarious story of war correspondents in Abyssinia. In *Authors Take Sides* (*c.* 1937), a questionnaire on the Spanish war published by *Left Review,* Waugh took his stand with Franco, and, if a choice had to be made, with fascism. Pound and Eliot professed neutrality.

[40] See Eliot's editorials and a dialogue in the *Criterion,* January 1925, February 1928, and *passim.* Eliot printed an article by Maurras, January 1928, and praised him, March and December 1928. Eliot's assistant editor, Herbert Read, however, called himself "anarchist, romanticist, and agnostic."

"classicist in literature, royalist in politics, and Anglo-Catholic in religion." These congenial positions, which, providing an emotional center, invited song, seem plainer than they are.

Paul Elmer More wanted to know why his friend, so austere and classical in his prose, should be so romantic in his poetry. To this Eliot replied that his prose reflects his ideals, his poetry the reality around him; and since this reality is romantic, his poetry can be no more than classical "in tendency." His classical prose reflects admiration of Benda, Maurras, Maritain, and above these, of Hulme. The two essays on Irving Babbitt and humanism, where Eliot rebukes his first master for secularity, restate ideas of Hulme. Eliot is after heretics again in *After Strange Gods* (1934), which, by references to racial homogeneity and "free-thinking Jews," falls into a familiar pattern. Since even in British politics the king is no longer or hardly ever an issue, Eliot's position as royalist must reflect that of Maurras, serve as the objective correlative of Midwestern aspiration, or else mean nothing but Tory. Tory standards alone could account for his disapproval of Milton and his approval of Kipling.[41] The essays on these poets are more conspicuous for feeling and tone than for sense.

[41] "A Note on the Verse of John Milton," *Essays and Studies by Members of the English Association,* XXI (1936). *A Choice of Kipling's Verse* (1943). *Selected Essays* (1932).

CHAPTER IV

Disenchantment and Fantasy

DISENCHANTMENT and its effects, the cynical, the disgusting, and the grotesque, though products of the first World War, existed before it as products of science and bourgeois self-contemplation. With these effects came others, the comic, the ironic, and the fantastic, the last of which appears an attempt of the disenchanted to recover enchantment. Attitudes of disenchantment, found at their happiest in the work of young Huxley and young Waugh, occur so abundantly that, like politics and religion, they discover the times.

"Come, my lad, and drink some beer," cries Dr. Johnson in one of his satiric ballads. But Shakespeare on golden lads and girls anticipates a commoner theme of A. E. Housman's *Shropshire Lad* (1896). In these poems, as every adolescent knows, gloomy, ironic Housman was preoccupied with lads dying, going off to nameless wars and getting shot or staying at home and getting hanged, especially the latter. To understand this obsession, we must remark his singular experience. Having decided at Oxford to be the greatest Latinist, he failed in his examination and went down with no degree. This failure, the center of his emotional life, explains the cruelty of his prefaces and his obsession with the lads. The hanging lad is not theme but symbol. As he hangs, youth and promise are frustrated and Housman flunks again. This obsession, after sinking into his unconscious, where it became more general than particular, emerged with dreamlike intensity. For this reason the poems of youthful frustration are poems.

His emotions remained the baffled undergraduate's. Because he never developed, his poetry, never developing, appeals to adolescents, whom it expresses; but, beyond these, it appeals to some who find his symbols the expression of our world. Within his limits and because of them he wrote some of the best "public" poems of our time, finer, on the whole, than Kipling's.

"Terence, this is stupid stuff" is among them because it expresses not the hidden self but what Yeats called the anti-self. Addressing Terence, the supposed author of these poems, Housman laughs at his sentimentality. Such wit, although it appears along with cruelty in the prefaces, is absent from most of the other poems. If he had not held with some earlier romantics that wit is inimical to poetry, he might have expressed the whole instead of part of what he was.

The Name and Nature of Poetry (1933) defines not poetry, of course, but Housman's romantic principles. Poetry, he maintains with the surrealists, is close to madness. To approximate this condition, or at least to quiet his intellect, he drank his beer and let the poetry come. It came like a secretion. But he was accustomed to improve the result. The first half of "Terence, this is stupid stuff" came by secretion, the second by conscious art. And for "coloured counties" he tried and rejected many adjectives before the right one came.

The result is excellently simple, though complicated at times by unintentional ambiguity; but many of the poems are less simple than obvious. Perfection of surfaces and epigrammatic felicity suggest depths of feeling and thought. But although Housman is a thinker, he thinks less than T. S. Eliot's man of sensibility, and although a feeler, he feels far less than that man. The famous poem of cherry trees is representative. Dismayed by blossoms, Housman feels that time is passing, he must age. "Now" at the end of the first line expresses this reaction, and occupying the remainder of the stanza, a suggestive image supports this ominous word. A Japanese poet would have stopped here. But Housman dilutes what is already thin, first by mathematics, then by stating what has been implied. Less final than it seemed at first, the examined poem becomes diffuse and tentative. Its merit is saying what the average man feels but cannot say as he would say it if he could.[1]

With Housman and Hardy, E. M. Forster belongs among the prewar ironists. Although he has the gifts of intelligence and humanity, resembling James at times and at others Lawrence, he somehow avoids their greatness. His aim, the exposure of his class, is more impressive than his achievement, the apparatus of exposure more elaborate than the results require. The trouble, perhaps, is that, unlike the exiles, he remained a resident critic, too near his kind and too far from others to see them properly. "It is impossible," he says, "to see modern life steadily and see it whole," but facing both ways, he tried. Refusing clear-cut issues and easy solutions, he approached comedy or tragedy.

Howards End (1910) and *A Passage to India* (1924) are generally considered the most complete and, by some, the

[1] *Last Poems* (1922), *More Poems* (1936), *Collected Poems* (1940). See also the prefaces to Housman's editions of Manilius (1903) and of Juvenal (1905). Laurence Housman: *My Brother, A. E. Housman* (1937). A. S. F. Gow: *A. E. Housman* (1936). Grant Richards: *A. E. Housman* (1941). Housman Supplement to the *Bromsgrovian,* October 1936. Edmund Wilson: *The Triple Thinkers* (1938).

most successful statements of his themes. At first glance *Howards End* appears another *Man of Property*, but upon consideration it appears far more complex and of greater value. Mr. Wilcox, like Soames, epitomizes the Philistinism and rapacity of the ruling class. The Schlegels, representing the culture and intelligence of that class, are almost outsiders. Leonard Bast, an instrument for revealing Wilcoxes and Schlegels, is not only an outsider, but a bounder who aspires to a culture belonging to his betters. Mysterious Mrs. Wilcox, a symbol like her house, represents the fine ignorance of the county, the unspeakable result of tradition, leisure, and Little England. These exemplary creatures are not so clear-cut as Galsworthy's. Wilcox may be a man of property who regards even that symbolic house as his, but he is the steady backbone of the nation, and her creator. Bast, his opposite, is not only pathetic but absurd. Seeing around and through his people, Forster sees them as they are, as mixed and dubious as gryphons. Although dull and, through most of the book, dead, Mrs. Wilcox alone emerges with full honors. Wilcox, compounded of bad and good, is real because Forster, wearing the same tie, knows him, but Bast, from whom he is separated by chasms of class and culture, remains unreal. The unreality of Bast, the principal instrument, is the defect of the novel. *A Passage to India*, a parallel exposure of the ruling class, is more effectual because Forster was more familiar with his instruments of exposure, the Indians, than with the lower caste at home.

The Longest Journey (1907), less successful than these but no less fascinating, concerns the nature of reality and of Cambridge. Reality is a cow and Cambridge is intellect, imagination, and humanism. Stephen Wonham, the child of nature, more or less conforms to the one, Ansell, the Jewish intellectual, to the other. But Rickie, untrue to nature and to Cambridge alike, weds conventional Agnes, who does not exist. Her effect upon him and her defeat by Ansell and Wonham, outsiders, agents and, despite their imperfections, ideals, constitute the plot. During its progress pompous Mr. Pembroke and his public school, mother of prigs, bullies, and imperialists, are destroyed, but all else, seen by the double eye of Cambridge, is mixed. Even Agnes and Rickie have upright moments, for in the pugilism of Cambridge every other punch is pulled.

In *A Room with a View* (1908) the Emersons, outsiders of low degree, occupy the place of Wonham and Ansell. Life, Passion, and Beauty, quarreling with middle-class emptiness, win a doubtful victory. Made a snob by his public school, Cecil is shown up. But Lucy, rising above the conventions of her class, elopes with young Emerson. Nothing, however, could be more painful than their Florentine honeymoon, for Passion and Beauty, remaining ideas in Forster's head, fail to emerge upon the scene. But if the Emersons are failures and if the ideas for which they stand remain unconvincing, the hotel full of clerics and old maids is a success.

Forster, who had one complicated thing to say, tried to say it again and again. The first and last attempts, on the whole, are best. *Where Angels Fear to Tread* (1905), the first, is the most nearly perfect among his novels and the most Jamesian. The suburban Herritons, sending ambassadors to Italy, are Forster's most disgusting Philistines. And Carella, the Italian who receives them, is as convincing as the Indians of *A Passage to India.* Like Lawrence's gamekeepers, Carella has the vitality vainly attributed to Emerson or Wonham. With his useful child, Carella reveals Harriet and her mother, improves Miss Abbott, and makes Philip aware of his powerlessness. Despite the ambiguity of Carella and the ironic inconclusiveness of the ending, the impact of the book is final. Even its melodrama serves the effect.

To make his defectives come alive and show themselves, Forster contrives for each of his novels a series of climaxes and melodramatic surprises. Although most of these do what they should, some are only odd, and some, after their violent introduction, are diminished by understatement or with a kind of public-school diffidence, deliberately avoided. His plots, somewhat old-fashioned and contrived, are excellently contrived for his purpose. His archaic intrusions, after the fashion of Fielding or Thackeray, compose an explicit chorus for what were better implicit. Urbanity of manner, irony, and occasional restraint expose more than Forster's subject. So exposed, the emotional defects of Philip or of Rickie and the wise incapacity of Mrs. Wilcox or Mrs. Moore seem withering comments by the author upon himself. Instead, however, of the silvery laughter that might accompany these comic practices, comes the smile of lucid pessimism.[2] This humor became that of the Cambridge-Bloomsbury school that called him master. Well beyond Rose Macaulay, Forster stands among his disciples a little this side of Virginia Woolf and Elizabeth Bowen.[3]

To understand the postwar disillusionment of literate civilians, the disillusionment of literate belligerents must be understood. Most of them were killed, but some—poets, novelists, and essayists—survived to unfold a tale of bungling, confusion, and horror that increased despair at home.

[2] Lionel Trilling: *E. M. Forster* (1943). Virginia Woolf: "The Novels of E. M. Forster," *The Death of the Moth* (1942). Rose Macaulay: *The Writings of E. M. Forster* (1938).

[3] Virginia Woolf's *Voyage Out* (1915), her first novel, is good imitation Forster. Rose Macaulay's *Potterism* (1920), an indictment of the ruling class, is obviously indebted to Forster. Her *Told by an Idiot* (1923), represents postwar disenchantment.

In *Disenchantment* (1922) C. E. Montague analyzes the soldier's disgust with the ruling class, its brass-hatted incompetence in France, its commercial shrewdness and hypocrisy in England. The ideas of this essay are illustrated in *Rough Justice* (1926), a Wellsian novel of adolescence and of war in which heroics, the public schools, caste, the newspapers, and politics are damned. There is hope, however, in men like Auberon, the solid squire, who, surviving school and war, returns to the common people and the simple life. *Right off the Map* (1927), a more entertaining novel, part adventure story, part allegory, starts out with a picture of British imperialism in South America, but, gathering speed, becomes an indictment of modern war. In the war between the republics of Ria and Porta, capitalists, journalists, and clergymen who provoked the war are responsible for military incompetence and a defeat that individual heroism cannot prevent.

The Spanish Farm (1924–7), a trilogy by R. H. Mottram, is of somewhat greater merit. The story, told from various points of view, amounts to a many-sided portrait of Madeleine, a French girl in the British sector, whose surroundings reveal the stupidity and waste of war and whose character reveals what is wrong with that sweet enemy France. Of the other war novels, all of which pursue patterns of disenchantment and disgust, the last two are best. Distinguished from the others by ambiguity, *Her Privates We* (1930) by Frederick Manning is a complaint about Fortune herself. *In Parenthesis* (1937) by David Jones is no less faithful to the themes of tedium and incompetence. But breaking now and again into a kind of verse, the horrors proceed in the syntax of Hopkins, Joyce, and the bards of Wales. This combination, however difficult to construe, brings solidity to the common nightmare.

Meanwhile Georgian poets provided equivalents in prose and verse of Barbusse and Remarque. The Sherston autobiographies of Siegfried Sassoon are the best in their kind. Sherston, a partial portrait of the author, embodies Sassoon's concern with venery (in the better sense) and war. Suavely malign, Sassoon allows his simple-minded hero to expose his irresponsibility and, after war had interrupted the chase, his innocent heroics. *Memoirs of a Fox-Hunting Man* (1928) was followed by *Memoirs of an Infantry Officer* (1930) and *Sherston's Progress* (1936). Conspicuously gallant but maturing, entrenched Sherston gradually becomes aware of war's futility, of official bungling and civilian greed. Finally, encouraged by Bertrand Russell, he announces his refusal to fight a war unnecessarily prolonged, but instead of the objector's martyrdom, receives the attentions of Dr. W. H. R. Rivers, the psychoanalytic friend of Robert Graves, and returns to the front. Sherston's story is Sassoon's minus poetry and intellect, which are attended to in another autobiography, *The Weald of Youth* (1942) and its sequel.[4] In *Good-bye to All That* (1929) Robert Graves, a fellow officer in the Royal Welch Fusiliers, repeats Sherston's progress. Honest and more pedestrian, Graves notes horrors of public school and war. He also suffered from neurasthenia, and, renouncing his caste after the war, also became a socialist.

Georgian by nature, Graves and Sassoon were encouraged by Edward Marsh, who published them in his anthology. *Fairies and Fusiliers* (1917), the war poems of Robert Graves, are not very good. A realistic description of "A Dead Boche," letters in verse to Sassoon and Robert Nichols announcing that "cherries are out of season," and the experimental Skeltonics are not above the Georgian average, but the childhood reminiscences into

[4] Other autobiographies: *The Old Century* (1938), *Siegfried's Journey* (1946). *Selected Poems* (1925).

which he retreated in his later collections are extraordinary. Improving, Graves wrote several good ballads on childhood and several poems in other measures.[5] Sassoon's war poetry, printed in *The Old Huntsman* (1917) and in *Counter-Attack* (1918), is more impressive. Converted from a conventional preoccupation with nature and music by the impact of Masefield, Sassoon used Masefield's colloquial diction and conversational rhythms for bitter ironic accounts of what he saw in France, "sodden buttocks" protruding from the "sucking mud" and other wastes of youth and courage. These poems, which keep within the metrical conventions of the Georgians, treat with greater condensation and force than Sherston's the reactions of Sherston. The last lines are monotonously withering. Aside from Owen's these poems are the best attempts at rendering an experience too enormous for poetry.

While at Dr. Rivers's hospital for the shell-shocked, Wilfred Owen met Sassoon, read his poetry, and was inspired. The poetry Owen wrote upon his return to the front is notable for its profound humanity and its technique. Discarding Georgian conventions, he used dissonance, assonance, and alliteration. He paired "world" with "walled," "shelling" with "shilling," and "fleers" with "feet." These discords, setting the teeth on edge, are what his horrors needed. But the poetry, as Owen said, "is in the pity." He was killed one week before the armistice.[6] Pity and dissonance alike commended him, long after, to the devotion of Auden and Day Lewis, but Yeats, making his anthology, refused to admit that unhappy warrior.

The reactions of Edmund Blunden, Robert Nichols, and W. W. Gibson conformed to the Georgian tradition, less

[5] *Collected Poems* (1938).

[6] *Poems* (1920), with introduction by Sassoon.

pastoral now than disillusioned.[7] To his fellow poets, the noble sentiments of Rupert Brooke, dead too soon, now seemed archaic. Even the imagists, discarding petals, shared Georgian bitterness.

Making a hokku of flowers one night in his trench, Richard Aldington was interrupted by a rat. For a time he had devoted his images and the decorous freedom of his verse to flowers, then to impressions, more sensuous than thoughtful, of immediate reality. The later verses of *Images of War* (1919) express disgust. In *Death of a Hero* (1929), one of the best war novels, he bitterly describes the war again and the despicable civilians who help make war what it is. Betrayed by these and depressed by former friends, the "hero" invites his death. The savagery of Aldington, which owes much to war, more to the success of friends, is at its most agreeable in "Stepping Heavenward" and the other satires of *Soft Answers* (1932).[8]

Herbert Read, another minor poet, is a better poet than Aldington or Graves. Commencing as disciple of Aldington, H. D., and Hulme, Read wrote poems in their manner. Tidy visual images in free verse convey impressions of accidental beauties and, increasingly, of battle and its mess. Some of his war poems are narratives, some dramatic monologues, some lyrics; but even the last are more

[7] Edmund Blunden: *Undertones of War* (1928), *Poems* (1930). Robert Nichols: *Ardours and Endurances* (1917). W. W. Gibson: *Collected Poems* (1926). Isaac Rosenberg: *Collected Works* (1937), foreword by Sassoon.

Poets of the second World War, working by indirection, concentrated their feelings of anxiety and guilt in images commonly irrelevant to war. E.g., Sidney Keyes: *The Iron Laurel* (1942), *The Cruel Solstice* (1943), *Collected Poems* (1945). Alun Lewis: *Raiders' Dawn* (1942). Alan Rook: *Soldiers, This Solitude* (1942). T. R. Hodgson: *This Life, This Death* (1943). Roy Fuller: *A Lost Season* (1944). Alex Comfort: *A Wreath for the Living* (1942).

[8] *Poems* (1934). *All Men Are Enemies* (1933), *Rejected Guest* (1939).

objective and serene than most, as *In Retreat* (1925), his brief history of a discouraging episode, is more detached than its longer parallels. Retaining in France something of the artist's aloofness, he used discouragement and atrocity less for personal complaint than as "focus for feeling . . . otherwise diffuse." After the war, following the development of Eliot and Pound, his imagistic colleagues, he wrote satiric quatrains, but his later work is closer than theirs to their flowery originals. Their happiest pupil, he sometimes approaches their effects.[9]

The sensibility of T. S. Eliot, who took Aldington's place on the staff of the *Egoist* when that angry man went off to war, was stirred, if not by war, by war's aftermath. The cynical quatrains of Sweeney, Bleistein, and the hippopotamus, written at the end of the war, and the images and people of *The Waste Land* express his reaction. No poet of our time has given greater finality to the mood of that decade or more thoroughly embalmed its bounders and parasites.

The "terrible gaiety" of Edith Sitwell and her luscious artifice parallel Eliot's austerities, conveying the same despair in fancier words. *Gold Coast Customs* (1929) is her *Waste Land*, footnotes and all. Emerging from her nursery in this, she confronted what she once transformed. *Street Songs* (1942), different in manner from her frivolities, contains "Lullaby," one of the best and most terrible reactions to the second war. The war poems of her brother Osbert (now Sir Osbert) Sitwell, who served at the front, concern the iniquities of civilians. These angry poems, in free verse or meter, which lament youth's slaughter for the profiteer, are less interesting than the satiric quatrains with which he expressed the peace. Instead of Bleistein and Doris, he used Mrs. Freudenthal, and instead of his own technique that of Eliot. But Sir Osbert the satirist is

[9] *Poems, 1914–34* (1934).

as good as Sir Osbert the mimic. He used couplets, quatrains, and free verse to castigate the loathsome age before lapsing, all passion spent, into his sister's manner.[10]

Sacheverell Sitwell, a better poet than his brother, belongs here for his discovery of the baroque, which, like Owen's dissonance or Donne's conceit, became a vehicle for the ambivalent and the polite. By interruptions of solidity, sublime irrelevancies, frivolous pomposities, the baroque diverted, while it expressed, the age. What had been the expression of magnificence and authority became the most florid expression of disenchantment. *Southern Baroque Art* (1924) and his other elegant studies, though anticipated by Germans, defined a cult already ensplendored by Edith Sitwell and Aldous Huxley. From these it broadened down to men of fashion and, after an interval, to critics and scholars.

Sweeney's mood was recaptured in the postwar novel of Aldous Huxley and Evelyn Waugh, for whom a form had been established by Norman Douglas. *South Wind* (1917), urbane and skeptical, is a symposium, plotless or all but plotless, in which opinions of eccentrics are interrupted by outrageous circumstance and innocents transformed by the spirit of place or the oddness of people. Pagan Mr. Keith, Miss Wilberforce, who undresses herself in public, and innumerable others, pious, gaga, or indecorous, became types and their eloquence a pattern for later novelists. Less immoderate than its successors, *South Wind* is mellow, golden, prewar; and far less dismayed, it supports against immoderation and repression a classical ideal. With its bland preposterous lives of the saints, its catalogue of fountains, its "luminous asides and fruitful

[10] *Collected Satires and Poems* (1931). Novels: *Before the Bombardment* (1926), *The Man Who Lost Himself* (1929). Stories: *Triple Fugue* (1924), *Dumb-Animal* (1930). Memoirs: *Left Hand, Right Hand* (1944), *The Scarlet Tree* (1946).

digressions," this panorama of Capri is as individual as *Tristram Shandy* and almost as fine. The exotic pedantry that Douglas shares with Sterne appears again in *Old Calabria* (1915), a travel book distinguished by lives of flying saints, and in the learned apparatus of *Some Limericks* (1928). Douglas, who wrote more novels than one, is a man of one novel.[11]

Huxley, a man of more than one but of none better, had a capacity for continual disillusionment. Nineteenth-century science and the war had made all meaningless. A solitary undergraduate in an Oxford depopulated by war, he became increasingly cynical and civilized. For a time he enjoyed his disillusionments and the feeling of irresponsibility that accompanied them, and it was long before he tried to restore a meaning. He made fun of those earnest mystics and vegetarians who were trying. But his pleasure was a kind of pain. Delighting like Swift in self-torment, he took his stand in the heart of a waste land where he forced himself to contemplate the disgusting and the inane.

Friendly with Sitwells, Huxley wrote strange poems, at once luscious, elegant, and desperate. Of these the philosopher's songs of *Leda* (1920) are typical. An idiot's merry-go-round became his image, and in the neighboring menagerie the "gorgeous buttocks of the ape" put him in mind of "sunsets exquisitely dying." These learned grotesques were followed by short stories of similar character, some owing shape to Katherine Mansfield, all their mood to war and peace, and all, as a character remarks, "the ingenious products of a very cultured and elaborate brain." Those of *Mortal Coils* (1922) are typical. As Mr. Hutton of "The Gioconda Smile" kisses his mistress he thinks of fabulous sea cucumbers in the aquarium at Naples. Sidney Dolphin, the decadent poet of "Permutations among the

[11] *Siren Land* (1911). *Looking Back* (1933), autobiography.

Nightingales," a one-act play anticipating Coward, sees life as a bad joke and love itself as meaningless. On these façades the curves are broken, the ornament is florid.[12]

Huxley's baroque novels are even better and more desolating. *Crome Yellow* (1921), a country-house symposium, made in the fashions of Douglas and Peacock, consists of digressions from nothing. Mr. Scogan, the commentator, fixes the point. "We all know," he says, "that there's no ultimate point." A gallery of fools and eccentrics proceeds to illustrate it, and innocent Denis is continually deflated. The Elizabethan privy proves that Huxley had read Sir John Harington, and the story of the dwarf that the period of Wilde and Beardsley was not wholly extinct. These grotesques compose Mr. Scogan's ideal for the novel: something fantastic, witty, erudite, and rich. Huxley was never more successful.

But *Antic Hay* (1923) is of equal value and shapelier, for the concentric meaningless circles and the arabesques surround a fixed, if empty center. While Coleman, a diabolist of the nineties, rapes, he lectures his girls upon the tediousness and pointlessness of debauchery. Shearwater's science is as futile as Gumbril's pneumatic trousers or Lypiatt's painting. Only Mozart and Christopher Wren emerge from the circles of Huxley's hell, which is symbolized by the night club and the taxi of Mrs. Viveash, the promiscuous and miserable. As she sees the twitching lights of Piccadilly, she has for a moment the illusion of being cheerful, but tomorrow, she knows, will be as awful as today.

Those Barren Leaves (1925) is less nearly perfect. Of the cynics, fools, and knaves at Mrs. Aldwinkle's house party, Chelifer, the masochistic editor of the *Rabbit Fanciers' Gazette,* is the most amusing and the most desper-

[12] Stories: *Little Mexican* (1924) (in the United States entitled *Young Archimedes*), *Two or Three Graces* (1926), *Brief Candles* (1930).

ate. But he and Cardan are less triumphant than Calamy, a mystic, for meaning was beginning to intrude upon a meaningless world. This mixture served to introduce *Point Counter Point* (1928), Huxley's most ambitious novel, in which the usual gallery of caricatures, now fixed and recurrent, is matched by hopeful specimens. Burlap in his tub belongs to the familiar world, but Rampion to another better. Philip Quarles, in betwixt and between, is a critical self-portrait. Far from being a natural novelist, Philip concludes, he does by intellect and fancy what others do by instinct. And the form of this novel, written by one of its own characters, helps to prove his contention. Based upon Gide's *Faux-Monnayeurs* and Bach's *Suite No. 2 in B Minor*, it illustrates elaborate heartlessness. This defect was soon to be remedied.

For this reason *Point Counter Point* is Huxley's last good novel. But even among his works of mystical vegetarianism traces remain of his talent for the disgusting and the bizarre. In *After Many a Summer* there are still baboons and antiquaries and the Marquis de Sade. The diary of the Fifth Earl is as good as the digression on plumbing in *Crome Yellow*, his fate as exquisite as Gumbril's beaver. But baboons and antiquaries are all but lost among the sermons of Mr. Propter. Although comparatively free from preaching, *Time Must Have a Stop* (1944) is comparatively tedious. From the wealth of meaning, however, Uncle Eustace's infantile lips protrude to suck a clear perfecto. That cigar, a relic of civilization, is, of course, a *Romeo y Julieta.*

While Huxley, the offended idealist, suffered from night clubs, Michael Arlen, once popular, took them as ideals. The manner of *The Green Hat* (1924) is warm, pink, and confidential. As Mayfair dotes on cocktails, he invokes the mews, and all the nymphomaniacs and drunks assume for him a kind of glamour. Arlen saw postwar society, but,

misunderstanding its meaning, made the desperate meretricious, the horrid shoddy.[13]

Evelyn Waugh, another idealist, differs from Huxley in being funnier and more savage, and from Arlen in almost every way. "All Mayfair," Waugh observes in one of his novels, "seemed to throb with the heart of Mr. Arlen." But it only seemed. Waugh's heartless Mayfair is also a "world that had lost its reason." Its occupants, who display with bright energy their indifference to value, their freedom from scruple, combine and recombine in situations so appalling that the weeping reader laughs aloud.

Decline and Fall (1928), the first of his excellent novels, is speedy, deplorable, and very funny. The central character, like all of Waugh's victims, takes what comes to him without reflection. This passivity increases the horror of what surrounds him: Oxford, the private school, Mayfair, and white-slavery. As symbol of this world Margot Beste-Chetwynde's chromium-yellow house lamentably obtrudes, its drawing-room embellished with octopuses, its conservatory with India-rubber fungi, and for its floor green glass. The people are outlines or shadows, their speech laconic, but standing without the support of the author's comment they have a kind of vitality. Their victim, who learns at last to cultivate his garden, returns to his theology. *Vile Bodies* (1930) is brisker and more sick-making as Miss Runcible, Miles Malpractice, or other Bright Young People would say. Mrs. Beste-Chetwynde, now Lady Metroland, gives parties, Mrs. Melrose Ape conducts her choir of synthetic angels, Father Rothchild, the omniscient Jesuit, intrigues, and society columnists report or invent these things for the *Daily Excess*. After

[13] Both before the war and after, Ronald Firbank, a corrupt dandy, composed arabesques in the most decadent style of the nineties. E.g., *Concerning the Eccentricities of Cardinal Pirelli* (1926). Cyril Connolly is his principal admirer. See *Enemies of Promise* (1939).

the symbolic motor race, Adam, a simpleton like Waugh's other victims, finds himself in the war his world has invited.

Waugh took the title for *A Handful of Dust* (1934), his best novel, from Conrad's "Youth" by way of Eliot's *Waste Land.* The allusion should have been to "The Heart of Darkness"; for the waste land's heart, shown here, was never darker. With quiet power this novel proceeds through gruesome comedy to tragedy. Pity and fear attend the fall of Tony Last, whose innocence and responsibility are out of fashion. His inevitable fate as idiot's reader is the more tragic for being absurd.

Put Out More Flags (1942) is somewhat less successful than its predecessors. But Waugh regained his power with *Brideshead Revisited* (1945), a sober review of the twenties and thirties from the vantage point of the second war, in which, deferring fascism, he served. The first part, concerning Oxford in the twenties, contains Waugh's most entertaining and most three-dimensional eccentrics: Sebastian with his Teddy bear, and Blanche, who paints his toenails red. The second part, far more serious than the first, concerns Sebastian's family, the ruin of Sebastian by his mother, and the conflict in their hearts between religion and the world. This subtle study of imperfect Catholics and of Catholicism triumphant is Waugh's most open treatment of his faith.[14] Like Huxley, Waugh found in religion a refuge from the world and a point of view from which to regard it; but unlike Huxley he remained an artist, leaving sermons to the clergy. His public religion, improving his art, gave to his moralities intensity and that monkish loathing by which he pleases.

Lytton Strachey is to biography what Waugh and Huxley are to the novel. Civilized, a member of the Cam-

[14] Waugh was converted in 1930. See his *Edmund Campion* (1935).

bridge-Bloomsbury set, he too found in satire and irony fitting expressions of the postwar world. During the war he had been a conscientious objector, and, when asked by the inquisitors what he would do if he found a German ravishing his sister, replied that he would try to get between them. Such reasonable ambiguity became his instrument.

The improvement of biography in our time is largely Strachey's affair. In the nineteenth century, biography had been scholarly or panegyrical, the one careless of art, the other of truth. Proposing to make biography once more a truthful art, he succeeded in making it an art. His merits and his defects come from his point of view, his manner, and his tone. These belong to his adorable eighteenth century and to France, on which he wrote his first book, *Landmarks of French Literature* (1912), one of the most sympathetic studies in English of the classical spirit. He adored that mildness of surface which hides a catlike malice; he adored the elegant, the urbane, and the aloof. He liked to use his ironies on what he disliked. The war having sharpened his instrument, he used it not upon the world around him but upon Victoria's world, which, with some reason, he held responsible for our condition.

The preface to *Eminent Victorians* (1918) states his purpose and defines the "new" biography. Lamenting those two fat volumes with which Victorians were accustomed to celebrate their dead, he proposes fact, not compliment; brevity and selection, not copious dullness. He will expose. In the essays that follow he exposes four Victorians who had been stuffed and whitewashed by their contemporaries. But the treatment of Cardinal Manning as an unprincipled politician seems unfair. This impression is not altogether unwarranted. Reference to Edmund Purcell's two-volume biography, Strachey's principal source, proves his facts correct but reveals his malice. In its interests his facts are selected, juxtaposed, or emphasized. The quotations are deadly, the sequences incongruous and anticlimactic. The result is swift, irreverent, readable; but truth is partial or colored. Dr. Arnold, an "earnest enthusiast" who is blamed for the public school, is destroyed by the same method; but General Gordon and Florence Nightingale, humanized a little, are improved.

In *Queen Victoria* (1921), perhaps the best biography of our time, this method has been refined. What had been crude at times or obvious is now easy and impeccable. Everything follows from the method. Victoria, absurd, middle-class, noble, admirable, becomes convincing and many-sided, and the portraits of the men to whom she was so susceptible are at once brilliant and lifelike. For suave malice nothing in English exceeds the portrait of Albert.

But this well-balanced book was followed by *Elizabeth and Essex* (1928), which lacks Strachey's particular merits. Irony has been succeeded by romantic enthusiasm, knowledge by ignorance. Strachey, at his best at what he detested, loved Elizabethans; and his many essays on the seventeenth and eighteenth centuries, though not without penetration, might have been composed by another.

Strachey had reason, in his essays on "Six English Historians," to commend the styles of Gibbon and Hume and to dismiss Macaulay's as "one of the most remarkable products of the industrial revolution." The classical virtues of clarity, elegance, and wit, so often wanting in the nineteenth century, were more than Strachey's instrument. They were his refuge from the times and, like Yeats's mask, the means to keep his own disorder down.[15]

[15] Strachey: *Books and Characters* (1922); *Portraits in Miniature* (contains "Six English Historians") (1931); *Characters and Commentaries* (1933); *Pope* (1925). Guy Boas: *Lytton Strachey* (1935). Max Beerbohm: *Lytton Strachey* (1943). Harold Nicolson: *The Development*

Before Strachey, Edmund Gosse in *Father and Son* (1907), a study at once kindly and detached of his father, anticipated many of the effects of the new biography. After Strachey, biographers abounded, moved by him, but all, save for their common preoccupation with the nineteenth century, dissimilar. Philip Guedalla, the most important of these, wrote *Palmerston* (1926) and *The Duke* (1931). Guedalla's intention as expressed in the preface to the first of these is Strachey's. But more scholarly than Strachey, Guedalla consulted documents, discovered facts, and left none except the unmentionable unmentioned. Where Strachey used a scalpel, Guedalla used a flashing shovel, each stroke so brilliant the effect is dull. Conclusions and character alike are left implicit in the heap. Re-creating the Whig aristocracy in *The Young Melbourne* (1939), David Cecil is swift, elegant, and urbane, but not inaccurate. This civilized book, the finest of Strachey's tradition, is the outstanding biography of its decade.

Noel Coward, no less postwar in attitude than these biographers and novelists, found his vehicle in the comedies of Wilde and Maugham, which it is necessary for their sake and his to review. The comedy of manners, as historians know the type, often departs from the tradition of Congreve toward sentiment, fantasy, or purpose. Whether true to type or not, its element is wit. Before the war wit was demanded by the decadence of society and after the war by the war.

Between 1892 and 1895 Wilde wrote four comedies, increasingly good, in which he cleverly combined the virtues of Congreve, Pinero, Ibsen, and W. S. Gilbert, who

of English Biography (1928). Mark Longaker: *Contemporary Biography* (1934).

Nicolson's preface to *Tennyson* (1922) states the aims of the new biography. His best book: *Some People* (1927), is autobiographical.

had restored the tradition of comedy. Unrealistic, these plays create a bright imaginary aristocracy who talk like Wilde himself in epigram and paradox. Since Burke's peerage, as Wilde's Lord Illingworth remarks, is the best example of English fiction, Wilde, like James, was compelled to invent what he could not discover. His middle-class fantasy pleased the middle class and flattered those members of the aristocracy who were still around. Giving his plays something of the appearance of Ibsen's gratified the advanced as the cordial reviews of Shaw attest. But that, while maintaining appearances, he avoided real problems and appeased the conservatives whom he excited is shown by his commercial success.

In his first three plays, dull virtue, confronted with glittering vice, is more or less victorious. In each there are a proper lady, a dandy, who carries the burden of antinomian wit, and several dowagers, sometimes witty too. As the ill-made play proceeds, with soliloquies and asides and creakings at the joints, a curious conflict develops between sentiment and wit, morality of theme and amorality of epigram. *Lady Windermere's Fan* (1892) and *A Woman of No Importance* (1893) are less comic on the whole than sentimental. Approaching pure comedy in *An Ideal Husband* (1895), which deals with political and financial unscrupulousness, Wilde almost achieved it in *The Importance of Being Earnest* (1895), where wit, for once at home with theme, shines in a moral vacuum.

Having learned his craft from Wilde and Jones, and disillusioned by science, Somerset Maugham commenced writing plays in 1903, his object, like Wilde's, money. *Lady Frederick* (1907) is Wilde minus sentiment, and Jones minus problem. Like most of Maugham's plays, it was a commercial success. Maugham defines the commercial play as one that people will go to see. Seeking delight, they want good construction, interesting theme, amusing characters and dialogue or, in two words, good theater. Since plays depend upon the many-leveled audience, most of which is indifferent to ideas, plays should avoid them.[16] This cynicism reappears in the entertainments he contrived for many-leveled London.

Of these witty plays *The Circle* (1921) is among the best. Here aristocrats in a country house keep reality at several removes, but enough of a problem is suggested and cleverly avoided to keep an audience in stitches and to please the cynical. That history repeats itself is at once familiar, hopeless, and amusing. If the purpose of the theater is not to inform or complain, this is the perfect play. *Our Betters* (1923), as savage as Wycherley, discloses wartime Mayfair, peopled with irresponsible aristocrats and rich Americans, mostly the latter, who have lost one code and failed to find another. These intruders almost transform Maugham's worldly tolerance into moral indignation. But this feeling, one feels, is what he felt his audience would feel. Equilibrium is restored with *The Constant Wife* (1926), which, taking its theme of woman's financial and sexual independence from the problem play, demoralizes it. Comic indifference had become an expression on the popular level of the postwar mind.

Having studied Maugham and the tempo of New York, Noel Coward gave the disenchanted the bitter sweetness they desired, uniting for them the worlds of Huxley and Arlen. Coward knew the theater and how to write a play. His craftsman's cunning made farces like *Hay Fever* (1925), thin when read, effective on the stage.

At once smart and moving, *The Vortex* (1924), though subsidized by Michael Arlen, presents a world as dark as Huxley's, symbolized, like his, by circling dancers. The vortex is postwar beastliness, in which mother and son

[16] In *The Summing Up* (1938) and in the prefaces to his *Plays* (1932), Maugham discusses his principles and plays.

revolve with the other flotsam of Mayfair. Even that tremendous final scene where the son confronts his mother's beastliness with his own promises nothing. The critics and the censor, less up to date than the audience, wanted to know why Coward chose unpleasant subjects and decadent types, why his characters drink cocktails, take drugs and lovers, or circle to the gramophone. In "The Author's Reply to his Critics" (*Three Plays*, 1925), Coward maintains that, far from trying to be shocking, he tries to express his view of reality and will continue to do so in the teeth of the middle class. Unlike cynics who regard the stage as a commercial opportunity, he regards it as the place of reality and art. Preserving these, he intends to provide an "evening's entertainment." He did that, and his plays helped retard the decay he laments in audience and stage.

Coward's well-made entertainments fall into two kinds, the ironic and the sentimental. Those of the first kind, called "brittle" by critics, are spare and swift, with splendid surfaces, their themes the moral anarchy of the times. *Easy Virtue* (1926) is an old-fashioned problem play on the conflict between a woman with a past and bourgeois respectability. But, faster in every sense than her predecessors, she is less victim than conqueror, and the open door at the end implies sophistication beyond Pinero's capacity. *Fallen Angels* (1925), slight, amusing, and symmetrical, concerns Mayfair wives and husbands and a Frenchman. No point is made, but the ambiguous ending seems to condone what moralists deplore. In *Private Lives* (1930), another symmetrical farce, Coward selects from the people of Waugh and Huxley two couples, who, intricately recombining, cut across conventions. Their lines are clever but not too clever, their conduct hilarious, and nothing, apparently, matters. This amusing play was followed by a better, *Design for Living* (1933), on a similar theme. What Ernest calls a "disgusting three-sided erotic hotch-potch" is illustrated by two men and one woman who love each other very much. At his words, as the curtain falls, the three laugh and laugh, but it is unclear at what—at him, at life, or at themselves?

Such pleasing ambiguities amused and reassured the audience, which understood, as many critics failed to do, that Coward's meaning was not to be confused with his surfaces. Beneath them beat a conventional heart, moral, sentimental, and serious, located, moreover, in the proper place. That the audience was correct is shown by his plays of the other kind. *Bitter Sweet* (1929), his favorite, spurns the jazzing world for what he calls "seminostalgic sentiment." Clever lyrics and a chorus of fairies serve only to reinforce this mood. *Post-Mortem* (1931), a poor thing, is a solemn indictment of those cocktail drinkers who have forgotten England's heroic dead. *Cavalcade* (1931), a pageant of enormously clever construction, of magnificent theater, expressed for wet-eyed Britons the pathos of empire and the ruling caste. In the final scene, amid the wreckage of depression, the Union Jack is discovered, spotlighted and glorious. It is not enough to say that these plays are what Coward's dramatic intelligence told him his audience wanted. They are also what he wanted. The curious thing about them is the importance, surely symbolical, of the cocktail. *Blithe Spirit* (1941) begins with dry Martinis, but this excellent farce of the husband and his shades, symbolical of nothing, is an entertainment.[17]

[17] *Play Parade* (1933), *To-night at 8:30* (1936), *Second Play Parade* (1939). *Present Indicative* (1937), autobiography.

A. A. Milne, best remembered for "The King's Breakfast" and excellent children's stories about very British Winnie-the-Pooh, which compare in value with Kenneth Grahame's *Wind in the Willows* (1908), shared the postwar stage with Coward but not the postwar attitude. He departs from pleasant comedy for whimsy in *Mr. Pim Passes By* (1920), and in *The Dover Road* (1922), for fantasy.

Before the first World War and after it other writers presented their world in comic novels or stories, some of which are sardonic, some sentimental, all more or less fantastic. A normal medium for Englishmen in our time, fantasy has enabled them to escape what they faced. With its aid it became possible to contemplate middle-class reality without the pain of Huxley or of Waugh, for reality, when passed through this medium, became agreeable. But the adoption of this protective enchantment argues a kind of disenchantment.

The precocious disenchantment that tempered Max Beerbohm's essays and fantasies of the Beardsley period reached dandier levels in *Zuleika Dobson* (1911), one of the best novels of our time. At once heroic and comic, this tender malicious story of Oxford takes the form of Greek tragedy with all the machinery of fate, the messengers and owls. The characters are caricatures in Beerbohm's manner. The Duke is the middle-class Englishman's ideal, Oover his most kindly idea of the intruding American, and Noaks his idea of the intruding proletarian. These portraits, which imply the class that made them, are matched by those of frigid Zuleika and the careless dons, who would be intolerable in another atmosphere. Fantasy is preserved not only by the preposterous plot, the perspiring Emperors, and the affair of the studs but by a style dandiacal, concerned with its own perfection, lucid, yet precious as Beardsley's, light, yet ensplendored with turns of classical rhetoric.[18]

However malicious, the comic fantasies of Beerbohm are sunny and urbane. Those of Saki (H. H. Munro) are savage. The callousness of his short stories, *The Chronicles of Clovis* (1911), for example, or *Beasts and Super-Beasts* (1914), is that of a sadistic child. His effect depends in

[18] *A Christmas Garland* (1912) contains excellent parodies of Henry James and other contemporary writers.

part upon regarding the affairs of the adult world with the cold-blooded eyes of such a child and in part upon brevity and casual speed. Appalling practical jokes, infantile revenge, and meaningless horrors compose a world (not unlike that of Kipling) peopled by children, carnivorous animals, and the ruling caste. After the child has been devoured by the hyena, the fox-huntress moves on to take her tea. Ascetic multitudes devour Filboid Studge while applauding Cousin Teresa and the big borzoi. It is hardly a surprise when the bishop is reported to be liquidating Jews with the assistance of Boy Scouts. Though these cruel stories present a vision of the world before the first World War, in which Saki died, they anticipate the world before the second, and from our point of view are less fantastic than they seemed.[19]

The world between two wars was oyster for Bertie Wooster and Jeeves, his man. By humorous exaggeration with the effect of fantasy, P. G. Wodehouse made unearned incomes bearable even by those who do not have them. It is unclear, however, whether he intended satire of the idle or their defense. As Wilde had made his idlers wits, Wodehouse made his fools, whereas most are neither. But as one or the other they are harmless, to all appearances, and tolerable. Whatever the intention, therefore, the effect was less satiric than protective, and the vogue of Wodehouse, assured by his hilarity, was reassured. When his young men in spats tool off to country houses to become involved with uncles and horsy ladies, from whom Jeeves, alone intelligent, will rescue them, their dilemmas are at once unlike and like what's what. For these pure and amiable distortions of Mayfair and the counties, no

[19] *The Short Stories of Saki* (1930). *The Novels and Plays of Saki* (1933). *The Unbearable Bassington* (1912), a novel, does not quite succeed though it recalls the wit of Wilde and anticipates the satire of Waugh.

more extreme in one direction than those of Waugh in another, Wodehouse invented an idiom parallel to that of polite society, but inimitable and far from tiresome.

Depending less upon word and situation, the humor of Angela Thirkell is inconspicuous. Her theme, like that of Wodehouse, is the gentry, not of Mayfair, however, but of the county, and the county, of course, is Trollope's Barsetshire. Her purpose, whether conscious or not, is their defense. As Wodehouse made them foolish, she made them charming, and the result, in a world they try to ignore, is pleasantly fantastic. Her self-contained province as displayed in *The Brandons* (1939) or *Northbridge Rectory* (1942) abounds with squires, their ladies, their vicars, and their servants. Some, like Mrs. Brandon, are helpless, and some, like Sir Edmund, are bluff, but all, as they enjoy their property, conceal hearts of gold. Their rounded characters, their placid idleness, and their diversions afford matter for comedy of manners. But into this lovely place the war intruded, and the later novels concern the impeccable reactions of these people.

The people of Barrie—or most of them—have hearts of gold, but while we are smiling about it we are asked to weep. His humorous fantasies are often sentimental, as everybody knows, but Barrie is neither as bad as he has been considered nor as good. His early work in imitation of the sentimental Kailyard school is best represented by *A Window in Thrums* (1889), sketches of village folk. A shrewd ear for speech and a shrewder eye for familiar detail of scene or character welcome all signs of goodness or of tears. It was against such sweetness that George Douglas directed *The House with the Green Shutters* (1901), a dour, nightmarish melodrama of the village Scot. Some years prior to this discouraging view of human nature, Barrie had published *Margaret Ogilvy* (1896), a tender portrait of his mother. Composed with love, this fascinating study reveals a relationship between Barrie and his mother that, not unlike that of Paul Morel with his, may account in part for the character of Barrie's work. As his mother wandered through his books, assuming the posture of heroine, he avoided adult reality or, when he met it, covered it with sentiment, whimsy, or fantasy.

These coverings, agreeable to the middle class, made Barrie a great success in the theater. *Quality Street* (1902), a charming play of old maids and a kind of love, concerns the Jane Austen period, and would resemble Jane Austen more with more sense and less sensibility. In *The Admirable Crichton* (1902), an amusing fantasy of caste, Crichton performs the defensive role of Jeeves. While inferior to the plays of Maugham, *What Every Woman Knows* (1908) is Barrie's closest approach to the comedy of manners. The philosophy that takes the place of problem is obvious, the characters are solid, the stage directions cute. His closest approach to social criticism is *The Twelve-Pound Look* (1910), but the character of his Philistine wants a firmer touch and a little bitterness. What we think of, unfortunately, when we think of Barrie's plays is *A Kiss for Cinderella* (1916), but only the mawkish first and last acts deserve our censure. The second act contains a subjective fantasy as good on the whole as the dream plays of most expressionists. *Dear Brutus* (1917), a fantasy involving Puck and the enchanted forest and what might have been, is almost cynical. The structure, as usual, is excellent.

Although some of these craftsmanlike commercial plays are free from sentiment and whimsy, such freedom was not Barrie's merit. Both are present in *Peter Pan*, his best work, whether as play or novel. In this fantasy of the boy who refused to grow up, as in *Margaret Ogilvy*, Barrie expressed what was nearest his heart. Instead of covering reality, the sentimental, the whimsical, and the fantastic became keys to what reality he could know.

The times or life itself being too hideous to contemplate, T. F. Powys mixed the real with the impossible. In *Mr. Weston's Good Wine* (1927) God and Michael, disguised as merchants, arrive in their Ford to interrupt the cruelties of Hardy's countryside. While the clock is stopped for judgment, Powys anatomizes with limpid objectivity the rapers, the sufferers, and the eccentrics. God, disguised as a tinker this time, attends to rural avarice in the first story of *The Left Leg* (1923), and the gods of *Mr. Tasker's Gods* (1925) are pigs.

Not unlike Powys in uniting earthiness with extravagance is A. E. Coppard, whose short stories, some realistic, some fanciful, have been collected in several volumes, of which *Adam & Eve & Pinch Me* (1921) is best. His dark ironic stories of actual life, indebted, of course, to Maupassant and Chekhov, and besides these to the folk tradition, explain by their bitterness his recourse to fantasy in others. Even his most realistic stories are a little strange. Some of the fantastic tales are as exotic as Dunsany's, some, on Irish themes in Irish idiom, as fanciful as Stephens's. The best, such as "Adam & Eve & Pinch Me" or "Big Game," present dream or unnatural experience or, like "Arabesque," his most famous, are formal arrangements of minor horrors. Good without greatness, these stories, better than Forster's, are inferior to those of Joyce, Mansfield, or Huxley. The style, meticulous and odd, is sometimes mannered.

These fantasts are distinguished for elegance of style. The clarity and ease of the eighteenth century were recovered by David Garnett for *Lady into Fox* (1922), a metamorphosis that all but equals Kafka's. The sobriety of the narrator, the adjustments of Mr. Tebrick to the foxiness of his wife, and his effort to abate her odor as they play cards or fondle each other give substance to the fancy. Falling somewhere between fantasy and whimsy, *A Man in the Zoo* (1924) discovers a Swiftian view of man as animal. As much a discoverer as Edward Garnett, his father, David Garnett encouraged T. F. Powys, Coppard, and Sylvia Townsend Warner, whose *Lolly Willowes* (1926) ornaments the fantastic tradition. If Garnett did not discover *His Monkey Wife* (1930) by John Collier, he should have.[20]

The moonlit fantasies of Walter de la Mare, like those of Machen, which they resemble, are responses to the world of science and the middle class. Uncanny and antiquarian, these stories draw atmosphere from the prose of the seventeenth century, which de la Mare loves and often approximates. In *The Return* (1910), a novel of morbid psychology, the hero, loitering at twilight in a churchyard, finds himself possessed by the tenant of a convenient grave. The displeasure of his suburban wife and his discovery of her nature and his own, providing an accompaniment of grisly humor, indict the world. Of the stories collected in *The Connoisseur* (1926), some are nightmares, others fantasies. Relying like Maeterlinck upon tenuous indirections, de la Mare approaches demons in "All Hallows" and nameless horrors in "Mr. Kempe." His best novel, *Memoirs of a Midget* (1921), is beautiful and strange, though somewhat Victorian in gait. His poppet's account of her relations with the normal world displays it as gigantic and incomprehensible. This vision, several fine characters, and the feat of penetrating, without loss of credibility, the mind of one so small are virtues of this fantastic romance.

[20] Other fantasts: Archibald Marshall: *Simple People* (1928). Bruce Marshall: *Father Malachy's Miracle* (1933). T. H. White: *The Sword in the Stone* (1939). Eric Knight: *Sam Small Flies Again* (1943).

The poems of de la Mare are similar in character to the stories, but more exquisite. His scenes are churchyards, forests, and ruined towers. His flora, from old herbals, is bindweed and dittany; his fauna the moth and vole; his people travelers, innocents, and revenants. Much possessed by death, he approximates the "metaphysical shudder" of Donne, and, renewing the Gothic, recaptures effects of Beddoes and Hölderlin. Freed by these antecedents from Georgian rhetoric, he is seemingly archaic, actually timeless. The title poem of *The Listeners* (1912), his best collection, is a conspiracy of suggestions. His happiest lines,

> Through what wild centuries
> Roves back the rose,

are not unlike the perfections of the seventeenth century. In this and his other volumes the flora, the fauna, and all the symbols of his private world maintain their enchantment, the incantation of sound and rhythm prolong the dream, and the simplest means add beauty to strangeness.[21]

At times in both his poetry and his prose de la Mare enters the province of the shocker, which, providing thrills of crime, espionage, or the supernatural, has enjoyed the addiction of multitudes. The purpose of the shocker is to reduce the tedium of the suburb and, by manageable horror, the horror of the world. Perfectly safe, the small fears of shockers can cure for a moment by a kind of homeopathy the fears and uncertainties of our condition. The dissolution of Victoria's world demanded the shocker as the world's instability toward the close of the eighteenth century invited the Gothic novel.

[21] *The Riddle* (1923), *Ding Dong Bell* (1924), *Collected Poems* (1941), *The Burning-Glass* (1945). Forrest Reid: *Walter de la Mare* (1929).

In the shocker, fantasy shows again familiar connections with reality. The vampires of Bram Stoker's *Dracula* (1897) vulgarize a preoccupation of a period no less occult than scientific; whereas *The Lodger* (1913) by Mrs. Belloc Lowndes preserves its more criminal excess. While Edgar Wallace tirelessly supplied its need, authors more respectable than he attempted rivalry, among them Sir Hugh Walpole. M. R. James, the provost of Eton, wrote horrid ghost stories. For the uses of Alfred Hitchcock, John Buchan (Lord Tweedsmuir) provided *The Thirty-Nine Steps* (1915) and Ethel Lina White *The Wheel Spins* (1936); and a few years later Eric Ambler, one of the most distinguished of his kind, wrote several thrillers, among them *A Coffin for Dimitrios* (1939), which combine international espionage with partiality for the political left. But John Buchan had used his Stevensonian entertainments, *The Three Hostages* (1924), for instance, to support the political right. These samples of this plenty show its purposes and its occasional excellence.

Many shockers, like those of Eric Ambler, involve detection and might be classified as well under what Frenchmen reasonably call the police novel. That one out of four recent novels in English has been a police novel may be accounted for in part by the tediousness or inanity of other popular fiction, and in part by what accounts for the shocker. For in the detective story a sample enormity, mimicking the large disorder of the times, is attended to by man's intelligence and the law. What we wish is symbolically fulfilled, and peril to the ruling class averted. To puzzling questions an improving craft has added character, psychological subtlety, wit, and a literate air uncommonly found in other popular fiction. As the police novel assumed the functions of the traditional novel, it threatened, for some of the more literate at least, to supplant it.

Ministers of state and, when the bombing began, the occupants of shelters were devotees.[22]

Diversion and the world itself are to be found in Baker Street, where in 1887 Sir Arthur Conan Doyle, full of Poe, Gaboriau, and Dr. Joseph Bell, established Sherlock Holmes. *The Adventures of Sherlock Holmes* (1892), *The Hound of the Baskervilles* (1902), and many lesser volumes proved attractive, not because Holmes is remarkable for detection, but because of his personality, dear Dr. Watson's, and all the furniture of gaslit London, real then perhaps, but now nostalgic. These period pieces started the fashion. The detective stories of Chesterton, making sin of crime, were followed by E. C. Bentley's masterpiece, *Trent's Last Case* (1913), which with wit, character, naturalness, and ingenuity of plot inaugurated the great period, the twenties and thirties, when increasing tension cried for suitable release. Agatha Christie's *Murder of Roger Ackroyd* (1926) displays rational sedentary Hercule Poirot at his best and the author at her unfairest. Dorothy L. Sayers is fairer and more notable. In *Murder Must Advertise* (1933) and *The Nine Tailors* (1934) Lord Peter Wimsey displays himself with literacy and wit and solves his puzzles. But his later exploits are impaired by love. Falling in love with Lord Peter, Dorothy Sayers conducts her affair through several volumes that are neither novels nor police novels. Like their excellent predecessors, however, these failures are celebrations of caste. Her high-Anglican devotions were succeeded by the thrillers of Nicholas Blake (C. Day Lewis) and of Michael Innes, the wittiest and most fantastic of his kind.

[22] Howard Haycraft: *Murder for Pleasure, the Life and Times of the Detective Story* (1941), contains full bibliography.

CHAPTER V

The Troughs of Zolaism

IN "Hydaspia," Wallace Stevens's Lady Lowzen thought what is "was other things." In England that was the trouble with some novelists until, enlarged by Zola and Flaubert, they tried to see life steadily and, if possible, whole. This effort is called realism or, in one of its forms, naturalism. Other English writers, more or less indifferent to the realistic French, were enlarged by science or by philosophies based upon it. For writers of both kinds the new reality was as knowable as a slot machine and not unlike it in character.

French realism itself was based upon science or deductions from it, partly upon the work of Darwin and of Claude Bernard, who applied the laws of matter to the study of creatures, and before these upon the Positivism of Auguste Comte, who in the first half of the century applied what he knew of physical science to the study of man in society. Matter and mechanics were triumphant. From their applications to man it was but a short step to literature. Taine took it, extending in the fifties and sixties the ideas of Comte and the scientists to the practice and criticism of literature. His *Histoire de la littérature anglaise* (1864) proved that literature, rigorously determined, illustrates the laws of cause and effect. For the instruction of novelists Taine held that psychology is physiology, that virtue and vice, like vitriol and sugar, are products of material causes. Justifying writers in the contemplation of any subject, however revolting, he became the philosopher of realism.

That Balzac, its first practitioner, had Comte in mind during the latter part of his vast inquest upon society is shown by the preface (1842) to *La Comédie humaine*, where he justifies himself as a student of "social species." Delighted, Taine saw Balzac's work as a collection of scientific documents on human nature. Balzac was not a scientist, though he presented actual life on every level. By his example, however, he pointed the way for subsequent realists, who with the aid of Positivism and science went further along it but not always as well. The development of realism by Balzac's followers is best represented by three great novels: *Madame Bovary* (1857), *Germinie Lacerteux* (1865), and *L'Assommoir* (1877). These novels were read and, to the limit of social or individual capacity, imitated by most French and English realists of the eighties, the nineties, and the new century.[1]

Although Flaubert denied that he was a realist and displayed throughout his life a taste for the exotic and the remote, he devoted *Madame Bovary*, his first novel, to a commonplace woman of the middle class whose like might be found in twenty villages. To Flaubert, Madame Bovary seemed less an individual than a type; for the novelist, working like a scientist, he held, should deal in "probable generalities." The authentic details, carefully observed and selected, that compose the life, character, and environment of his heroine are presented with divine aloofness and impersonality. This attitude, so moving in its effect, was one of Flaubert's contributions to the novel. The other was his care for art. Maupassant, Flaubert's disciple, makes this

[1] For French realism see P. Martino: *Le Naturalisme français* (1923).

plain in his preface (1885) to *Bouvard et Pécuchet* and in the preface to his own *Pierre et Jean* (1888). Painfully searching for the precise word, the one noun, adjective, verb, the one rhythm that would distinguish a particular janitor or horse from others, Flaubert immortalized his observations of common things and their uncommonness. *Bovary,* so composed by the greatest artist among realists, became the Bible of realists, turning some to thoughts of art, others to thoughts of life.

Germinie Lacerteux, a servant, is a woman of lower degree than novelists had been accustomed to handling; and during the course of the novel she becomes still lower. The stages of her degradation, presented without reticence, proceed from illicit love to drunkenness, lying, theft, sexual debauch, tuberculosis, and rupture of the bowels. This infamous decline follows logically from her passionate, generous nature and from her environment. The brothers Goncourt, her creators, regard her with sympathetic detachment as the victim of circumstances. Social historians and, to some extent, Positivists, they applied historical method to modern horror. Recording what they found, they produced a "documentary novel," which to most early reviewers seemed *"littérature putride."*

But when Émile Zola reviewed *Germinie Lacerteux* in 1865, he admired the "excessive and feverish," yet somehow scientific character of the documentation. In 1868 he visited the brothers Goncourt to express his adoration and that same year he published *Thérèse Raquin,* his first "scientific novel." This novel owes its character not only to the Goncourts but to Taine, whose materialism Zola exaggerated. Almost immediately Zola conceived a plan, as large as Balzac's but more systematic, of studying the history of a family through five generations. The two branches of this family would evolve under the influence of heredity and environment through all the strata of society. Having read a book on heredity, Zola provided the original Rougon-Macquarts with suitable distempers. During the twenty volumes of their "natural history" these unfortunates, who become merchants, peasants, priests, laborers, or prostitutes according to their surroundings, display, according to their inheritance, the symptoms of hysteria, imbecility, scrofula, ataxia, and alcoholism.

Le Roman expérimental (1880) is the clearest expression of Zola's plan. This manifesto is based upon *L'Introduction à la médecine expérimentale* (1865) by Claude Bernard, who applied the methods of physical science to medicine, previously considered an art. Substituting the word "novelist" for "doctor," Zola paraphrased Bernard. The novelist, says Zola, must be a scientist, indifferent to moral convention and art, using hypothesis, examination of evidence, and verification of hypothesis. The laws of nature that his experiments confirm are, of course, heredity, environment, and the physiological nature of the sentiments. The conduct of fictional characters is determined by these laws. "A like determinism," said Zola, "will govern the stones of the roadway and the brain of man."

But Zola's science was pseudo-science, and his faith in it was premature. Carried away by his enthusiasm, he was unaware that the laboratory method requires a laboratory. As he pursued the laws of heredity and environment, he forgot that a family so tainted as his could not have survived three generations, still less five; and he forgot that a dog born in a stable is not necessarily a horse. But his faith in what he took for science stimulated his imagination and his zeal for fact. His novels are less experimental than documentary.

In *L'Assommoir*, the most nearly perfect illustration of Zola's method, Gervaise Macquart, like Germinie Lacerteux, is the victim of temperament and environment. Her marriage to Coupeau, at first a sober worker in zinc, is happy until, having fallen from a roof, he learns the charm of idleness and drink. She borrows money of a tender bolt-maker, starts a laundry, supports her degenerating husband. But her generosity and his excess bring them to ruin. They starve in a dismal room. Their daughter Nana, to whose career Zola devoted another volume, goes bad. Coupeau expires of delirium tremens, Gervaise of starvation.

Already familiar with the slums of Paris, Zola visited them again, notebook in hand. He studied public wash-houses, bolt-factories, home industries, flower-factories, dance halls, tenements, and the outer boulevards. He recorded the smells, sights, and sounds of laundries and saloons. He observed marriage feasts, birthday feasts, confirmations, fights among women, and wife-beating. He consulted police reports, read books on alcoholism. From a mass of notes and observations he constructed, not a plot in the usual sense, but a logical chain of causes and effects. He described environment and typical conduct in detail; for environment, the chief element in the book, produces the characters, and however tedious at times his descriptions, none is irrelevant. Forgetting, now and again, his scientific pretensions, Zola abandoned dispassionateness for gusto and, not infrequently, elevated objects, like the steam engine of the wash-house, into symbol.

Au Bonheur des Dames (1883) concerns a great Parisian department store. In this environment clerks illustrate Darwin's struggle for existence, and the store itself, which puts its less efficient rivals out of business, illustrates the survival of the fittest. Here, as in *L'Assommoir* the documentation is relevant; but in many of his novels, carried away by a natural desire to use his notes, Zola forgot that description should be used where needed, not where not. As some of his novels are over-documented, some are inadequately documented, especially those that deal with the life of the upper classes, the clergy, or farmers, where neither ignorance nor imagination could supply the background. At times a tendency to melodrama injured his scientific demeanor.

Zola called his novels naturalistic. By naturalism, a term for critics to quarrel over, he meant scientific or, better, Positivistic realism, which he hoped by this name to distinguish from the artistic realism of Flaubert. Naturalism is an exaggeration, with the aid of Comte, Taine, and the scientists, of the methods of Balzac and Flaubert. Although *Germinie Lacerteux* is as naturalistic as *L'Assommoir*, it is customary to reserve the label for Zola's novels and the work of his followers, the early novels of Huysmans, for example, and the stories of Maupassant. The naturalistic novel usually differs from the realistic in the kind of reality it includes. Realists contented themselves with average reality, but naturalists, carried away by their scientific or humanitarian ardor, delighted in revealing what decorum had hitherto concealed. Their novels are filled with brutality, ugliness, and degradation. A novel about the slums that contains wife-beating, drunkenness, and sexual promiscuity is usually naturalistic. But this test is not infallible. Some novels with these ingredients are sentimental melodramas; others, like *Au Bonheur des Dames*, which lack these ingredients, are thoroughly naturalistic. It might be best, avoiding these difficulties, to call the realistic novel realistic.

French critics are accustomed to consider realism antithetical to romanticism, but their definitions are traditional and a little academic. There is every reason to consider realism as romantic as transcendentalism. In their search for a wider reality romantics not only soared above the old limits but descended below them. Back to nature, a romantic cry, means not only back to flowers but back to life as it is. The slums and their inhabitants were as attractive to these later romantics as flowers to their predecessors. The war between idealists and realists, in which Zola was a champion, was a war between romantic factions.

The last of these romantic realists to influence the English was Maupassant, whose first short story, "*Boule de Suif*," appeared in 1880 with the blessing of Zola. Though Maupassant belonged to the group of Médan, his realism is closer to Flaubert's than to Zola's. From Flaubert he learned the art of exact and lucid prose, the attitude of ironic detachment, the habit of minute observation, and hatred for the middle class. For his three hundred stories of Norman or Parisian life he had no need to study documents, for he wrote of what he knew. Maupassant differs from his master chiefly in his increasing pity for mankind. *Une Vie* (1883), his first novel, is the story of an innocent provincial woman, who, though disillusioned by husband, mother, and son, says at the end: "Life is never as good or as bad as one thinks." *Pierre et Jean* (1888) is an "objective" novel, in which actions and speech take the place of psychological analysis. The black pessimism and the physical horror of man that complicated Maupassant's sympathy are implicit in his impersonal art.

Meanwhile, when Victorian novelists confronted reality, they generally kept within limits set by middle-class decorum. When they examined brutality, bastards, and slums, they softened the focus by sentiment or by moral conclusions. Personal intruders, they had little use for the aloofness of scientist or artist. They imposed artificial plots upon observed reality or turned it into melodrama. These distortions were necessary; for their novels, issued in three volumes, were dependent upon the great circulating libraries and these upon public opinion. George Moore changed all that.

When Moore went to Paris in the latter seventies, he

discovered naturalism. In *Confessions of a Young Man* (1888) he tells of reading *L'Assommoir,* which he considered abominable, and, later, the propaganda of Zola. This converted him. Awed and excited by the "new art based upon science," which embraced all of life, avoiding puerility of plot and of imagination, he sought out Alexis, of Zola's school, and the Goncourts. He read Flaubert, Huysmans, Balzac, and resolved to become the first English naturalist. On his return to London in 1880 he wrote *A Modern Lover* (1883).[2] This novel, which anticipated Maupassant's *Bel-Ami,* concerns an artist who makes unscrupulous use of women to pursue his ends. The reviewers who found traces of Zola in this book were too acute.

Moore's first naturalistic novel, the first in English and still one of the best, is *A Mummer's Wife* (1885). The epigraph from Victor Duruy is significant: " 'Change the surroundings in which man lives, and, in two or three generations, you will have changed his physical constitution, his habits of life, and a goodly number of his ideas.' " Taking a respectable woman of the lower middle class, the wife of a nonconformist, asthmatic shopkeeper in a pottery town, Moore causes her to elope with an actor. Her temperament, her romantic reading, and her dismal environment, of course, lead her to this step. She is gradually coarsened, takes to drink, has an illegitimate child, and finally marries the actor, who is not a bad sort. She beats him. Finding this very tiresome, he is compelled at last to leave her. She drinks until her liver rots, and, nursed by a madwoman, she dies. For this relentless sequence of

[2] Rewritten as *Lewis Seymour and Some Women* (1917). For Moore and Zola see Joseph Hone: *The Life of George Moore* (1936). For the effect of French realists upon the English see William C. Frierson: *L'Influence du naturalisme français sur les romanciers anglais de 1885 à 1900* (1925); P. Yvon: *L'Influence de Flaubert en Angleterre* (1939); M. L. Cazamian: *Le Roman et les idées en Angleterre,* Vol. I, *L'Influence de la science* (1923).

cause and effect Moore took his notebook to the pottery district, traveled with actors, and mastered the symptoms and progress of alcoholism. Like Zola he provided detailed descriptions of the motivating environment: asthma, the shop, the potteries, the theater. His attitude is sympathetic but aloof. He refuses to moralize, to soften or distort. The novel is massive, the action appears inevitable, and the portrait of Kate is convincing. Her character is drawn in part from Madame Bovary's and her career in part from *L'Assommoir,* but she is independently alive.

Reviewers found the book "repulsive" or, at best, "a powerful study of the commonplace." Tennyson, reflecting opinion as a laureate should, appears to have alluded to Moore in "Locksley Hall Sixty Years After" (1886):

> Authors—essayist, atheist, novelist, realist, rhymester, play your part,
> Paint the mortal shame of nature with the living hues of art.
> Rip your brothers' vices open, strip your own foul passions bare;
> Down with Reticence, down with Reverence—forward—naked—let them stare.
> Feed the budding rose of boyhood with the drainage of your sewer;
> Send the drain into the fountain, lest the stream should issue pure.
> Set the maiden fancies wallowing in the troughs of Zolaism,—
> Forward, forward, ay, and backward, downward too into the abysm!

Mudie's circulating library was of the same opinion. In *Literature at Nurse, or Circulating Morals* (1885) Moore attacked Mudie for restricting, in accordance with middle-class morality and commercial prudence, the freedom of the artist. To circumvent the libraries, Moore had persuaded Vizetelly, his publisher, to issue novels in a single volume. By this device Moore and his publisher liberated the novel, for many readers, interested in science and hence in scientific fiction, proved to be more tolerant than librarians or critics.

Vizetelly, who had published translations of Flaubert, now undertook translations of Zola. Moore provided the enthusiastic preface for *Piping-Hot* (1885), a translation of *Pot-Bouille.* These translations, though somewhat expurgated, proved intolerable. The National Vigilance Association, charging Vizetelly with obscenity, brought him to official notice. The publisher was tried and fined in 1888, and, after renewed offenses, imprisoned for three months in 1889 despite a petition signed by Hardy, Moore, Havelock Ellis, and Gosse. But Vizetelly prospered during the nineties. And when Zola visited England in 1893 he received almost universal homage.

Moore, who was largely responsible for this development of middle-class taste, met Zola on this occasion. But he had been corresponding with the master since 1881 and, as recorded in "A Visit to Médan," had visited him. Moore's letters to Zola and his continual propaganda show a disciple's devotion.

A Drama in Muslin (1886) presents the Irish upper class and the marriage market of the Dublin season. However elegant the theme, this documentary study of silks and ballrooms, as Moore informed Zola, is fundamentally naturalistic. But there are significant intrusions from René Ghil, Jane Austen, and Balzac; and Moore's new concern for style shows other influences. For Moore was turning from Zola at this time under the influence of Pater, Huysmans, and the symbolists. Confessing in *Confessions* his inability to recapture his old ecstasy over naturalism, Moore saw Zola as crude and wanting art. In *Impressions and Opinions* (1891), praising Balzac and Turgenyev,

Moore condemned Zola as too objective to be realistic and, in later essays, as too unspiritual.

But before Moore had got quite clear of the "shallows and mudbanks of naturalism," he wrote *Esther Waters* (1894), his last novel in the manner of the French realists and one of his best. This excellent story of a servant girl and her illegitimate child conforms to naturalism in theme, documentation, and detachment. Moore was full of his subject. In his *Confessions* he speaks of a servant girl whom Dickens would have sentimentalized or laughed at. But Moore, with French eyes, "studied the horrible servant as one might an insect under a microscope. 'What an admirable book she would make. . . .'" Like the Goncourts, however, Moore tempered detachment with sympathy; and although declaring it his intention merely to "exhibit life," he was as pleased as Zola with the moral effect. Smith's circulating library banned the book. It enjoyed great success.

With "Mildred Lawson" of *Celibates* (1895) Moore bade a farewell to the school of Balzac. *Evelyn Innes* (1898) and *Sister Teresa* (1901), second-class novels of love, music, and religious experience, distantly resemble the later novels of Huysmans. For the details Moore consulted friends familiar with music and nunneries.

George Gissing was an imperfect realist. A self-centered man, he was at his best in semi-autobiographical fiction like *New Grub Street* (1891) and *The Private Papers of Henry Ryecroft* (1903) where, enamored of his subject and full of pity for it, he could display his sentiment or his mellowness. Although in *Workers in the Dawn* (1880) he wrote about the slums, where poverty once compelled him to live, he described their victims with a fastidiousness that confirms his later confession of hatred for them. Even hatred failed to give him detachment. He is always personal, intrusive, emerging for exclamations and asides, pointing morals and social deductions. His style is crude, his observation limited, his occasional humor or irony ponderous. No writer could be further from Flaubert. Yet Gissing was aware of Flaubert and Balzac, whom he mentions in his study of Dickens (1898), and he was to some extent affected by the French realists. His achievement in novels of the lower classes was to confound Zola with Dickens.

The Unclassed (1884), described by Gissing as pure narrative without moral, deals as he says "in a romantic spirit with the gloomier facts of life." His heroine, investigating a slum, finds bad smells and a dead baby in the garbage. Among less gloomy facts are unhappy marriages, poverty, and prostitution. Ida, the heroine, is a prostitute. Driven to this profession by economic necessity, she does well at it until her "nobility of character" moves her to become respectable. She finds a job in a laundry, inherits riches from her reappearing grandfather, and spends her virtuous days in rebuilding Grandfather's slum or taking poor children on picnics. The intricate, sentimental plot with which Gissing distorted probability saved him and his readers from the dangers of his subject. Waymark, the hero, who marries Ida, is a realistic novelist like Gissing. His job of rent-collecting in Grandfather's slum gives him the materials for his art. He plans a novel, he says,

> such as no one has yet ventured to write, at all events in England. . . . The novel of every-day life is getting worn out. We must dig deeper, get to untouched social strata. Dickens felt this, but he had not the courage to face his subjects; his monthly numbers had to lie on the family tea-table. Not *virginibus puerisque* will be my book, I assure you, but for men and women who like to look beneath the surface, and who understand that only as artistic material has human life any significance.

Elsewhere Waymark modifies this position of artistic detachment by announcing that art should be "the mouthpiece of misery." When his novel appears, reviewers class it with "the unsavoury productions of the so-called naturalist school." If Waymark's novel resembles *The Unclassed,* and the implication is that it does, these reviewers are ignorant of Zola. But it is probable that *The Unclassed* is the closest approximation of Zola that English convention, always too strong for rebellious Gissing, allowed him to make. Intending Zola, he produced Victorian melodrama.

The Nether World (1889) is no less dismal. From Zola come the long descriptions of the environment that determines the viciousness and brutality of Gissing's London slum. But upon this Zolaesque material Gissing once more imposed an artificial, melodramatic plot, filled with improbable coincidences, vitriol, nicks of time, and missing wills. And Jane Snowdon, the heroine, whose purity is unsullied by her slum, is a sentimental invention. The trouble is that Gissing's characters, intellectually conceived, are unfelt; and all his "hapless spawn of diseased humanity" remains a little inhuman.

It would have been better for Gissing had he resembled Harold Biffen, the realist in *New Grub Street* who wrote a novel called *Mr. Bailey, Grocer,* "unutterably tedious" but true to life. This fictional fiction has no drama, no art, but only cold serious reporting. Biffen says:

> What I really aim at is an absolute realism in the sphere of the ignobly decent. The field, as I understand it, is a new one; I don't know any writer who has treated ordinary vulgar life with fidelity and seriousness. Zola writes deliberate tragedies; his vilest figures become heroic from the place they will fill in a strongly imagined drama. I want to deal with the essentially unheroic, with the day-

> to-day life of that vast majority of people who are at the mercy of paltry circumstance. Dickens understood the possibility of such work, but his tendency to melodrama on the one hand, and his humour on the other, prevented him from thinking of it.

But Gissing, who also understood this possibility, resembled his own unfortunate Reardon, and it was left for others to follow Biffen's plan.

Among others were the short-story writers of the nineties, who found form and attitude in Maupassant and Flaubert, theme, sometimes, in Zola. In the first issue of the *Yellow Book* a realistic story by Hubert Crackanthorpe, the best of these Englishmen, appeared together with an attack by Arthur Waugh upon the clinical grossness of George Moore. In the following issue Crackanthorpe defended realism against the morality of Waugh and Mrs. Grundy. Crackanthorpe's first collection of stories, *Wreckage* (1893), is distinguished by an epigraph from *Germinie Lacerteux.* But the detachment, irony, economy, and pessimism of the stories suggest Maupassant. Of these "The Struggle for Life" is best. It concerns an idle worker, whore on knee in pub, who brutally drives his wife to prostitution to feed her children. Other stories present mistresses, promiscuity, incompatibility. In *Sentimental Studies* (1895) there are suggestions of Flaubert. Before the appearance of the third collection, *Last Studies* (1897), the desperate realist, unable to swim, had thrown himself into the Seine.[3]

In *Tales of Mean Streets* (1894) Arthur Morrison studies with humorous detachment the bestiality of the slums. "Lizerunt," the best and most frightful of these

[3] Among others in the realistic tradition: George Egerton (Mary Bright): *Keynotes* (1893), *Discords* (1894); Richard Whiteing, *No. 5 John Street* (1899). Even Kipling wrote a naturalistic story, "The Record of Badalia Herodsfoot," *Many Inventions* (1893).

stories, includes a proletarian holiday, a pickle-factory, and the kicking of pregnant women when they are down. The humorous attitude of the author, which makes bad worse, is in part his defense against sentiment and in part the recognition by a man of higher caste that nothing else can be expected of outsiders. This humor, however, had the effect of making Zola's reality palatable to lovers of Dickens, who liked a bit of fun with a slum. In *A Child of the Jago* (1896), his novel of the slums, Morrison tells with detached jocularity of Dicky, a victim of environment. His slum has everything a slum must have but sex. Somerset Maugham's slum has everything. *Liza of Lambeth* (1897), his first novel, resembles Morrison's "Lizerunt" in theme, humor, and detachment. But Maugham's medical experience conspired with his peculiar talent in this story of a factory girl to produce a completer reality. From the first, Maugham could tell a story.[4]

For these realists reality consisted of what earlier Victorians had endeavored to avoid. Unlike Zola, these morally detached or semidetached observers had no scientific pretensions; but the level of reality they observed was also limited by scientific materialism to environment and to predictable responses. Nothing mysterious, nothing above or below the conscious, the mechanical, or the social could intrude. Within this area, as limited in its way as that of their decent predecessors, the realists found their reality in prostitutes, wife-beaters, and servants (preferably with illegitimate children) or in the tedious affairs of the lower middle class. These French subjects were more or less adapted to English taste by humor or by judicious reticence.

[4] In *The Summing Up* (1938) Maugham explains his adherence to the doctrine of determinism, telling how he was affected by Darwin, Spencer, Maupassant, the Goncourts, and Morrison. Cf. The preface to *East and West* (1937), on Maupassant.

In spite of Moore's success, the English public was not altogether at home with the new realism. Enough readers were converted to assure a moderate success for moderate realism, which the excesses of Wilde and the æsthetes had made appear comparatively innocuous. But Philistines remained true to their ideals. Arnold Bennett, while making the new realism commercially profitable, felt to the end the need for compromise; and the banning of *Ulysses,* which defined middle-class capacity, justified his prudence. It was enough for realists to contemplate the dregs without stirring them up.

Arnold Bennett belongs with Moore among superior products of France. During the nineties Bennett read the French realists, learned of cause and effect from Taine and Herbert Spencer, and with Moore and James came to share Flaubert's idea of the novel, not as so much material, but as art, selective, impersonal, final. He made elaborate technical studies of form and development; and he counted verbs. Of English realists Moore, whose *Mummer's Wife* Bennett read three times, seemed most admirable. Like Moore and Zola, Bennett recorded what he observed in notebooks and in the *Journals* he kept after the fashion of the Goncourts. Priding himself, like Moore, upon knowledge of women, whom he observed with and without his notebook, Bennett arrived at the point of being astonished at nothing. By his own devices this provincial man had freed himself from the puritanism of his youth to arrive at a moral disinterestedness unusual among Englishmen. He freed himself, that is, to a point; for like his heroes he remained in part the creation of his lower middle-class commercial and religious environment. He was all the French can do to a Wesleyan Methodist.

A Man from the North (1898), Bennett's semi-autobiographical first novel, concerns a young clerk from

Bursley, who, coming to London with literary ambitions, is frustrated and doomed to the suburbs by heredity and circumstance. This "natural history" reflects Bennett's admiration of Zola, Gissing, and especially Huysmans, whose *A vau-l'eau* is the closest parallel. This was Bennett's apprentice work in amused detachment. He did better in *Anna of the Five Towns* (1902), a serious study of a commonplace woman in the pottery district, a satire on Methodism and parental tyranny, and a firm re-creation of environment. The extensive, often ironic, descriptions of the potteries, of the revival meeting at the chapel, and of Anna's kitchen are less irrelevant than they seem; for they serve to account for their creatures. With this admirably restrained story of dullness and frustration Bennett found his subject and his manner. *Leonora,* which followed this in 1903, is of less value. The excellent portrait of a woman of forty is injured by an improbable plot and left unsupported by the surrounding caricatures. Bennett was attempting to combine realistic psychology with something that would appeal to popular taste. He wanted a yacht.

This natural desire led Bennett about this time to the composition of what he called commercial fiction, novels designed by their worthlessness to please the reader and make their author rich. The best of these sensational novels is *The Grand Babylon Hotel* (1902). Though this "fantasia on modern themes" reflects Bennett's own provincial devotion to urban splendor, it is otherwise unserious. It concerns dark doings at the Savoy: trapdoors, secret passages, abductions on yachts, a disappearing corpse, poisoned wines, gilded adventurers, rouged girls, international crooks. The American capitalist who buys the hotel to spite the head waiter is always lifting a bottle of "Heidsieck Monopole, Carte d'Or" and the heroine exclaiming: "You can't play games with me. You've just got to remember that I'm . . . a Yankee girl." When she marries the Prince, Nella gets fifty millions from Papa.

Along with these thrillers Bennett produced several humorous novels of merit, *A Great Man* (1904), for example, and *Buried Alive* (1908). Alice Challice in *Buried Alive* is one of Bennett's best portraits; and the triumph of his craft is nowhere more evident than in Priam Farll's emotion at his own funeral. *A Great Man* is a hilarious account of the popular writer and of his publishers, critics, and readers. Henry Shakespere Knight is puzzled by his gift: "I just sit down and write," he says. "And there it is! They go mad over it!" Arnold Bennett differed from Henry Shakespere Knight in being a knave.

That the same man at the same time could have written *The Old Wives' Tale* (1908) increases the wonder of Bennett's capacity. This novel, one of the best of our time, is one of the best in the French tradition. As he tells us in the preface, he found his theme in a Parisian restaurant where he observed an eccentric lady, once young. His novel would concern women and time. Instead of eccentric he made his heroine commonplace, as the realistic tradition required. Maupassant's *Une Vie*, he said, was his model. But one woman was too easy for a student of women and insufficiently illustrative of heredity and environment; so he provided his heroine with a sister of different temperament. Placing them, like an experimental novelist, in the environment of a drapery shop in Bursley, he removed one to another environment, reunited them after a while, and observed that however different their lives and tempers, time had brought both to a common end. With what he called "an infinite number of infinitesimal changes" he revealed his provincial women in the grip of heredity, environment, and time. Of these, time, which levels all, is chief. To convince the reader of its passage he resorted to many technical devices—concentration, monotony, selection here, detail there, and, more dramatic than these, generations of dogs and deaths of husbands. The book is an epic of dull lives and of all life, the more moving and tragic because aloof in manner, restrained in style, and filled with what Bennett himself called a "lofty nobility." Lafourcade cannot be blamed for finding this romantic novel a monument of classical art.

Bennett's sources were observation and notebook and, for the melodramatic and somewhat inferior scenes in Paris, newspapers of the time. From Maupassant came Constance's relationship with her son. But a principal model seems to have been Moore's *Mummer's Wife,* and it was probably this book that showed Bennett the literary possibilities of the Five Towns. As Moore's heroine is lured away from her draper's shop in the pottery town by a traveling actor, so Bennett's Sophia from hers by a traveling salesman. These travelers are but devices to effect a change of environment. Their similarity means perhaps that Moore and Bennett alike were in the naturalistic tradition.

Bennett's virtues, his patient building of external reality, his mastery of the illusion of time, his understanding of character, simple or complex, in relation to environment and time, reappear in *Clayhanger* (1910), which belongs with *The Old Wives' Tale* among masterpieces of realism. Edwin's life in solidly constructed Bursley, his development as an individual, and his frustrated love for Hilda are presented in humdrum scenes selected from a period of thirty years, crystallized now and then by small symbolic climaxes designed to flash the meaning: the Sunday-school centenary, for instance, and the death of Darius. The clinical details of Cheyne-Stokes breathing, the steam printing shop, the streets and squares and kilns are re-created in the spirit of naturalism; but the psychology of Edwin and Hilda, who rise mysteriously above their surroundings to heights of complexity, is indebted to Stendhal and Dostoyevsky. In *Hilda Lessways* (1911), the second volume of the trilogy, Bennett told the same story from Hilda's point of view. The mistake of explaining her mystery makes this novel inferior. *These Twain* (1915), the third volume, concerns the commonplace marriage of Hilda and Edwin. The trick was to sustain interest in their minor quarrels and delights without the aid of adultery, cruelty, or the other paraphernalia of drama.

Given courage by the war, Bennett dared in 1918 to brave middle-class disapproval with *The Pretty Lady,* his *Nana.* Christine, the elegant cocotte, unlike the shameful heroine of Gissing, is a craftsman, proud of her craft. Aside from this excellent portrait, however, the novel is poor, popular stuff. *Riceyman Steps* (1923), the story of a book-selling miser and his appropriate death is a triumph of realism, dull and inevitable.

Bennett's last important book, *Imperial Palace* (1930), unites his interest in detailed environment, his knowledge of women, and his love of luxury. The plot and the characters of the capitalist and his daughter are contrived in Bennett's best commercial manner. But the hotel represents the climax of naturalistic documentation. Notebook in hand, Bennett had explored a luxury hotel, its laundry, kitchens, stores, its housekeeping, catering, and accounting departments. The portrait of this elegant machine is the single point of the novel and its success. Equally romantic but more frivolous, *The Grand Babylon Hotel* was a first study for this portrait. For years Bennett had been fascinated with hotels, department stores, and steamships, which assumed in his eyes the importance of symbols, representing not only the repressed provincial's dream but the world in little. The resemblance between this microcosmic novel and Zola's *Au Bonheur des Dames,* his study of a department store, is far from accidental.[5]

By the time of Bennett's greatest novels, objections to realism by reputable critics were less commonly moral than æsthetic or metaphysical. In *Notes on Novelists* (1914) Henry James complained on æsthetic grounds of Bennett's excessive and irrelevant materials. If reality is an orange, said James, in reading Bennett we are immersed, to be sure, in its juice, but to what end? This objection to Bennett's naturalism by the disciple of Flaubert repeats Flaubert's objection to Zola. But it is odd that James should have rebuked for want of art one who was no less preoccupied with art than he or Moore and no less a part of the French tradition. When Virginia Woolf attacked Bennett, together with Wells and Galsworthy, in *Mr. Bennett and Mrs. Brown* (1924), her complaint was that Bennett's reality is unreal. His materialism, his elaborate concern with surroundings, fails, she said, to convey life itself. Amid so much well-constructed solidity and such craft, character and soul as well are lost. This metaphysical objection to realists' reality marks a change in the nature of reality to something perhaps no more real. But for the generation of Mrs. Woolf, though he was certainly as much a realist as she, Bennett was out of fashion.[6]

During his long career and after, other realists were around. Frank Swinnerton, who wrote in 1912 a study of Gissing, in 1917 wrote *Nocturne,* one of the finest, most delicate, and most selective novels of the London slums. During the twenties, when the troughs of Zolaism were relatively untenanted, novelists flew above or burrowed

[5] *The Journals of Arnold Bennett* (1932–3). Georges Lafourcade: *Arnold Bennett* (1939).

[6] Oscar Wilde had attacked realism on æsthetic grounds in "The Decay of Lying," *Intentions* (1891); Stephen Spender attacked it as bourgeois and photographic in *The New Realism* (1939).

below them. In the thirties, however, when the terror of Virginia Woolf's displeasure had somewhat abated, the naturalistic tradition resumed with James Hanley, who writes of sailors and of slums. Claiming Balzac and Turgenyev as his ideals, Hanley resembles the naturalists in his pictures of squalor. *The Furys* (1935) is chiefly remarkable for the character of Mrs. Fury, whose attempt to raise her family above its environment is defeated. Street scenes during the general strike have all the quality of Zola's nightmare. Violence and extravagance take the place of customary dullness, for Hanley and his Liverpool slum are Irish.[7] Richard Llewellyn's *None but the Lonely Heart* (1943), though melodramatic and subjective, is among the more recent ornaments of the slummy tradition.

While disciples of Zola or Flaubert were reaffirming the possibilities of their reality, other English writers, more or less immune to France, were learning similar realities from science. Thomas Hardy is the most eminent of these. Early in his development he read Darwin, Spencer, and Colenso, lost his faith in revealed religion, and, seeking no substitute for it, faced the universe like an Englishman. Natural selection and mechanical determinism had taken the place of special creation and design. Man was cog or victim of a machine. The governing forces, laws of Newton's physics and of Darwin's biology, determining and themselves determined, seemed casual at best or at worst malign. This deplorable universe was also Zola's. But Hardy differed from Zola in being sad about it instead of happy. Where Zola saw cause and effect, Hardy, seeing them as they seem, saw chance and made it plain by arbitrary plot. Reading Greek tragedy, he read chance for

[7] *The Secret Journey* (1936) continues *The Furys*. *Boy* (1931); *Stoker Bush* (1935). *No Directions* (1943) is an excellent nightmare of a London tenement during an air raid.

fate. References in *Tess of the D'Urbervilles* to Huxley and Æschylus fix the frame he imposed upon observed reality.

Of Hardy's novels in our time, *The Mayor of Casterbridge* (1886) and *The Woodlanders* (1887), like some of the earlier novels, are tragedies of Darwin's man in Newton's universe and Mrs. Grundy's parlor. *Tess of the D'Urbervilles* (1891) and *Jude the Obscure* (1895), as dramatic in form, are closer to Zola's reality. What is true of these, however, is more or less true of all. Their power comes from the feeling with which Hardy contemplated human significance and insignificance, their irony from the disparity he found between chance and will, their density from love of native soil, a love the more intense (as Darwin fought inside him with Wordsworth and Lord Nelson) for his awareness of nature's cruelty or indifference. By the English and by those who like them Hardy is valued above his great merit for being so English, a quality he shares with Samuel Butler, A. E. Housman, and T. S. Eliot.

Tess is another servant with illegitimate child. Like Germinie and Esther Waters, she is the blameless victim of nature and of social convention, which wears in middle-class England the aspect of a natural force. Chance in the ordinary sense is there. Tess's letter goes under instead of over the rug. But chance is less important than usual in Hardy. Here for the most part chance in the sense of determinism operates like Darwin's selection through heredity and environment. Tess does what she has to do because half D'Urberville, half peasant; and Angel, torn between theological emancipation and moral convention, acts according to his half-lights. Tess is sex, Angel, in his degree, intellect. Under "cruel Nature's law" they converge in a social environment ill adapted to their natures or desires. The background is half the book, for it is the environment out of which the victims grow and in which they move. It is there to reflect and intensify their moods. When happy, Tess milks idyllic cows at the dairy farm; when sad, digs turnips on the blasted heath. The background is there because nature is fellow sufferer of nature. A value of Hardy's books, and often all that one recalls of them, is their atmosphere and setting. This value of *Tess* and the tragedy of its people are marred by melodrama. Alec, the Gothic scenes in the ruined chapel, and the baptism all show that Hardy had learned his art from Wilkie Collins. The continual intrusions of the author to announce the pity of it, to blame the First Cause, or to make a terminal flourish grow tiresome. The style is heavy. It is easy to see why Moore, amorous of the impersonal art of France, found Hardy intolerable. Too amorous of France, however, Moore could not see native virtue or tragedy in homely dress.

The genteel protests to which Hardy, protesting truth, responded in the preface to *Tess* were nothing to those occasioned by *Jude*. The book was banned by the circulating libraries, defended by Havelock Ellis, and publicly burned by a clergyman. Even the last of these actions is understandable; for, attacking caste, Hardy presented the clergy of Oxford as agents of respectability alone. And at his hands the sacrament of marriage appeared to be endangered. Having read Ibsen, and thinking of the Parnell case and his own affairs, Hardy arranged the four people of *Jude* in displeasing marital or extra-marital combinations. Of Jude, victim not only of society but of Darwin's universe as well, Hardy says: "Nature's logic was too horrid for him to care for." Jude's ideals are defeated by the blind forces of nature, by sex, for example, which compels the scholar to embrace a woman little better than a beast. He knows the folly of free will; but even Hardy's littlest victims are not regardless of their doom. Little

Father Time has Hardy's view of things before he is old enough to take it. Among other victims Sue is the most disturbing, as complex and unpredictable as someone from Dostoyevsky. With these unnatural creatures and the natural laws, Hardy was attempting Greek tragedy with Darwin in place of the Eumenides. He failed. The pattern was too capriciously imposed; and evil is unrelieved by good. Wanting catharsis, the gloomy reader is forced to conclude that, however violent, this is a morbid book.

Hardy was even more explicit about determinism in the cantankerous lyrics he wrote. In "Hap," for example, and "In Vision I Roamed" he deplores "that Universe taciturn and drear," and in "The Ivy-Wife" and "In a Wood," the struggle for existence among vegetables. These dismal little philosophies, whose virtues are irony and crabbedness, fail as poems. Perhaps, as T. S. Eliot observed in the *Criterion,* Hardy is a minor poet; and it is certain, as Yeats observed in his anthology, that Hardy "lacked technical accomplishment." He was a poet, but not enough of a poet to invent or discover an appropriate form for his individual feeling. As Victorian form takes one line and Hardy's matter another, agreeing and disagreeing, the effect is contrapuntal. From this his failures and his triumphs. But form and mood happily conspire in *The Dynasts* (1903–8), his most successful work.

This grandiose mixture of epic and drama, of blank verse and lyric chorus, is modeled upon Shelley's *Prometheus Unbound.* Since there are nineteen acts and one hundred and thirty scenes, many of which are cosmic, the play is ill adapted to the stage and even worse to the closet, for which it was written. For years Hardy had been fascinated with the Napoleonic Wars, partly because an ancestor had received Lord Nelson's last exclamation. But *The Dynasts* surveys the wars from the point of view of Darwin and Newton. Fancying free will, Napoleon is determined; and even Englishmen are puppets of Schopenhauer's Immanent Will. The pointlessness of mechanical determinism is expressed by a machinery of celestial observers, Spirits of the Years and Choruses of Pities. As the First Cause blindly works Its clocklike laws or like a vast fermenting-vat brews evolution, the Spirits sing:

> Of Its doings if It knew,
> What It does It would not do!

The conflict between Pities and Years, the one a projection of human sentiment, the other of Flaubertian indifference, reveals the theme of the play, the conflict between will and chance. However philosophical their demeanor, these spirits are there to tighten structure, effect transitions, and, like a Greek chorus, provide the obvious comment and some relief. Although philosophical, the play is less philosophy than vision. As T. S. Eliot tolerantly observed, Hardy apprehended his matter as a poet should. But Chesterton, confronted with Hardy's exploitation of the nineteenth-century universe, an exploitation as great as Zola's, heard only the "mutterings of the village atheist." [8]

Although Catholic, Joseph Conrad shared Hardy's view of nature and of man. In a letter of 1897 to Cunninghame Graham, that eupeptic idealist, Conrad explained the nature of the universe. It is a machine, he says, that evolved itself

> out of a chaos of scraps of iron and behold!—it knits. I am horrified at the horrible work and stand appalled. I feel it ought to embroider,—but it goes on knitting. . . . The infamous thing has made itself: made itself without thought, without conscience, without foresight . . . with-

[8] David Cecil: *Hardy, the Novelist* (1946). William R. Rutland: *Thomas Hardy* (1938). Florence E. Hardy: *The Early Life of Thomas Hardy* (1928), *The Later Years of Thomas Hardy* (1930). *Cakes and Ale* (1930), one of Maugham's best novels, is generally supposed to be an irreverent portrait of Hardy, but Maugham denies the likeness.

> out heart. It is tragic accident,—and it has happened. You can't interfere with it. . . . It knits us in and it knits us out. It has knitted time, space, pain, death, corruption, despair, and all the illusions,—and nothing matters.[9]

Like Hardy, Conrad considered man's consciousness his tragedy. Like Hardy, he had a gloomy temper.

By storms and calms and jungles Conrad presented the indifference or malevolence of nature, against whose alien might man's life is struggle. The sea of *The Nigger of the Narcissus* (1897) is the "terrible sea," and the jungle of "The Heart of Darkness" holds the "horror" of Kurtz's final lucidity. Marlow, obsessed with the machinery of chance, speaks in *Lord Jim* (1900) of the "working of the implacable destiny of which we are the victims—and the tools."

But Conrad differed from Hardy in the belief that nature, claiming victims, may create heroes. Testing men, she may increase their moral stature, discovering courage, honor, and integrity. In *Typhoon* (1903), Captain MacWhirr confronts his tempest like a teapot. Refusing to change his charted course, attending to the neatness and order of his hold, he emerges with his engineers and the builders of his ship as a symbol of human integrity. In *The Shadow Line* (1917) the young captain confronts his calm. Bringing ship and crew through their ordeal and gaining moral maturity, he becomes no less symbolic.

Nature, which made Conrad the moralist of emergent occasions, explains the invention of Marlow, his moral detective. This cynical sentimentalist, obsessed with man's integrity, is compelled to spend his time assuring himself of its existence. Lord Jim was his most fascinating case. Faced with two accidents, Jim succumbed to one, unsettling Marlow, and, cheering him, conquered the other by

[9] From: *Joseph Conrad, Life and Letters,* by G. Jean-Aubry, copyright 1926, 1927 by Doubleday & Company, Inc.

death. This equivocal victory foreshadows that of Heyst in *Victory* (1915). Trying to defend himself by insularity from man and nature, Heyst falls victim to accident, in the person of Mr. Jones, to his own nature, and the nature of man. His elegant refusal to fight is atoned for, however, by the gesture of death, somehow an assertion of defiance and contempt. The defeat of Lingard in *The Rescue* (1920), Conrad's most complicated morality, amounts to success because of that hero's scruples. Torn between loyalty to his rajah and to the woman he adores, frustrated by circumstance, Lingard has done what man can do.

Like most of those concerned with circumstance, Conrad owed something to the French realists. From Flaubert and Maupassant, whom he admired with moral reservations, Conrad took not method but attitude and some notions of style. He admired their disinterested art, and, using morality as matter alone, he refrained like them from preaching it. He admired their ideas of diction, and, hunting precise words, he endeavored to make the reader see, hear, smell, and taste experience. But never satisfied with the precise word, Conrad used many precise words, succumbed to the vice of word-painting, and blanketed his stories with description that, far less evocative than drama, defeated its end. Few can read the first chapter of *The Rescue,* where for page after page Conrad describes the sea, the ship and its sails, and then the sky. At last someone comes on deck to light a cigar.

This ponderous motion, however, helps create a vision of life no less than the dullness of these heroes. Lord Jim is far from bright; Lingard is dumb, and Nostromo simple. Incapable of thought, these moralists brood, and Conrad, wisely disdaining analysis, broods over their brooding. Nothing comes quite clear. Motions and punctilios emerge from wading-glue. But this effect, the portrait of his world, is Conrad's triumph.[10]

Science, which made Hardy regard and distort reality, made H. G. Wells regard, discuss, and try to change it. Wells was excited by Huxley's lectures on biology at the Normal School of Science. Duller lecturers on physics, geology, and astronomy bored him. But his mind was formed by these studies, and his knowledge, though superficial, was greater than that of other literary men. While Kipling optimistically sang of piston and connecting rod and saw in the evolution of caveman to imperialist a promise of larger imperialists, and while Henley in his "Song of Speed" complacently fondled the pipes and cylinders of the horseless carriage, Wells, better informed, saw danger in complacency and optimism. Science had shown him that nature is cruel or at best indifferent, that the position of man, dwarfed in the perspectives of astronomy and evolution, is precarious, that more science and more wisdom are required. He devoted his scientific fantasies to grave warnings. *The Time Machine* (1895), ostensibly a frivolous romance of the fourth dimension, shows that evolution may produce degenerates, that the future is likely to belong to giant crabs, and that, according to the second law of thermodynamics, sun and earth must die. The horrors of *The Island of Dr. Moreau* (1896) blasphemously reveal the cruelty of the Creator, the animal nature of the highest creatures, and their liability, despite moral ideals, to relapse. *The War of the Worlds* (1898), another assault upon complacency, demonstrates the insignificance of man and the dangers of intellectual

[10] For Conrad's aim as an artist see the preface to *The Nigger of the Narcissus*. *Notes on Life and Letters* (1921) contains an essay on Maupassant; and two stories in *Tales of Unrest* (1898) are close imitations of Maupassant. In his letters, however, Conrad is hostile to the external realists.

development. Wells was not a scientist but a critic of science and, unlike Jules Verne, with whom he was often confused, a moral philosopher. In his romances the fantastic occupies the commonplace. *The Invisible Man* (1897), despite a preposterous premise, concerns actualities of London and Kent, and the manner, pedestrian and easy, suits things as they are.

Wells had little use for Frenchmen. When he turned to the realistic novel, he used Dickens and Gissing as models. But Gissing, at whose death-bed Wells presided, lacked science and in Wells's eyes was little better than a humanist. It was science that gave Wells his air of examining as in a laboratory the human specimens before him. Science had nothing to do, however, with the gusto that complicated his view of the trials and errors of little men in bad environments. From *Love and Mr. Lewisham* (1900) and *Kipps* (1905) down to *The History of Mr. Polly* (1910), many of Wells's characters are caricatures; but the exaggerations are of observed reality. *Tono-Bungay* (1909), "a cross section of the British social organism," is at once typical and transitional. The servants' basement, the bakery, the chemist's shop, and all the other sets are substantially presented. Nicodemus Frapp and Ponderevo are Dickensian grotesques. But while Ponderevo puffs his worthless potion, George, the potential savior of society through science, experiments with flying machines and talks. As he talks, what began as novel threatens to become essay. Managing this transition without awkwardness by the autobiographical method, which enables George to present or to interpret as he pleases, Wells happily balanced his interests and his talents.

In *The New Machiavelli* (1911) and in the later novels, ideas of reality increasingly take the place of reality; imagination and concreteness are replaced by abstract monologues. But science, more abstract than concrete, was also behind this development. Dreams of the New Republic and of natural aristocrats are scientific dreams of order, clarity, and foresight, of all that is opposite to muddle. No longer used to examine muddle, science is used to show the way out of it. Wells cheerfully admitted that he had become less interested in character and circumstance than in ideas about them. And as for the art of the novel, dear to most realists, he rejected it with violence. He quarreled with Henry James, Bennett, and Conrad over Flaubert's empty ideals, and called himself a journalist. "A Digression about Novels" in *Experiment in Autobiography* (1934) reaffirms his denial of realism and art. And in his preface to Swinnerton's *Nocturne* Wells claimed, forgetting his earlier works, that he had never "presented" life.[11]

Wells, Bennett, and Galsworthy, grouped by long custom, have little in common save, as Virginia Woolf insisted, a common materialism. John Galsworthy, though in a sense a realist like the others, had little to do with science and, though a follower of Flaubert and Turgenyev at a suitable distance, little to do with France. But science and realism were at large in the atmosphere, and *The Forsyte Saga* is a monument to cause and effect, heredity and environment.[12] Even sports like young Jolyon, who have attained the power of self-analysis, have the sense of property. Although this sense is probably the product of middle-class environment, young Jolyon, when speaking of it or defining a Forsyte, implies an evil heritage. The

[11] During his Fabian period Wells wrote *This Misery of Boots* (1907) and other tracts. Typical of the utopianism that lifted him above the actual is *A Modern Utopia* (1905), a cross between a novel and a treatise. Geoffrey West: *H. G. Wells* (1930).

[12] Galsworthy's pattern, combining with Zola's, produced many sagas, among them G. B. Stern: *The Rakonitz Chronicles* (1932); Louis Golding: *Five Silver Daughters* (1934); Storm Jameson: *The Triumph of Time* (1932); Henry Handel Richardson: *The Fortunes of Richard Mahony* (1930).

metaphors of the preface imply a scientific purpose, as if Galsworthy thought of himself as pickling a species for some museum.

The Man of Property (1906), the first of the novels that compose the *Saga*, is best. The trouble is that Irene and her Bosinney, symbols of beauty, never come to life, whereas Soames, whom Galsworthy understood, is enormous and vital. As the *Saga* proceeds through a series of family dinners and conferences, of rather obvious symbols of house, hat, mutton, or picture, the matter disintegrates into the unconvincing affairs of Fleur, Jon, and Mont, creatures of the fast twenties, whom Galsworthy could not know and could not wish to know. What started as excellent satire upon a class that he could anatomize if not transcend is lost in tenderness or, as D. H. Lawrence savagely remarked, in "fake."

Heredity and environment and the effort to escape them are also the theme of the novel of adolescence. This form, which had flourished throughout the nineteenth century, producing *Wilhelm Meister, David Copperfield,* and *Richard Feverel,* received new life toward the end of the century from the science of biology and later from psychology.[13] In novel after novel sensitive lads are apprenticed to life, formed by its forces, rebelling against them, sometimes failing, sometimes emerging in victory. Their trials and errors, like those of rats in a maze, are painfully displayed. And all the horrors of adolescence, the theater of biology and spirit, are examined. The popularity of this form may be traced in part to the philosophy of determinism and in part to the growing revolt against it. The danger, since these novels are commonly autobiographical, is sentimentality. From 1903 onwards almost every first novel by a serious novelist was a novel of adolescence.

[13] Justin O'Brien: *The Novel of Adolescence in France* (1937). Susanne Howe: *Wilhelm Meister and His English Kinsmen* (1930).

So usual was the practice that Aldous Huxley in *Crome Yellow,* his first, congratulated himself too soon on having avoided the dangerous tradition. But it produced some of the best novels of the early twentieth century.

The Way of All Flesh (1903), which started the vogue, is not one of these. Samuel Butler wrote this book between 1872 and 1884 to express hatred for his father, admiration for himself, and his dearest prejudices. He could not publish it at once for fear of being disinherited, and since he was his father's parasite, this fear was not irrational. Mainly autobiographical, the book concerns Ernest's apprenticeship to life, his revolt against his father, and its success. His ancestry is traced in an essay on heredity, which in its ebb and flow, says Butler, tends to skip a generation. This happy circumstance keeps Ernest from resembling his father. Ernest's own children, however, inherit his acquired maturity; for, hating Darwin, Butler followed Lamarck. As for environment, Ernest's education through trial and error in religion, money, caste, and marriage occupies the rest of the book. He learns that money is all that matters, that inherited money is the only conceivable kind, that "tangible material prosperity in this world is the safest test of virtue," that "nice people" or those, like Towneley, of superior caste alone are nice, and that there is an impassable gulf between the classes. This Philistine position at which Ernest arrives after all his trials was Butler's own. In his maturity Ernest does what Butler did, thinks what Butler thought, but, happier than he, is able to avenge himself upon his father by inheriting money from another. The trials that precede this victory are painful. He loses money in the stock market, mistakes a nice girl for a whore and lands in jail, marries a bibulous servant girl because he thought he had to. Cambridge, which had failed to teach him about the stock market, nice girls, and whores, was to blame. From this sentimental story one caricature emerges, that of Theobald Pontifex, the father, who is good because hatred gave Butler detachment. Hypocrite, bully, Victorian clergyman, this Philistine is less Philistine than his son and far more lovable.

Addressing the reader, depending upon statement instead of drama or symbol, Butler evaded art. The isolated man, driven in upon himself, could not separate himself from Ernest. But the book is not without incidental merit. The style is straightforward. Scenes, especially Theobald's courtship, are excellent, and the epigrams are clever.

The Way of All Flesh was a tremendous success. Time, which explains much, explains this. The age, prepared by Ibsen and Shaw, was ready for another attack upon the Victorian family. Converted to Butler, Shaw, a master of publicity, converted others. At the annual dinners in Butler's honor, at which Shaw, for his own purposes, presided, his assurance that Butler was "advanced" kept diners from perceiving his middle-class conservatism and enabled them to confuse personal revenge with criticism. The publication of the *Note-Books* (1912), which Butler indexed for posterity, and of Jones's carefully whitewashed biography (1919) expanded the cult. While intellectuals were finding their affinity in Butler's ideas, romantic authors found in his happy form the vehicle they had looked for. Novels of adolescence, each with hateful father or, sometimes, uncle, abounded. Some are better than *The Way of All Flesh,* but none was of more importance.

In *Clayhanger* (1910), Bennett, who liked Butler, followed his pattern. The quarrel with the father, the struggle of the sensitive boy to escape the environment which had partly formed him, the experiments in life are there. Bennett's troubles with his own father gave pattern point. But Bennett made Darius Clayhanger, the father, a credible human being; and Edwin, the son, though in part the author's portrait, is an independent creature. The vengeance vowed against his father for thwarting his æsthetic and amorous desires turns to pity. And his struggle with environment is unsuccessful. For Butler's fantasy of wish-fulfillment Bennett substituted reality.[14]

The novels of adolescence that have appeared in England since 1920 depart from Butler's tradition, which departed for America and flowered again in Thomas Wolfe's *Look Homeward, Angel.* Dylan Thomas's *Portrait of the Artist as a Young Dog* (1940), consisting of brilliantly original stories of the poet's youth, is a quieter evocation of the strange world of his poetry. Exceeding other novels of this sort in frankness and most in value are *Maiden Voyage* (1943) and *In Youth Is Pleasure* (1945) by Denton Welch. With childlike precision, close to preciousness, he follows two holidays in the career of the neurotic hero, whose deviations, elevated by his innocence and the author's detached lucidity, are refreshing. But the best books in this tradition are *Of Human Bondage* (1915) by Somerset Maugham and James Joyce's *Portrait of the Artist as a Young Man* (1916).

Philip, the victim of Maugham's clinic, has an uncle in place of the father. Uncle, of course, is a Victorian clergyman, a hypocrite, and a Philistine. Thwarted by uncle, oppressed by nature, Philip endeavors to assert his individuality, only to accept at last the lot of a country doctor. His character and his career are determined by his club foot, his sexual instinct, and circumstance. "He acted as though he were a machine, driven by the two forces of

[14] Among other novels of adolescence: J. D. Beresford: *The Early History of Jacob Stahl* (1911–15); Compton Mackenzie: *Sinister Street* (1913–14). In 1910 Gilbert Cannan translated Rolland's *Jean-Christophe,* one of the best French examples of the type. Forrest Reid's *Peter Waring* (1937) and most of his other novels, L. A. G. Strong's *The Garden* (1931), Stephen Spender's *The Backward Son* (1940), belong in the tradition with Lawrence's *Sons and Lovers* and Sinclair's *Mary Olivier.*

his environment and his personality." He sees at last that all men are "helpless instruments of blind chance." This Hardyesque determinism presides over his trials of accountancy, of art in Paris, of medicine, of speculation in the stock market, of entanglements with women. His affair with Mildred, the waitress, is almost too painful. Like obscure Jude, he is compelled to love his "vulgar slut" despite all reason and his loathing and to return to her again and again. This mechanical experience, however, helps him to understand the meaning of life. He sees that, like the figure of Cronshaw's carpet, it has no meaning. This knowledge, which he has sought for years, brings acceptance at last and a kind of happiness. If his philosophizing sounds like a sophomore's, it must be remembered that he is young and that Maugham, as he showed again in *The Razor's Edge,* is fascinated by adolescent philosophy. Maugham's style is plain but not, as in the Ashenden stories, felicitous. His detachment, ironic to the point of indifference, is scientific. He differs from Butler, his chief model, not only in this but in adherence to the arts of Maupassant. These auspices and his craft produced one of the most depressing masterpieces of English realism.[15]

Compared with Philip, Joyce's Stephen Dedalus is successful in life. *A Portrait of the Artist* concerns his formation by the Jesuits, whom he disliked, and by his country, his experiments with sin and repentance, his conflict with father and mother. For the sake of artistic integrity he determines to detach himself from environment, and though he remains essentially attached, he succeeds to the point of using what he is. The pattern of his struggle and

[15] Although somewhat apart from the main tradition of the novel of adolescence, Henry Handel Richardson's *Maurice Guest* (1908), one of the best novels of the period, is comparable in many ways to *Of Human Bondage.* Her study of music students at Leipzig is not only an excellent picture of adolescent bohemianism and exile but one of the most harrowing of love stories.

development is the pattern of this kind of fiction. That Joyce had Butler in mind is shown by Simon Dedalus, the father, whom literary convention made Stephen despise. Joyce liked his father, an agreeable man, capable of saying when shown Brancusi's abstraction of his son as a bed-spring: "Well, Jim hasn't changed much." Joyce followed the pattern, but the pattern directed genius. The *Portrait* is by far the greatest English novel of adolescence. Its early version, *Stephen Hero,* first printed in 1944, enables us to admire the selection, emphasis, and style, the attached detachment, of Joyce's artistic maturity. It was this maturity that prevented the dangers of sentiment. Like all novelists of adolescence, Joyce was writing about himself and his conflict with the hostile world, but he regarded himself as another. The essential words of his title, as he himself observed, are *as a Young Man.* In presenting him Joyce approximated Stephen's ideal of the artist, who, "like the God of the creation, remains within or behind or beyond or above his handiwork, invisible, refined out of existence, indifferent, paring his fingernails." In *Ulysses,* however, the author's adverbs applied to Stephen in the first chapter suggest the sentimental eye, and the portrait of Shem in *Finnegans Wake,* though jocular, is almost sentimental.

Ulysses (1922), which continues the story of Stephen, brings to their English climax the French traditions of realism and art. The bright, solid reconstruction of Dublin and the scenes of degradation owe something to Zola. The impersonality, form, and firmness of the whole are in the tradition of Flaubert. To his tradition also must be ascribed the style, the fixing of the unique impression by the precise noun, adjective, verb, and rhythm. This great novel, which combines these traditions with symbolism, is less scientific than humane, but the penultimate chapter, the return of Odysseus to Ithaca, is the logical development of the scientific method in literature—and its parody. Proceeding by scientific or catechismal question and answer, this chapter reduces all things to matter, space, and motion, presents man in the world of mechanical physics, and provides a cross-section of the scientific mind, Bloom's mind in contrast to Stephen's.[16]

The fiction of cause and effect (naturalism and, to some extent, the story of adolescence) declined because the universe it celebrated died. Pure mathematics took the place of mechanism and biology, determinism with all its causes and effects gave way to atomic free will and statistical probability. No longer a machine, the universe became a thought, matter a wave, and wave a fiction. Time complicated space, which unimaginably curves. In short, the universe of the engineer-physicist, where Darwin's creatures grew, gave place, if there is place, to the universe of the mathematical physicist and he alone can think it; for he alone can multiply the time-space continuum by the square root of minus one, which does not exist. This unthinkable universe is the creation of Max Planck, whose quantum theory (1900), all but destroying cause and effect, made nature discontinuous, and of Einstein, who in 1905 welded space with time. Since, as Jeans observes, this universe is mysterious, news of it took time to descend from laboratory and thinking-room to literary circle. Even Wells, though he spoke of four dimensions in the nineties and in an essay cast doubt upon predictability, waited until the 1920's to say more. It was in this decade that philosophical mathematicians, possessed of limpid style and poetic imagination, spread the news. As far as literary people were concerned the new physics was an invention of the twenties. *The Mysterious Universe* (1930) by Sir James Jeans is the clearest of these books. Proceeding by

16 Herbert Gorman: *James Joyce* (1939), biography. Harry Levin: *James Joyce* (1941), criticism.

concrete analogy, his admirable prose leads almost to the understanding of what words cannot express.[17]

The effect of these books, though in some cases no doubt indirect, was pervasive. They confirmed the old romantic distaste for mechanism and matter, supplying the war waged by Lawrence, Woolf, and Aldous Huxley on both. To these romantics Hardy's universe seemed antiquated, Zola's objective reality unreal. And the new physics, unlike the old, could not deny the religious possibilities of which they dreamed; for if electrons have free will, and matter is thought, there may be a place in the crumpled continuum for angels or a god. The new physics encouraged the subjective novelists, already encouraged by psychoanalysis. Although the stream of consciousness was designed before the discontinuous continuum, and consciousness is thought by Jeans to lie outside it, the stream of consciousness is as discontinuous as the stream of quanta. Although the illogical conduct of heroines and heroes in these novels and those of Lawrence owes much to Dostoyevsky and Freud, their attractiveness may have been increased by the conduct of matter. The new physics, hastening the rejection of Taine's historical criticism in favor of the analysis of separate virtues, immune to cause and effect, affected criticism. This is not to say that William Empson or Stephen Spender read Jeans and immediately applied him; but he had created a climate where critics too must live. Physical discontinuity as well as psychological free association may lie behind the incoherence of poetry, in which casual meetings and departures parallel the behavior of electrons. If it is the business of literature to arrange or to reflect reality, there is nothing

[17] E.g., A. N. Whitehead: *Science and the Modern World* (1925); Bertrand Russell: *The A B C of Atoms* (1923); Arthur Eddington: *The Nature of the Physical World* (1928). After reading Whitehead, Herbert Read combined the quantum theory with Kierkegaard to justify romanticism: *Annals of Innocence and Experience* (1940).

odd about the appearance of a discontinuous literature in the age of physical discontinuity.

Without better evidence than parallels and the former laws of cause and effect provide, all this, of course, is tentative. But some important works unmistakably illustrate the new physics. *The Waves* (1931) by Virginia Woolf is a symbolical demonstration of Jeans's statement that all is waves. Having little use for such symbolism, Shaw made his talkers talk about the new physics. Although he attacked it in *St. Joan* (1923) as evidence of modern credulity, he was delighted with the death of determinism, which he had religiously defied. In *Too True to Be Good* (1931) The Elder, an old-fashioned materialist, laments the end of Newton's universe. The capricious electron obeys no law, he complains, and "the calculable world has become incalculable."[18] In *Finnegans Wake* (1939) Joyce presents the universe of relativity, and, in spite of Jeans, of cyclical regeneration. The private universe Joyce created is finite, discontinuous, and curved. That he had the new physics in mind is proved by his references to the quantum theory, the "abnihilisation of the etym," and the expanding universe, and by such phrases as "Eins within a space" and "whorled without aimed."[19] As Hardy's *Dynasts* is the greatest exploitation of the old universe, so *Finnegans Wake* of the new.

[18] In *Geneva* (1938) Shaw ends worry over politics by the news that the earth has jumped to its "next quantum." Talk of space-time complicates O'Casey's *Within the Gates* (1934). Several of James Bridie's plays deal with physics, biology, or medicine; e.g., *Babes in the Wood* (1938), *The Last Trump* (1938). Among poets who have used the new science for frame, image, or background are William Empson, W. J. Turner, and Charles Madge.

[19] *Finnegans Wake,* pp. 149, 152, 263, 272, 333, 353.

CHAPTER VI

The Hunt for a Father

FROM Blake's time to Lawrence's, men of feeling lamented a world in which physics, displacing metaphysics, limited reality to matter. The world of their desire extended from matter to spirit. In that world a chain of being, connecting all things by correspondences, linked microcosm or man himself with macrocosm. That was the world of the astrologers, who, since celestial and human bodies were analogous, could predict man's future by the stars and earn a decent living. It was the world of the alchemists, who, by increasing the spiritual contents of baser metals, could turn them into gold. And it was the world of those who could speak with assurance about choirs of angels, music of the spheres, and siren song. Although it would not work, it was a good world and a hopeful one in which all things, whether souls or metals, could be promoted a little or refined.

This happy order, made to fit man's emotions and his need for unity, was so tightly constructed that doubt cast upon one part imperiled the whole. Copernicus and Galileo cast such doubts. The new philosophy, said Donne, as his world fell about his ears, puts all in doubt. Indifferent to poets and their anguish, followers of Bacon and Newton gave a kind of unpoetic stability to the eighteenth century by omitting metaphysics from the universe of their design. Safe in the horizontal world of physics, few regretted the vertical. Poets became exact and descriptive, scanning lines without presuming God to scan.

But this universe, which denied so much, was too limited and artificial to last. Long before it died in its turn men of feeling had rebelled against it. The transcendental revolt that began in the eighteenth century, impairing its stability, has continued to our time. Even after the universe of Darwin and Newton yielded to the newer physics, which replaced determinism early in the twentieth century, the spiritual revolt against materialism persisted because news of the new disorder was slow to get around among poets who had not taken calculus. Where it did get around, the physics of discontinuity, permitting various kinds of truth on different levels, encouraged spiritual exercise.

Some turned to Rome, some, for whom science had made Western orthodoxy untenable, found comfort in Hinduism or Theosophy, others in amateur religions like vitalism. Seeking the reunion of matter and spirit, these transcendentalists sought personal integration. The reunion of matter and spirit symbolized union of self and world and, beyond this, of the unconscious with the conscious. Religions offered ends and means. If these religions had been kept out of polite literature, they would not concern us, but they have had an enormous effect, at times producing sermons, at others poetry.

Samuel Butler, the first of these romantic men in our time, was destined for holy orders. After going down from Cambridge in 1858, he became a lay worker in the slums. But he was unsettled by a difficulty: the good little boys in his care had not been baptized, the bad ones had. This, together with inconsistencies he detected in the Gospels, led him to refuse ordination. His disappointed father sent young Butler to New Zealand, where instead of becoming a pastor he became a shepherd.

To increase his disillusionment he read Strauss and the other "higher critics" who were examining the Scriptures with scientific zeal, and in 1861 he read Darwin. In "Darwin on Origin of Species" (1862), the first of three articles Butler contributed to New Zealand newspapers, he announced his acceptance of the new doctrine, chance variation and all. He was answered, to his delight, by a bishop. In hope of another, he devoted "Darwin among the Machines" (1863) and "Lucubratio Ebria" (1865) to playful applications of Darwinism. Machines, he said, developing by the same mechanical laws that control animal and man, may supplant us; and since "a fertile union between two steam engines" is unlikely, man, a slave to machines, will serve to reproduce them. In the second of these articles Butler saw machines as limbs and those who possessed most limbs as fittest. No bishop disputed this capitalistic sentiment.[1]

These articles provided Butler on his return to England with the main ideas of *Erewhon* (1872), a Utopia in reverse. Seeing the danger of being supplanted by machines, the Erewhonians had abolished them. This book with its excellent introductory narrative, its direct style, its effective satire against church, university, and criminal code, is imperfect only because Butler, unable to decide where he stood, could not maintain a tone. He is sometimes serious, sometimes ironic, always too copious. The ironic accounts of Chowbok's baptism and of the Musical Banks reflect the author's recent emancipation from sham. Higgs,

[1] Henry Festing Jones: *Samuel Butler* (1919). Malcolm Muggeridge: *The Earnest Atheist* (1936), a corrective to Jones. Butler: *A First Year in the Canterbury Settlement* (1914) contains the New Zealand tracts.

Mrs. Humphrey Ward's *Robert Elsmere* (1888), the most popular and the most earnest novel of the eighties, takes its theme from the higher criticism. Clerical Elsmere reads Germans, gets doubts, succumbs.

the hero, is at once the author's spokesman and his victim. The section on machines, the best in the book, is serious; for Butler, in the odd position of accepting Darwin's mechanical system while rejecting machines, seems to have seen something of the danger to man in his growing dependence upon them. The efficient prose is the triumph of all the ideas of utility that scientists, Puritans, and men of business had carefully fostered from the time of Bacon. In all but his fear of machinery Butler proves himself in this book to be the child of science and his class.

Fair Haven (1873), his chief contribution to the higher criticism, exposes the inconsistencies of the four Gospels and the myth of the Resurrection. Pious reviewers, unaccustomed to irony, mistook it for earnestness and Butler's mock defense of faith for its defense; and even Darwin, to whom Butler sent a copy in the hope of impious applause, was not amused. Darwin and the pious reviewers were more discerning than Butler, who, distracted with admiration of his wickedness, failed to see that his book, in which irony quarrels with sentiment and skepticism with vague aspiration, is more earnest than wicked. For irony a point of view is requisite. Of his models, Swift had faith, Gibbon skepticism. But Butler, betwixt and between, reflects the confusions of his age.

In *Erewhon Revisited* (1901), a sequel to *Fair Haven* and *Erewhon,* Butler shows the development of a religious myth. The ascent of Higgs in a balloon had been interpreted with some reason by the unmechanical Erewhonians as the Ascension and exploited by the clergy. Attempting wickedness again, Butler succeeded in being more tiresome and much more sentimental.

Butler was less ironic shepherd than lost sheep. But Darwin, who had made return to the Church of England impossible, offered no solace for the yearner. Butler began to resent Darwin for destroying what he could not replace. Moreover, at tea one day with Darwin, misinterpreting Darwin's British demeanor as the sign of coldness and contempt, Butler found himself hating the scientist. Driven by his need and his dislike, he proceeded to invent a substitute for the religion Darwin had destroyed, something that would satisfy mind and feeling at once and baffle Darwin.

The idea of evolution still appealed to Butler, but evolution by chance variation offended his need of spiritual design. He made a private religion by removing Darwin from evolution and substituting Lamarck, whose giraffe owed his neck not to chance but to desire. The religious tracts that Butler proceeded to write attack the mechanical, mindless universe of Darwin and, replacing luck by cunning, reintroduce mind and purpose into nature.[2] "Faith and hope," said Butler, beckon the world of chance and blindness to his dream. Ignorant of science, he attributed equal ignorance to Darwin and Huxley, whose foolish theory of protoplasm Butler demolished. That later men corrected Darwin does not make faith or hope a better instrument of correction. He wisely ignored the pugnacious amateur, who, failing to correct him, liked him less.

This one-sided quarrel had no common terms. Darwin, according to his tradition, inhabited the world of physics. Butler, in revolt against this tradition, demanded metaphysics. Darwin was concerned with immediate causes, Butler with final causes. Darwin asked how, Butler why. Less one-sided than Darwin, Butler was trying to combine physics with metaphysics again. But their unfortunate separation needed stronger glue than his.

The religion of Samuel Butler may be called vitalism. This neo-Lamarckian faith celebrates the progress of the

[2] *Life and Habit* (1878), *Evolution Old and New* (1879), *Unconscious Memory* (1880), *Luck or Cunning* (1887).

life force, which penetrates matter and, improving it by desire, design, and purpose, makes spottier bodies or longer necks. In his later years Butler called his hopeful faith Broad Church, a name as good as another for evolution without Darwin and Christianity without Christ. This religion is expounded in *Erewhon Revisited;* and it is to this religion that Ernest turns after his trials and errors.

Having attended to Darwinism, Butler turned to other heresies and shams. In free-verse poems he disconcerted the entrenched rhymesters, in tracts the entrenched and indifferent scholars.[3] In *Narcissus* (1888), a Handelian cantata, he confounded the entrenched musicians. These confusions of heresy illustrate that final success of Protestantism in which every man his own church assails from within its walls the heresy without. His transcendentalism, as divided as his age, carried him above all matter but money and above all categories but those of caste. In his last years, not quite alone in his belief, he found a convert in Bernard Shaw.

In the preface to *Man and Superman* (1905) Shaw declares himself a preacher with a popular method, and his conscience the "genuine pulpit article." When he said that, he smiled; for what he said, however odd it sounds, is true enough. Although as Protestant as Butler and more of a puritan, Shaw as a boy had little religion to lose, soon lost what he had, and spent much of his subsequent career seeking a suitable substitute for what he should have had. He had had no formal creed, but he had the religious impulse, which, like Freud's sex, when repressed in one place, reappears in another. In a more favorable time Shaw might have been Bunyan, whom he admired above

[3] *The Authoress of the Odyssey* (1897); *Shakespeare's Sonnets Reconsidered* (1899). Of the poems (printed in *The Note-Books*) the best, and Butler's most successful work, is "A Psalm of Montreal" (1878).

most other men; but in the nineteenth century he was compelled to become a playwright. It is not altogether correct to say that his plays are sermons; for, confusing the two, he produced something with the beauties of both kinds and few of their defects.

Every age has its idiom. That of the nineteenth century was not religious. At first Shaw expressed his religious ideas under the guise of socialism, as during the seventeenth century, when the idiom was religious, lay preachers expressed their social ideas under the guise of religion. However satisfactory socialism was to his intellect, it left his emotions unappeased. In 1896 Nietzsche, newly translated into English, presented in the idea of the unsocialistic superman an object for Shaw's groping devotion. The name rather than the idea was new to Shaw, for supermen, equally beyond good and evil, had served him as heroes of his novels and plays for many years. Provided now with a name and a more splendid destiny, Shaw's hero acquired from Wagner's Siegfried an even more heroic deportment and took his place alongside Bunyan's Christian in a private pantheon.[4]

Dick Dudgeon, the hero of *The Devil's Disciple* (1899), a Nietzschean superman, is compared not only to Siegfried but to Shelley's Prometheus. A puritan by inclination, he is forced by the nature of society to abandon organized religion, now the property of the middle class, and take the Devil's side or romantic private religion. This excellent allegory, which reflects Shaw's own nature and development, rejects materialistic society as well as philosophical materialism.

[4] "Nietzsche in English," *Dramatic Opinions; The Perfect Wagnerite* (1898); preface to *The Devil's Disciple* (1899). See Eric R. Bentley: *A Century of Hero-Worship* (1944).

The preface to *Androcles and the Lion* (1913) is Shaw's principal attempt at the higher criticism. Like this excellent farce, *Major Barbara* is an attack upon conventional Christianity.

Taken with old unsuccessful Butler, whom he met in 1897, Shaw permitted him to lecture on Nausicaa before the Fabians, six of whom attended. Not content with this, Shaw persuaded a publisher to accept *Erewhon Revisited*, and after Butler's death, in 1902, he secured too late by ceaseless propaganda the fame that Butler had always wanted. This propaganda began with the preface to *Major Barbara* (1905), in which Shaw credits Butler with the discovery of "mystical vitalism." It was this that Shaw took from Butler to add to his private religion. The superman of Nietzsche and Wagner was to be produced by Butler's Lamarckian life force, struggling through matter with the aid of desire and purpose. This up-to-date religion involved, like Butler's, the excommunication of science. By its happy union of physics with metaphysics it satisfied emotions and intellect as well.

The attack upon the science of medicine in *The Doctor's Dilemma* (1906) follows from Shaw's religious position, which was fully expounded in *Man and Superman*. This work, says Shaw in his preface, is a Bible for the "modern religion of evolution." The heroine of the play, directed by the life force, seeks a father for the superman and, despite his protests, finds one. The interlude, which interrupts this pursuit, is a round-table discussion of Shaw's religion by the characters of Mozart's *Don Giovanni*. Hilarious and tedious by turns, this work seems badly designed for its stated purpose. But suitably expurgated, stripped, for example, of Tanner's speeches and the interlude, it would make a capital play. By such expurgation the movies made a vehicle for actors out of *Major Barbara* and showed how fine a dramatist Shaw was.

In *Back to Methuselah, a Metabiological Pentateuch* (1924) "the most advanced man" of his time, having come across Bergson ten years late, added creative evolution to his vitalistic synthesis. The preface to this play, one of the best commentaries upon the battle between science and aspiration, is an attack upon the "materialistic nihilism" of the nineteenth century, under which the soul starved. As antidote to Darwin and food for the soul, the "vitalist philosopher," as he calls himself, offers Butler's Lamarckian evolution once again under its new name, and, he says, he awaits disciples. The play that follows this interesting preface is less interesting.

Saint Joan (1923), Shaw's most popular play and one of his best, also concerns the life force. But instead of making his creatures sit around talking about it, Shaw discussed it himself in the preface and dramatized it in the play. He approved of Joan, for although her imagination made use of an old-fashioned religious iconography to express the life force, she was a superwoman whose religion is nearer the truth than the gospel of St. Louis Pasteur or the other saints created by modern credulity. Taking her from the Papists and saving her from materialists, Shaw makes her a saint of his own faith. But almost alone among human beings she appealed to him less as a representative of something else than as a person. For this reason he could create a living woman with a life independent of his intellect. Yet much of her strength comes from the significance he alone detected and for once artistically used.

Subsequent years saw the cooling of Shaw's religious fervor. Increasingly political in character, as the times demanded, his prefaces and plays continue to mention his diet and his faith. But he became so lukewarm about them that in the preface to *On the Rocks* (1933) he refers to his creed of creative evolution as a "provisional hypothesis," a "useful illusion," differing from older creeds in this and, unlike them, continually adapted to the times. For the coming state he tolerantly advises creeds for different capacities. In the preface to *The Six of Calais* (1934), removing another of his prophetical robes, he says:

> Now a playwright's direct business is simply to provide the theatre with a play. When I write one with the additional attraction of providing the twentieth century with an up-to-date religion or the like, that luxury is thrown in gratuitously; and the play, simply as a play, is not necessarily either the better or the worse for it.

The playwright with a private religion, since he constitutes his church, must be priest as well as artist, and though it may be his business to write plays, it is his plain duty to preach. According to the doctrine of art for art's sake or the æsthetic theory of Stephen Dedalus, the art of such an artist, being didactic, cannot be good. If the artist is good enough, however, whatever his intention, his work is likely to be art. Shaw, like Bunyan, was usually good enough.

The religious impulse, which turns literature to tract, has no power to injure tract. For this reason the works of Samuel Butler escaped all injury. And the only effect of this impulse upon Shaw was to make those abstract interminable dialogues longer and more abstract. Intellectual by nature, and more at home in essay or debate than play, Shaw wrote prefaces that sometimes dwarf their plays. And many of the plays, avoiding character, action, and symbol, ape their prefaces in explicitness. Shaw, said Shavian Beerbohm, would be a good dramatist if he wrote plays. Under these circumstances religion could but add at times to the intellectual load a transcendental straw.

Not always plays in the usual sense, Shaw's plays brought new intellectual vigor to the theater and with it brilliance, grotesqueness, gaiety, a few substantial characters, and Shaw's bright inhuman smile. These virtues, creating a kind of drama, give life to the roundest tables. Shaw is not unlike the man who told Dr. Johnson that although he had tried to be a philosopher, cheerfulness would break through.

The religion of H. G. Wells is no less symptomatic of our disorder. Half schoolmaster, half visionary, he arrived in his later years at a religion of humanity, secular and benevolent, not unlike that of Comte. The high priests of this unmetaphysical faith, which he offered as a substitute for old theology, were scientists, its prophet Wells. It ill became pious Mr. Eliot to call this rival faith "ersatz."

The Open Conspiracy (1928), the key to Wells's later work, is the bible of this religion. "This is, I declare," says Wells, "the truth and the way of salvation." Though once deficient in a religious sense and a rebel against religion before he had any, he now feels that what is wrong with the world is the want of religion. The old religions are of no use to order chaos. Only a new one will do; and the best of new religions is the world state. It is his hope that religious men, reading his books to one another, will advance his plan. Far from being a union of physics and metaphysics, this modern religion is the elevation of physics by faith and hope to a plane where it may move men's hearts.[5]

Wells regarded his later works, both expository and fictional, as tracts for this religion. The purpose of his outlines and guides is clear. And in "A Digression about Novels" he explains the purpose and character of his later novels. The objection that he fails to write the old kind of

[5] During and shortly after the first World War Wells had restated his religion in somewhat more theological terms in *The Soul of a Bishop* (1917) and *The Undying Fire* (1919), novels, and in *God the Invisible King* (1917), a tract.

novel is irrelevant, he says; for, driven by his hope, he is writing a new kind of novel based on Plato's dialogues and the Book of Job. *The World of William Clissold* (1926), that monstrous monologue on all things, serves to illustrate what social purpose inflamed by piety can do to fiction.

Butler, Shaw, and Wells revived religion and adjusted it to the world about them. More transcendental than these, Yeats, Lawrence, and Huxley, turning back the clock, recovered a former piety. They saved self and world not by reuniting physics with metaphysics, but by fleeing to a time when they were united. This happy time is represented by the Oriental or the occult, by Hinduism, alchemy, or the wisdom of Mme Blavatsky.[6]

"I am very religious," says Yeats in his *Autobiography*, "and deprived by Huxley and Tyndall, whom I detested, of the simple-minded religion of my childhood, I . . . made a new religion, almost an infallible church, of poetic tradition." His scriptures were the spiritual, the old, and the imaginative, his prophets adepts or poets. The arts, he says in an essay, "are about to take upon their shoulders the burdens that have fallen from the shoulders of priests." At first a refuge from the middle class, this poetic church excited his imagination and provided for a time the illusion of unity.

The works of Shelley and Blake were among Yeats's sacred books, and to them he soon added those of the Theosophists. Theosophy, founded by Mme Blavatsky in 1875, is a synthetic religion that, embracing the Oriental and the occult, is good for those who are weary of Huxley

[6] In *The Integration of Personality* (1939) Carl Jung discusses the Oriental and the occult as means of integration for those for whom the symbols of Christianity have lost their power.

See W. Y. Tindall: "Transcendentalism in Contemporary Literature," *The Asian Legacy and American Life* (1945), edited by A. E. Christy, and J. B. Coates: *Ten Modern Prophets* (1944).

and Tyndall. A. P. Sinnett was Blavatsky's apostle to the British, and Colonel H. S. Olcott her apostle to the Americans. In 1885 Yeats read Sinnett's *Esoteric Buddhism* (1883), an account of reincarnation. Excited, he showed the book to A. E. and Charles Johnston; and together they founded in Dublin a Hermetic Society, which Sinnett chartered in 1886 as the Dublin Lodge of the Theosophical Society. At their meetings these vegetarians discussed Blavatsky's *Isis Unveiled* (1877) and, when it appeared in 1888, her *Secret Doctrine.* They listened to lectures by Annie Besant and Mohini Chatterjee, Blavatsky's Hindu disciple, to whom, years later, Yeats addressed a poem. Colonel Olcott lectured on elementals; and, seated for safety in a magic circle, Yeats and A. E. invoked these intolerable spirits. On Blavatsky's arrival in London in 1887, Yeats visited her and was permitted to smell spectral incense, hear spectral bells. Following her advice, he placed the ashes of a rose in the receiver of an airpump, reduced the pressure, placed the apparatus in the moonlight, and watched all night for the ghost of the rose.

When, in 1885, Yeats also became a poet, his poems, of course, reflected his spiritual interests and the nature of society. The heroine of the closet drama *Mosada* (1886), summoning phantoms by her art, exclaims: "I'm eastern-hearted once again." Such fancies, whether Eastern or Western, offered the poet refuge from men of science, "merchants grey," and from time, change, and confusion.

Yeats improved his wisdom in 1887 by joining in London the Order of the Golden Dawn, a Rosicrucian, cabbalistic, and alchemical cult under the direction of MacGregor Mathers. References to the cabbala and to famous alchemists like Lully, Flamel, and Paracelsus began to appear in Yeats's poetry and his prose. Pledged to read all occult literature he could come by, Yeats seems to have been faithful to his vow.

MacGregor Mathers enjoyed familiar relations with two societies in France, the Martinists, under Papus, a follower of Eliphas Lévi, and the Kabalistic Order of the Rosy Cross, under Stanislas de Guaita, the "magus," who offered magic and alchemy as antidotes to materialism.[7] And to French poets rebelling against the bourgeoisie, he offered that "unity of being" which was the desire of the nineteenth century. Through the doctrine of Hermes, "as above, so below," the seekers of his time might discover that harmony of matter and spirit for which they looked. Seeking these things, Yeats visited the Martinists in Paris during the nineties and on one occasion at least saw great Guaita at his home. Excursions to these awful places, where mysteries were celebrated under the image of the Sabbatic Goat and alchemists sought the formula for Hermetic gold, gave Yeats the pleasing sense of being magus as well as poet. In 1896 Yeats drew upon Guaita to furnish his Rosicrucian story "Rosa Alchemica." Michael Robartes, the hero, is a magus, using alchemy for spiritual exercise. But it is Yeats's poems that bear in theme and image the weight of this wisdom.[8]

In "Fergus and the Druid," King Fergus abandons the real world of politics to become an Irish magus and poet. Immediately he is oppressed by unspeakable knowledge. Politics was bad; magic and metempsychosis are worse. The occult, Yeats felt, was what a poet needed in order to free himself from matter; but at the same time he knew that a poet's place is the real world, not the world of

[7] Guaita served Huysmans as villain in *Là-bas* (1891), the best account of Parisian occultism.

[8] Michael Robartes, Yeats's symbol for his occult interests, also appears in "The Tables of the Law," a story, and in many poems. In "A Song of the Rosy-Cross" (*Bookman,* October 1895) Yeats celebrated the Order. The "fire-born moods" of his poems are Zoroastrian creatures, and "the everlasting voices" are elementals. Many passages in *The Countess Cathleen* illustrate his occult interests.

dream. Oisin, who flees time, change, and the implacable laws of nature for the Land of Youth in *The Wanderings of Oisin,* is unhappy there; for evil is needed for happiness as well as good. "To Ireland in the Coming Times" expresses fear that the occult may separate the poet from his nation, and hope that, though haunted by elemental spirits and the "red-rose-bordered hem," he may yet be one with Davis, Mangan, Ferguson.

"Who Goes with Fergus?" the most enigmatic and the best of the early poems, can be understood only in the context of these poems and this situation. Noting the ambiguity of "will" and "now" in the first line, William Empson wonders in *Seven Types of Ambiguity* whether warning or invitation is intended, and concludes that the poem owes its charm to meaning nothing in particular. The charm of the poem does owe something to the quarrel between finality of form and vagueness of substance; for if taken alone as a text for explanation or in connection with the other poem on Fergus, the substance is puzzling. But if its setting in *The Countess Cathleen* and Yeats's notes in the early editions are considered and the poem is examined in a larger context, the meaning Yeats had in mind is too unambiguous to merit the notice of Empson. Fergus is a poet or magus who, like Yeats, has abandoned reality, not politics this time, but love; for Yeats was suffering his first disappointment with Maud Gonne. Fergus has regressed, like Oisin, to the Land of Youth, that "woven" or integrated place where love can bother him no more. An invitation to leave this world with Fergus and be as happy as children in the womb, this poem celebrates a passing mood. Such retreats, whether to infancy, the Lake Isle of Innisfree, or the occult, brought Yeats a bitterness that drove him to confront and flee again his love, his nation, and his world.

These poems, representing in rhythm, tone, and diction

all that was opposite to his world, seemed sentimental to older Yeats. The occult, which had helped give them this character, now seemed no less unsatisfactory. Far from giving Yeats the integration he desired, the occult had replaced the chaos of the world by a more shadowy chaos. In 1899 he quarreled with Mathers and left the Golden Dawn. He confronted Ireland, and the world of the middle class that he had fled was now his arena. His poems became harder, colder, more precise. But Yeats's old interests were dormant, not dead.[9]

"The Phases of the Moon" (1919), a didactic poem, announced an occult system of his own, fully expounded in the prose of *A Vision* (1925). At first he ascribed this system to the researches of Michael Robartes, but after some further attempts at mystification he confessed in *A Packet for Ezra Pound* (1929) that certain benevolent demons had dictated the whole business to Mrs. Yeats, a medium. Their revelation, which presents the nature of man, his history, and the progress of the soul under the symbolism of the moon and its twenty-eight phases, seems, however, to be the poet's work. Rewriting it in 1937, Yeats made it even more complicated and less readable. But that a poet of the Celtic twilight could command that intricate geometry improves the effect by wonder.

Around the great wheel of the month, souls move through the phases, each of which (except the full and the dark) represents the incarnation of a psychological type according to the proportion of light and dark. The brighter half of the wheel includes the better sort of men —statesmen, poets, honest wives—and the darker half the

[9] See the two essays and the learned notes Yeats provided for Lady Gregory's *Visions and Beliefs* (1920); *Per Amica Silentia Lunæ* (1917), his essay on Cambridge Platonism; and his introduction to the *Gitanjali* (1912), of Rabinranath Tagore.

butchers, saints, and hunchbacks. The better sort are subjective, the worse objective. Each soul makes the circuit of reincarnation four times before escaping from time and fate into nirvana. Between incarnations the soul follows a course of dream and purgation. The course of history follows that of the soul, and empires rise and fall in cycles. Having begun with Mary, the present cycle is now ending in disorder as the previous cycle, which began with Leda, had ended.

For this system, inspired perhaps by Blake's, Yeats seems to have combined astrology, Plato's great year, the Hindu symbol of light and dark fortnights, and the Buddhist wheel of destiny with Sinnett's metempsychosis. On the whole the system may be regarded as a simplification of astrology. The moon is taken, like the stars, as a sign of that union of microcosm and macrocosm which enables one to account for present, past, and future. Yeats used astrological and alchemical symbols on his diagram of the wheel. The moon and wheel, like the earlier rose, appear to signify unity and generation.

This system made Yeats at home in the world. Reconciling spirit and matter, self and world, it gave him the framework our age desires and with it unity and myth. Yeats's poems now, like Dante's, could depend for image and reference upon something external to themselves. By explaining confusion as part of a great order, Yeats could confront and use what he abhorred, and almost alone could be man of the world and poet too.

Yeats's system had further values. Ridding him of abstractions that had plagued him for years, it left him free to write the poems it inspired. And sending him for corroboration and support to the records of the past, it gave him a liberal education, such acquaintance with the European tradition from Homer to Jung that he could fill his poems with common images and references to familiar knowledge. Through his private system he became a public poet.

To be sure, some of the later poems, such as "The Double Vision of Michael Robartes," which refers to the first and fifteenth phases of the moon, are unintelligible without reference to *A Vision,* which Yeats published to help readers through poems like this. And though "Byzantium" has every appearance of unity and though such images as the dome are readily intelligible, the poem remains enigmatic in parts even with the help of *A Vision.* Such privacy is uncommon.

That apocalyptic poem "The Second Coming," presenting the disintegration to be expected at the end of a cycle, presents a vision of our time. In a nightmare from Blavatsky's Anima Mundi or Lévi's Astral Light, Yeats sees how the Sphinx, a symbol of the previous cycle, was vexed at the rocking cradle of Christ, and he wonders what symbolic beast will represent the approaching cycle. Despite the elaborate implications, the images are plain to the common understanding. Even more public in character, "Two Songs from a Play" requires no reference to *A Vision,* for Yeats presented his idea in images that have been familiar for two thousand years. His virgin is the Virgin [10] and his wheel is Plato's year.

Public and private at once, "Sailing to Byzantium," like all great works of art, says what cannot be said another way. Sense cannot be separated from sensation nor sensation from rhythm, feeling, and tone. But while the whole remains inexplicable, the parts may be explained and their functions determined. "The mackerel-crowded seas" summarizes the world's condition, struggle, limited survival, and time. Part of its power comes from the unconscious symbolism, part from inevitable statement, and part from

[10] The virgin is also Vergil's Astræa and one of Frazer's ladies.

contrast with neighboring abstractions, "those dying generations" and the trite, mysterious trinity of "fish, flesh, or fowl." The single word "commend" is by position and tone the central magic of the stanza. Caught in that noble rhythm, the dissonance of time yields in the last couplet to anticipations of timelessness. But even here the tone is complex, and one becomes aware that compulsory timelessness is but an old man's substitute for time. The idea of this voyage, having come from Yeats's unconscious, had smoldered so long in his consciousness, forming many poems, that now, glowing, it emerged final, easy, and triumphant.

Noting that his later poetry had gained in assurance and power, Yeats ascribed the improvement to his wheel. But one may wonder with Katharine Tynan how far a man of his intelligence believed what he professed. "Some will ask," says Yeats in *A Packet for Ezra Pound*, "if I believe all that this book contains and I will not know how to answer." This important question, however, had been answered earlier in other essays. Of his occult studies in Paris he had said: "My critical mind . . . mocked, and yet I was delighted." Not intellect but imagination needed the excitement, myth, and unity that our age could not provide. He intelligently invented what he wanted. The pragmatic occultist, never as transcendental as he seemed, was first of all a poet.

Reproving the folly of Yeats, Lawrence, and Wells, I. A. Richards in *Science and Poetry* (1926), the neatest of his books, observes that science, which deals with references, is right, religion, which deals with emotive terms, wrong. To satisfy our emotions without the danger of believing what is wrong, Richards suggests that poetry, which also consists of emotive terms and pseudo-statements, may take the place of religion. Annoyed by this pragmatic attitude toward belief, T. S. Eliot accused Richards of confusing poetry with religion. He might have been accused more reasonably of confusing Yeats's religion with religion; for he failed to see that Yeats's substitute for religion was as pragmatic as his own.

But in his last years Yeats returned to Hinduism. Poems in *The King of the Great Clock Tower* (1934) celebrate this return and his friendship with a learned yogi named Shri Purohit Swami, whom he met in 1931. His introductions to the swami's works assert that Hinduism, seen at last without Blavatsky's aid, satisfies mind and feeling and gives unity to the chaos of occult experience. In his new enthusiasm he wrote an essay on the "Mandookya Upanishad" for Eliot's *Criterion,* and with the swami's help translated *The Ten Principal Upanishads* (1937). Yeats, though old and ill, undertook these labors to provide young poets with a more public myth than his *Vision,* to which he referred less and less. And the excellent poetry of these final years is secular.

Unlike Yeats, George Russell (A. E.) was a mystic. He also became a member of the Dublin Lodge, where he read the Upanishads, the yoga aphorisms, and the works of Mme Blavatsky. His paintings and poems[11] are the product of mystical raptures with which critical intelligence was not permitted to interfere.

The Candle of Vision (1918) is A. E.'s spiritual autobiography. Given to trances and visions from early youth, he says, he spent half his time in Anima Mundi, whence he returned to paint pictures of what he saw there or write poems about it. In *Song and Its Fountains* (1932) he tells how easy it is for a mystic to write verse. Going into a trance, he receives the poem from spirits and sets it down with automatic hand. On waking, the poet reads with surprise and gratitude the finished poem. These early

[11] *Homeward: Songs by the Way* (1894); *The Earth Breath* (1897); *Collected Poems* (1913).

Theosophical visions are diffuse and misty, typical in diction, feeling, and tone of the softer romanticism. Later his visions lost their intensity, and he was compelled to write his own verses.

The practical side of A. E. is represented by his work for Sir Horace Plunkett's Agricultural Society. Going about on a bicycle, A. E. persuaded farmers by talk of fairies to establish co-operative dairies. Of his many books on politics and economics, *The National Being* (1916), advocating rural communism and Anima Mundi, is representative. Essentially a prophet, though the most agreeable of men, he made economics and art serve piety. Even young Joyce attended A. E.'s Sunday evenings.[12]

Arthur Machen, another Celt, was preoccupied like Huysmans and Yeats with black magic and its horror. To Machen, too, nature seemed a veil embroidered with signs of a reality unveiled at peril, but useful for counteracting science and Maupassant. Enormities are evoked in *The Great God Pan* (1894), in which Helen Vaughan, an initiate, sends men mad with knowledge. *The Three Impostors* (1895) discloses the doings of an occult society off Oxford Street in Babylonian London, their Sabbatic rites, and their vengeance upon a faithless member. Perhaps the strangest part of this Stevensonian fantasy is Miss Lally's story of the initiate who relapses into semiliquid corruption on the floor. The stories of *The House of Souls* (1906) are similar, "A Fragment of Life" dealing with a clerk who renounces the suburb for a kind of theosophy, and "The White People" with a little girl who, having learned something of sorcery and the Sabbath, succumbs before an ancient image in a place of mounds and hollows "with a terrible voor over everything." "The Inmost Light"

[12] *The Living Torch* (1937) is a posthumous collection of his shrewd kindly essays from the *Irish Statesman,* which he edited. Appearing as a character in Joyce's *Ulysses,* A. E. represents mysticism.

shows the danger of suburban experiments with alchemy. These stories, which gain their effects through indirection, are chiefly remarkable for their exquisite style. Like "Rosa Alchemica," they unite the worlds of Pater and Huysmans, and like it are less indicative of worship than of refuge in spiritual horror from the greater horrors of the world.

In contempt of the world that had destroyed the Primitive Methodism of his youth, D. H. Lawrence also found relief from matter and reason in Theosophy. Between 1912 and 1915 he read the works of Mme Blavatsky. Mixing this spiritual literature with anthropology, he made a private religion, which he preached in his novels and essays. Lawrence was an enthusiast and, unlike Yeats, was prophet before poet or novelist. Prophetical purpose sometimes gives his novels of the unconscious a didactic and allegorical character foreign to their substance and makes what should be lyrical a little grim.

In *The Secret Doctrine,* Mme Blavatsky had described Atlantis as a spiritual Utopia from which, after the Flood, swimmers had carried fragments of the truth to shores where today they may be found in the doctrines and symbols of Hindus, American Indians, and Etruscans. Theosophy is an attempt to reassemble this secret doctrine from its fragments and to return in spirit to a better past. That Lawrence shared this endeavor is evident from the preface to *Fantasia of the Unconscious* (1922). And his best novel, *The Plumed Serpent* (1926), recovers the truth of Atlantis from its Aztec vestiges. Here Lawrence, seduced perhaps by the splendor of Mexico, assimilated what he preached and subdued it to purposes of art.

He was familiar with the Vedas and the Upanishads and, as might be expected, was devoted to yoga. For this his principal source was *The Apocalypse Unsealed* (1910) by James M. Pryse, one of Blavatsky's twelve disciples and one-time member of the Dublin Lodge along with A. E. and Yeats. Pryse's book is a Theosophical interpretation of the Apocalypse of St. John in terms of yoga. The centers or chakras through which Lawrence's unconscious flows in *Psychoanalysis and the Unconscious* (1921) come from Pryse, whom Lawrence preferred to Freud. The spiritual exercises of Don Ramon in *The Plumed Serpent* are those of the yogi, and Quetzalcoatl, the Aztec serpent, is Pryse's Kundalini, the serpent coiled at the base of a yogi's spine. Lawrence's *Apocalypse* (1931), adored by young poets, closely follows Pryse. Transcendental and occult, this tract is of value for the strange brilliance of its symbols, archetypes, according to Jung, of the unconscious and means of integration. But, unable to find himself as Yeats had done or to adjust himself to reality, Lawrence spent his last years reproving it, flying above it, or retreating, with the method of a relapsed Methodist, to Blavatsky's paradise. That his uncentered work did not suffer more is a tribute to his powers of flight.[13]

Sometimes, as Lawrence says, a "demon" shook a poem out of him. From Hardyesque descriptions of nature, rhymed but irregular in metre, he progressed to songs of his mother, his body, and his religion. "Virgin Youth," which celebrates his genitals, anticipates the religious preoccupation of his maturity. But the characteristic early poems are those in which he loves his mother, "Piano," for instance, that fine Proustian memory restored by the "great black piano appassionato." These poems have the energy of something overcharged and suddenly released. Burningly personal, evading censor and objective correlative alike, they leave him almost naked. When symbols inter-

[13] For more about Lawrence's occultism see W. Y. Tindall: *D. H. Lawrence and Susan His Cow* (1939). See also *The Letters of D. H. Lawrence* (1932), edited by Aldous Huxley.

rupt directness, they are Freud's, used unconsciously at first, then consciously, but—of the most public sort—they complete exposure.

After Lawrence discarded rhyme, an uncongenial impediment, and adopted the rhythms of Whitman, he was even better able to follow the contours of passion. His best poems, those of *Birds, Beasts and Flowers* (1923), express him entirely. Conversational, tender, fierce, and incandescent, they draw morals from figs and other natural things, and prove the poet a Georgian who, having read wonderful books, has left the suburb for a distant pulpit. There like a medieval friar he uses the *exemplum* to compose his bestiary. But whereas Hopkins and the friars used nature to celebrate God, Lawrence, by turns chatty and apocalyptic, uses nature to celebrate nature. His poems of peach, goat, and snake, models of didactic art, are among the first religious poems of our time. Besides satiric trifles, *Last Poems* (1932) contains a few vital lyrics on gentian, for example, and whale. But, death upon him, Lawrence was declining into abstraction. "The Ship of Death," though symbols of apple and ship remain unreconciled, is a good poem, stricter than the others and final by circumstance.[14]

The crusade against science that Lawrence preached by allegory and symbol seems less absurd today than it used to seem. And Aldous Huxley's contention that science has gone far enough is proved by atomic fission and the irresponsibility of scientist, capitalist, and politician. About to be decomposed, we can return with understanding to these prophets. Surely, what we need is one religion or another, preferably both.

Aldous Huxley, Lawrence's disciple, was an apparent

[14] *Collected Poems* (1928); *Pansies* (1929); *Nettles* (1930). See Horace Gregory: *Pilgrim of the Apocalypse* (1933).

cynic when he met the prophet in 1915. War and science had destroyed all meaning; and to express his disgust with the world, Huxley was writing desperate verses and planning elegant novels. Lawrence invited Huxley to join him in a Utopia he was going to establish in Florida. Touched by sincerity and passion, Huxley accepted; but, circumstances preventing Utopia at that time, cynicism resumed. In *Antic Hay* (1923) Huxley made fun of Lawrence's chakras. But longing for unity and truth expressed itself in *Those Barren Leaves* (1925), whose hero retires from fools and cynics to meditate; and when Huxley met Lawrence again in 1926, both were ready and Huxley succumbed. Rampion, a spiritual man among knaves in *Point Counter Point* (1928), is Huxley's interpretation of Lawrence. Huxley remained a disciple until Lawrence's death and, after it, piously edited his letters. The savage from New Mexico who dies a martyr to H. G. Wells in *Brave New World* (1932) is Huxley's second portrait of Lawrence. In the absence of Lawrence's attractive presence, Huxley's fervor cooled, and after going to Mexico to check up on Lawrence's Indians, as Huxley confesses in *Beyond the Mexique Bay* (1934), he was disenchanted. But Lawrence, softening Huxley's intellect, had left the former cynic ready for Gerald Heard.

No less attractive than Lawrence, Heard had the advantages of respectability and omniscience. For years he had delivered over the B.B.C. his famous lectures on all things, and he had written books on the same subject. Anthropology, psychoanalysis, and intuition prove, he says in *The Social Substance of Religion* (1931), that man's disunity and that of the world may be cured by religion. Huxley fell under the influence of the new prophet in 1934 or 1935. After writing tracts for the Peace Pledge Union, which promoted "the redeeming power of Love" as a refuge against bombs, Huxley and Heard prudently left for America.[15] As they traveled, they composed almost identical tracts, Heard *The Third Morality* and Huxley *Ends and Means,* both published in 1937. The mechanical philosophies of Newton, Darwin, and Freud, they say, have made life meaningless by ignoring the spirit. Man needs a new religion to embrace all levels of reality. Samuel Butler and Lamarck have shown the possibility of spiritual evolution. The wise men of the East have revealed the power of a vegetable diet and, through yoga and Buddhistic contemplation, the proper training of the mind-body unit. Heard and Huxley propose, therefore, the improvement of man by spiritual and physical exercises, a diet of vegetables, and systematic meditation.

In *Eyeless in Gaza* (1936) Huxley had told of his conversion to Heard and his system. Anthony Beavis, the hero of this religious novel, meets Mr. Miller, who advises yoga, vegetables, and enemas as cure for skepticism. Immediately convinced, Beavis practices, eats, and takes these things. Meditation and mystical ecstasies improve his sermons for Mr. Miller's Peace Pledge Union.[16] This is the story of Huxley and Heard up to their departure for America.

Finding little to their purpose in the East, they departed for the congenial West, where in Hollywood Heard wrote *Pain, Sex and Time* (1939), a further exposition of his religion, and Huxley *After Many a Summer Dies the Swan*

15 Heard and Huxley: *Pacifism* (1935). *An Encyclopedia of Pacifism,* edited by Huxley.

16 Mr. Miller is Heard combined with Canon Dick Sheppard of the Peace Pledge Union.

The transcendental career of J. Middleton Murry, Huxley's Burlap, has paralleled Huxley's. The preface to *God* (1929) is Murry's spiritual autobiography. A mystical experience led him to reconcile physics and metaphysics in a private faith, with Shakespeare, Keats, Jesus, and Marx as saints. See *The Necessity of Communism* (1932) and *Christocracy* (1942).

(1939), a fictional twin to Heard's tract. In this novel Mr. Propter presides in California over a little cult of meditators. This neo-Brahmin, like Heard, spends his time transcending personality and time when he is not preaching to the materialists who surround him. He has a greenhouse for the vegetables. *Time Must Have a Stop* (1944), more allusive on the whole, leaves particular treatment of Huxley's religion to the notebook at the end. But Uncle Eustace's limbo is a warning to materialists; Rontini is a reminiscence of Lawrence; and the desperate hero, of course, is converted.[17]

Huxley is less to blame for his decline than our times, which, making writer prophet and writing tract, invite correction or escape. The later novels of Huxley illustrate that indifference to art which he proclaims in *Time Must Have a Stop.* Although it is foolish to blame for æsthetic failure one who has abandoned the plane of æsthetics for a higher one, the pity is that good cynics are uncommon in English literature and preachers are a dime a dozen.

Since 1940 Huxley has been under the influence of Swami Prabhavananda of the Ramakrishna Mission, who, in his miniature Taj Mahal in Hollywood, expounds the Hindu scriptures on Tuesdays and Thursdays. So instructed, Huxley writes for *Vedanta and the West,* the magazine of the Vedanta Society, and in 1942 contributed a foreword to Swami Nikhilananda's *Gospel of Sri Ramakrishna.* Living in the desert with no neighbors but his cows, Huxley assumes yoga postures, breathes deeply, and meditates.

For a time the altar boy, if that is the name for him, of

[17] Huxley's spiritual development may also be traced in *Grey Eminence* (1941), *The Perennial Philosophy* (1945), and *Science, Liberty and Peace* (1946). For further details of this development see W. Y. Tindall: "The Trouble with Aldous Huxley," *American Scholar,* XI (Autumn 1942). For a general survey of Huxley's work see David Daiches: *The Novel and the Modern World* (1939).

Huxley's Hollywood temple was Christopher Isherwood, late novelist and collaborator with Auden in left-wing plays. Having more or less abandoned the world, Isherwood assisted Swami Prabhavananda at services, helped him edit *Vedanta and the West,* and prepared himself with austerities for the priesthood.[18] The example of Isherwood appears to have inspired Somerset Maugham's *Razor's Edge* (1944), a novel about a worldly boy who, converted to Hinduism, leaves his inheritance for the holy life. Similar in theme to Huxley's later novels, this novel differs in other respects. Seeing his material with a novelist's eye, Maugham is content with the wonder of human nature.

Less need be said of those who in despair of modern or exotic remedies found what they required in a Western church, usually that of Rome or Canterbury, since the appeal of Geneva has visibly declined. The effect of conversion upon Catholics and Anglo-Catholics has been great, but not, on the whole, injurious. Because their churches maintain a salaried clergy, the convert may allude to what is commonly known or celebrate it, leaving the preaching to the proper authorities. Under different auspices, Huxley and Eliot left time for eternity. The result of one departure is tract and of the other poetry.

Although a preacher of a sort in his sermons, Gerard Manley Hopkins was a poet in his poems. He is not only the greatest religious poet of England in our time, but one of the greatest poets. He was not a mystic like Huxley, A. E., or Lawrence, but a poet who used his art for the greater glory of God.[19]

[18] *Vedanta for the Western World* (1946), edited by Isherwood, contains contributions by Huxley, Heard, and Swami Prabhavananda. In 1944 Isherwood and the swami translated the *Bhagavad-Gita.*

[19] *The Note-Books and Papers of Gerard Manley Hopkins* (1937). G. F. Lahey, S.J.: *Gerard Manley Hopkins, a Biography* (1930). John Pick: *Gerard Manley Hopkins, Priest and Poet* (1942). Martin D'Arcy,

While at Balliol in the 1860's, Hopkins was attracted by the higher criticism of Jowett and Strauss, and his sensuous nature was stimulated by the teaching of Pater. But the Oxford Movement and the defection of Newman, proving more congenial to his temper, made him aware of the void left by skepticism and sent him, in the endeavor to fill it, to former certainty.

With the extravagance of the convert he became a Jesuit. The Society of Jesus promised an austerity that seemed opposite to his own sensuousness and to the doctrine of Pater. Ordained in 1877, Hopkins remained faithful to his vows—indeed, somewhat overscrupulous—and as happy as his neurotic constitution permitted. After he had preached in the seventeenth-century manner a sermon upon the church as a cow, whom we must milk and feed and whose moo we must follow, his colleagues came to regard him as one who would be better employed perhaps as a schoolteacher. In this capacity he spent his later years at that university in Dublin which Newman founded and Joyce was to make illustrious.

Hopkins tried to repress his eccentricity, his sensuousness, and his dangerous delight in nature. He burned his verses. But the possibility of compromise appeared in Loyola's permission to employ sensuous beauty for God's sake. Far from impairing his poems, as several critics have held, his vocation improved their quality, gave them character and exciting matter, and disciplined their romantic confusion. Since he became a great poet, his vocation did not prevent him from becoming one. It is idle to suppose that under other circumstances he might have been greater.

His poems, written between 1876 and 1889, were published in 1918. Their editor, Robert Bridges, has been

S.J.: "Gerard Manley Hopkins," *Great Catholics* (1941), edited by Claude Williamson.

blamed for delaying so long, but he was wise to wait until the times, prepared by other excesses, could receive poems so peculiar for rhythm, diction, metaphor, and syntax.

Sprung rhythm, in which Hopkins composed, is the rhythm of *Piers Plowman,* but he developed it from the choruses of Milton's *Samson Agonistes.* With syncopated accents and effects of counterpoint, sprung rhythm looks formidable, but it raises few problems of scansion; for as Hopkins observes, it is the "natural rhythm of speech," and though elaborately composed is easily read.[20] Like Whitman's verse, sprung rhythm is a major development in prosody, an attempt to complete the romantic revolution, which, correcting words, had let rhythm alone. But Hopkins was conservative in rhyme. Retaining it at the cost of awkwardness and—in the "Eurydice"—of bathos, he prized it as an extra value.

His diction, though he had no German, Anglo-Saxon, or Middle English until late in life, seems Germanic. He knew Welsh prosody, however, and his alliteration, his kennings, his internal rhymes and dissonances, as "blood-gush blade-gash" or "lush-kept plush-capped," exaggerate Welsh usage. Such oddities, at once sensuous and uncouth, kept him at several removes from Tennyson.

That "naked encounter of sensuality and asceticism" which offended the nineteenth-century reverence of Robert Bridges excellently describes the metaphors of Hopkins, who, combining Pater and piety, made discordant concords of heaven and earth. Unlike the dry metaphysical conceit, these sensuous emblems present the spirit so palpably and flamboyantly that they approach the grotesque. But the sensualization of spirit, as in the images of barn, stallion, and deliquescent sloe, is redeemed by ec-

[20] For Hopkins's explanation of sprung rhythm see *Poems* (1930), edited by Charles Williams. For Hopkins's comments on his poems see his letters to Robert Bridges (1935) and *Further Letters* (1938).

stasy. All material things, however common or mean, sanctified by the Incarnation, comprised a store of poetic contraries, agreeing and disagreeing with spirit in pleasing tension. Hopkins differed from the other Jesuits of his time (who, while admitting the rule of "*tantum quantum*," inclined to severity) in having recaptured the baroque spirit that inflamed Crashaw and his Jesuits, leaving as it swept through Europe a trail of florid churches with voluptuous altars.

Prizing singularity and encouraged by Duns Scotus, its philosopher, Hopkins called the essence and the underlying design of a thing its "inscape." His endeavor to be true to his inscape and his theme's, making him singular and, he feared, repulsive at first reading, demanded those distortions of syntax, the ellipses, the grammatical improvisations, that make his poetry difficult. In this interest and for intensity he condensed as he distorted. So made and charged with the profound experiences of his faith, his poems seem not recollections in tranquillity but experience in progress. Songs of becoming, not of being, they are opposite in kind to the perfections of Yeats.

"The Wreck of the Deutschland," Hopkins's first great poem, improves upon acquaintance. Dealing with the problem of evil, this ode unwinds in three congruent strands, the first of Hopkins and God, the second of the wreck, the third of nuns and God; and the point is discovered in the broken exclamations of the twenty-eighth stanza.[21] Following this tumultuous success, Hopkins wrote those sonnets of nature that comprise his most agreeable achievement. "God's Grandeur," a marvelous unity of rhythm, sound, and meaning, proceeds from the

[21] See the explications by John Pick and by W. H. Gardner: *Gerard Manley Hopkins*, Vol. I (1944). Cf. The Kenyon Critics: *Gerard Manley Hopkins* (1946). Among recent poets who have studied Hopkins with profit are Auden, Day Lewis, Barker, and Thomas.

conceit of the Leyden jar to the traditional image of the Holy Ghost, redeemed from commonness by a magical "Ah!" "The Windhover," a more incredible sweep of pace, harmony, and image, puzzles by its ambiguities. Is the falcon a bird, the critics ask, or the poet or Jesus Christ? He is, of course, all three at once, but in the last three lines is dominantly Christ addressing Hopkins, priest. The theme is the apparent conflict between two kinds of beauty, that of vocation and that of life.

Poems of men, Purcell, Scotus, Felix Randal, follow with tenderness and past imperatives; and these in turn are followed by the self-questioning poems of the eighties, "Spelt from Sibyl's Leaves," tortured and grim, and the sonnets of the "terrible" period, of which "Carrion Comfort" and "No worst" are best, their theme his own unworthiness and, as a reader of William James should know, of normal religious experience. But even these cries of anguish reveal the passionate grammarian. The wonder is not that Hopkins, confined by self-imposed puntilios of syntax and prosody, wrote poems so good, but that he wrote poems at all. Their excellence is a tribute to his constant burning faith, for only by this fire could that syntax and that prosody prevail.

Almost to a man, the Paterites of the nineties, having pursued hedonism to its limit, turned for relief to the Church of Rome as Huysmans had done before them. In an essay on Huysmans, Arthur Symons said that Catholicism is the religion of the decadence "for its venerable age, valuable in such matters as the age of an old wine, its vague excitation of the senses, its mystical picturesqueness." Dorian Gray in his search for odd sensation delighted not only in flowers and rugs, but in the ritual of the church. Oscar Wilde, going further, became a convert. So did Lionel Johnson, Ernest Dowson, Henry Harland, John Gray, Aubrey Beardsley, and Frederick Rolfe or, as he preferred, Baron Corvo, author of *Hadrian the Seventh* (1904). The literary results, except for the religious poetry of Johnson and Dowson and the eccentric novels of Rolfe, were meager.[22]

While the Catholicism of G. K. Chesterton was more medieval in character than that of Hopkins or Rolfe and more jovial, it served a similar purpose. The scientific materialism and the decadence of the nineties left him dissatisfied. Groping for something better, he was attracted, as he tells in his *Autobiography* (1936), to Theosophy. He met Yeats, considered Blavatsky and the Celtic twilight, but preferred the London fog. The only trouble with Yeats's *Land of Heart's Desire,* he said, is that "the heart does not desire it." In 1905 he devoted *Heretics* to Shaw, Wells, and others whose solutions were eccentric. The optimistic pantheism that attracted him at this time underlies that fine, fantastic novel *The Man Who Was Thursday* (1908). Policemen and anarchists and the insane light in which they move indicate the personal nightmare of nihilism, materialism, and æstheticism from which he was beginning to emerge; and Sunday is his provisional god. That same year, however, he wrote *Orthodoxy.*

The appeal of order and tradition had led Chesterton to the company of eminent Anglicans and then to Father John O'Connor (Father Brown), who told him about sin. Chesterton became a Catholic at last in 1922 and devoted his journalistic brilliance, his paradox, wit, and outrageous simplicity to tracts in verse and prose. This happy man

[22] A. J. A. Symons: *The Quest for Corvo* (1934). *The Last Letters of Aubrey Beardsley* (1904), edited by John Gray.

The richly metaphorical poems of Francis Thompson (e.g., *Sister Songs,* 1895) recapture the baroque lusciousness of Crashaw and Marvell and the drier wit of Donne. "The Hound of Heaven" (1893), more austere, triumphs by the scenery of dream, but that it is overelaborate can be seen by comparison with George Herbert's "Collar." Cf. "The Shepherdess" and the other sweet, delicate verses of Alice Meynell.

combined the qualities of Shaw and Eliot, resembling Shaw as poet, and as thinker Eliot.

Eliot expressed despair in his early poems and, in the poem on the hippopotamus, irreverence as well. Elegantly allusive, he piled fragments of culture about the ruins. That culture was not enough becomes evident in "Gerontion," a desperate monologue on the need and unlikelihood of salvation. *The Waste Land* (1922) objectifies the spiritual desert in which he felt half alive, a cross between Dante's Hell and London. The second part of this excellent poem proves the desert moral. Hindu and Buddhist overtones, dark references to ruined chapels and the Resurrection of Christ, which accompany the regenerating rain, point the way to salvation. Images from Dante's Purgatory and Limbo, together with cactus and stuffed shirts, define "The Hollow Men." But these spiritual allusions are so oblique that I. A. Richards may be pardoned for thinking Eliot happily represented freedom from all belief. To correct this error and to make his conversion plain, Eliot announced in 1928 his adherence to the more pompous faction of the Church of England. That he could find spiritual refuge there is not as unlikely as it appears, for the established church, representing what is least American, promised immunity from Bleistein and Sweeney.[23]

Although Eliot has emphatically rejected the idea that his church is respectable, he is deceived. But it is not true that his religion is simply a matter of caste. If his essays on dogma, on ecclesiastical affairs, and on the less pleasing bishops contained nothing more than their apparent snobbishness, they would not have their power to enrage the reader. This power must come from something genu-

[23] Eliot's spiritual career is presented as a saint's life by Richard Aldington in "Stepping Heavenward," *Soft Answers* (1932). Eliot did not become a Roman Catholic because, as he says in the *Criterion* (October 1927), Anglicanism is essentially Tory and Catholicism in our time is essentially American and democratic.

ine hidden beneath manner and tone and the colorless, odorless, tasteless prose.

It is difficult, however, to detect the piety that must underlie Eliot's exposure of such heretics as Yeats, Lawrence, and Hopkins. It is even more difficult to detect the piety that must underlie *The Idea of a Christian Society* (1939). In this incredible document Eliot offers a kind of theocracy as the only substitute for liberalism, democracy, and godlessness. He excludes America and the Dominions from comprehension in his state because the mixture of people in those places makes them irredeemable. Not all Englishmen, however, are worthy, for not all have attended the better public schools. In England the lower orders, incapable of religion, will be kept within the Anglican frame by the "Community of Christians." The "distinguished theologian" to whom Eliot submitted his book had reason for fearing that this community might be interpreted to mean the "nice Christianly-minded people of the upper middle class."

Yet Eliot writes good devotional poetry, little inferior to the religious poetry of Hopkins. It is true that *The Rock* (1934), a pageant composed for an ecclesiastical occasion, is heavy. But *Murder in the Cathedral* (1935), also written for an ecclesiastical occasion, is a successful play of great emotional power. This play and *The Family Reunion* (1939) are his most public poems.

In his essays lamenting the separation of poetry and drama Eliot had asked how our craving for poetic drama could be satisfied. Not, he replied, by imitating the Elizabethans, but by creating a form. Since drama must be popular, he suggested the development of some popular technique, that of the music hall, for instance, or of the Mass. For *Sweeney Agonistes* (1932), an exercise for the closet, he employed the Greeks, jazzed to our capacity by the uses of the music hall. The speedy rhythms, vulgar diction, and hypnotic repetition add horror to an American theme, a bathtub murder, and to those typical Yankees Sweeney, Doris, Krumpacker, and Klipstein. This fragment approaches Eliot's ideal of the many-leveled play with plot for the simple, character and conflict for the more complex, words for the literate, rhythm for the musical, and a meaning, gradually unfolded, for men of sensibility.

Contemptuous of closet and private stage, he realized his ideals more nearly in *Murder in the Cathedral,* which, far from being produced by a little theater, was produced by Canterbury Cathedral and, in America, by the W.P.A. This fine play, one of the best of the thirties, unites good poetry and good theater. From the Greeks came mumbling chorus and the sense of doom, from the morality play the expressionistic tempters, and from the advanced little theater the enlargement from Ibsen's peepholed chamber. Always dramatic in his poetry, Eliot had transferred his talent to the stage. In *The Family Reunion* or Æschylus in modern dress the Eumenides, now working for the Church of England, embody not only the need of expiation but all the evils of family and society that had been suggested in *The Waste Land* and "The Hollow Men." The ultimate integration of Harry, their victim, must be applauded by psychoanalyst and theologian alike. Remarkable verse, combining the flatness of conversation with the relaxed intensity of the *Quartets,* maintains the actual and elevation above it. Too subtle perhaps for the public stage where it was presented and too interior in its climax, the play is redeemed for the vulgar by rhythm, mounting terror, and the reality of the victims. Not least among these attractions is the chorus of aunts and uncles.[24]

24 In *The Quest for Salvation in an Ancient and a Modern Play* (1941), Maud Bodkin compares Eliot with Æschylus. For Eliot's essays on the poetic play see *Selected Essays* (1932) and *The Sacred Wood* (1920).

In *Ash Wednesday* (1930), the best of his religious poems, liturgical incantation and the clear allegorical images he took from Dante objectify a penitential mood and his desire to desire faith. In *Four Quartets* (1943), less purgatorial than heavenly, bare, incantatory statements of time and eternity reveal a feeling that almost redeems Mr. Eliot's Sunday morning service.

Essays Ancient and Modern (1936) announces that the poet has no objection to being called a bigot. Although one may be inclined to separate his bigotry from his poems or, dismissing it, praise them, the two are inseparable and the poems are bigotry's excuse. In bigotry—and for one of his temper nothing less would do—Eliot found the integration a poet needs. The "still point" of the turning *Quartets,* a symbol of God, is also the symbol of this integration. As Yeats's queer system provoked poems, so, after long silence, did Eliot's.

For the Time Being (1944) by W. H. Auden suggests the later work of Eliot. The oratorio is a dramatization of Christian material that proves, whether poetic exercise or profession of faith, that Auden's powers have not been injured by the exile into which, by a kind of reverse lend-lease, he followed Eliot. Although Auden's creed seems Anglican, it has been tempered to his individuality by admixture of Kierkegaard. By this device Auden has improved the pleasure of piety by the assurance of fashion.

During the forties Auden's favorite among the Fellows of Magdalen, C. S. Lewis, became the foremost apologist for Anglicanism. Converted from atheism after a career of brilliant scholarship, he began to deliver lectures and to write tracts, distinguished by logic, wit, and ease, on the case for Christianity. In *The Screwtape Letters* (1942), his cleverest book, one devil advises another upon the promotion of impiety. In his three interplanetary fantasies Lewis uses the frame of H. G. Wells and the manners of Kafka and Michael Innes to dramatize the war of good and evil, matter and spirit. *That Hideous Strength* (1945), the last of these transcendental thrillers, does for our time what John Bunyan did for his.[25]

It is curious that James Joyce, the writer in our time most deeply penetrated by Christianity, was converted from, not to, it. As Cranly observes in *A Portrait of the Artist,* the mind of Stephen Dedalus is saturated with a religion in which he no longer believes. The hero of *Stephen Hero* confirms this observation. "I am," he says, "a product of Catholicism." Even Eliot, hunting heretics, found Joyce orthodox.

The detachment from religion that Joyce thought necessary for art was never as complete as he desired. A tradition that Eliot painfully pursued and almost caught remained Joyce's heritage. His art is good because it is traditional and detached, and difficult for the same reasons. His detachment sometimes amounts to privacy, and his traditionalism is beyond those outside his traditions. *Finnegans Wake,* for example, is permeated with Catholicism. The fall of man and his redemption, sin and repentance, the obsessive presence of Lawrence O'Toole and the other saints, the canonical hours, litanies, prayers, and the formulas of the sacraments compose a private nightmare.

Ulysses provides a symbol as potent for our time as *The Waste Land.* The hunt of Telemachus for Odysseus, repeated by Stephen Dedalus, who has lost both earthly and heavenly father, reflects our longing for support. That his

[25] *The Allegory of Love* (1936) is one of the ornaments of medieval scholarship. Tracts and lectures: *The Problem of Pain* (1940), *Broadcast Talks* (1942), *Beyond Personality* (1944). Romances: *Out of the Silent Planet* (1938), *Perelandra* (1943).

Ruth Pitter has directed her capricious muse to the celebration of Anglicanism: *A Mad Lady's Garland* (1935), *A Trophy of Arms* (1936), *The Spirit Watches* (1940).

hunt for a father should result in Mr. Bloom is unfortunate, but not without parallel.[26] Wiser than most literary men, however, or able to walk alone, Stephen, after drinking his cocoa, rejects his substitute father and departs.

[26] Mr. Bloom symbolizes the father on at least three levels, Homeric, divine, and personal. For Bloom and Jesus see S. Foster Damon: "Odyssey in Dublin," *Hound and Horn,* Fall 1929.

CHAPTER VII

The Forest of Symbols

IN his sonnet "*Correspondances*" Baudelaire speaks of the forest of symbols. It is this Baudelairian forest that the most enterprising French and English poets have been exploring ever since, and from it they have returned with the best as well as the most inscrutable poetry of our time. Among the French pioneers were Rimbaud, Verlaine, and Mallarmé, whose poems guided Valéry, Apollinaire, and the surrealists. Spreading across the Channel in the nineties, symbolism gave the more advanced English poets a new manner and new substance and, after 1910, new method. Oscar Wilde, Arthur Symons, T. S. Eliot, Edith Sitwell, and Dylan Thomas learned much of their art from the symbolist tradition of France. And Yeats, a more important poet, is in a parallel tradition.

Symbolism became dominant in modern poetry because it is adapted to the needs of poets exiled from middle-class society. The best vehicle for the expression of their ingrowing sensibilities and of their tenuous relationships with the world, it is at the same time another, and the most æsthetic, variety of transcendentalism, of the attempt to escape the external, the material, and the Philistine and to soar above them to a more satisfactory plane. To understand the English poets of this tradition it is necessary to know something of the French.[1]

Baudelaire, the father of the symbolist movement, was a decadent, a transcendentalist, and probably the greatest poet of the nineteenth century. On first looking into *Fleurs du Mal* (1857), one is struck by the strangeness and morbidity of the poems. There is, for example, "*La Géante*," in which Baudelaire finds himself living with a giantess, crawling over her enormous knees, and going to sleep "nonchalantly" in the shade of her breasts "like a peaceful hamlet at the foot of a mountain." Lying with his "*affreuse Juive*," he plagues himself with thoughts of ideal beauty. In "*Une Charogne*" a putrescent horse reminds him of another mistress. And there are macabre poems, surpassing those of Poe, whom he adored, and many others that are blasphemous, disgusting, or bizarre.

The "hypocritical reader" was disturbed. Baudelaire was prosecuted and compelled by the judgment of Paris to remove several of the more offensive poems. But later on it became apparent that, far from being depraved, Baudelaire was an idealist who, like Swift, liked to torture himself with what revolted him, who found in ugliness a sort of back door to beauty. Verlaine saw only the "ineffable delicacy" of Baudelaire's poem about the decomposing horse and his "inconsolable nostalgia for the ideal." Later critics have seen a moral and almost Christian Baudelaire. "*Voyage à Cythère*," which at first sight seems merely disgusting, is medieval allegory. The evil flowers of his title appear to have been the seven deadly sins. Filled with two conflicting sentiments, the horror and the ecstasy

[1] Marcel Raymond: *De Baudelaire au surréalisme* (1934). Pierre Martino: *Parnasse et symbolisme* (1925). André Barre: *Le Symbolisme* (1911). Peter Quennell: *Baudelaire and the Symbolists* (1929). Enid Starkie: *Baudelaire* (1933), *Arthur Rimbaud* (1938). Albert Thibaudet: *La Poésie de Stéphane Mallarmé* (1929).

of life, looking at life with the fresh senses of the perpetual convalescent or the child, Baudelaire extracted beauty from horror and eternity from time.

Among Baudelaire's most disturbing poems are the "*Tableaux Parisiens.*" Here, with horror, compassion, and equanimity, he presents the sad, swarming streets of Paris, the garbage carts, rags, sewers, mud, the monstrous old men and women. Similar images fill the prose poems of *Le Spleen de Paris* (1869), where, he says, the growth of enormous cities has given him the "obsessive ideal" of presenting in selected images their "desolating suggestions." "I love you, O infamous capital," he exclaims, ". . . hospital, *lupanars,* purgatory, hell." The "depraved phantasmagoria" of stone, fog, and gaslight composes "the great desert of men." It is plain that to him, as to a later idealist, this desert and this hell represented sin and death. Baudelaire differs from Eliot, however, in contemplating the desert and its creatures with charity.

Baudelaire was not a naturalist presenting catalogues of the infernal metropolis. Far from copying nature, the artist, he says, must select significant images, heighten them, and use them to project his vision. "In certain almost supernatural states of soul," he says in *Journaux intimes,* "the depth of life is revealed in ordinary everyday happenings. Ordinary life then becomes the Symbol." Swedenborg had seen a web of "correspondences" between the worlds of matter and spirit. Following Swedenborg, Baudelaire believed that the symbolic images of his poems accosted the ineffable. But proceeding beyond Swedenborg, he maintained that images from the external world corresponded to his own inner life, so that his poems about Paris were also portraits of himself, formulas for expressing his mind and soul. The meaning of these poems is not their ostensible themes, but the interaction between the symbol and the spiritual or subjective state symbolized. Proceeding still further, Baudelaire maintained in "*Correspondances*" that the senses correspond to one another in such a way that it is possible to hear color and see sound.

The confusion of nature became order, and matter acquired significance. Baudelaire the transcendentalist was appeased and Baudelaire the poet provided with a system of meanings and images that enabled him to employ what he detested and to remain in and out of the world at once. The visible world was only a store of images and signs to which his imagination through the "evocative magic" of words gave place and value. To glorify the cult of images, he says in *Journaux intimes,* became his passion. He was not alone, he felt, for there were Delacroix, whose paintings could be heard, and Wagner, whose music evoked color and color idea.

When correspondences proved insufficient, Baudelaire found relief from the natural in the unnatural. Opium permitted visits to an "artificial paradise." In the landscape of "*Rêve Parisien,*" the record of one of these holidays from nature, no animal or vegetable life injures arrangements of water and mineral, fountains, flights of stairs, and gigantic colonnades. To the disgust of his fellow romantics, he announced in "*Éloge de maquillage*" a preference for artifice. By unnecessary rouge, natural woman becomes supernatural, and by dandyism man can follow her. The dandy, whose outer elegance is the symbol of an inner perfection, is the last champion of human pride against the encroachments of nature and the commonplace.

A dandy in verse as well, Baudelaire was a perfectionist and a craftsman. His contrived effect lies in the contrast between the classical, impeccable, final surface and the romantic interior, between his imperturbable aloofness and his matter. Verlaine, seeing him as the unmoved mover, calls attention to the masterly change of pace and mood in "*Les Petites Vieilles,*" where, after seeming moved for once, the poet deflates himself with a casual "*Avez-vous observé . . . ?*" and follows this with the "phlegmatic impertinence" of "*méditant sur la géometrie.*" Only an artist in full control of his material could have managed such effects, and only a man of profound humanity and imagination could have produced the situation upon which the effects depend. Although his ideas, his feelings, his stately rhythms, his images with their reverberating overtones move the reader, it is the control of the artist that gives his poems their inexplicable glory.

Baudelaire subscribed to the tenets of Théophile Gautier to the extent of praising art for art's sake; and though he did not perfectly illustrate that doctrine in his poems, which are very moral, Baudelaire was acceptable on the whole to the Parnassians, whose longing for "impassibility," plastic and sculptural façades, and pagan themes found no offense in his surface and manner. Paul Verlaine, also on the ultimate slopes of Parnassus, was among the earliest admirers of Baudelaire, from whom he had learned the art of the melancholy evocative landscape and the Parisian nocturne. Into *Fêtes galantes* (1869) Verlaine put tender, gay, and bizarre poems about an imaginary Versailles. "*Colloque sentimental*" is elegantly sad, "*Les Ingénus*" is pure Watteau, and "*Fantoches*" resembles the early poems of Wallace Stevens. because perhaps early Wallace Stevens had read this poem with profit.

Later, under the influence of Rimbaud, "his infernal spouse," Verlaine abandoned the Parnassians and, recapturing the simplicity of ancient songs, bent his efforts toward verbal music and the liberation of metrics from the rules to which Baudelaire and Gautier had remained more or less faithful. "*Art poétique,*" a poetic exposition of liberated metrics, tells of his devotion to music, nuance, tenuous sensation, and to that marriage of the vague and the precise which is suggestive of one knows not what. Illustrating his new rhythms, undulating and broken, "*Il pleure dans mon cœur*" and the other melancholy landscapes of *Romances sans paroles* (1874) are not descriptions of the objective Parnassian world, but internal landscapes, projecting his moods. Although the poems of *Sagesse*, written after his conversion to Catholicism, have a fresh childlike quality, they have proved less interesting than some of the later poems, "*Je suis l'Empire à la fin de la décadence*," for example, and the celebrated "*Parsifal*."

To the young of the 1880's and '90's, Verlaine was first of all a legendary bohemian who by his life illustrated disregard of middle-class convention. For a time he attracted the young symbolists, who found his sadness and his interior landscapes congenial. Chiefly, however, they hailed him as a liberator of metrics until, learning of his debt to the more considerable liberties of Rimbaud, they transferred their praises to the makers of free verse. What made Verlaine great, his original pure lyric gift, was inimitable and for this reason comparatively ignored by the followers of schools.

Commencing as poet in 1870 at the age of fifteen, Rimbaud wrote at first in the Parnassian manner, then in the manner of Baudelaire, then in the manner of Rimbaud. His early poems, filled with outrageous comparisons, grotesque rhymes, sudden shifts in tone, are the poems, as Marcel Raymond says, of a bad boy, but, it is clear, one of a superior kind of badness. "*Comédie en trois baisers*" (1870), with its magical phrase "*les grands arbres indiscrets*," and "*Mes petites amoureuses*" (1871), with its strange technical and colloquial words, prove that his rebellion was also directed at poetic proprieties. By 1871 he had reached maturity. "*Le Cœur volé*," which appears to be a frivolous romp among neologisms and slang ("*ithyphallique et pioupiesque*"), is regarded by Enid Starkie as the terrible record of a terrible experience with the amorous soldiers of France. If her interpretation is right, this poem anticipates by its indirection the symbolist ideal of the eighties. "*Les Chercheuses de poux,*" another poem of the same year, is even more complex. The elegant louse-hunt, the suave, malign tone of the poet, the ambiguous atmosphere, all serve to produce a portrait of young Rimbaud and a comment upon society so delicate that it could not be stated.

These ironies were not impalpable enough to detain Rimbaud for long. Hungry for experiences, he became, like Baudelaire, a "*voyant*" or visionary. By magical correspondence and incantation he proposed to cheat his senses and rise above them. Not Swedenborg but Eliphas Lévi, the Christian cabbalist, the magus who was to lead so many tired Frenchmen and Englishmen to more spiritual places, led Rimbaud not only to the idea of correspondence but to the idea of salvation. By occult, Eastern power he hoped to restore the materialistic West to its primitive glory.

A letter of May 15, 1871 is Rimbaud's manifesto. "The poet," he says, "makes himself a visionary through a long, immense and reasoned derangement of all the senses." With the discipline of an ascetic, subjecting himself to every form of degradation, he must confound his senses until in their confusion they can surprise the unknown. In a special language "of the soul and for the soul, summing up all, perfumes, sounds, colors," he will suggest his visions or state their formulas. The result of this transcendental plan is great poetry.

In the sonnet on the vowels, a playful, serious poem, Rimbaud uses infant memories of a colored alphabet for Lévi's incantation. Correspondences of color and sound bring him face to face with worlds, angels, and violet eyes. Under the symbolism of a voyage on, above, and under the sea, "*Bateau ivre*" expresses romantic impatience with limits and almost mystical desire. Baudelaire's "*Voyage*" approaches the "unknown"; Rimbaud's plunges through its immaterial scenery. A drunken boat is the proper vehicle for the course he sets. Rimbaud had never seen the sea. His imagery came from Coleridge, Jules Verne, and, above all, his own imagination. Shelley's Alastor, desiring the infinite, also enters his boat, passes through sea, river, whirlpool, and putrid marsh. The resemblance means, however, that Shelley and Rimbaud were of the same tradition. Rimbaud differs from Shelley in stature and from Coleridge in method. While the voyage itself seems to be the subject of "The Ancient Mariner," Rimbaud's voyage is the symbol for something else.

Illuminations, written in 1872 and 1873, is a deeper voyage into the unknown. The title suggests fireworks or mystical raptures. Rimbaud was not a mystic, however, but a magus, a disciple of Lévi, who used incantation to compel what mystics are given. Like the poems of A. E., those of Rimbaud are sometimes descriptions of what he saw; but more often they are formulas, like the words of a magician, to create what he could see. The incoherent flood of images that his method released is like nothing previously recorded save for the Apocalypse, perhaps, or the records of literate madmen.

The poems in verse, though simple in appearance, are enigmatic. The poems in prose are even more ambiguous and more interesting. Some years earlier Baudelaire had invented a poetic prose, which he described as "musical without rhythm or rhyme, supple and bold enough to adapt itself to the lyric movements of the soul, to the undulations of reverie, to the somersaults of the consciousness." Some of his prose poems record his opium dreams, but Rimbaud's go further. His prose poems present hallucinations, dreams, infant memories, and all the rich nonsense of the unconscious. In one of his nightmares Mme X "established a piano on the Alps." *Une Saison en Enfer* (1873), his spiritual autobiography, explains her conduct:

> I discovered the color of the vowels. . . . I discovered a poetic language available to all the senses. I reserved the rights of translation. . . . I noted the inexpressible. . . . I accustomed myself to hallucination: I saw a mosque in the place of a factory, a set of drums played by angels . . . a parlor at the bottom of a lake. . . . Then I explained my magical sophistries with the hallucination of words.

Convinced of failure, Rimbaud abandoned poetry. Stéphane Mallarmé, also plagued with a sense of failure, persisted. Although impressed by the discrepancy between his ideal and its poetic realization, he resigned himself to "the grief of the inexplicable Penultimate." The famous poem of the swan in ice symbolizes his frustration. He need not have worried. "*Hérodiade*" and "*L'Après-midi d'un faune*," symphonies of indirections, exceed the Penultimate. To Mallarmé a poem was a means of communicating between matter and idea, exhausting matter, image, and word in the process until only idea was left. Unaware of verbal alchemy, the reader might take the poem at its face value as if it were about a faun or Salomé. The later poems, however, have small face value to mistake. In place of palpable subject "*Prose* (*pour des Esseintes*)," for example, offers impalpable vibrations.

To do their transcendental job, words had to be relieved of their normal meanings, removed from their familiar contexts, until, purified, they could provoke reveries, resonances, ineffable suggestions. Poems built by meticulous craft from words deprived of syntax could suggest things too fugitive for expression and meanings at once precise and multiple. Poems built in this way were absolute. Free from meaning in the usual sense, they were also free from time, chance, life, passion, and matter. A symphonic relationship among the parts of the poem took the place of comprehensible relationships with external things. The poem, said Mallarmé, "is a mystery to which the reader must hunt the key." Abandoning the hope of a single interpretation, he must discover the main images, observe the effect upon them of the peripheral images, and guess the idea generated by their interaction. Mallarmé explained these matters to his disciples on Tuesday evenings.

For many years Mallarmé, Verlaine, and Rimbaud remained relatively unknown. But in 1884 their fame began. Turning away from naturalism in *A rebours,* Huysmans discovered Mallarmé; and Verlaine in *Poètes maudits,* advertised Rimbaud, Corbière, Villiers, and Verlaine. These poets immediately became the idols of the Decadents, a self-conscious group, who published the magazine *Le Décadent.* In *La Revue Wagnérienne* others began to advance the cult of Wagner and of poetry as music.[2]

But their idols were individuals, hardly representing a tendency, still less a school. That would never do. The younger poets founded a school, elected themselves and their elders to membership, and, after a few unsuccessful tries, named one another symbolists. The name was not inappropriate for Baudelaire, Mallarmé, and Rimbaud, who held the doctrine of correspondence in common; it was almost appropriate for Verlaine; and it served to cover youth with a glamour so thick that the middle class was baffled again. Defining symbolism in his manifesto of September 18, 1886, Jean Moréas followed Mallarmé:

> Enemy of explanation, of declamation, of false sensibility, of objective description, symbolist poetry tries to clothe the Idea in a palpable form, which, nevertheless, is

[2] *Les Déliquescences d'Adoré Floupette* (1885), parodies of Mallarmé, Verlaine, and Laforgue by Vicaire and Beauclair, was good publicity.

> not an end in itself, but which, while serving to express the Idea, remains subject to it. The Idea in its turn does not let itself be seen without sumptuous trains of exterior analogies; for the essential character of symbolic art consists in never going to the conception of the Idea in itself. Thus in this art, pictures of nature, actions of men, concrete phenomena are not there for their own sake, but as simple appearances destined to represent their esoteric affinities with primordial Ideas.

"It is true," observed Anatole France, "that M. Moréas explains symbolism, but it is also true that his explanation is not easy to follow."[3]

Moréas, René Ghil, Stuart Merrill, Gustave Kahn, and the others praised and wrote "symbolist" poems. Sometimes the symbol was an image, like Mallarmé's swan, or a system of images; sometimes it was a suggestive rhythm or combination of sounds; and sometimes it was a whole poem, a symphony of sounds, images, rhythms approximating the condition of music. To be symbolist was to be subjective, oblique, bizarre, difficult, transcendental, Wagnerian, "*anglais,*" or even symbolic.

With the help of the English tradition the symbolists, going further than earlier French romantics, freed themselves from the domination of the rules. But except for a poem here or there, the symbolists do not resemble the Englishmen and Americans who assisted them toward liberty; for coming after the climax of their tradition, they transformed what they took from their predecessors. The decadence and individuality of the symbolists permitted later Englishmen to come to them with a sense of discovery for aid in remaking the English tradition or escaping it.

The example of Walt Whitman and rebellion against the rules led the symbolists to free verse, which may be

[3] See Moréas: *Les Premières Armes du Symbolisme* (1889), for the symbolist manifestoes and the resultant controversy.

defined as rhythm responsive to mood, or the attempt to give words their musical value, or what is left after the rules of prosody have been abolished. Rimbaud appears to have been the first to use it. Verlaine less adventurously followed him, but Mallarmé, like Baudelaire before him, remained technically conservative until near the end of his life when in "*Un Coup de dés*" he anticipated the vagaries of E. E. Cummings. Laforgue, Kahn, Dujardin, and Whitmanesque Verhaeren all availed themselves of metrical liberty. Gustave Kahn, their theoretician, defined and justified the new poetic instrument.

With Maeterlinck and Villiers, symbolism entered the theater. New little magazines published new little poets. By 1895, however, there was some falling away from the symbolist ideal. Moréas turned to classicism. Verhaeren, after following Baudelaire through "hallucinated countrysides" and nightmare cities, began to celebrate factories, railways, and power. By 1900 symbolism was pronounced dead, but despite repeated pronouncements by the best authorities it maintained a hidden vitality and made appearances. Paul Valéry emerged as Mallarmé's most faithful disciple, as mysterious as his master and as great a poet. Guillaume Apollinaire revived the most bizarre excesses of the Decadents and invented the word "surrealism." In the twenties surrealists rediscovered the tradition of Rimbaud and Lautréamont. Exploring the unconscious, André Breton and Paul Éluard returned with metaphors.

II

The poets of England who followed the symbolists took from them what their times, their circumstances, and their capacities permitted. From the 1870's some English poets were aware, and later more were aware, that the way to revive their exhausted tradition was the way of the French.

During the nineties the English knew something of all the symbolists.[4] Not all, however, had news for Englishmen; for some Frenchmen, further advanced in method, manner, and decadence, were beyond the comprehension of their Victorian admirers. The English saw part at least of what Baudelaire meant and profited by what they saw. They admired, misunderstood, and translated Mallarmé. They translated and imitated Verlaine. Some knew of Rimbaud, Laforgue, Verhaeren, and Merrill. And to some Maeterlinck seemed what the world of Darwin required. From each they took what they could in response to their needs, and English poetry or some of it became exotic, decadent, and new.

To the *Spectator* in 1862 Swinburne contributed the first review in English of Baudelaire's poems. Sadistic, Lesbian "Dolores" and "Anactoria," which seem to owe something to Baudelaire's "*Femmes damnées,*" are so successfully transposed into the lilies and languors of Swinburne that the debt is not immediately apparent. "*Ave atque Vale,*" an elegy on Baudelaire, expresses Swinburne's mistaken conviction that Baudelaire was a kindred spirit.[5]

Late in the seventies George Moore, who had fled the English Philistines for the bohemians of Montmartre, met Villiers and, through him, Mallarmé. Moore was fascinated with *Fleurs du Mal.* His *Flowers of Passion* (1878) were plucked, as the title confesses, from Baudelaire's wicked garden. "These bloomless blossoms," Moore announces, are "symbol flowers." But it is hard for a reader today to detect either symbolism or Baudelaire in the boyish imitations of Swinburne that, at first glance, seem to compose the volume. It is in the morbid poems on corpses, prostitutes, and Lesbians that Baudelaire's mark is dimly appar-

[4] Ruth Temple's forthcoming book is the authoritative treatment of symbolist influence upon the English before 1900.

[5] Georges Lafourcade: *Swinburne* (1932).

ent, in "The Corpse," for example, "Ode to a Dead Body," or "A Sapphic Dream."

> Wondering I gaze upon each lineament
> Defaced by worms and swollen in decay,
> And watch the rat-gnawed golden ringlets play.

As Moore considered another corpse, that of a prostitute this time, his memory of Baudelaire, passing through the Victorian tradition, produced these lines:

> Poor shameful lips! that never knew a kiss
> Of innocence, I wis.

In *Confessions of a Young Man* (1888) Moore tells what Baudelaire's "poisonous blossoms" meant to him. "The children of the nineteenth century go to you, O Baudelaire, and having tasted of your deadly delight, all hope of repentance is vain. Flowers, beautiful in your sublime decay, I press you to my lips." That is not what Baudelaire meant, but what Moore needed and what he found; and it pleased him to think that Baudelaire disbelieved in goodness, truth, and life itself. It is not surprising that a reviewer of *Flowers of Passion* called Moore "a bestial bard." With the publication of *Pagan Poems* (1881) his imitations of Baudelaire fortunately ceased, but not his interest in the symbolists.

Moore tells in *Confessions of a Young Man* of his acquaintance with René Ghil and Gustave Kahn, of his admiration of Kahn's "strange, abnormal, and unhealthy" poems, two of which he quotes, and of the decadent charm of Verlaine's *Fêtes galantes.* He quotes the sonnet on Parsifal. Moore had enjoyed the talk at Mallarmé's on Tuesday evenings, but he confesses that he never enjoyed the master's poems. "*L'Après-midi*" seemed absurdly obscure, though lucid in comparison with the "brain-curdling enigmas" of the later poems. He knew that these poems were symbolist. "What is symbolism?" he asks. "Vulgarly speaking, saying the opposite to what you mean." And he proceeds to give an account of the making of a symbolist poem in which each unexplained image stands for an idea. This pedestrian, gay, and all too literal interpretation of Mallarmé's method is balanced by Moore's translation of two of Mallarmé's prose poems, which are interpreted as "aberrations of a refined mind, distorted with hatred of the commonplace." Longing for decadence as an antidote to the commonplace or as irritant to the "hypocritical reader," Moore saw only the decadence of the decadent French.

It was probably from his friend René Ghil and from Baudelaire's "*Correspondances*" that Moore learned that confusion of the senses which gives an inappropriately symbolist air to *A Drama in Muslin* (1886), his novel about the superior daughters of Ireland, whose dancing at the Shelbourne Hotel seems an "allegro movement of odours . . . interrupted suddenly by the garlicky andante, deep as the pedal notes of an organ, that the perspiring armpits of a fat chaperon exhaled slowly." As Moore had been the first in England with a volume of Baudelairian poems, so he was the first in England with French synesthesia. He was the first to read and praise Huysmans's *A rebours* and to imitate it; and he was the first to write critical essays on Verlaine, Rimbaud, and Laforgue.[6] Moore is important less for what he said about symbolism or for what he did with it in his novels and poems than for his services in making it known to literate Englishmen.

Moore's guide and adviser in Paris was Édouard Dujardin, editor of the *Revue Wagnérienne*, pioneer in free verse, and author of *Les Lauriers sont coupés*. With Dujardin, Moore visited Verlaine the day he wrote "*Parsi-*

[6] *Impressions and Opinions* (1891).

fal," and with Dujardin he shared an admiration for Laforgue's *Moralités légendaires.* Dujardin led Moore through the mazes of the symbolist reviews, told him about Wagner, and later on, out of his considerable Biblical scholarship, provided Moore with material for *The Brook Kerith* (1916). In *Conversations in Ebury Street* (1924), expressing his debt to his friend, Moore celebrates their wanderings through symbolist Paris.[7]

Oscar Wilde knew of the French almost as soon as Moore. While still an undergraduate at Oxford in the late seventies, he incurred the loathing of honest men by talking of Baudelaire and the beauty of evil. *Poems* (1881), though generally in the English romantic tradition, shows some traces of Baudelaire, especially "*Impression du Matin,*" one of the few successful poems in the volume. This clear, visual piece about a harlot confuses Whistler's landscapes with Baudelaire's infernal city. It was by following the Baudelairian line of this poem that Wilde was destined to improve himself until during the nineties he attained the status of minor poet. "The Harlot's House," written during the eighties, combines the macabre, the urban, and the grotesque with a sudden, disconcerting prettiness, more horrible than what preceded it. From this discord comes surprise and with it poetry. Even the bizarre rhymes, which in Wilde commonly occur for their own sake, conspire toward the intended effect. He had captured the externals of Baudelaire, and he was no less successful in "The Sphinx" (1894). Taking theme and images from Flaubert, Huysmans, and Baudelaire, he devoted his exotic verbalism and imagery to an evocation of theatrical evil. But his purple corridors (rhyming with moaning mandragores), his basilisks, nenuphars, gilded galiots, and monstrous hippopotami somehow escape absurdity; for though one may smile, one is impressed

[7] Moore's letters to Dujardin, 1886–1922, were published in 1929.

against all judgment by the density of the atmosphere surrounding his "lovely seneschal . . . half woman and half animal." That such an air can be exhaled by the stanza of *In Memoriam* deepens one's impression. Perhaps the poem does belong to what T. S. Eliot dismissed as the dead-cat aspect of Baudelaire, the only one Wilde was fitted by nature to isolate, but his cat exhales an equivocal scent, the more compelling for its isolation.

To Wilde, Baudelaire, a symbol of sin, sensuousness, and exoticism, meant beauty separated from morality. A portent to frighten Philistines, he is paraded through *Intentions* (1891). Criminal Wainwright of "Pen, Pencil, and Poison" becomes, like Baudelaire, a "delightfully artificial person." Throughout these essays Baudelaire's artifice or Whistler's surpasses nature. To Baudelaire *Dorian Gray* (1891) owes the dandyism of Lord Henry, the opium, and the Wagnerian music. But it is, of course, to Huysmans's *A rebours,* Lord Henry's favorite book, that Dorian owes his symphonies of flowers and odors. Recognizing these origins, a reviewer described *Dorian Gray* as "a tale spawned from the leprous literature of the French decadents—a poisonous book, the atmosphere of which is heavy with the mephitic odours of moral and spiritual putrefaction." Wilde had realized his intentions.

Wilde's most thoroughly symbolist work, *Salomé,* published in 1893, is the most successful approximation of symbolism to that time in England.[8] Wilde wrote it with the advice and correction of several symbolists with whom he enjoyed a kind of friendship. Paul Fort, who was managing the symbolist Théâtre d'Art, helped him. So did Stuart Merrill, Marcel Schwob, and Adolphe Retté,

[8] Wilde wrote this one-act play in French in 1891. The English translation is by Lord Alfred Douglas. Wilde's Salomé is modeled upon Flaubert's Salammbô, Laforgue's Salomé in *Moralités légendaires,* and the Hérodias of Flaubert and of Mallarmé.

a poet who was assisting Fort in his production of Maeterlinck's *Aveugles.* With such aid it is little wonder that Wilde achieved the authentic manner, nor is it surprising that after the British censor had denied Sarah Bernhardt a license to produce the play in London, it was accepted (in 1896) by Lugné-Poe for his Théâtre de l'Œuvre. This theater, founded in idealistic reaction against Antoine's naturalistic Théâtre Libre, was the citadel, if so definite a word may be used, of symbolist drama. Here Lugné-Poe had offered Maeterlinck, Hauptmann, Strindberg, and symbolical Ibsen. The sound of wild ducks, of footsteps down empty corridors, and of sunken bells surrounded this spiritual place.

Maeterlinck, who started as a symbolist poet in 1889, was the first to succeed in transporting the symbolist ideal to the stage. For a long time Mallarmé had dreamed of a theater in which a union of music, poetry, and gesture could be kept from the audience by a veil. Maeterlinck's talents did not extend to music or poetry, but he did provide a sort of veil in the dreamlike atmosphere, the circumambient fears, and that uncertainty of time, place, and character which seemed to favor the infinite. Since the finite cannot depict the infinite or words express the inexpressible, Maeterlinck undertook to suggest the infinite and the inexpressible by childish words, overtones, and silences. Rebelling in his turn against external reality, he suggested interior and superior realities. Critics praised his *Intruse* (1890) for suggesting death without presenting it on the stage, and they saw in *Les Aveugles* (1890), *Les Sept Princesses* (1891), and *Pelléas et Mélisande* (1892) the ceremonies of a future religion. The symbolist theater, like a symbolist poem, concerned something else than it concerned.

Wilde studied *Les Sept Princesses* and *La Princesse Maleine* as well, but his sensuous and extravagant nature interfered with a faithful reproduction of Maeterlinck's manner. Exotic jewels, green flowers, white peacocks, mouths like "the red cries of trumpets," and the other furniture are Wilde's own or else Flaubert's, Laforgue's, or Mallarmé's. Apprehending Mallarmé's technique of making each ornament and gesture suggest more than it could, Wilde made *Salomé* as symbolist in its degree as the work of the master. Using Maeterlinck's simple dialogue with overtones and his habit of understatement, except, of course, in passages where sensuousness overcame him, Wilde evoked what was not presented, the problem of hedonism, Jesus, and man's regeneration. These moral and religious implications arise from a symphony of their opposites. Wilde's symbolism, crude compared with Mallarmé's, is not inferior to Maeterlinck's. Take, for instance, the behavior of the moon. At first merely strange, it becomes hysterical, turns red as blood, then hides behind a veil as a cold wind passes by. Observing these things, Hérode says to comfort himself: "One must not find symbols in everything one sees." But in a symbolist play one must. Moreover, the sense of impending horror, the beating of unseen and unheard wings, and the cistern show how well Wilde had learned the lesson of the symbolist theater. On the whole his play has weathered time as well as any of Maeterlinck's, though perhaps that is not saying very much.

Maeterlinck was also responsible for *Vistas* (1894) by William Sharp, who, since he was addicted to mysticism, found the Belgian congenial.[9] In 1891 Sharp read *Les Aveugles* and *La Princesse Maleine* and, blinded by the mist toward which he had been groping, proceeded to compose closet dramas. "Finis," the first "interlude" of *Vistas,* is a dialogue in Maeterlinck's most childlike man-

[9] In 1892 Sharp visited Verlaine and Moréas. In March 1892 his article on Maeterlinck appeared in the *Academy.*

ner between a soul and a phantom lost in "an obscure wood" through which nameless terrors sigh. Nothing is evoked beyond atmosphere and mystery, which deepen when the soul of the soul's wife strangles the soul. "A Northern Night," concerning two lovers in a tower, is also filled with things that are not there. Always hearing noises, the lovers ask: "What is it that is moving so softly to and fro?" No one knows.

Through the work of Arthur Symons symbolism reached a wider public. His criticism interpreted the French to the readers of magazines, his translations gave some idea of the nature of symbolist poetry, and his original verses followed the French as well as they were able. Coming closely on the heels of Moore, Symons began in the early nineties to write his essays on French poets, most of whom he had met.[10] He had attended Mallarmé's seminar and, suitably impressed, could not wait to tell the news to England. In "The Decadent Movement in Literature" (1893) he says that though the literary movement of France is variously called symbolist, impressionist, and decadent, decadent alone suits Verlaine's "exquisite depravity of style," Mallarmé's symbols, by which the "deeper meaning of things" is obscured, and the deliberate singularity of Moréas.

The Symbolist Movement in Literature (1899), where the word is symbolist, is Symons's masterpiece. Though there is little understanding of Rimbaud, who had nothing to say to Englishmen of the nineties, the essays on Verlaine, Huysmans, and Maeterlinck are adequate, and the essay on Mallarmé is excellent. This and the introduction, which remains the best English survey of symbolism, give the book its value.[11]

[10] These essays are reprinted in *Studies in Prose and Verse* (1904), *Dramatis Personæ* (1923), and *Figures of Several Centuries* (1916).

[11] This collection also includes essays on Villiers, Laforgue, and Nerval.

Symons's translation of the last part of "*Hérodiade*" leaves much to be desired, but it must be remembered that Mallarmé is untranslatable. With the poems from Verlaine's *Fêtes galantes* and the melancholy song from *Romances sans paroles* Symons was more successful. Later he turned to Baudelaire, and for remaking him into something out of *A rebours* deserved and received the rebuke of Eliot. The ungrateful critic, however, had forgotten that he owed his first acquaintance with symbolism to this imperfect interpreter.

Symons wrote little about Baudelaire during the nineties, but he modeled his own verses on what he could assimilate from that poet. At their best they are wicked and bizarre, and at their worst sentimental. The favorite themes—opium, city landscapes, derelicts of the streets, alcoves, and morbid mistresses—are Baudelaire's.[12] His too is that love of artifice confessed in "*Maquillage,*" a poem in praise of rouge and powder. "Why," Symons asked the indignant Wordsworthians, "should we write exclusively about the natural blush, if the delicately acquired blush of rouge has any attraction for us?" As for him, he preferred perfume to new-mown hay, gaslight to sunlight, and city to country. Amid these delights of artifice he paused to taste audible odors and other confusions of the senses.

Although these verses were inspired by his idea of France, they belong in diction and sentiment to the Victorian tradition. Under the Baudelairian rouge he continued to "swoon in ecstasy divine" and, when he drank, to "drain the winepress' fruitage up." But it is difficult

[12] "To One in Alienation" is a version of the "*affreuse Juive.*" "City Nights" and "At the Cavour" are scenes from the infernal city. "The Old Women" is a sentimental version of "*Les Petites Vieilles.*" Other poems show the effects of Verlaine and Mallarmé. See *Collected Poems* (1902).

During the nineties Theodore Wratislaw, Lord Alfred Douglas, and Victor Plarr followed Symons and Wilde in imitations of the French.

for a minor poet who finds his tradition exhausted to place himself in a more advanced tradition. Later poets with his help and example were better able to do what he attempted.

Ernest Dowson, a finer poet than Symons, was also indebted to France. The famous poem on Cynara transposes Baudelaire's "*affreuse Juive,*" and many of Dowson's most fastidious pieces reproduce the autumnal music of Verlaine. From him Dowson learned to divest his verse of moral, social, and philosophical preoccupations and by all the skills of prosody to perfect his isolated moods.[13]

Like others in the nineties, Dowson understood Verlaine because that Frenchman was the most English of the symbolists. What made his poetry novel in France made it familiar in England. Moreover, he visited England in 1893, lectured at Oxford and London, and while staying with Symons, met the English poets.[14] Thoroughly comprehensible, he was decadent enough to be attractive, and his disreputable life was another point in his favor with those trying to forget or annoy the middle class.

John Gray's translations from Verlaine, Baudelaire, and Rimbaud show command of decadence. Even the malign early manner of Rimbaud, now first attempted, survives the process. Gray's own excellent poems in *Silverpoints* (1893) are very decadent. "*Les Demoiselles de Sauve*" combines the elegance of *Fêtes galantes* with a bizarre lusciousness. "The Barber" exceeds in preciousness all previous celebrations of artifice. After such delicate excesses it is as well, perhaps, that John Gray left his world for the priesthood.

Aubrey Beardsley's *Under the Hill* (1896) is the cli-

[13] "*Colloque Sentimental*" and "Spleen" are translations from Verlaine. *Pierrot of the Minute,* a poetic play, approaches the manner and tone of *Fêtes galantes.*

[14] In the *Savoy,* April 1896, Verlaine describes his visit to England and interprets the French poets.

max, in England at least, of decadent artifice. This prose fragment, which Arthur Symons printed in the *Savoy,* presents "blond trousers," "intelligent curls," "little mutinies of ruffle and cravat," and little else. The model for this arabesque is the *Moralités légendaires* of Laforgue, whose mixture of the bizarre, the humorous, and the precious Beardsley was enabled by nature to improve.[15] Whereas Laforgue's prose sketches burlesque the legends of Salomé, Hamlet, and Lohengrin, Beardsley's improvement plays with the Wagnerian conceit of Tannhäuser and Venus.

As a critic of symbolists Edmund Gosse was second only to Symons. In 1875 Gosse had met Mallarmé at Swinburne's home in Chelsea, and from that time maintained a kind of uneasy friendship with the "eloquent and mysterious" poet, whose "*Après-midi*" he ventured to paraphrase in prose. During the nineties he composed many essays on the French. Free from any taint of decadence and thoroughly British, he condescended a little to these foreigners. In 1895, accompanied by Henry Harland, he went to Paris on a decadent-hunt and, ascending the boulevard Saint-Michel, looked into each café. There was Jean Moréas at his table and there Verlaine at his (in a clean shirt), speaking "with a veiled utterance, difficult for me to follow." Everywhere he heard verses he could not understand and could not have understood had he been a Frenchman.[16] This humor reappears in his obituary on "poor, charming Mallarmé." Although Gosse

[15] Aside from this, Laforgue had little effect on men of the nineties, and Rimbaud was beyond the comprehension of most. But T. Sturge Moore in *The Vinedresser* (1899) made an excellent translation of "*Les Chercheuses de poux.*" His "Response to Rimbaud's Later Manner," *Poems,* Vol. II (1931–3), is an excellent parody. Moore also adapted poems of Baudelaire and Valéry. At his best, Moore is an excellent poet.

[16] *Savoy,* April 1896. His other essays on the French were reprinted in *French Profiles* (1905). His paraphrase of Mallarmé is in *Questions at Issue* (1893).

discusses Mallarmé's method with some understanding, he deplores his effect upon the young, whom he has driven to nonsense and affectation. It is to Gosse's credit, however, that in his essay on Samain he separates the Satanism of Baudelaire, which up to then had preoccupied the English, from that lofty severity which "his horrors at first concealed." It is to Gosse's credit, moreover, that he failed to confuse the symbolists with Donne. A lesser critic perhaps than T. S. Eliot, Gosse was a greater scholar.[17]

Symbolism was more cosmopolitan than most suspected. Although the English preferred him as a social critic, Ibsen, as Frenchmen knew, was also a symbolist, and so were Gabriele d'Annunzio and Stefan George, not to mention the Russians. First in the field, Frenchmen attracted Englishmen first, and for years monopolized their attention. Taking quick looks and sometimes mistaking what they saw, the English poets of the nineties were content with exotic surfaces. Few if any of their poems are symbolist according to Mallarmé's ideal or the prescription of Moréas, but many of them show what Eugene Lee-Hamilton in his sonnet on Baudelaire calls "the gorgeous iridescence of decay." These are the issue of the marriage, unhappy as yet, of exhausted English romanticism with French romantic decadence.

The French to whom the English aspired were great poets and the aspirers small. Unable to write great poems, they succeeded, however, in spreading a novel conception of the poem as a self-contained, harmonic system, remote from society, philosophy, and politics. They expanded the themes of poetry to include the ugly, the disgusting, and the bizarre. They used theme and tone as weapons against the Philistines. But the Philistines, turning at last, used the exposure of Oscar Wilde, whose

[17] Gosse's life of Donne (1899) had almost as much to do as Grierson's edition (1912) with the vogue of metaphysical poetry in our time.

association with France was notorious, to disparage the symbolist tradition. Whether or not social pressure succeeded, symbolism or its externals, so carefully fostered in England for more than a decade, expired around 1900, to be resurrected only after ten years of triumphant convention. But the minor poets and the critics of the nineties had done their work, and it was on foundations they established that poets and critics of greater capacity were to build. The generation of 1910, desiring in turn to remake the romantic tradition, captured what had eluded the grasp of the nineties.

The portrait of Enoch Soames in Max Beerbohm's *Seven Men* (1919) provided an epitaph for this decade. Taking his absinthe at the Café Royal, Soames wrote a book of incomprehensible essays called *Negations* in imitation perhaps of Mallarmé's *Divagations*. *Fungoids,* the strange poems Soames wrote in imitation of the French, were generally neglected. In pity for this symbolist, Beerbohm quotes several poems from *Fungoids,* among them:

> Pale tunes irresolute
> And traceries of old sounds
> Blown from a rotted flute
> Mingle with noise of cymbals rouged with rust,
> Nor not strange forms and epicene
> Lie bleeding in the dust. . . .

"Nor not," that exquisite violation of grammar, reminded him of Mallarmé.

III

When Arthur Symons, dedicating his *Symbolist Movement in Literature* to William Butler Yeats, called his Irish friend "the chief representative of that movement in our country," he meant a general European movement of which the French were leaders. Later critics have been less precise. C. M. Bowra in his *Heritage of Symbolism* (1943) assumes that Yeats is heir to the French. Joseph Hone, also accepting Yeats as heir to the French, asserts in his *Life of W. B. Yeats* (1943) that Yeats was familiar with the "*Hérodiade*" of Villiers de l'Isle Adam, an assertion that would carry more weight if Mallarmé had not written it and if Yeats had been familiar with it. These critics, whose confusions suggest only that the matter is confusing, may be forgiven for their desire to impose cause, effect, and order upon something that seems to deny these satisfactions.

Yeats was a symbolist. That much is clear. But it is also clear that his knowledge of French was so slight that he was unable to read the difficult poems to which he is supposed to be indebted. His French, which he picked up here and there without much benefit of schooling, was adequate for adapting Ronsard's sonnet "When You Are Old" unless, of course, he had found an English version. "Ephemera," another early poem, resembles Verlaine's "*Colloque sentimental.*" Ronsard and Verlaine, however, are comparatively simple, and neither could have become the basis for a system of symbolism such as Yeats was to devise.

The case for *Axël* by Villiers de l'Isle Adam is stronger. Probably between 1890 and 1892 Yeats read this play slowly and laboriously, for, as he says, his French was very poor. "That play seemed all the more profound," he adds in the preface he wrote for an English translation of *Axël* in 1925, "because I was never quite certain that I had read a page correctly." On February 26, 1894 he went to Paris to see the production of *Axël* at the Théâtre Montparnasse, in company with Maud Gonne, who assisted his memory by explaining the words of the actors. She or another helped him through the almost surrealist obscurities of Jarry's *Ubu roi* at the symbolist Théâtre de l'Œuvre in 1896. On his return from Paris in 1894, Yeats reviewed *Axël* in the April *Bookman* as part of the spiritual reaction of his time against science, externality, and the realism of Zola and Ibsen. Yeats saw no hope of a London production of this transcendental play, for the public was ready only for Pinero and Jones. That the reading of *Axël* had a lasting effect upon Yeats is proved by "Rosa Alchemica" and "Out of the Rose," short stories of the nineties. And his symbolic play *The Shadowy Waters* (1900) is a translation of *Axël* into nautical terms.

Aside from *Axël* and a number of treatises on the occult, there is no available evidence that Yeats read anything in French. But he was acquainted with the plays of Maeterlinck in English translation. Although he was less enthusiastic about Maeterlinck's plays and essays than about *Axël,* he regarded them as significant protests against the external, and he was fascinated with Maeterlinck's repeated symbols of mysterious intruders, lighthouses, and wells in the woods.[18]

With the other symbolists Yeats was less familiar. In 1894 he visited Verlaine in the rue Saint-Jacques and spoke with him in English, "for I had explained the poverty of my French." They talked of *Axël* and of Maeterlinck. When he met Stuart Merrill in Paris, they talked not about poetry but about socialism, toward which both temporarily inclined. But at this time, perhaps, Merrill undertook the translation into French of three of Yeats's poems.[19] Maud Gonne and William Sharp conducted

[18] *L'Intruse* was produced in London, January 1892; the other plays were produced and published in London during the nineties. Yeats reviewed Sutro's translation of *Aglavaine et Sélysette* for the *Bookman,* September 1897. Casual references to Maeterlinck occur in Yeats's essays and reviews from 1894.

[19] Yeats tells of his visit to Verlaine in the *Savoy,* April 1896. His essay concerns Verlaine's character and life, not his poetry. Marjorie Henry:

Yeats among the French during the nineties; and in later years Iseult Gonne, Maud's daughter, took their place. It was she who kept Yeats up to date, reading and translating for him poems of Claudel, Péguy, and Valéry, none of which seem to have had the slightest effect on his work.

Yeats managed to supplement these inconsiderable contacts with France during the late nineties through his friendship with Arthur Symons, his next-door neighbor in the Temple and fellow member of the Rhymers' Club. As he finished them, Symons read Yeats his translations from Verlaine and Mallarmé. Yeats was impressed, he tells in his *Autobiography,* with Symons's selection from Mallarmé's "*Hérodiade,*" which increased his own inclination toward an art separated from circumstance, character, and "everything heterogeneous and casual," toward a poetry as unlike that of the Victorians as possible, but like the self-contained, socially isolated, and integrated poetry of Mallarmé. These translations, Yeats continues, "may have given elaborate form" to his *Wind among the Reeds* (1899); and he will never know, he adds, how much his theory and practice owe them. It is possible, as Yeats suggests, that the verses of Symons had these effects. It must be remembered, however, that Symons's translation from "*Hérodiade*" is not a good one and that any elaborateness communicated by it is from Symons, not Mallarmé. But the case for theory is a stronger one; for it must be supposed that Symons, who understood the theories of Mallarmé, talked as much as he read, and that Yeats must have acquired some knowledge at second hand of symbolist intentions. Moreover, Yeats read *The Symbolist Movement in Literature* when it appeared in 1899 and based his essay "The Symbolism of Poetry"

La Contribution d'un Américain au symbolisme français, Stuart Merrill (1927).

(1900) partly upon what he had learned. "When sound, and colour, and form are in a musical relation . . . to one another," Yeats says in this essay, "they become as it were one sound, one colour, one form, and evoke an emotion that is made out of their distinct evocations and yet is one emotion." This is Mallarmé by way of Symons. That phrase about the trembling of the veil of the temple which Yeats was continually quoting comes from the *Divagations* (1897) of Mallarmé. Since this book, if not this phrase, is difficult, Yeats received it, no doubt, from Symons, who had sat on Tuesdays at the feet of the master.

A man who cannot read Mallarmé cannot be affected by Mallarmé. But it is unnecessary to look to him or to any Frenchman for the symbolism of Yeats, who was a symbolist long before he had heard of the French. He based his symbolism upon the poetry of Blake, Shelley, and Rossetti and, above all these, upon the occult. In 1886, as we know, Yeats joined the Dublin Lodge of the Theosophical Society, and two years later the Order of the Golden Dawn. From the works of Mme Blavatsky, Yeats learned that Anima Mundi, a reservoir of all that has touched mankind, may be evoked by symbols. From Swedenborg he received the doctrine of correspondences, from Eliphas Lévi the doctrine of magical incantations and symbols that have power over spiritual and material reality, and from Boehme the similar doctrine of signatures. The Emerald Tablet of Hermes Trismegistus informed him that things below are as things above. And the symbolic ritual of the Rosicrucians confirmed these ideas. A rebel against the world of matter, Yeats learned that all material things correspond to ideas in the world of spirit and that through the use of material objects as magical symbols the adept may call down disembodied powers. The essay "Magic" (1901) expresses his conviction that the great memory of nature "can be evoked by symbols." Like Baudelaire, who had read Swedenborg before him, Yeats became a poetic visionary, and like Rimbaud, who had followed Eliphas Lévi, Yeats became a magus, a master of magic, who through poetic symbols and trances could surprise reality. Although he had not heard of Baudelaire or Rimbaud when he read Lévi and Swedenborg, Yeats belonged, with these poets, to the great transcendental movement of the nineteenth century and turned naturally to the same supernatural sources. Material reality became for him as for them a chaos of symbols through which a poet could discover spiritual order. The example of Blake, also an occultist, taught Yeats the use in poetry of magical symbols; and the poems of Shelley, which he carefully analyzed, confirmed his symbolic system. Like Blake, Baudelaire, and Rimbaud, Yeats saw the poet as magus and priest, but as poet before magus and priest. Knowing what he was about, he went to the occult in the first place to discover, if he could, the laws of the imagination, to find ways of inducing trance and vision through which he could confront the inner and higher realities he needed and to find symbols for his poetry.

By 1890, before Yeats knew about the French symbolists, he had been writing symbolic poems for several years, and when Symons and others told him about the French poets, he welcomed them as fellow travelers on the road he was following, as fellow transcendentalists and occultists who had, like Blake and Shelley, hit upon symbolism as the only possible way to express what they had experienced. Maeterlinck was a kind of theosophist. Villiers was a student of Eliphas Lévi and of the Rosicrucians. Occult considerations led Yeats to the laborious reading of *Axël,* and it was probably MacGregor Mathers, the Rosicrucian, who introduced him to this congenial play.

To see how congenial it was, a synopsis is necessary. This play concerns the well-born Sara, a novice in a nunnery, who has read a collection of Rosicrucian works carelessly left around in the convent library. As she stands before the archdeacon in her bridal robes about to take the veil, she is overcome with longing for a more spiritual life and for a treasure she has learned about. Seizing an ax and assuming a fierce demeanor, she locks the archdeacon in a tomb, climbs out of a window, and departs. Meanwhile Count Axël of Auërsperg, living in exile from the world in his Gothical castle in the Black Forest, pursues Rosicrucian studies, attempts the "Great Work" of alchemy, and practices magic according to the precepts of Eliphas Lévi, under the supervision of Master Janus, an adept. Indifferent to the world of matter, from which he desires to detach himself for the sake of perfection, Axël refuses to hunt for the treasure buried somewhere on his premises. He speaks eloquently of Hermes Trismegistus, Paracelsus, and the Magi. During an interminable conversation with Master Janus, however, he suddenly renounces his spiritual aims and decides to use his magic to secure the treasure. Descending into the vaults beneath the Gothical castle, he comes upon Sara, who has already discovered the treasure. She shoots him. Enchanted by her cruelty and her shape, he covers himself in her long hair and breathes the spirit of dead roses. He proposes that they take the treasure and have a good time in Paris, Kashmir, Heliopolis, London. But she shows him her cruciform dagger and her faded rose (the Rosy Cross), which are the symbol and "correspondence" of her belief, her soul, and the nature of things. He is moved. Therefore, in expiation of their passing infidelity to the spirit of the Rosy Cross, and in contempt of world and love, they resolve to die—and die. This spiritual allegory, filled with symbols of castle, lamp, treasure, and the like, immediately became one of Yeats's "sacred books," surpassing even *Prometheus Unbound* in his favor.

The symbols of Yeats's early poems, like those of Villiers and of Lévi, are occult in character. Aware that Anima Mundi or the great memory of nature may be evoked by symbols drawn from Irish legends, Yeats used the symbolic characters of Oisin or Aengus, for example, the hound with one red ear, the white deer with no horns, and the island in the western sea. But equally characteristic are his arbitrary occult symbols of rose, cross, lily, bird, water, tree, moon, and sun, which he could find in the cabbalistic, Theosophical, and other profound works that constituted the greater part of his reading. The two trees in his poem of that name are the Sephirotic tree of the cabbala and the tree of knowledge. The "Powers" of his poem "The Poet Pleads with the Elemental Powers" are Mme Blavatsky's elemental spirits, the "Immortal Rose" is Rosicrucian, and the "Seven Lights" are the seven planets of Theosophy. The "Ineffable Name" of "To Some I Have Talked with by the Fire" is the cabbalistical *Shem Hamphorasch* or Jehovah, whose unspeakable four-lettered name in Hebrew characters admits of seventy-two combinations, as Yeats, practicing with the cabbalists in Paris, knew by experience. These symbols differ from those ordinarily employed by the French in being traditional, systematic, more arbitrary and definite in outline. But though they are first of all magical symbols, hence impersonal, as used by Yeats they become as personal, reverberating, and mysterious as the symbols of the less systematic French.

Of these early symbols the rose is the most complex. Most of the rose poems are to be found in *The Rose* (1893), written in his first enthusiasm after reading *Axël* with its Rosicrucian roses. But as a member of the Order of the Golden Dawn Yeats had no need to pilfer *Axël*, for the symbolic ritual of his society centered in the rose and cross. The society, of course, was secret; but Aleister Crowley, a member, violating dreadful vows, exposed its ritual at great length in the September 1909 and March 1910 numbers of the *Equinox,* a magazine he edited. This ritual does much to make Yeats's poetic symbolism plain.

The novices of the Golden Dawn were confronted with the Sephirotic tree of life, the seven planets, the Sphinx, and the symbols of the four elements. Candidates of the fourth grade, who were called Unicorns from the Stars (a phrase that Yeats took as the title for one of his plays), learned the doctrine of correspondences between microcosm and macrocosm and at one point in their spiritual development were permitted to inhale the perfume of a rose. But only the higher initiates were admitted to the secret of the Rose of Ruby and the Cross of Gold, "the fadeless Rose of Creation and the immortal Cross of Light" or life itself, ecstasy and suffering, and union with God. Light, fire, and the color red symbolized, as in Zoroastrianism, the highest good. In the vault of initiation there was a rose on the ceiling, a rose with a cross on the floor, and the vault was lit with the ray of a luminous rose. Father Christian Rosenkreutz, about whom Yeats wrote an essay, was regarded as the founder of the society; and the symbols of dagger, cup, and rose, which appear in Yeats's diagram of the Great Wheel, were conspicuous in the ritual. Even "Hodos Camelionis," which makes its appearance in Yeats's *Autobiography* as "Hodos Chameliontos," occurs in the course of this awful ceremony.

But to return to the symbol of the rose in Yeats's poems and stories: it is even more complex than this ritual would imply, for Yeats was personal as well as occult and he used the rose to mean more than Father Christian Rosy Cross or MacGregor Mathers intended. In "The Rose of

Peace" the rose means earthly love as in a popular song; but, serving as refuge from earthly love, the rose of "The Rose of Battle" symbolizes spirit in the battle of spirit against matter. The rose in "To the Rose upon the Rood of Time," as the title of the poem implies, is the Rosicrucian rose, but it is also the power of the creative imagination and occult philosophy too, which, Yeats fears, may remove him so completely from the present world that he will cease to be a poet. A similar fear plagues the hero of the story "Rosa Alchemica," an adventure in spiritual alchemy in which the rose as in Eliphas Lévi means the "Great Work" of transmuting matter into spirit. Taken to the headquarters of the Order of the Alchemical Rose, where adepts ceremoniously dance with spirits, the hero joins the dance. On the dancing-floor is a great cross and on the ceiling a greater rose.[20]

More and more Yeats feared the isolation of spirit from matter, as he had feared the isolation of matter from spirit, and with these fears the rose came to mean what he called "unity of being" or the harmony of self, world, and spirit. These meanings are present in the rose or around it, but they are not all that it suggests because from each context come reverberations enriching the symbol as it in turn enriches its context. The value of a symbol, said Yeats, is this richness or indefiniteness of reference, which makes it far more mysterious and potent than allegory with its single meaning. A hundred men, he continued, would advance a hundred different meanings for the same symbol; for "no symbol tells all its meaning" to any man.[21]

[20] In the story "Out of the Rose," Yeats's Rosicrucian knight wears a militant rose of ruby and flame. The acting version of *The Shadowy Waters* has a passage on the rose and cross as symbol of the union of body and soul, life and death, sleep and waking.

[21] For his observations on symbolism see his edition of Blake's *Prophetic Books* (1893), his essays on Shelley, the two essays called "Sym-

The Wind among the Reeds (1899) gives "dumb things voices, and bodiless things bodies." Reviewing this book, Arthur Symons hailed it as a triumph of symbolist indirection. Through the swooning diction, the musical, individual rhythms, the harmonies and overtones, and the interaction of many traditional but mysterious images each poem becomes the symbol of an unstated idea or mood. Although Yeats employed description and statement more lavishly than the French were accustomed to do, this book is closer in feeling and method to the works of the symbolists than any other that appeared in England during the nineties. It resembles these works not because it is their debtor but because, coming from the same revolt against matter and surface, it is their parallel.

Some of Yeats's plays resemble those of the symbolist stage not only because they are also transcendental reactions against the realistic stage, but because he had Villiers and Maeterlinck in mind when he wrote them. The debt of *The Shadowy Waters* to Villiers is clear. *The Countess Cathleen* (1892), however, which has all the atmosphere of Maeterlinck, was written before Yeats knew of him. It is difficult to say what part of Yeats's other plays comes from the French and what from the so-called Celtic twilight or the English romantic tradition.

The poems of *The Wind among the Reeds* and the earlier poems owe part of their richness and depth to something apart from the conscious use of occult symbols and wavering rhythms. Like Rimbaud, Yeats had discovered a way to evade the interference of his intellect and to explore his unconscious in search of symbols. Rimbaud had done this by a systematic derangement of the senses through drugs, fatigue, and depravity. Yeats, who was too prudent for such excesses, found in the occult a way of

bolism in Painting" and "The Autumn of the Body," and his introduction to *A Book of Images* (1898), by W. T. Horton, a fellow adept.

doing the same thing. Inclined by nature to waking visions and trances in which he saw wonderful things, he found that through the use of ritual and hypnotic symbols he could enjoy deeper and more effectual trances in which new images swam before his eyes. Magic, by putting his active intellect to sleep, permitted him to secure for his poems the wealth of his unconscious. Naturally he tried to give these floating images an occult value, but this did not prevent them from carrying with them to his poems, whatever his conscious intention, the richness of man's deepest reality. Like Rimbaud, then, and with the aid of Rimbaud's tutor, Eliphas Lévi, Yeats discovered a poetic country that had been neglected in England except by occasional madmen since the time of Blake. Yeats differs from Rimbaud, however, in the formal, conscious pattern he forced upon his images.

In the second part of *The Wanderings of Oisin* (1889) he tells of his hero's battle on an island in the sea with an elderly demon who keeps a lady in a cave. This episode, Yeats told Katharine Tynan, came to him in a kind of vision, which plagued him night and day and left him in a state of collapse. "Under the guise of symbolism," he told her, "I have said several things to which I only have the key." The story, he continued, was for the common reader who would remain unaware of the symbolism, yet "the whole poem is full of symbols." Aware that these unconscious symbols would bear neither an occult nor a legendary explanation, Yeats seems in this letter to Katharine Tynan, written long before Freud commenced his study of such symbols, to apprehend some part of their significance.[22]

From his interest in semiconscious vision, Yeats was led by his occult interests to examine his dreams for their oc-

[22] See Morton Irving Seiden: "A Psychoanalytical Essay on William Butler Yeats," *Accent,* Spring 1946.

cult meaning and for poetic themes and images. "The Cap and Bells" (1899) is, he assures us, a dream recorded exactly as he dreamed it. Here the images of queen, garment, hair, cap and bells, window, and the colors would have interested Freud. In a note Yeats says that this poem meant much to him, but, as with all symbolic poems, its meaning was never twice the same.

The first two stanzas of "The Song of Wandering Aengus" (1899) are obviously another dream, which is rationalized in the third stanza. The change of fish into girl is dream material. The images of wand, stream, berry, and fire are from man's sleeping consciousness. But the sun, moon, and apple of the third stanza, however Freudian they seem, are conscious occult symbols meaning intellect, imagination, and the tree of good and evil. Aengus was introduced afterwards to impart an Irish character to the mysterious and lovely poem.

After 1900 Yeats's poetry became colder, plainer, and more classical until in its "lofty severe quality" it came to resemble the poetry of Baudelaire. Feeling left the surface and vibrated beneath it. Far from following Baudelaire, still farther from following Moréas, who had turned to a kind of hardness before him, Yeats was responding bitterly to circumstance and self. The satiric and occasional poetry of the 1910 period, however, appeared symbolist to George Moore, who was unable to get Paris out of his head. Speaking in *Vale* of a poem Yeats wrote about a house, "What house?" Moore asks. "Mallarmé could not be darker than this." Had Yeats and Mallarmé ever met, he adds, they would have "got on famously." But Moore was exaggerating. The only indirection or obscurity of "Upon a House Shaken by the Land Agitation" is Yeats's failure to mention Coole Park.

After 1917 Yeats returned more or less to symbolism, retaining nobility of tone and classical surface, and with this return came greater obscurity. Dissatisfied with the Golden Dawn, he announced in 1925 a system of his own. One of the demons who had dictated it to Mrs. Yeats informed her husband of its purpose: "We have come," he said, "to give you metaphors for poetry." Yeats used them in many of the poems he wrote between 1917 and 1935. "Leda and the Swan," which springs from the system, is symbolist in the sense that the manifest level is there to suggest unstated themes, the union of matter and spirit, of god and man, of Dove and Virgin, and all the cycles of history that begin with these unnatural conjunctions. In like manner "The Saint and the Hunchback," which has a dramatic, comprehensible level, implies three attitudes toward life symbolized by the saint, the hunchback, and Alcibiades, the last of whom stands for that aristocratic wholeness toward which Yeats aspired. "The Delphic Oracle upon Plotinus," a gay, preposterous poem, filled with mysterious overtones, concerns the philosopher Plotinus, swimming through turbulent waves toward a shore where Plato, Minos, Pythagoras, and Rhadamanthus await him with all the choir of love. This poem seems to be more surrealist than symbolist. As the title suggests, however, the author is not Yeats but the Delphic Oracle, who composed the poem in Greek long ago. By suppressing much and by selecting such beauties as the "golden race" and the "choir of love," Yeats made of her indifferent stuff, the stuff of poetry.[23] As for its meaning, the Delphic Oracle, according to Porphyry, intended her sym-

[23] Yeats found the Delphic Oracle's poem in Porphyry's "Life of Plotinus" in Stephen MacKenna's translation of Plotinus. The following lines of Marcilio Ficino's Latin version of the poem indicate the use Yeats made of the oracle:

Aurei generis magni Jovis ubi agitant
Minos et Rhadamanthus fratres: ubi justus
Æacus: ubi Plato, sacra vis: ubi pulcher
Pythagoras, et quicunque chorum statuerunt amoris.

bols to imply the journey of Plotinus through the chaos of time and death to the Elysian Fields. Her symbols of sea and island attracted Yeats whose unconscious had persistently offered them to him. Like Milton, moreover, he was unable to resist the richness of names, especially those of Pythagoras and Plotinus, who were among his favorite adepts. No doubt the swimming of Plotinus toward his shore had a very personal significance to Yeats, not unlike that of the voyage to Byzantium, to the island of Innisfree, or to the Land of Youth.

These symbolic poems, which seem at first so French, owe little or nothing to the French. But many of the later poems, "Among School Children" or "Sailing to Byzantium," have a tight logical structure and a dependence upon statement rarely found in French symbolist verse. Until the end, where the symbols of chestnut tree and dancer represent unity of being, "Among School Children" is more classical in method than symbolist, and its difficulties are those of any compressed, coherent whole of thought and feeling. The misprint in stanza six may be responsible, of course, for some perplexity, but "golden-thighed," which glimmers so strangely in the same stanza, is only a classical epithet applied to Pythagoras by Plutarch in the life of Numa Pompilius.

Whatever the occult bearing of Yeats's poems, they are also personal and worldly. In his most dramatic poems, those on Aengus or on the saint and hunchback for instance, Yeats had his own problems in mind. Whatever his romantic contempt of the world, it was never as thorough as that of Mallarmé, who saw the world merely as a store of symbols for something else. Even in his Rosicrucian days Yeats wanted to reconcile world and spirit and to integrate himself with world and spirit. His symbols, like his mask, gave him a way to do this. By their triple reference to self, world, and spirit they achieve on the æsthetic plane a unity of being impossible in life.

The greatest poet of the symbolist tradition in England, Yeats was the greatest poet of his time. It is hard to say in what the greatness of a poet consists; for it is a response by the reader, far below the level of his intellect, to the poet's poems. The response of the reader comes from what the sense, rhythm, tone, and images of the poem imply about reality and from what reality they compose. The response to Yeats is not only to rhythm, tone, and elaborate interconnections, but to the symbols, which are charged with the deepest reality. Such symbols convey more than can be said. It is for their reverberations and the art of producing and arranging them that Yeats is great.

IV

Between 1900 and 1910, when Yeats became satiric and more or less objective, such poetry as England produced, though not eminently Victorian perhaps, was thoroughly British. When symbolism resumed its course after this uninteresting decade, the poetry inspired by Frenchmen was better than that of the nineties because better poets with greater understanding now found the French congenial.

The Georgian poets, who undertook the revival of English poetry in 1912, were not of this kind. But some of the contributors to *Georgian Poetry* who knew about the French rose by their aid a little above the common level of their fellows. In his opulent, Oriental verses James Elroy Flecker, for example, followed the Parnassians. And to the Georgian anthology of 1918 Edward Shanks contributed "*Fête Galante*," a long poem in free verse, which recaptures some of the elegance of Verlaine.

The imagists, contemporaries of the Georgians, used the French to better purpose. Imagism is unusual among English poetic movements for having commenced with theory. In 1908 T. E. Hulme, the Bergsonist philosopher, founded a club with the object of restoring poetry to England. Looking at the declining Victorian tradition, he dismissed it as Wordsworth had dismissed the declining tradition of Alexander Pope, proposed a return to nature, to the language of common speech, and, going beyond Wordsworth, to a more natural rhythm. Late Victorian poetry seemed abstract, rhetorical, and vague. To remedy these evils Hulme advised brevity and precision, free verse, and concrete images. Some idea of the advice he gave at the sessions of his poets may be had from his "Notes on Language and Style."[24] True to the anti-intellectual position of Bergson, Hulme says in this essay that the poet must escape the limits that perception imposes upon the flow of experience. Evading logical statement, he must try to embody his feelings and sensations in precise physical analogies. Such metaphors and similes may convey the inexpressible, but any suggestions surrounding them must be controlled by the poet in order to avoid vagueness of reference. The reader of this imagistic, illogical poetry, with its limited suggestions and its economy, must work as he reads and share the task of creation. Hulme was no poet; but he carefully composed five poems to illustrate free verse, economy, and the image.[25]

Although Hulme based his theories on Bergson, who was reacting like the symbolists against externality and logic, he seems to have known nothing of French poetry until told of it by his young disciple F. S. Flint, who joined the second of Hulme's conventicles in a Soho restaurant

[24] *Criterion*, July 1925.

[25] Printed by Ezra Pound in *Ripostes* (1912), and in *Speculations* (1924).

in 1909. Flint had been reading the free verse of Fort, Jammes, Claudel, Gourmont, Régnier, and Verhaeren. Combining Hulme's theories with his own knowledge of the French, Flint became their chief interpreter.[26] It was he who told Richard Aldington and Ezra Pound, new members of Hulme's circle, about the French. Pound's subsequent articles about them confuse the ideas of Flint and Hulme; and *Six French Poets* (1915) by Amy Lowell owes more to them than she was willing to admit. These imagists were lost in admiration of Rémy de Gourmont's *Problème du style,* which announced ideas like Hulme's about emotion, concreteness, and the exact word.

Flint and Aldington were the principal English poets of the group. Aldington's early poetry, inspired by the Greeks, the Song of Solomon, and Whitman, was unaffected by the poetry of France. In *Cadences* (1915) Flint published imagistic poems that distantly reflect Verhaeren, his favorite. Poems by Aldington and Flint appear in *Des Imagistes* (1914), edited by Pound, the first imagist anthology. Although the rather French verse of Flint is even less memorable than the rather Middle Eastern verse of Aldington, Flint's poem on the swan in *Des Imagistes* is a more instructive example of imagism than any of Aldington's because it can be compared with an earlier and a later version. As it first appeared in 1909 the poem explains the feelings of the poet; but in *Des Imagistes* the feelings are presented by an image with a briefer explanation, and the last version, in *Otherworld* (1920), thoroughly objective, allows the image to speak for itself.

However Parnassian their themes or transcendental their implications, imagist poems never attained the impassibility of Parnasse or the indefinite suggestiveness of symbolism. The classical pretensions of the imagists, which seem odd in poets who, like Aldington, wanted to be

[26] E.g., "Contemporary French Poetry," *Poetry Review,* August 1912.

petals or who could weep at the color of a tile, come less from their Parnassian antecedents than from the classical pretensions of T. E. Hulme. No poets, however, have been less classical in feeling, and few have been so trivial.[27]

The importance of the imagists is greater than the slightness of their poems would suggest; for by their example of brevity and precision they destroyed the vestiges of Victorian expansiveness. By making concrete pictures do the work of statement, they made poetry dramatic. By their rhythms they liberated verse. But having cleared a way, they found themselves unable to take it. Their failure may be explained in part by their incapacity and in part by their indifference to intellect.

The difference between imagism and symbolism becomes evident when Flint's final image of the swan is compared with Mallarmé's image of the swan in "*Le vierge, le vivace et le bel aujourd'hui.*" Mallarmé's image is surrounded with suggestions, feelings, and ideas about his position, his poetic ideals and failures, and art, society, matter, and spirit. The image, there to create its ghostly surroundings, is lost in what it creates. Flint's image, on the other hand, is relatively simple. It is there not to create but to represent the sensation and feeling of the poet at a particular moment. It takes the place of statement by dramatizing what a statement could do, whereas Mallarmé's image does more than a statement could do. An image is direct and representative, a symbol indirect and endlessly evocative. An image is a denuded and limited symbol. This difference, which owes something to a difference in poetic theory, owes more, perhaps, to a differ-

[27] For imagism see Glenn Hughes: *Imagism and the Imagists* (1931), René Taupin: *L'Influence du symbolisme français sur la poésie américaine de 1910 à 1920* (1929), and the introductions by Hughes and Ford Madox Ford to the *Imagist Anthology* (1930). Cf. Aldington: *Life for Life's Sake* (1941), autobiography. For Herbert Read's connection with imagism see *Annals of Innocence and Experience* (1940).

ence between poets; for Mallarmé, a great poet, had much to say, and Flint, a small poet, had little.

Of the Englishmen who went on from where the imagists left off, T. S. Eliot is the most respectable. While at college in America, he discovered the French through Arthur Symons's *Symbolist Movement in Literature*. To his admiration of Webster and Donne he added an even greater admiration of Baudelaire and Laforgue, especially the latter. Between 1907 and 1910 Eliot contributed several Laforguian poems to the *Harvard Advocate*,[28] and while still at college he wrote his "Portrait of a Lady" (1909) and "The Love Song of J. Alfred Prufrock" (1910) in the manners of Webster and Laforgue. This adolescent, generally ignored by French critics or, when remembered as a decadent of the eighties, dismissed as a poet of the third class, had what Eliot required.

The essays of Jules Laforgue tell almost as much about him as his verse. Inflated at first with transcendental yearning, he was deflated, he says, by Darwin. Hence the inflation and deflation of the poet's metaphors and the painful joy of punctured sentiments. But in Hartmann's theory of the unconscious Laforgue found peace and a literary method. It was the job of a poet, he felt, to follow the vagaries of the life force beyond limits, categories, and reason. "The wind of the unconscious blows where it will," he exclaims. "Let it blow." Meanwhile the poet's face assumed the expression of the clown, the "*fumiste*," and the man about town. Slang of the boulevards, images from botany and zoology, and impressions of the suburb conceal a bleeding heart. In his prose poems, while men lean vacantly from windows, there are smells of frying, and all the "quotidian" ennuis of restaurants, pianos, and advertisements. The poems in free verse are streams of consciousness in which images of middle-class life float by

[28] See Eliot Number of the *Harvard Advocate*, December 1938.

in free association. To this procession the flippancy or nonchalance of the poet gives a disconcerting movement. In a letter to one of the mature women who attracted him he said: "Life is sad, history a nightmare," and I, like Pierrot, am "dilettante, virtuoso, guitarist. . . . Do you still find me young?"

Laforguian "Prufrock" is a dramatic monologue of that living dead man who, in "The Hollow Men" and other poems, was to become Eliot's specialty. Suffering from emotional anemia, repression, and weakness of will, J. Alfred owes part of his character to Henry James, more to Laforgue. But through the convenient mask of Laforgue, Eliot spoke with his own voice of his own condition, dramatizing it by images of coffee spoons, bald spots, and "lonely men in shirt-sleeves." Raised by these desolating particulars from the personal, the poem as a whole becomes a symbol of our condition and our world. It is for this value that "Prufrock" has undone so many. But this value, depending upon more than images, is a conspiracy of these with rhythm, structure, and tone to compose the symbol. The inflation and deflation, the vagaries of free association, pleasing while they perplex, are of course Laforgue's. The masterly rhythms, however much they owe to Laforgue and Webster, are Eliot's.

Wherever one looks in Laforgue there are similarities: "*Oh, qu'ils sont pittoresques les trains manqués.*" It is unnecessary to multiply such lines or to cite the lines and images that Eliot lifted from his master; for they have been cited [29] and he has justified his habit. A poor poet imitates, he observed; a good one steals, and improves

[29] By Edmund Wilson, in *Axel's Castle,* and by René Taupin. In his preface to Pound's *Selected Poems* (1928) Eliot says that the form in which he began to write was based upon Laforgue and the later Elizabethan drama. For resemblances to Henry James see F. O. Matthiessen: *The Achievement of T. S. Eliot* (1935).

what he takes by making it part of a new system of thought and feeling. Taking what he needed from Laforgue, Eliot made arrangements, like the "Portrait of a Lady," which are better than anything of Laforgue's. Distinguished by rhythm and brilliance of imagery, these are among the most original British poems of our time.

For a long time Laforgue continued to enchant him. "*Conversation Galante*" follows Laforgue's "*Autre Complainte de Lord Pierrot.*" Deflation by Laforguian irony reappears in Part II of *The Waste Land* during the conversation between the hysterical woman and the man about town. Tags from popular songs and scientific terms used out of context repeat the lesson of the master. And the dead geranium, which preceded the rose in Eliot's favor, is from the window-box of Jules Laforgue.

While enamored of Laforgue, Eliot also fancied Donne and Marvell, whose fusion of sense and intellect, according to "The Metaphysical Poets" (1921), was recaptured by Laforgue. This attractive confusion of logical Donne with illogical Laforgue, while pleasing to the sensibility, has done much to obscure the nature of Laforgue, who as a disciple of Hartmann did his best to suppress his intellect. Eliot's resemblance to logical Donne is far less than his resemblance to illogical Laforgue.[30] In *The Waste Land* logical progress has been replaced by Laforguian sequences of feeling.

For the autobiographical poem "*Mélange Adultère de Tout*" Eliot took not only his title but his manner from Tristan Corbière, a jaunty and more virile predecessor of Laforgue. "*Le Directeur,*" also in French and one of Eliot's most fascinating poems, seems to owe its strangeness to

[30] The characteristic of metaphysical verse is the elaboration of a metaphor according to its logical possibilities. The initial metaphor has definite relations to external reality. In symbolism the initial metaphor, often private and noncommunicative, is multiplied by free association. There is little resemblance between Donne and Laforgue or Mallarmé.

Guillaume Apollinaire. "The Hippopotamus," as René Taupin shows by parallel columns, is a reproduction of Gautier's Parnassian "*Hippopotame*." These instances, which serve to show Eliot's reverence for tradition, make the originality of his poems appear more wonderful.

While at college Eliot also discovered Baudelaire, who proved to be almost as useful as Laforgue. In "Baudelaire in Our Time," an essay reprinted in *For Lancelot Andrewes* (1928), Eliot reviews the translation by Arthur Symons, who, says Eliot, made Baudelaire a poet of the nineties. More childish than Huysmans, Symons saw only the evil, the romantic unhealthiness, and the perversity of a poet who is almost as classical as Racine and "essentially Christian." After thinking these matters over for a while, Eliot softened his conclusions in another essay.[31] Classical only in tendency, Baudelaire is not so Christian as Eliot had thought, though Christian in tendency.

This essay is of value for comments upon Baudelaire's imagery, which explain Eliot's. Baudelaire had a romantic stock of images: "mulattoes, Jewesses, serpents, cats, corpses," pleasing to Symons and Wilde, perhaps, but displeasing to men of sensibility. On the other hand, says Eliot, Baudelaire used images of modern city life. Taking a suitable image from café, street, or gutter, Baudelaire presented reality as it was, yet, making it represent something more than itself, raised it to "first intensity." Through his discovery of desolating city images he gave later poets expression for themselves and their world. It is difficult to distinguish Laforgue's city images from those of Baudelaire, his master, but it is probable that the "sawdust restaurants" of "Prufrock," the rusty springs in vacant lots, the cigar butts, the rancid butter in the gutter, the

[31] In *Selected Essays*. An introduction to Christopher Isherwood's translation of *Journaux intimes* (1930).

boarding-houses, and all the smells of Eliot's early poetry are from Baudelaire's preferable stock. The "unreal city" of *The Waste Land* is sufficiently identified by quotations from Baudelaire and Dante as Baudelaire's city and our hell. Eliot found his disgusting images in Baudelaire, but he missed as completely as Symons had the compassion behind disgust. He had gone to Baudelaire and Laforgue, however, not to improve his nature, but to find ways of expressing it.

When Eliot met the followers of Hulme in 1915, he was already an imagist of sorts, and, finding the followers of Hulme congenial, he became one of their number, succeeding Aldington as assistant editor of the *Egoist*, the principal organ of imagism. Eliot adopted the theories of Hulme, which clarified his own practices; and, like his friends, he conceived a moderate passion for Rémy de Gourmont's "*Litanies de la Rose*," which he imitated years later in the second part of *Ash Wednesday*. "Preludes" and "Rhapsody on a Windy Night," the first poems he composed upon his arrival in England, are imagist poems, not of petals, however, but of vacant lots. With the aid of Baudelaire, Eliot made imagism more masculine and, with the aid of Laforgue, more complex. For the single image of most imagist verse he substituted long sequences of images; and for verse he substituted poetry. Though he soon turned with Pound to the quatrain of Gautier, Eliot remained a Laforguian imagist for many years. The first part of "Gerontion" is imagistic, and *The Waste Land* is a subtle suite of images.

However customary it is to class young Eliot with the symbolists, he was closer to the imagists. The particularities of his cold youth bear little resemblance in method or effect to the work of Mallarmé or Rimbaud or to the principles of Moréas. The images of these early poems are dramatizations of definite feelings about self or society, not evocations of the inexpressible. Finite, not infinite, they have little mystery about them; and their overtones, narrowly beamed by the poet, lack the expanding rings of the symbol. His cigar butt is far more precise in meaning than Yeats's rose. From Baudelaire Eliot took, not the theory of correspondences, but a stock of images for less metaphysical purposes. Laforgue, from whom he took more, is more properly classed with the Decadents than with the symbolists, with whom he has little in common. The ceaseless praise of objectivity and impersonality that fills Eliot's essays reflects Gautier, the Parnassians, and the imagists. His ideal of the "objective correlative," something outside the poet that embodies something inside him, is Hulme's ideal of the image. And that fine definition of poetry (from the essay on metaphysical poets) as the "verbal equivalent for states of mind and feeling" is another reflection of Hulme and Flint, not of transcendental Baudelaire, Rimbaud, and Mallarmé. Limiting himself to the psychological and social levels of symbolism, Eliot, content to project himself, was careless of eternity.

As Eliot approached Christianity in his later poems, he approached the symbolists. Abandoning Laforgue's manner as he approached them, he began to state his case. It is true that the symbolists had substituted indirection for statement; but, making statement musical, Eliot made it do the work of indirection. By this method, which first appears in the Sweeney poems and the latter part of "Gerontion" and reappears in "The Hollow Men," *Ash Wednesday*, and *Four Quartets*, he evokes idea and feeling less by images than by rhythm, by prosaic statements that say less than they mean, and by incantation with fragments of thought. The images within these incantations, the broken column of "The Hollow Men," or the window and winding stair of *Ash Wednesday,* or the roses of the *Quartets,* differ from the earlier images in being clear and mysterious, precise and imprecise.[32]

The theme of "East Coker," the second of the *Quartets,* is time and eternity or humanism as represented by Sir Thomas Elyot, and piety as represented by Mr. Thomas Eliot. Elegant allusions to Heraclitus, St. John of the Cross, Milton's *Samson,* and *The Hound of the Baskervilles* show need of death before rebirth; and masterly changes of pace support the references. The structure, indicated by the general title, is musical, following the development of a five-part quartet, the first part a sonata, the second part two themes with coda, the fourth perhaps a rondo. These poems, which belong with *Point Counter Point,* the fugue of *Ulysses,* and the poems of Mallarmé, those earlier attempts to make words do what music can, are no less successful.

Edith Sitwell, Eliot's contemporary, discovered the symbolists independently during an attack of measles in 1912. She read Arthur Symons, Baudelaire, Verlaine, Rimbaud, and, after reading Eliot, Laforgue. *The Mother* (1915), her first volume of poetry, contains imitations of Baudelaire and Rimbaud that she excluded from her *Collected Poems* (1930) as too derivative. Excluded by her French demeanor from the conservative Georgian

[32] Eliot contributed an essay on Mallarmé to the *Nouvelle Revue Française,* July 1926. The "Garlic and sapphires" of "Burnt Norton" are adapted from Mallarmé. In 1924 Eliot wrote an introduction to Mark Wardle's translation of Valéry's *Le Serpent.*

For the *Quartets* see Raymond Preston: *"Four Quartets" Rehearsed* (1946); Elizabeth Drew and John Sweeney: *Directions in Modern Poetry* (1940); James Sweeney: "East Coker," *Southern Review,* Spring 1941.

For explications of the earlier poems see Cleanth Brooks: *Modern Poetry and the Tradition* (1939); Ruth Bailey: *A Dialogue of Modern Poetry* (1939); F. R. Leavis: *New Bearings in English Poetry* (1932); Leonard Unger on *Ash Wednesday, Southern Review,* Spring 1939; Grover Smith on *Waste Land, Accent,* Summer 1946.

anthology and by her strangeness from the pretty collections of the imagists, she established *Wheels* (1916–21), an annual anthology of her own.

Poetry and Criticism (1925) is Edith Sitwell's manifesto. It was her purpose, she says, to renew the exhausted romantic tradition. By "rag-time rhythms," grotesque words, and abstract patterns, like those of Picasso, Stein, and Stravinsky, by nonsense, synesthesia, and flippancy she composes antidotes to Wordsworth. In one of the series of articles she wrote for the *New Age* in 1922, she says that, spiritual and elegant like Villiers de l'Isle Adam, she too is plagued by the middle class. "Lullaby for Jumbo," "Trio for Two Cats and a Trombone," and her other poems, at once fantastic and sensuous, were admirably calculated to astonish this class.

These ninetyish poems were inspired by France. From Baudelaire Miss Sitwell took dandyism and the exotic artificiality of "*Rêve Parisien.*" Proceeding with his aid to transform Wordsworth's nature, she put bustles on the cherry trees. If a simple cherry tree is romantic, a cherry tree with a bustle on it, though no less romantic, is also decadent.

Elegant artifice was a refuge from the terror of the world. Retreat to childhood was another. In this Miss Sitwell was encouraged by the example of Rimbaud, who had ransacked his unconscious for infant memories. "Pleasure Gardens," a section of *Troy Park,* which celebrates her infancy, owes epigraph, atmosphere, and theme to Rimbaud. The synesthesia that she cultivated more systematically than any other English poet was inspired by Rimbaud's "*Voyelles*" and Baudelaire's "*Correspondances.*" Welcoming Rimbaud's derangement of the senses, she heard colors and smelt sounds. That she thoroughly understood Rimbaud, however, is questionable; for in one of her articles in the *New Age* she says she liked him because he is decorative, exquisite, and formal. But in her introduction to Helen Rootham's translation of *Prose Poems from the Illuminations of Rimbaud* (1932) she is more orthodox. Here what she likes about Rimbaud, besides his irrational incantation, is his recovery of childhood, his abandonment to the unconscious, and his freedom from meaning.

In Miss Sitwell's preface to *Children's Tales from the Russian Ballet* (1920) she finds Laforgue's "terrible gaiety," like Petrouchka's, another refuge from the postwar world. Her poems on clowns are terribly gay. At the feet of Eliot's master she learned the arts of free association, mannered disillusionment, and verbalism. Equal admiration of Verlaine's *Fêtes galantes* is apparent in the nostalgic eighteenth-century elegance that interrupts the terrible gaiety. She learned her lessons well. Her early poems are generally agreeable, often good. Fresh impressions from startled senses, original patterns, and the resonances that assure her a place in the symbolist tradition make her poems richer than they seem.[33]

That, like Yeats and Eliot, Edith Sitwell could develop is shown by *Street Songs* (1942) and *Green Song* (1944). As the first World War had made her rococo, so the second made her human. Retaining her virtuosity, her elegance of rhythm and texture, she used bones, apes, and carrion birds for general despair, which she expressed more movingly than most of her juniors. Age led her to the weathers and all the common things she had missed.

In *Do What You Will* (1929) Aldous Huxley attacks Baudelaire as a nasty Satanist whose present cult among the English is explained by their hunt for what expresses

[33] For her admiration of Symons, Verlaine, Baudelaire, and Rimbaud see *A Poet's Notebook* (1943). In *Street Songs* she turned to Éluard.

them. In *Point Counter Point,* a year before this allusion to T. S. Eliot, Huxley had modeled Spandrell's disgusting career upon Baudelaire's. But the Laurentian Huxley of the late twenties was forgetting earlier benefits. He too had found congenial expression through Baudelaire. Commencing as a disciple of Edith Sitwell, Huxley had contributed to *Wheels,* and his early volumes of verse maintained on their level a course parallel with hers. Convinced like her of the emptiness of all things, he had followed her not only to Baudelaire, but to Laforgue and Rimbaud.

"Back Streets" is a Baudelairian prose poem on the degraded life of a modern city. "Morning Scene," in verse, and many of the other poems from *Leda* reflect the horrors of Baudelaire, whose *"Femmes damnées"* Huxley translated. He resembled Baudelaire in dandyism, elegance, and preoccupation with what he detested.

Something of an æsthetic snob, young Huxley found Laforgue to his taste. In "The Walk," a poem on the banality of the suburb, the rhythms and the quotidian piano are Laforgue's, and the knowing parade of French slang is Huxley's. Other poems and the portrait of Denis in *Crome Yellow* (1921) present Laforgue's Prufrockian hero. From Laforgue, Huxley also acquired his habit of using scientific terms in startling contexts and a keener taste for exotic prose. Whereas Eliot improved Laforgue, Huxley reproduced him.[34]

Rimbaud gave intellectual Huxley a refuge from too much intellect. Incapable of imaginative holidays when well, he found that when fever was upon him his intellect softened. Under these conditions, he could approxi-

[34] Among Huxley's Laforguian poems are "Uncertainty to a Lady" and "Valedictory" in *The Defeat of Youth* (1918). In *Music at Night* (1931) Huxley commends Laforgue's ironic juxtapositions of the scientific and the religious or sentimental. See Ruth Temple: *"Aldous Huxley et la littérature française," Revue de Littérature Comparée,* January 1939.

mate that derangement of the senses which permits the combination of unrelated objects.[35]

Huxley's translations of Rimbaud's *"Chercheuses de poux"* and of Mallarmé's *"L'Après-midi,"* generally considered the best that have been made, express, like the best of his original poems, the decadence rather than the illuminations of the French tradition. A decadent young man of great talent and great intellect, he went with the help of the symbolists as far as talent and intellect allowed. If he could have discovered a better way to suspend his intellect, he might have become a considerable poet.

James Joyce, who adapted symbolist methods to the English novel, was familiar with a number of symbolists. In 1902 Yeats presented young Joyce to Arthur Symons, whose *Symbolist Movement in Literature* Joyce immediately read. In 1903 or earlier he studied Hauptmann and Strindberg, and for years he had admired Ibsen. Stephen Dedalus, who, before his trip to Paris, was able to talk of Rimbaud, Nerval, and Maeterlinck, was able on his return to talk of Mallarmé, Villiers, and the correspondences of Swedenborg.

It has been said that the symbolism of *Ulysses* consists in Joyce's subtle adaptation of rhythm, sound, and texture to his purpose. In *Stephen Hero* (1944), Stephen reads Rimbaud's sonnet on the vowels. Inspired by this poem, he puts his own poems together letter by letter "to fix the most elusive of his moods," and permutes the vowels to make words for his emotions. Since this practice, which obviously has some bearing upon the verbal technique of

[35] Huxley: "Fever," *Harper's,* June 1929. Among Huxley's imitations of Rimbaud are the prose poems of *Leda* (1920), "Zoo Celeste," *Wheels* (1918), and "The Reef," *Selected Poems* (1925).

Roy Campbell closely imitated Baudelaire, Rimbaud, and Valéry. *The Flaming Terrapin* (1924) is a version of *"Bateau ivre."* See *Adamastor* (1930). Justin O'Brien: "Poet on Horseback," *Kenyon Review,* IV (Winter 1942).

Ulysses, is based upon Rimbaud's, it is symbolist; but if it is peculiar to symbolism, Flaubert and Alexander Pope are symbolists. The doctrine of "epiphanies" announced by Stephen in *Stephen Hero* is more plainly symbolist. An epiphany, he says, is a "sudden spiritual manifestation" of an object, however trivial and quotidian, the radiance of a moment. This idea, which resembles Baudelaire's,[36] seems to underlie the short stories of *Dubliners,* fragments of life, trivial moments, which reveal through their reverberations something beyond themselves.

It is often supposed that *Ulysses* is a symbolist novel because it is filled with symbols. To be sure, the book is filled with symbols. Most of its parts symbolize organs of the human body, and most the human arts. Each part contains a symbol expressing the essence of that part. The action is symbolic, and while the Homeric parallel is maintained by means of allusions, hints, and symbols, the three principal characters, representing three kinds of man, symbolize man. Subsidiary symbols fill the book—the loss of keys, the breakfast, wave and tower. But this symbolism is more medieval than modern. Joyce compared his book with Phineas Fletcher's *Purple Island.* And it must be recalled that Joyce, immersed in the Catholic tradition, loved Dante.

Although on one level *Ulysses* is a realistic study of a day in Dublin, on its symbolic levels it is as universal as Dante's *Comedy* or *The Romance of the Rose.* On these levels the book concerns the modern world, man's nature, and his arts. The symbolism by which these are revealed is sometimes odd. The scene in the newspaper office symbolizes the lungs on the organic level and rhetoric among

[36] Baudelaire believed that in "certain almost supernatural states of soul the depth of life is revealed in ordinary everyday happenings. Ordinary life then becomes the Symbol."

the arts. On the Homeric level the office symbolizes the cave of Æolus, and the headlines that interrupt the text suggest the office and our world. The scene in the Ormond Bar, which represents the Sirens and the ear, has music as its symbol. Music in turn is indicated by punning allusions ("Tenors get women by the score") and by fugal structure. Since Joyce used symbols to represent the ideal and the eternal against which the narrative moves, the symbolism is half the book. If it is held that the symbolism complicates and interferes with the narrative, it might be held with equal justice that the narrative interferes with the symbolism. On the whole, however, the two get along comfortably together and the complexity that each imposes on the other is nothing to that of the world we live in.[37]

To the symbolists Joyce turned for other things. His chief debt is to Édouard Dujardin, whose *Lauriers sont coupés* (1888) is the first symbolist novel. Trying like other symbolists to find a medium for subjective deformation of outer reality, Dujardin invented a stream of consciousness. Except for this technique the result is uninteresting; but Joyce developed its possibilities and, with the help of other symbolists, proceeded to explore the mind.[38]

The verbal distortions of *Ulysses,* the grammatical improvisations, and the cunning incompatibilities of image belong generally to the tradition of Mallarmé, as the employment of dream and hallucination, whatever the specific source, belongs to the tradition of Rimbaud. On

[37] For a catalogue of Joyce's symbols see Stuart Gilbert: *James Joyce's* Ulysses (1930). The elaborate color symbolism of *Ulysses* is probably based upon the synesthetic correspondences of Rimbaud and the other symbolists.

[38] Dujardin: *Le Monologue intérieur* (1931) celebrates Joyce's use of *Les Lauriers sont coupés.* Cf. Dujardin's preface to the 1924 edition of his novel.

the whole *Ulysses* fulfills the ideal of the symbolist novel as stated by Jean Moréas in the manifesto of 1886. In this ideal novel

> a unique hero moves in places deformed by his hallucinations and his temperament. Mechanical beings move around the unique person, serving as pretexts for his sensations and conjectures. Mythical phantoms are evoked. Disdainful of the puerile method of naturalism, the symbolist novel bases itself on subjective deformation.

Ulysses does not altogether follow this pattern, for it has a generous admixture of naturalism; but *Finnegans Wake* follows it precisely. With his overtones, rhythms, tortured and sometimes melted language, Joyce went further than the symbolists and approximated the surrealist ideal. From Flaubert on the one hand, and from the entire symbolist tradition on the other, Joyce had learned how to present conscious and unconscious reality by all the arts of definition and suggestion. Such arts, though they may excite our wonder, are of less value for themselves, of course, than for the reality they express. That Joyce was a master of reality is recognized, if not by many Englishmen, by most American and Continental critics. To most of them *Ulysses* seems revolutionary, but it is plain by now that it looks backward, not forward, and that like other epics it comes toward the close of a period, summarizing it. A complete expression of the romantic period, *Ulysses* includes all romantic materials and all exploratory techniques. What Dante's *Comedy* did for the Middle Ages or *Paradise Lost* for the Renaissance, *Ulysses* does for the age of the middle class.

Inspired by Joyce, other novelists of the twenties and thirties turned to indirection, symbols, and the stream of consciousness. Virginia Woolf owed her technique in part to Joyce, and the symbols that interrupt her subjective stream, the leaden circles of Big Ben in *Mrs. Dalloway*, for example, are Joycean or French. The curious obliquity, the symbolic fish and sea of *Rainbow Fish* (1937) by Ralph Bates, are similar in character. The symbolism of such novels and of Lawrence's, no longer the rather wooden kind of Galsworthy, is enigmatic and suggestive.

What cannot be expressed directly can be expressed indirectly. Of the poets who had also learned this lesson under French masters, none had learned it better than the poets of the late thirties. At this time Baudelaire and Laforgue, who had served poets as masters, were succeeded by Rimbaud and, sometimes, Mallarmé.[39] Although recalling Rimbaud's "*Bateau ivre*," Dylan Thomas's "Ballad of the Long-Legged Bait" is not an imitation, but an original poem of the same kind. Poems of Lawrence Durrell and Peter Yates, no less indebted to the French tradition, are no less original.

Durrell hunts *A Private Country* (1943) for "precise emotion by clues." Arrangements of thought and feeling, inseparable from their odd fastidious expression, bring Wallace Stevens to mind. And in line behind him the shades of Rimbaud, Mallarmé, and Apollinaire fix Durrell in the symbolist tradition at its most bizarre. His songs and elegies of Greece use the Ægean past not so much as refuge from the unmentionable present but as medium through which to pass it. Prismatic refractions compose his country and its climate. Dandyism, the adjustment of ruffle and cravat in a vacant lot, gives an air to "The Sonnet of Hamlet" and "The Death of General Uncebunke," his most elaborate sequences. An amorist of parts, he is

[39] The revival of interest in Mallarmé is shown by Roger Fry's literal translation: *Mallarmé, Poems* (1937), and, for example, by the translations by Francis Scarfe in *Inscapes* (1940).

not unlike Don Giovanni, that fortunate man, who kept a private orchestra to play him *Figaro.*[40]

Yates, a philosophical poet, thinks in symbols about man's condition. His chiseled poems, seeming lucid, are difficult, but, like poems of Valéry on another, parallel plane, yield when the clue is found. On second reading, the repeated symbols of mirror, bone, and pole communicate, and the reader discovers that *The Expanding Mirror* (1942) reflects horror of life. Confined within "the cube of now," the poet seeks a formula for time, space, and prisoner. But every formula, while bringing magic and elegance to shape, adds pressure to the "is of this." His second collection, *The Motionless Dancer* (1943), promises escape. The dancer is a statue, surrounded by river, love, and falling leaf, immune to change. Out of nature, he becomes a symbol of timeless perfection, of living death, like Yeats's golden bird, Eliot's Chinese jar, or Huxley's Heard. Even the purity of bone, though inferior to such perfection, seems better to Yates than the rose with "paranoiac wings." These thoughts, repeating the death-wish of our time, are not original—Hardy had them and Omar too (with wine)—but these poems, of value this and that side of thought, are.

Whether Thomas, Durrell, Yates, or the other poets of their generation drew directly or indirectly upon the French is unimportant. What matters is that English poetry, inflamed by France and freed at last from all Victorians but Hopkins, had been renewed.

[40] *Cities, Plains and People* (1946), his second collection, is simpler but equally strange.

CHAPTER VIII

The Stream of Consciousness

THE romantic movement has been exploratory. Among the most fruitful of new countries to be opened up and surveyed with wonder is the conscious mind. What, its explorers asked, is the nature of experience and what the nature of self? Is reality to be found without the mind, as naturalists had thought, or within it? Is consciousness simple or complex, discrete or continuous? Does it proceed on one or many levels? What part does memory play, or time? Romantics of our time were not the first to ask these questions, but they were among the first to use novels for the answers.

There were other motives for introspection. For some it was an escape from the outer world, increasingly awful, to an inner refuge—an escape, sometimes, from one chaos to another. For others, despairing of external certainty, faced with the apparent impotence of action and intellect, the inner chaos, however relative, became an absolute. Reality had moved from brothel and slum to the lonely head. Explorer and refugee alike, attempting a greater reality than realists had known, belong with transcendentalist and symbolist to the great rebellion against the external, the material, the logical, and other impediments to truth.

Entering new lands ahead of English novelists, philosophers surveyed the interior and determined its economy. William James and Henri Bergson, the chief among these romantics, made explicit what others could feel and directed future feeling by map and guide. In "The Stream of Thought," a chapter of his *Principles of Psychology* (1890), William James, commencing the "study of the mind from within," found constant change and a "teeming multiplicity of objects and relations." Science, reducing life to simplicity, had tried to make consciousness clear and logical, said James; but looking within, he could see only the fringes and penumbras that surround, obscure, and give significance to images. Far from being discrete, consciousness proved on introspection to be continuous flow. "A 'river' or a 'stream' are the metaphors by which it is most naturally described. In talking of it hereafter, let us call it the stream of thought, of consciousness, or of subjective life." Having given novelists a place to float in and a name for it, James passed to the consequent problem of identity. We are nct one self, as scientists and novelists had thought, but many selves; in fact, a flux of identities without determinate outlines. Novelists soon found themselves wondering if they were James or Virginia or Marcel and if their characters were characters or streams of experience or waves.

Simultaneously in France, Henri Bergson, Proust's relative and brother-in-law to Yeats's spiritual adviser MacGregor Mathers, was also rebelling against scientific externality and mathematical abstraction. By intuition or intellectual sympathy he discovered reality in "the indivisible flux" of consciousness, which he called "duration." Made continuous by memory, which charges each moment with its past, duration involves a present that, like Gertrude Stein's, is "always beginning again." The trouble with science, logic, and clocks, said Bergson, is their imposition of concept upon flowing reality. Logical and scientific novelists, he continued, had distorted and simplified reality. Ticketing characters, they had drawn outlines around them and framed their thoughts. He advised novelists to get inside their heroes by intuition and, forgetting logic, clock, and all the traditions of character, to flow.

Long before James or Bergson, Turgenyev had evolved a subjective technique for *Smoke* and other novels, and Chekhov, discarding logic, outline, and plot, had devoted his short stories to small situations that reveal the depths of personality and release those vapors of mood in which reality seems to float. Dostoyevsky, looking within himself, had discovered, if not the stream of consciousness, the problem of identity. Raskolnikov in *Crime and Punishment* has two identities, one projected as Svidrigailov. The characters of *Notes from Underground* and of other novels suffer from split, contradictory, and multiple personalities. "Do you know," says Versilov in *A Raw Youth,* "I feel as though I were split in two? . . . It's just as though one's second self were standing beside one; one is sensible and rational oneself, but the other self is impelled to do something perfectly senseless. . . ." According to André Gide, his disciple, Dostoyevsky explored vast regions of the soul, revealing the baffling complexity that earlier novelists had tried to make logical and consistent. His novels, translated into English during the eighties, found English novelists unready to make use of his discoveries. But the translations by Constance Garnett, coming after 1912 upon the heels of Bergson and Freud, found them ready and willing.

Bergson was right in seeing himself and James as parts of a tendency much larger than themselves. Over in France, Édouard Dujardin had discovered the stream of consciousness before William James wrote about it, and in *Les Lauriers sont coupés* (1888) had invented a technique with which to present it. In England writers of fantasy had discovered multiple personality before their more serious compatriots. Stevenson's Dr. Jekyll and Beerbohm's happy hypocrite are as divided as Gertrude Stein's Teresa, who is one self indoors and another out.

The effects of this pioneering by philosopher and novelist were not immediately evident in England except in the works of Henry James, Conrad, and, to some extent, George Moore. But after 1916 the course of English fiction for many years was determined by these explorations and by those of the psychoanalysts. Seen from within, the characters of this new fiction lack definite outline and, often, connections with things external to themselves. Their selves are multiple; their conduct is not infrequently irrational. Mysterious organisms, not mechanisms, they have souls. The novels in which these fluid creatures move are sometimes as deficient in outline as the fluid creatures themselves. Looking back at the "typical" novels of this period—*Ulysses* and *The Waves*—William Butler Yeats found them deluges of experience "breaking over us and within us, melting limits whether of line or tint," and their people swimmers or "the waves themselves."[1] Noting this "self-dissolving introspection, the generally heightened awareness of the goings on of our own minds, merely as goings on," I. A. Richards found Joyce his best and most sensitive example. The inner world of Stephen Dedalus is "composed of images which shift and flow and merge with an intricacy" beyond the power of intellect to follow.[2]

Among the first in England to adjust his technique to the demands of flux was George Moore, who had commenced his career as novelist in the objective tradition of

[1] *Wheels and Butterflies* (1934).
[2] *Coleridge on Imagination* (1935).

Zola. But, as we have seen, Moore gradually turned away from the scientific and the external. This reaction was assisted by *Les Lauriers sont coupés* of his friend Édouard Dujardin and by the example of Turgenyev, whom Moore distantly imitated in the short stories of *The Untilled Field* (1903). *The Lake* (1905), an expansion of one of the stories in this volume, is the first unmistakable sign of Moore's new narrative method, which, although not a stream of consciousness in the later sense of that term, achieves a kind of flow in which objective and subjective dissolve and merge. By rhythms and imperceptible transitions the reader is washed along sometimes within the hero, sometimes without. This method was brought to perfection in *The Brook Kerith* (1916), a book with currents so insidious and palpable that the reader is put to it to penetrate the surface or, sometimes, to stay awake. By a triumph of style, which maintains a melodious flow of its own above the matter it is intended to carry, Moore obtained effects that other writers were obtaining by point of view. For his autobiographical sketches, commencing with *Memoirs of My Dead Life* (1906), he contrived a method that, though not dissimilar, proved more successful because perhaps his matter fascinated him. *Hail and Farewell* (1911–14), the outstanding memoir of our times, is an extended stream of memories, proceeding capriciously by free association, and revealing by nuance and tone not so much the people of the story as the selves of its creator.

Henry James, who went further than Moore toward a suitable method, was also in revolt against naturalism. An admirer of Turgenyev, whom he knew in Paris, and brother to the philosopher of the stream, James hunted ways of presenting the mind in moral and social situations. It appears from his prefaces, however, that his methods owe less to Turgenyev and William James than to the necessities of art. For the sake of unity, drama, irony, and suspense he employed for his subjective purposes narrative in first person and the more penetrating technique of impressionism.

He found the first person singular of use for presenting delusions that the narrator cherished in his mind and projected upon external reality. In *The Turn of the Screw* (1898) James, an expert in the unmentionable, used all his arts of indirection. The story is told in first person by the governess not only because the ambiguities must not be injured by intervention of the author but because, an apparent neurotic, she must be allowed to expose the workings of her mind, upon which in the end our interest must center. In *The Sacred Fount* (1901), another study of delusion, the narrator is permitted to display himself. His week-end at a country house is made fascinating by his hypothesis about the relationship, the worse the better, of two couples. He snoops, interprets, and dodges around corners to corroborate his ingenious obsession, until, tiring of the metaphysical game, Mrs. Brissenden confronts him with the facts. " 'I think you're crazy,' " she observes. "It naturally struck me. 'Crazy'? I remember just wondering if perhaps I mightn't be."

In the technique of "impressionism" James found a better method for presenting more normal processes of mind. His impressionism, which must not be confused with impressionism in painting, is a method whereby an observer's mind is the stage upon which all action occurs. But the impressions of the observer are recorded in the third person by the author, peering through a window in the observer's head. Since the author tells what is occurring on this subjective stage, he can limit the narrative by selecting what he thinks relevant or suitable and maintain an artist's control over the flow of experience. The most objective of subjective novelists, an extrovert compared with Virginia Woolf, James generally limited the flow to levels of polite intercourse and to things external to the observer, who looked out as James looked in.

This method, which James first used in *The Spoils of Poynton* (1897), was brought to perfection in *What Maisie Knew* (1897), a tale of divorce, adultery, and the consequent difficulties of Maisie, a child. Because she occupies the center of this situation, James chose Maisie's consciousness as his stage. "The one presented register of the whole complexity," he says in his preface, "would be the play of the child's confused and obscure notation of it." That it should be presented through a child's awareness of it was required by convenience, economy, art, and above all by the fact that it afforded a "most delightful difficulty." For though the female young have "no end of sensibility," no child of six or eight could know all that the observer must know. Looking into her head, James told what she saw and did not know, expressed what she could only feel, and, by judicious interference assisted the reader through her perplexities. As we look through Maisie's eyes and feel what she feels and listen to the helpful asides of James, we discover in what might have been a common domestic tragedy the mystery, drama, and suspense that for some of us surround our own affairs.

By this point of view James gave similar immediacy and excitement to other stories that otherwise might have seemed familiar or banal. *The Wings of the Dove* (1902) cover British designs upon American innocence and wealth. Milly, the American girl, is so sensitive, and Kate and Merton, the British designers, are so delicate, that almost no words are necessary among them. To interpret their gestures, silences, and intimations four observers are required, two British and two American; but for all this observation we never know what Milly is dying of. Is it anemia or leukemia or consumption? The suspense is maddening; but, as in a symbolist poem, we are never told. *The Ambassadors* (1903) discovers an American, Chad, who has acquired a mistress in Paris. Strether, the American observer, who is sent to find what is detaining the lad, is assisted in his interpretations by a confidante, a happy device for the aid of observer, author, and reader alike. With her aid we follow the gradual expansion of Strether's awareness as he approaches civilization and life until at last he realizes Chad's condition. The development of awareness has been so carefully limited to the limited observer, however, that few readers can have anticipated him in this exciting discovery.

For bloodless creatures, eternally spinning and projecting upon the outer world their webs of speculation and fancy, the subjective approach is fortunate. By its aid even the sanguine reader can find excitement where it seems unlikely. James's method is as dramatic as exploratory; but many readers used to find the results impalpable or dull. Remarking the "copious emptiness" of these novels, H. G. Wells in *Boon* (1915) compared them to a church "without congregation to distract you, with every light and line focused on the high altar. And on the altar, very reverently placed, intensely there, is a dead kitten, an egg-shell, a bit of string. . . ." But Conrad, Dorothy Richardson, and Ford Madox Ford hailed James as master, and, with his example before them, embarked upon further explorations of the inner world. And it is clear today that James anticipated Proust not only in the analysis of a decaying society but to some extent in method. Associations of *The Middle Years* (1917), an autobiography, expand in rings from a nuclear memory as in Proust, and as in Proust each ring is subjected, as it expands, to analysis and qualification in expanding sentences. James read *Swann's Way* on its appearance before the war, but before he could make use of it for the enhancement of his parallel method or, indeed, before he could do more than receive the Order of Merit from a royal hand, he died.

James's earliest disciple, Joseph Conrad, who has been justly considered a nautical variety of his master, saw James in *Notes on Life and Letters* (1921) as a great artist with a "conscience troubled by the nice discrimination of shades of conduct." This describes Conrad better than James. To settle doubts of human values, to support faith in man lost in a careless universe, Conrad created Marlow, a kind of detective of conscience, whose consciousness is the scene of several important stories and novels.

In his prefaces and here and there in the novels Conrad speaks of the inner truth, the real meaning of life, and of the difficulty of getting at it. The technique of impressionism, which he learned from James and suitably modified for his own purposes, provided a way. Marlow became the observer and in his own words "went gravely about trying to account . . . for a lot of things no one would care to bother one's head about." Marlow is a many-sided character, a union of sentiment, morality, cynicism, and curiosity. His impressions of reality distort it before passing it on to the reader, and before Marlow receives it, it has been distorted by the temperaments and memories of those who report to him. As in *Lord Jim* (1900) Marlow usually works upon impressions at several removes from the facts. Interested in Jim's honor, he questions those who have seen Jim or who have talked to those who have seen him. Sometimes the facts have passed through the refracting media of three or four minds, augmented, distorted, and changing color at each passage, before Marlow in turn can impose his share and focus the result. The story, therefore, is less the story of Jim and his search for honor than the passage of this story through minds of which Marlow's is the point of interest. In his passion for truth Marlow discards chronological sequence and tells the story in fragments as he received it. Students of morality may rejoice with students of memory and subjective deformation, but the reader who goes to *Lord Jim* for adventures in the South Seas goes mad.

Jim's personality, in so far as we can disengage it from Marlow's contributions, is complex, and his motives are obscure. If Jim has any depths below the moral level or heights above it, however, they are not explored. Flora de Barral, the heroine of *Chance* (1914), on the other hand, is far more than a moral problem for Marlow: she is a tortured soul whose obsessions seem Freudian, or at least Russian. Innocent of Freud, and indifferent to Dostoyevsky, whom he liked far less than Turgenyev, Conrad seems to have drawn this study of father-daughter relationship and of psychological trauma, as Hardy drew Sue Bridehead, from his own observation. Marlow is fascinated; and as he pieces the story of Flora together from many reports, he illustrates again the arts of impressionism and obliquity.

Conrad used Jamesian impressionism to penetrate solitary regions that James preferred to hint at and conceal. Conrad used obliquity of structure, as James used the device of expanding awareness, to give reality its due. But subjecting reality to a longer sojourn in the mind, Conrad made more use of memory and took advantage of its nature. *Youth* (1902) is the reflection by mature memory of youthful illusion, and *Victory* (1915) brings memories of many observers to bear upon man in an exotic corner of the alien universe. James never brooded about the universe. The heaviness by which Conrad distorted what was already distorted makes his work seem profounder than James's elegant webs of colloquialism, qualification, and astonishing metaphor. But except for occasional excursions both of them pursued reality upon the same level, that of conscious experience.[3]

Dorothy Richardson admired James and Conrad. On commencing to imitate them she discovered, however, that their technique was too remote from what she thought reality. From their impressionism she independently developed a technique in which the flow of experience is conveyed not by the analysis of observer or author but by letting experience flow. Far more realistic than impressionism, her stream of consciousness is an attempt to record the contents of the mind without that selection by which James maintained the canons of art and the demands of decorum. Thoughts, feeling, images from the senses, and the endless, inexplicable irrelevancies that constitute waking life and complicate it by pursuing several simultaneous courses—in short, the rich confusion described by Bergson and William James as our immediate reality—became her material, and fidelity to this rich confusion provided her technique. Placing herself inside the head of Miriam, she recorded in flowing sentences or at times in disjointed fragments the flow of Miriam's mind. This flow, which began with *Pointed Roofs* (1915) and continued through nine other novels, was collected in *Pilgrimage*.

If Dorothy Richardson had attempted to record every moment of Miriam's life, she would have required more than ten volumes, but she contented herself with selecting short periods of tedium or intensity. Within these selected periods there is no selection. But the necessities of truth and silence imposed upon the novelist by the nature of the stream were fatal to structure. Held together only by

[3] For *The Moon and Sixpence* (1919) Maugham adopted Conrad's observer and his structural obliquity. Cf. the role of Ashenden in *Cakes and Ale* (1930). For Maugham's interest in the many-leveled character see his autobiography.

continuity of person, such as it is, *Pilgrimage* falls into separate fragments. Plot and action have virtually disappeared, character has lost its elegance of shape, and personality has been all but replaced by a series of reactions; for the interest is no longer centered upon what occurs without, but upon what flows within. That we may know what Miriam looks like, Richardson has her sit before a mirror. If we can trust her own impression, Miriam is plain. It is not surprising that almost nothing happens to her. Following her heroine as she teaches school, takes tea, walks on an Alp, or enjoys a botanical rapture, the novelist bores from within. It is difficult to quarrel with Frank Swinnerton, who, while recognizing Dorothy Richardson's development of technique, wishes that Miriam had died young.[4]

Rebellion against old-fashioned fixity of character and against the imposition of plot led Dorothy Richardson in pursuit of an internal reality undistorted by concept to a formlessness that is realistic enough, but monotonous and æsthetically unsatisfying. James Joyce, her contemporary and fellow explorer, showed that the new fluidity could be reconciled with form. In place of the string of sausages into which Miriam's selected and interrupted experience falls, Joyce provided symphonic structure, which, while satisfying the requirements of beauty, is closer to reality and to a greater area of reality. In place of the adequate but uninteresting prose of Miriam's stream, Joyce brought all the resources of poetry to bear upon the illustration of consciousness. Suggestion, symbol, rhythm, dramatic changes of tone, texture of language, conceits, and neologisms express the richness of experience. A virtuoso of

[4] Frank Swinnerton: *The Georgian Scene* (1934). W. L. Myers: *The Later Realism* (1927). May Sinclair: Introduction to *Pointed Roofs* (1919 edition). Louise Morgan: "Dorothy M. Richardson," *Everyman*, October 22, 1931. J. C. Powys: *Dorothy M. Richardson* (1931).

language, reminding one in turn of Shakespeare, Flaubert, and the symbolists, Joyce could command rhythm and sound for such effects as this: "Grossbooted draymen rolled barrels dullthudding out of Prince's stores and bumped them up on the brewery float."

Although several of the stories in *Dubliners* (1914) belong to the objective tradition of Maupassant and Flaubert, certain of the stories, such as "Araby" and "An Encounter," with their obliquities and unresolved situations, are impressionistic. In the latter story the presentation of adult depravity through the childish consciousness repeats the triumph of *What Maisie Knew*. Joyce was acquainted with some of the works of Henry James, but for these stories he may have been equally indebted to Turgenyev or to his own invention. In "Clay," Joyce turned the objective method of the naturalists to the implication of inner barrenness. "Counterparts" and "The Dead," suggesting by trivial incident and mood more than they contain, reveal, in the manner of Chekhov, the depths of personality and of human relationship. These cold and masterly stories of frustration, the first and among the best of those we recognize as "modern," were rejected by a Dublin publisher because real shops and King Edward were named. For permission to name Edward, Joyce wrote to George, who, if he had answered, would be a famous man.

A Portrait of the Artist as a Young Man (1916) is impressionistic autobiography. Selecting, like Dorothy Richardson, the moments of importance, Joyce penetrated below and above the level of decencies on which James, Conrad, and Richardson moved. At the beginning, by selection, memory, and suitable incoherence he presented the quality of the infant stream of consciousness, if not the stream itself, and later he presented from within the feelings, emotions, and intellectual life of a hero at once more emotional and more intellectual than anyone in

James or Conrad. The refusal of English and Irish publishers to accept this book reveals the extent to which Joyce, departing from conventions, had enlarged the scope of the novel.

The method with which Joyce experimented in the *Portrait* was perfected in *Ulysses.*[5] This great comedy was immediately banned by English-speaking countries because Joyce had explored the corners of the mind and all its levels. For many years English and American tourists came home from Paris with copies bound as prayerbooks or hidden under shirts. At last, in 1933, John Woolsey, judge of the United States District Court of New York, remembering that since we inhabit the corners of our minds we might as well read about them, allowed Americans to do so. The officials of England, broadening up from precedent, grandly ignored the subsequent appearance of *Ulysses* in London. But the theocratic Irish have found themselves unable to comply.

The third chapter of *Ulysses* concerns Stephen's walk along the beach at Sandymount. In this section (Proteus on the Homeric level) Joyce symbolized change and flux by the waves, the dissolving and rebuilding of the shore, and the flow of thought through Stephen's mind. Adapting Dujardin's technique, Joyce made Stephen's stream of consciousness a bright parade of thoughts, memories, sensations, and feelings linked by free association. Isolated words and phrases or formulated sentences express the

[5] *Ulysses* was written in Zurich and Paris, 1914–21, printed in part in the *Little Review*, 1918–20, and in the *Egoist*, and published in Paris, 1922. See Frank Budgen: *James Joyce and the Making of Ulysses* (1934); Stuart Gilbert: *James Joyce's* Ulysses (1930); Édouard Dujardin: *Le Monologue intérieur, son apparition, ses origines, sa place dans l'œuvre de James Joyce* (1931).

More Pricks than Kicks (1934) and *Murphy* (1938) by Samuel Beckett, the best of Joyce's Irish followers, are precious, elegant, and absurd. In *At Swim-Two-Birds* (1939) Flann O'Brien uses several of Joyce's techniques to say nothing elaborately.

intricate, many-leveled flow of experience, verbalized sometimes by Stephen, sometimes by Joyce. The mental tone is alert, for he always suited means to purpose, and Stephen serves as his symbol of intellect and imagination. In the fourth chapter, the Calypso episode, we enter the mind of Mr. Bloom and flow with his stream of consciousness as he visits Dlugacz's butcher shop, cooks breakfast, feeds cat and wife, and meditates in the jakes. Although Mr. Bloom's stream also consists of fragments and sentences and also reveals the total contents of his mind, it has a quality and rhythm of its own, opposite to Stephen's; for Mr. Bloom is the average man, the citizen of cities, the indifferent audience that men like Stephen fled. Mrs. Bloom's interior monologue, which we encounter in the last chapter, is different from both of these. Without the interference of intellect, her confusion of desire, feeling, and memory moves in a long gush, from which, in order to indicate its cowlike character, Joyce omitted all marks of punctuation. Mrs. Bloom represents the flesh, and her final word is suitably affirmative.

Far from dissolving the limits of character, Joyce's streams establish them. The effect of *Ulysses* is not liquefaction, but a curious solidity and, despite subjective flow, immobility. One wonders why Yeats chose *Ulysses* and *The Waves* as his examples of contemporary dissolution, for though they are both subjective, no two books could be less alike. Joyce's solid, brilliant reconstruction of Dublin, a symbol of the modern world and his private obsession, corresponds to nothing in *The Waves,* which have washed external things away. Though Joyce created external solidity, he shied away from external action, deterred perhaps by a conviction of its unimportance or perhaps by his inability to deal with it. His interest, moreover, was not action but being or "whatness" and psychological readjustment within a family, the change in relationship between Mr. and Mrs. Bloom that night, or between Mr. and Mrs. Earwicker. Admirably adapted to this purpose, the stream and the other subjective techniques prove inadequate for action. For an artist as conscious of means and limitations as Joyce, commitment to flow was a farewell to movement. If it seems odd that a novel based upon the *Odyssey* should be so static and marmoreal, the limitations of purpose and technique should be considered. And one may admire the art by which Joyce drew his glittering structure from chaos, disgust, and dissolution without impairing that sense of them which is the privilege of our times.

Part of Joyce's solidity comes from his use of other means to supplement the stream. Mr. Bloom is the most fully realized character in recent fiction because we see him from within and without by the aid of many arts. He is as definite as sculpture. Yet we know his interior, the levels of his mind both conscious and unconscious, and, apart from these, his actions and his effect upon others through whose minds his image passes. To achieve this triumph of characterization Joyce used every known point of view and invented others. About one third of the book consists of parody, which he made an instrument for displaying or examining human nature. For another third he used drama, objective question and answer, musical development, and even traditional narrative.

The Nausicaa episode, in which Gerty MacDowell and Mr. Bloom become aware of each other on the beach, is divided into two parts, Gerty's consciousness and Mr. Bloom's. Gerty's is presented in the style of a cheap Victorian novel in order to suggest a mind that can cast a glamour even over Mr. Bloom. His is presented in the earthiest of interior monologues. This shocking disparity not only fixes each character from within, but serves, since each mind reflects the other, to externalize the other. In the hospital scene (Oxen of the Sun) Joyce used parodies of English literature in chronological sequence. Illustrating virtuosity, these parodies also present, while they almost conceal, the conversation of the medical students, Stephen's state of mind and its literary character, and the birth of a son to Mrs. Purefoy. The technique, said Joyce is "embryonic": "While the baby is being born upstairs, English literature is being born downstairs." The parody of the Reverend Alexander J. Dowie at the end of this sequence suggests decay and growing intoxication. The scene in the cabman's shelter (Eumaeus) is written in a fatigued style to suggest the state of Bloom and Stephen. The trick is brilliant, but the danger after almost fifty pages is that the reader too may be fatigued. Joyce never realized, and this is his principal fault, that there may be too much of a good thing. The return of Mr. Bloom with Stephen to 7 Eccles Street (Ithaca) is treated objectively by means of question and answer in the barren style of a catechism or of a scientific text. On the conscious level, fatigue, ending in sleep, is suggested, and on the anatomical level the skeleton. The cold, exact point of view of science, of a too well-established church, or of a legal inquiry provides the antithesis to the stream of consciousness and helps to establish the sculptural effect. Let us see, the author seems to say, what science or religion would make of this palpitating material. The last two pages, which place Mr. and Mrs. Bloom in relation to the points of the compass, the orbit of the earth, and the universe of stars, resolving fatigue and wandering in sleep, are as fine as anything in Joyce.

Each of these methods carries many meanings on many levels, and each episode, whatever its method, is linked to the others by common themes and mazes of allusion. This labyrinthine structure is epitomized in the central chapter (the Wandering Rocks), in which eighteen brief episodes, some subjective, some objective, are elaborately tied by theme and reference to each other and to the rest of the book. If this chapter is the epitome of the book, it follows that the book itself is a labyrinth; and it is not for nothing that Joyce named his hero after that famous carpenter who assisted Pasiphaë in her strange amours. By the creation of his labyrinth, which reflects the confusion of our world while imposing order upon it, Joyce was able to control his fluid materials. The discipline imposed upon his youth by the Jesuits gave the mature artist the detachment and control required to bring intricate form to flow and chaos. Joyce's interior monologues, however unselected and realistic they appear to be, are as thoroughly controlled for the ends of art as the impressions of the observer in Henry James. Yeats was more nearly right about Joyce when he saw him not as a victim of contemporary dissolution but as "the scholastic Irishman."

Jesuitical Stephen Dedalus, who brought "to tavern and to brothel the mind of witty Aristotle," distrusted, says Joyce, "aquacities of thought and language." Virginia Woolf adored them, and her novels, far more representative than *Ulysses* of Bergson's ideal and that of William James, mark the ultimate in deliquescence. But there can be virtue in deliquescence. Unimpeded by witty Aristotle, Virginia Woolf became an artist of the stream of consciousness, of which her works provide the most perfect examples.[6]

In "Modern Fiction" Mrs. Woolf speaks of reading *Ulysses*, which was appearing in the *Little Review*. By his subjective approach, his spirituality and sincerity, she says, Joyce reveals the "flickerings of that innermost flame

[6] There are studies of Virginia Woolf by David Daiches (1942), Winifred Holtby (1932), Floris Delattre (1932), E. M. Forster (1942), and Joan Bennett (1945). Cf. Herbert J. Muller: *Modern Fiction* (1937), J. W. Beach: *The Twentieth Century Novel* (1932), Edward Wagenknecht: *Cavalcade of the English Novel* (1943).

which flashes its messages through the brain" and brings us face to face with life itself. He sheds light on the dark places of the mind, which for moderns are the one consuming interest, but his light is too brilliant, its focus too precise. He has shown by his technique the way to interior truth, but, she fears, there is something hard and narrow about him, a kind of intellectual angularity, inhuman and sterile. He deals in flow, to be sure, but he lays pipes for it. Avoiding the plumbing, she will make use of his stream.

"Modern Fiction," which repudiates the objective methods of Bennett, Wells, and Galsworthy, is the manifesto of this streaming art. Her account of what she proposes to do with Joycean method purged of Joyce is the best description of the stream of conscicusness:

> Examine for a moment an ordinary mind on an ordinary day. The mind receives a myriad impressions—trivial, fantastic, evanescent, or engraved with the sharpness of steel. From all sides they come, an incessant shower of innumerable atoms; and as they fall, as they shape themselves into the life of Monday or Tuesday, the accent falls differently from of old; the moment of importance came not here but there; so that if a writer were a free man . . . if he could base his work upon his own feeling and not upon convention, there would be no plot, no comedy, no tragedy, no love interest or catastrophe in the accepted style, and perhaps not a single button sewn on as the Bond Street tailors would have it. Life is not a series of gig lamps symmetrically arranged; but a luminous halo, a semi-transparent envelope surrounding us from the beginning of consciousness to the end. Is it not the task of the novelist to convey this varying, this unknown and uncircumscribed spirit, whatever aberration or complexity it may display, with as little mixture of the alien and external as possible? We are not pleading merely for courage and sincerity; we are suggesting that the proper stuff of

> fiction is a little other than custom would have us believe it. . . . Let us record the atoms as they fall upon the mind in the order in which they fall, let us trace the pattern, however disconnected and incoherent in appearance, which each sight or incident scores upon the consciousness.[7]

The Voyage Out (1915) and *Night and Day* (1919), her early novels, were promising, but conventional in method. With "The Mark on the Wall" (1919), a short sketch reprinted in *Monday or Tuesday* (1921), she entered her new domain and fulfilled at once the promise of her early novels and of her manifesto. This sketch, which epitomizes her work, is the reverie of a woman who allows an unidentified mark on the wall to provoke a train of free associations. From the mark her mind wanders to thoughts on the uncertainty of life, to Shakespeare, to tables of precedence at court, to remains of the past, and back to the mark. The external world is represented by the mark, which turns out to be a snail. But no matter: the point is not the nature of the mark, but the flow of consciousness, and the interest lies in the workings of the mind for their own sake.

Snails were at home in the world of Virginia Woolf, but not so much as fish, which became her favorite metaphor for illustrating the progress of the soul through the waves of consciousness. The reader, swimming her waves, becomes a fish, and, if he is not careful, he loses shape, like the soluble fish of André Breton, and becomes a wave. And why not? If flow is our reality, and if the aim of the

[7] "Modern Fiction," written April 1919, was reprinted in *The Common Reader* (1925). For Mrs. Woolf's hostility to the naturalists see also *Mr. Bennett and Mrs. Brown* (1924). Bennett's *Accident* (1928), an experiment in the stream of consciousness, seems to be his answer to Mrs. Woolf. Both Bennett and Wells had been interested in multiple personality; e.g., *Clayhanger* and *Marriage* (1912).

realist is immersion of self and reader in the flow, if life has no meaning except the sense of immersion and flow (and she seems to hold these truths to be self-evident), by all means let us dissolve, admiring the arts by which we are transformed. It was not accidental that Virginia Woolf, a symbolist to the end, cast herself into the river Ouse and drowned.

Casting herself, before this, into the stream of her heroine's consciousness, Mrs. Woolf abandoned herself in novel after novel to her idea of ultimate reality. In *To the Lighthouse* (1927) she flows with Mrs. Ramsay, who sits on the terrace reading a story to her little boy. The words of the story occupy part of her consciousness, but she is also aware of her husband striding up and down; simultaneously she thinks of Mr. Carmichael and the rumor that he was addicted to drugs, and she thinks of the marriages of friends. Across this section of an ordinary mind on an ordinary day leaps the thought: "the bill for the greenhouse would be fifty pounds."

But Virginia Woolf was not, as this would seem to imply, a recorder of the stream; she is its poet, suggesting immersion and the quality of thought, often below the level of consciousness, by means of rhythm and symbol. Mrs. Dalloway sits sewing:

> Quiet descended on her, calm, content, as her needle, drawing the silk smoothly to its gentle pause, collected the green folds together and attached them, very lightly to the belt. So on a summer's day waves collect, overbalance, and fall; collect and fall; and the whole world seems to be saying "that is all" more and more ponderously, until even the heart in the body which lies in the sun on the beach says too, That is all. Fear no more, says the heart, committing its burden to some sea, which sighs collectively for all sorrows, and renews, begins, collects, lets fall. And the body alone listens to the passing bee; the

> wave breaking; the dog barking, far away barking and barking.

This beautiful passage does not convey the substance of Mrs. Dalloway's thought, for she is not thinking of wave, beach, or dog. But by these symbols and rhythms Virginia Woolf gives us the feeling of Mrs. Dalloway's thought, the emotional halo that surrounds it, and the tone of her experience. By the more abstract symbolism of the alphabet Mrs. Woolf gives us in *To the Lighthouse* not the reasoning of Mr. Ramsay, the philosopher, as he confronts the limit of his intellect, but the feeling of this frustration. If thought is like the alphabet, he had reached Q, a point seldom reached in the whole of England, but as he strained for R with "qualities that would have saved a ship's company exposed on a broiling sea with six biscuits and a flask of water—endurance and justice, foresight, devotion, skill," as he strained for R and failed, he knew himself a failure. Novels should generalize, not analyze, says Mrs. Woolf in "Notes on an Elizabethan Play," and, suggesting mood by symbol, should occupy a plane above reality while expressing it.

No doubt James, Conrad, Dorothy Richardson, Chekhov, and Dostoyevsky helped to confirm Virginia Woolf in her subjective ways; for she read everything, including Laurence Sterne, who, in his rebellion against eighteenth-century rationalism, had provided her with a model of free association, subjective vagary, and freedom from plot.[8] But *Mrs. Dalloway* (1925), her first important work, is indebted primarily to Joyce. His three complementary

[8] Virginia Woolf's reviews of Henry James are reprinted in *The Death of the Moth* (1942), her essays on Conrad and the Russians in *The Common Reader*. Her essay on Sterne serves as the introduction to the Oxford edition of *A Sentimental Journey* (1928). Bergson's disciple Proust, whom she read in 1922, had considerable effect upon her later novels. *Night and Day* was inspired by Dostoyevsky's *Idiot*.

characters, Bloom, Mrs. Bloom, and Stephen, are matched by her Septimus and Mrs. Dalloway. His episode of the Wandering Rocks, in which several minds are linked by the passage through Dublin of the viceregal cavalcade, is matched by the scene in the park in which she links several minds by a sky-writing airplane.

To Winifred Holtby, Virginia Woolf remarked that she had not read Bergson, with whom Floris Delattre associates her. But she lived in Bloomsbury, where Bergson was a fad. Her sister-in-law, Karin Stephen, published a study of Bergson in 1922, and ten minutes with a Bergsonist would be enough. Whether or not Mrs. Woolf read Bergson, she seems to have been familiar with him. Her novels reflect his hostility to concept, logic, character, and external time, and his fidelity to flux.

In the early twenties it was the fashion of intellectuals to be anti-intellectual. Inspired by Bergson, Freud, and Dostoyevsky, they exploited the possibilities of the irrational. To Virginia Woolf, intellect appeared to be the enemy of fluid life. Sir William Bradshaw and Miss Kilman in *Mrs. Dalloway* represent this enmity, especially Miss Kilman, whose raincoat, inimical to waters, symbolizes her condition. Mr. Ramsay in *To the Lighthouse* shows by his pursuit of Q and R the limitations of Sir Leslie Stephen's Victorian intellect. Lily sees him as one who neglects flamingo sunsets for "angular essences" in the shape of kitchen tables "when you're not there." Mrs. Woolf's work abounds in similar symbols and in direct attacks upon concept. Her characters who, discarding intellect, abandon themselves to the mysterious flow of life are good, the others defective. Those who flow possess their souls; for however secular she appeared to be, Virginia Woolf was not without transcendental impulses. In the absence of religious instruction, public or private, she confused the soul with the flow of consciousness, evil with intellect, and spiritual exercise with the subjective method.

As Mrs. Woolf's novels seem to illustrate Bergson's romantic fluidity and transcendentalism, so they seem to illustrate his ideas of time.[9] The duration or inner time of Bergson flows in her stream of consciousness. Outer time intrudes with the striking of Big Ben, whose leaden circles, punctuating the reverie of Mrs. Dalloway, mark the disparity between real and mechanical time. Parts one and three of *To the Lighthouse* are duration or time lived through, but the middle section, called "Time Passes," is external time in which the decay of the empty house takes the place of the clock. In *The Waves* the interludes of wave, sun, snail, and vegetable represent external time, while the rest of the book records the more elastic progress of duration. In *Orlando* Mrs. Woolf plays with Bergson's times. Born in the age of Elizabeth, Orlando is thirty-six years old in October 1928. Three hundred years and thirty-six represent inner time and outer time or vice versa. And time is complicated by memory, through which several times, says Mrs. Woolf, may proceed simultaneously. The expansion or contraction of inner time with the intensity of experience is discussed in the little essays on clock time and inner time that she inserted to perplex the unphilosophical reader.[10]

[9] The general preoccupation with time was increased by J. W. Dunne, who in *An Experiment with Time* (1927) explained his prophetic visions by the hypothesis of serial time. To an observer in the fourth or fifth dimension, present, past, and future are present. This difficult but attractive position explains *Berkeley Square* (1928), a play by J. L. Balderston and J. C. Squire, and *Time and the Conways* (1937), a play by experimental J. B. Priestley. It is likely that the past, present, and future of "Sailing to Byzantium" (1927) represent Dunne's absolute time as well as that of the occultist; for Yeats was fascinated by Dunne.

[10] Orlando's home is Knole, home of the Sackvilles. See *Knole and the Sackvilles* (1922), *The Land* (1926), and *The Edwardians* (1930), by V. Sackville-West, who served as the principal model for Orlando. In *All Passion Spent* (1931), her most successful novel, V. Sackville-West examines a divided personality.

Bergson had advised novelists to discard the hard old outlines with which they had identified, solidified, and distorted their characters. In her subjective novels from *Jacob's Room* (1922) to *The Waves* (1931) Mrs. Woolf dissolved away the limits of character until nothing was left but duration. Unlike Joyce, who dramatically modified the flow to suit the character, Virginia Woolf presented one flow, which may be identified with her own. Her works are as free from characters as from external action. Indistinguishable flow has taken the place of both. In *The Waves*, one of the central expressions of our time, we flow by turns within six consciousnesses at selected periods of their lives. As each delivers the dramatic monologue that takes the place of the stream of consciousness and performs the same service, it is hard to tell who is there. This is not surprising, for in his final monologue on Monday or Tuesday and the uncertainty of life Bernard finds himself merging, all boundaries gone, with others. Is he Bernard, he wonders, or Susan or Neville; is he male or female? He is but a wave rising from and lapsing into a common sea with which he mystically unites himself, differing from earlier mystics in uniting himself with time instead of eternity. The liquidation of Bernard met its antithesis in "Solid Objects," a story in *The Haunted House* (1944). Walking along the flowing beach one day, the hero of this story finds a piece of glass. He is so pleased by its character that he neglects career and friends in the pursuit of other solidities. It is unfortunate for the cause of solidity that this man is mad.

This madman and Septimus in *Mrs. Dalloway* owe their condition to Virginia Woolf's interest in abnormality, but her interest was directed and increased by Dostoyevsky. Septimus and Mrs. Dalloway, who think in similar images, are halves of a split and projected personality like Raskolnikov and Svidrigailov. The multiple personalities that

Orlando finds in herself, however, seem to owe more to William James.

Virginia Woolf did not substitute chaos for plot as her adherence to the doctrine of dissolution might lead one to expect. In place of conventional structure imposed from without, she developed flexible organic forms from within. For *Jacob's Room* she created a ring of minds around an absent center. *Mrs. Dalloway* is kept from formlessness by unity of time and by the device of complementary persons; the division of *To the Lighthouse* into three parts is æsthetically satisfying; and the sequences of symbolic interlude and monologue in *The Waves* are rhythmic and suitable.

After *The Waves* Mrs. Woolf's powers declined. *The Years* (1937), which deals with external time, is tiresome, though a best seller in its time, and *Between the Acts* (1941) is confused and unreadable. But she had proved herself a novelist of rare distinction and an artist who, whatever her dependence upon tradition, had something original to say. She surpassed her contemporaries in sensitive fidelity to the most evanescent movements of consciousness. Better than Pater she provides the sense of passing moments. Her defects are obvious and pardonable. It matters little that her novels are without action or character. One goes to them for other things. It matters more perhaps that her sensitivity was limited to people of her own class, that she misunderstood those who had not attended a public school or belonged by birth to those who had. Far from being a snob, however, she extended her compassion to the unfortunates who are so ill at ease in Mrs. Dalloway's garden. But flow is flow even within superior people, and we go to her novels for the sense of it. Her achievement is a style, a style of wit and intelligence, of odd conjunctions of particular with general, of rhythms, of exclamations and parentheses, that made her, as she was aware, a Bloomsbury equivalent of Laurence Sterne.

Meanwhile Mr. Eliot lay deep in Mr. Eliot's hell, the stream his Styx. It is fitting to recall that "Prufrock" and *The Waste Land,* on one level at least, are personal streams of consciousness, interrupted by selection, progressing by images, linked by free association. Free association is what symbolists substituted for logic. Eliot's Laforguian stream, identical with Dujardin's, points to the common source of Eliot and Joyce. Although neither owed much to the English novelists, "Portrait of a Lady" proves Eliot an admirer of Henry James.

Of lesser writers, Ford Madox Ford was closest to mid-stream. In one of his autobiographies, *Return to Yesterday* (1931), he tells of friendship with James and of collaboration with Conrad, at whose knees he learned the technique of impressionism, which James and Conrad had learned, he says, from Turgenyev. Basing his method on that of *What Maisie Knew,* with hints from Conrad, Proust, and others, Ford wrote a tetralogy of Tietjens, whose troubles in love and war provide the theme.[11] His stream of consciousness, unselected, complicated by the simultaneous flow of sensation, thought, and memory, seems more immediate and completer, though less excellent, than James's decorous selections. From Conrad, Ford took structural obliquity and the technique of memory flash-backs, which permit past to jostle present in the flow of consciousness. In *A Man Could Stand Up,* for example, Valentine Wannop stands telephoning on Armistice Day in her classroom.

[11] *Some Do Not* (1924), *No More Parades* (1925), *A Man Could Stand Up* (1926), *The Last Post* (1928). Ford, who changed his name from Hueffer during the first World War, wrote a memoir of Conrad (1924) and a study of James (1913). Autobiographies: *Ancient Lights* (1911), *Thus to Revisit* (1921).

In *Myrtle* (1925) and other novels Stephen Hudson, who translated part of Proust, experimented with the subjective technique.

She learns with difficulty through the noise of the class and of the celebration without that Tietjens, her lover, has returned. Through these sensations rivers of memory flow in and out, mingling past with present. This confusion, reproducing the richness of the mind, also serves for exposition and characterization. Her experience, which takes about twenty minutes, requires about a hundred pages to relate; for at such moments of intensity the mind expands our time. Another of Ford's entertaining autobiographies, *It Was the Nightingale* (1933), uses the time-shift to enrich the present with the past. Ford pauses on the curb at the beginning of the book with one foot in the air. Memory intervenes, and the foot descends in the last chapter.

Katherine Mansfield used the short story to surprise inner truth behind conventional façades. Equaling Virginia Woolf in sensitivity, surpassing her in common humanity, she was prevented by circumstance from using her gifts as she might have done. What she did do, though as delicate as anything of Virginia Woolf's, appears to come from a more limited talent.

Miss Mansfield learned her individual art from many masters. From "dull turgid" James she received an occasional "sweet shock." But like J. Middleton Murry, her husband, D. H. Lawrence, her friend, and the other Bloomsbury literates, she received more from the Russians. She read Dostoyevsky and Turgenyev, and, her husband informs us, Chekhov, whose art seems to have had the profoundest effect upon her. Her stories, like many of Joyce's, belong to Chekhov's tradition. She discarded plot and action for mood or situation, conventionally important moments for moments of hidden intensity, and—slicing life thin—peered through the sections. Like the symbolist poets, she often worked by indirection, allowing overtones, hints, and silences to suggest more than the situation seems to hold. As she said in her *Journal,* she wanted to write stories "with a radiance, an afterglow . . . I want to write poetry. I feel always trembling on the brink of poetry." Whether she employed an objective technique or worked obliquely by hints and symbols or used impressionism or the stream of consciousness—and she used all these devices—her aim was always the penetration of surfaces.

Editors, save of course J. Middleton Murry, were slow to recognize work so penetrating and odd, and before 1919 Katherine Mansfield was little known, though she had been writing stories since 1908 and had published a collection, *In a German Pension,* in 1911. "The Tiredness of Rosabel" (1908), her first story, is without important incident. A London shopgirl, home at last, indulges her fancy with a daydream of her life with a dashing customer. Pursuing within a mind this contrast between illusion and reality, Katherine Mansfield discovered her destined territory. Though their interest lies in what underlies events, many of the later stories round to a climax and have a suggestion of plot, "*Feuille d'Album*" and "A Dill Pickle," for example, and "*Je ne parle pas français.*" In the last of these, however, the plot is truncated, explanations are left to the reader, and the situation is unresolved. The trivial surfaces of these stories, like the manifest content of dreams, vibrate with a tension that, sometimes breaking, allows glimpses of what lies beneath.

Bertha in "Bliss" experiences a mood of happiness, beyond analysis, that can be expressed to herself only by the symbol of a blooming pear tree. When her nameless bliss and her desire are broken by a hint of the infidelity her former coldness had provoked, the tree becomes external fact again. This delicate and indirect projection of marital failure and of three lives compares favorably with "The Dead" by Joyce, and "Ma Parker" approximates the effect of Joyce's "Clay." Following a stream of memory, Katherine Mansfield penetrates the unlovely surface of Ma Parker to regions of pathos of which her employer, the literary gentleman, is unaware, and to all the sorrows of "a hard life." Sympathy, humor, and bitter understanding fill "The Daughters of the Late Colonel" and "The Fly," the first a picture of genteel frustration, the second, rivaling Chekhov, a disclosure through casual sadism of one man's nature and, through this, of other men's.

From 1916 to 1920, driven in upon herself by the death of her brother and by the war, Katherine Mansfield turned to memories of her New Zealand childhood. "Prelude," "At the Bay," "The Doll's House," and "The Garden Party," which embody these memories, are her best. The first two are fragments, parts of a projected novel, but their very shapelessness allowed her talents an appropriate liberty. Getting by turns into each member of the Burnell family, from young Kezia to Aunt Beryl, as they pursue their blameless day, she makes each incident imply its significance and each moment a life. The other two stories, beneath their pleasant exteriors, are terrible disclosures of caste, but they are more than that. After the dancing and the sandwiches and the death of the young man in the neighboring slum, Laura exclaims: " 'Isn't life . . . isn't life—' But what life was she couldn't explain. . . . 'Isn't it, darling?' said Laurie."

Katherine Mansfield's aim was truth. She always feared that in rounding her stories she had distorted truth or had become artificial, sophisticated, or too clever. None of her work, when she reviewed it in her *Journal,* seemed quite good enough to her. She was never satisfied in her endeavor "to be simple as one would be simple before God."

It was partly to purge her soul of affectation and her style of preciousness that she entered the spiritual retreat at Fontainebleau, where she died of other troubles. She was too severe a critic of her own sincerity and of her slight, sensitive accomplishment.[12]

Look at All Those Roses (1941) by Elizabeth Bowen contains stories that are even less conclusive and direct than those of Katherine Mansfield, and no less excellent. In "A Love Story" several maladjusted lives are implied in the glimpses we are given of guests at an Irish hotel. "Look at All Those Roses" is a fragment of experience in which possibilities are left unpursued. As maddening and suggestive as a symbolist poem, this story also resembles a classical tragedy in which, though everything happens offstage, there are no messengers or chorus. "The Apple-Tree" concerns traumatic hallucination; and the nameless sorrow of the little weeper in "Tears, Idle Tears" seems to imply the sorrow of the world and all the mystery of human nature. Elizabeth Bowen's stories, which employ irrational actions, unnatural children, adhesive mistresses, and summer hotels, preferably deserted or open out of season, as subject and symbol, are at once elegant and sinister. The stories of wartime England known in England as *The Demon Lover* (1945) and, more felicitously, in America as *Ivy Gripped the Steps* suggest by small terrors a general state of mind made more harrowing by impingement upon it of an equally terrible past. Of these symbolic interludes of neurosis, hallucination, and decay, the two that provide the titles of the English and American collections are at once the most gruesome and the most delicate. The elliptical, inconclusive form of these stories, though reflecting

[12] *Journal* (1927); *Letters* (1928). Her best collections are *Bliss* (1920) and *The Garden Party* (1922). *The Short Stories* (New York, 1937).

Mansfield and Chekhov, no doubt, is an additional commentary on the times.[13]

Innocence disconcerting civilization, the theme of *What Maisie Knew,* is the theme of Elizabeth Bowen's *Death of the Heart* (1939), one of the best and bitterest novels of recent years. The heart of Portia, sixteen, orphaned, seeking heart in the heartlessness of upper middle-class society, finds only betrayal and death. This moving story, which implies the death of more hearts than hers, is subjective but analytic in method. Character sketches in the grand manner and sententious reflections upon life are made to carry the tone of experience if not its details. The similarity to James is more evident in *The House in Paris* (1935), an impressionistic account of neurotic adults and even more distressing children. The most Jamesian of Miss Bowen's books, however, is *Friends and Relations* (1931), a charming novel in which tenuity of theme is supported by an elaborate preciousness of manner and by characters who maintain an empty reticence by implication.

In *The Hotel* (1927), the happiest of Miss Bowen's books, she does better than E. M. Forster what he did well in *A Room with a View.* It is not easy to determine the position from which these subtle studies of upper middle-class society proceed. Her birth in Ireland seems to have provided a suitable detachment, but whether this detachment is ironic, sympathetic, or neutral cannot be told from the novels, nor whether she intended her characters to

[13] Other collections of stories: *Encounters* (1923), *Joining Charles* (1929). *The Last September* (1929) is a fine sinister novel on the attempt by Irish gentry to ignore the "troubles" around them. Cf. *Bowen's Court* (1942), the story of her Irish home.

Men and Wives (1931) and the later novels of Ivy Compton-Burnett almost equal those of Elizabeth Bowen in subtlety and art.

Subtlety is popularized in Rumer Godden's *Take Three Tenses, a Fugue in Time* (1945), which echoes Woolf and Eliot, and in Rosamond Lehmann's *The Ballad and the Source* (1945).

be as awful as they seem. In *To the North* (1932) the climax appears to indicate an ironic intention like that of James. One wonders how these sterile people get married and reproduce themselves, and by what virtue their class is preserved. As a character in *Look at All Those Roses* remarks:

> The blood of the world is poisoned . . . who shall stem the black tide coming in? There are no more children: the children are born knowing. The shadow rises up the cathedral tower, up the side of the pure hill. There is not even the past: our memories share with us the infected zone. . . .

Exploration of the mind by so many women and men has given recent novelists, whether subjective or not, new conceptions of personality and form, new centers of interest, and new methods. Tight imposed plots have almost disappeared. Conventional narrative, though still in use, is often supplemented by interludes of impressionism or of the stream. Character is often replaced by many-sided or sideless personality, and personality by the experience of the moment. The old fictional character, says Aldous Huxley, was like the victim of one of Ben Jonson's humors, neatly circumscribed; the new is as uncircumscribed as Hamlet. When experience has taken the place of personality, those who receive experience must be so sensitive, as a famous critic once observed, that, like Stephen Dedalus, they continually vomit. Such vomiters are peculiar to our period.

But even in the twenties, at the high-water mark of the stream of consciousness, critics found the subjective novel wanting in shape. Herbert Read, discussing the modern novel in *Reason and Romanticism* (1926), objected to the decay of structure, the decline of action, and the increasing emphasis upon temperament and duration in the work of Conrad, Joyce, and Proust, in whom he found a "terrible fluidity." But from these strictures Read exempted James, who mastered flux with analysis. In *Time and Western Man* (1927) Wyndham Lewis, supporting classical outline and sculptural solidity, attacked Joyce, whom he also misunderstood, and the followers of Bergson, who were menacing Western culture by their indecent abandonment to time, disintegration, and flow. The stream of consciousness reminded Lewis of nothing so much as the conversation of Mr. Jingle. In Lewis's *Childermass* (1928), intended as a satire upon the cult of time, figures representing Joyce and Gertrude Stein wander about in a limbo of relativity and flux, the world of Bergson, Alexander, and Einstein. Although recognizing the advancement in sensitivity achieved by the subjective novelists, I. A. Richards, in *Coleridge on Imagination* (1935), saw the need of better form, not the old external form advocated by classicists, but a new one evolving from new sensitivity. And Yeats, joining the classicists in *Fighting the Waves* (1934), looked with alarm at symbolic waves engulfing Cuchulain or human integrity. Over in France, Julien Benda, the champion of clarity, order, and detachment, devoted *Belphégor* (1918) to the feminine fluidities of those who had betrayed art itself for a mystical union with their materials.

Not these severe rebukes, but circumstance at last discouraged the subjective novelists who had done so much to change and improve the novel. The depression of 1929 marked the beginning of their decline, and the war of 1939 almost finished them off. External action was demanded, not further exploration of ivory towers; and as the occasional detective stories attempted in this medium have amply demonstrated, the stream of consciousness, whatever its fidelity to inner movements, is ill adapted to outer movement. Social, economic, and political problems, increasingly pressing, were beyond the capacity of the interior monologue, even on its most intellectual levels, as *The World of William Clissold* serves to prove. When men of these turbulent times became aware of the mind at all, it was no longer the conscious levels that attracted them but deeper levels revealed by psychoanalysis and surrealism. For these levels, which symbols alone could fathom and irrational conduct illustrate, the stream of consciousness seemed far too shallow.

CHAPTER IX

The Unconscious

UNCONSCIOUS of the unconscious, we may be conscious of its effect upon our actions and our thoughts. Freud's discovery in the nineties and his ceaseless publication of the news in the early years of this century slowly altered man's values, his idea of his own nature, and his notions of morality and art. Unsettling a world unsettled by Darwin, Planck, and Einstein, Freud brought order to settle it again and light to country that Rimbaud, Dostoyevsky, and many more had ignorantly explored.

It will be enough perhaps to recall that Freud found the unconscious, man's deepest being, to be sexual, primitive, and childish, hence abhorrent to the civil ego and carefully suppressed. He found that little children are incestuous or narcissistic by nature and that unless during puberty they are able to direct their affections to a suitable object, they suffer the fate of Œdipus or, retreating in other ways to childhood, become neurotics, perverts, artists, or madmen. Neurosis and insanity, he found, are symptoms of the thwarted id and the ego's defenses against the thought of it. Our most trivial acts—washing the hands, slips of the tongue, or falling downstairs—acquire a terrible significance. Dreams, too, may lead to the center of man's labyrinth. But dreams require interpretation, for their manifest content has been distorted and condensed by the censorship of the ego. But symbols of dream are universal, constantly recurring in the night of every man and in the myths, literature, and popular sayings of his ancestors. This fortunate arrangement gave Freud a clue and artists a method.

His early works, *The Interpretation of Dreams* (1900) and *Three Contributions to a Theory of Sex,* translated in 1910, became the favorites of literary men. Poets, novelists, and critics, convinced again that they had keys to meaning and creation, found in Freud's account of the dream-work new ways of expressing the self or understanding it. Novelists, attracted most by infant sexuality and family relationships, adopted repression, complex, and neurosis as the mechanics or substance of their art. Taking what they wanted, loosely using what they took, ignoring Freud's later work, they became Freudian in the most general sense. But their heroes in the grip of the unconscious became more abnormal and irrational than Dostoyevsky's. From 1910, when Freud's doctrines were first received in England, new conceptions of the personality and of the motives of conduct, new ideas of good and evil, gave the novel a character that filled the conservative with discomfort and sometimes alarm. The battle of novelists against moralists surged with Freud's help almost to victory, for belated Victorians, fearing as they fought that the good are indeed the repressed and the wicked the uninhibited, fought no longer with the strength of ten. Their feeble cries went unheeded while the young of the postwar period illustrated the new morality in their conduct as their immediate elders had done in the novel. Biographers, though somewhat less affected, found a new approach to the understanding of man in Freud's case histories or in his analysis of Œdipus and Hamlet. In these analyses and in the book of dreams, critics, becoming conscious of what lies below the form and rhythm of art, found clues to value and meaning. Poets were slower to respond, but during the thirties they consciously exploited the unconscious, provoking conflict between ego and id, using dream and hallucination as Rimbaud had done before them to reach man's central reality, and brought to symbols at last an awareness of their significance. From the syntax, the ambiguities, the condensation of dreams they took madness for method. The symbolist tradition, renewed with the aid of Freud, flowered into surrealism.[1]

Enamored of unity and order, Freud was led by his loves to extravagance and, some say, error. His dissenting disciples, Jung and Adler, objected to sex as the solitary inhabitant of the labyrinth; and others, seeing other motives than wish-fulfillment in their dreams, accused him of substituting dialectics for evidence. Correcting the master, as Darwin's disciples corrected Darwin, but without undervaluing his real achievement or altering the faith in it of literary men, Adler gave them the inferiority complex and Jung the theories of introversion and the collective unconscious with its archetypes.

The sexual pathologists, who were investigating one of Freud's themes before he had started, provided case histories for the use of writers. Krafft-Ebing, Havelock Ellis, Edward Carpenter, and many others made useful studies of perversion, which, with the aid of Freud, gave literature for some years a pathological coloring. These matters were by no means new in literature, but Freud and the pathologists gave scientific assurance to the romantic exploitation of the perverse.[2]

Romantics, yearning ever for the mysterious and the

[1] See Frederick J. Hoffman: *Freudianism and the Literary Mind* (1945); E. M. Forster: *The Development of English Prose between 1918 and 1939* (1945).

[2] See Mario Praz: *The Romantic Agony* (1933).

perverse, welcomed the unconscious and its effects. Although Freud was brilliantly intellectual and a follower of scientific method, his field was so inscrutable as to prove attractive to enemies of science and lovers of mystery. And to the romantic enemies of reason the dethroning of reason by Freud gave encouragement. But the exploratory and more admirable romantics owed him a greater debt.

Of exploratory critics Robert Graves was first. Shell-shocked during the war, he was treated in 1918 by psychoanalysts, in whom, especially W. H. R. Rivers, he became interested. Rivers, one of Freud's followers, and like most of them a dissenter in some things, made the conflict of unconscious personalities his theme. *On English Poetry* (1922) adopts it as the clue to poetry's nature. Here Graves defines poetry, both controlled and uncontrolled, distinguishing classic from romantic, real from fake. Real or romantic poetry is the expression of a conflict in the unconscious. When the conflict is finally resolved, the poetry—that of Wordsworth, for example—dries up. But however useful to the critic, says Graves, psychoanalysis must be supplemented by historical scholarship and æsthetic analysis. In *The Meaning of Dreams* (1924), where Graves, reviewing the theories of Freud and Jung, discusses dream and poetry, the analysis of "La Belle Dame" by Keats and "The Gnat" by Graves is psychoanalytic. *Poetic Unreason* (1925), a sequel to these, repeats them. This work is valuable, however, for the more elaborate distinction between good and bad poetry—the good from the unconscious, serving needs of poet and reader, the bad from the consciousness, serving no need at all. The key to value is the theory of secondary elaboration, the conscious attempt to expand or mimic the real thing. "As in dreams," he concludes, "so also in poetry."

While Graves was soberly applying denatured Freud, Roger Fry was austerely rejecting him. In *The Artist and*

Psycho-Analysis (1924) he asserts that Freud's theory of art as wish-fulfillment defines bad art alone, the cinema or the calendar or the popular novel. The sexual basis of art fails to explain its value, and nothing, Fry says, can be more contrary to good art than dream or symbol. Good art, the formal relation of part to part, is elevated above dream, symbol, and desire to regions where only the pure may follow it. This seems to be, but is probably not, the last gasp of art for Whistler's sake.

As Herbert Read tirelessly decided between romanticism and classicism or reconciled them, he called upon Jung and Freud for help, drawing character from ego, personality from id when favoring Freud or filling the void between introversion and extroversion by phantasy when favoring Jung. When feeling superior, he called upon Adler. With their aid, the eclectic hoped to commend or to express the whole personality. In "Psycho-analysis and Criticism," an essay in *Reason and Romanticism* (1926), he proposes the improvement of criticism by psychoanalysis. Although it is concerned with the process of creation and criticism, with the product's value, psychoanalysis, he says, can do more for critics than find art neurotic or trace the complexes of artists. It can test the value of their symbols, helping to distinguish between the "real" and the neurotic, the collective and the eccentric. What is more, it can solve the old dispute between classicism and romanticism as easily as it solved the problem of Hamlet.[8] In practice, as in the essay on the Brontës in this volume or the one on Bagehot in *The Sense of Glory* (1929), Read's psychoanalysis was allusive or trivial until he encountered the problem of Wordsworth, which tested his instruments.

[8] Dr. Ernest Jones caused a stir among Shakespearians by his pioneer application of Freud: "A Psycho-analytic Study of Hamlet," *Essays in Applied Psychoanalysis* (1923).

For Read see Henry Treece, editor: *Herbert Read, an Introduction to His Work* (1944).

Wordsworth (1930) is devoted to an analysis of the poet's childhood, his relations with women, and the inhibitions and sublimations that might explain his exuberance and his decline. By this analysis Read solved a literary problem that had baffled, and will baffle, others. *In Defence of Shelley and Other Essays* (1936) defends the psychotic poet. Tracing his images back to prenatal experience, Read explains their character. As he had hoped, psychoanalysis, increasingly eclectic, permitted him to explain creation and judge it. In *Form in Modern Poetry* (1932), still preoccupied with romanticism and classicism, character and personality, he goes for aid to Freud's id. Deciding again in favor of personality, Read surveys poetry and, noting value here or there, dismisses Joyce and Hopkins as characters. Of these essays, however, all that seems valuable or clear is the character of Read, at once solemn, enthusiastic, and confused.

As knowledge of psychoanalysis increased, other critics made use of it, though Richards and Eliot remained aloof, the one adhering to another school, the other filled with scruples. But their liberal followers followed Freud or felt his influence. William Empson, for example, brought Freud's idea of dream-condensation to bear upon the seventh type of ambiguity.[4]

Bound as a Marxist to quarrel with Freud, Marx's opposite in diagnosis and cure, Christopher Caudwell, while denouncing Freud, made better use of him than other English critics because, perhaps, he was more brilliant than others. In *Illusion and Reality* (1937) he compares poetry with dream, and though he finds Freud's dream private and bourgeois, he finds Freud, reinterpreted by

[4] F. L. Lucas in *The Decline and Fall of the Romantic Ideal* (1936) used Freud to define romanticism as "a liberation of the less conscious levels of the mind." In *Archetypal Patterns in Poetry* (1934) Maud Bodkin finds Jung's archetypes behind the imaginative appeal of great literature from the Greeks to Eliot and Lawrence.

Marx, to be the clearest guide to poetry's nature. Poetry is dream with manifest and latent levels, and creation is allied to dreaming, but poetry is public or inverted dream with Marx manifest, Freud latent.

Of exploratory biographers Harold Nicolson is among the more eminent. In *The Development of English Biography* (1927) he sees two courses open for biographers, the fictional and the scientific, the latter following Freud, Havelock Ellis, the students of glands, and the economists. Nicolson's *Tennyson* (1922), like his *Swinburne* (1926), took the latter course. Peering with the aid of psychoanalysis beneath Tennyson's Victorian façade to discover sex, the fear of it, and maladjustment, the biographer finds the laureate repressed by circumstance, but capable of sublimation. Enid Starkie in her *Baudelaire* (1933), after noting the nonsense written about that poet's Œdipus complex, implicitly follows Freud in her account of it. In *Son of Woman* (1931) J. Middleton Murry performs the same service for D. H. Lawrence, his friend. These samples indicate a trend that became so general that Lytton Strachey himself descended from his classical eminence to imply the sexual difficulties of the Virgin Queen. *Elizabeth and Essex* (1928) was injured by a science for which Strachey had no talent.[5]

Two writers who approached Freud's province without his help call for notice before we notice the Freudian novelists. It is curious to find Shaw one of these. Discussing sex like a sociologist, he alludes to Havelock Ellis in the preface to *Getting Married* (1908), and, discussing family relationships in the preface to *Misalliance* (1910), he describes what seems the mother complex. In *Pygmalion* (1914) it leaves preface for play. Eliza rejects the ineffec-

[5] Of autobiographers J. C. Powys is most deeply indebted to the psychoanalysts and pathologists for self-knowledge: *Autobiography* (1938).

tual advances of Higgins, as Shaw explains in a note, because she considers his mother "an irresistible rival." While it is possible that Shaw had heard of Freud by this time, he usually followed the latest thing after an interval of ten years, and it is likelier that, for Higgins, Shaw had consulted his own experience. Some years later, however, we know he knew of Freud. In the preface to *Saint Joan* (1923) he compares psychoanalysts with Christian Scientists and laughs at the "Edipus complex." No less afraid of love, Conrad devoted *Chance* (1914) to a study of father complex, Lesbianism, and psychic trauma. He noted his dreams, spoke in his letters of his unconscious, and tried, by drawing upon it, to give his stories a dreamlike quality.[6]

Under the spell of Shaw and Wells, May Sinclair had written many novels on the self-fulfillment of women before *Three Sisters* (1914), in which she put Freud to service in the feminist cause. This novel, based loosely upon the situation of the Brontës, concerns, like *The Way of All Flesh*, a country vicarage, a proper place for the study of repression. The vicar gets his satisfaction by keeping his daughters from theirs. Unaware of the meaning and causes of his acts, he seems to himself "the image of righteousness." This familiar anti-Victorian theme is given depth and new significance by Freud, who provides two levels, conscious and unconscious, and drama in the conflict between them. Deprived at last of his only satisfaction by the revolt of his daughters, the vicar solves his problem by suffering a stroke and defense amnesia, which enable him to enslave Gwenda. She remains sane, however, for although a victim of self-sacrifice, she manages to sublimate her desires. Mary, under the guise of womanliness,

[6] Henry James's symbols of tower and lake in *The Turn of the Screw* (1898) have invited Freudian speculation: Edmund Wilson: *The Triple Thinkers* (1938).

refuses to admit to "the lighted front" of her mind the unscrupulous sexual needs that compel her. Alice, driven to hysteria and almost to insanity, blindly seeks the marriage that her unconscious knows will relieve her. But she fears the bestiality of the only available man. "Expert in disguises, in subterfuges," her mind substitutes a lesser fear in place of the fear that would prevent her fulfillment, and once it has served its purpose, this substitute fear is gone. These creatures with their hidden selves and apparent motives are many-sided and convincing, but, though the materials of tragedy are there, curiously wanting in tragic significance. Too clear and intellectual to be moving, defining the irrational motives of her people too well, May Sinclair has the air of penetrating mysterious recesses with a guide book in her reticule.

Mary Olivier (1919), which owes its subjective method to Joyce and Dorothy Richardson and its pattern to Samuel Butler, is May Sinclair's best and most Freudian novel. Mary and her brother Mark have a mother and father. This is sinister. Mark, in love with his mother, becomes incapable of marriage. His exemplary case history is surpassed in pathos by that of Aunt Charlotte, who suffers delusions of approaching marriage, plays, to the scandal of her family, with naked dolls, and departs at last for the asylum. Mr. Olivier, jealous of Mark, his son, takes refuge from his domestic sorrows in drink, then apoplexy. But Mary, translanting Euripides, writing verses, and enjoying mystical raptures while she sacrifices normal fulfillment and feminist career to the mother who has thwarted her, can sublimate.

Mary's unnatural understanding of Mark's condition and her own can hardly be explained by her reading of Spinoza and the Upanishads. It is still less easy to account for her mother's occasional self-analysis. But the brilliant light of science in the hands of May Sinclair, dissipating one mystery, created another, and careful selection cleared away what might obscure the understanding. The novel is less mechanical in effect, however, than this would make it seem. Her subjective approach, permitting, if not the feminine penetration of Woolf or Mansfield, at least an intellectual approximation of it, permits Mary to take her place beside Dorothy Richardson's Miriam. The girls who serve the female novelists of this period as heroines are a little gruesome.[7]

Amnesia, which defended the egos of the vicar and Mrs. Olivier, is the principal subject of *The Return of the Soldier* (1918) by Rebecca West. The hero, losing his memory in the war, ostensibly of shell-shock, really loses it to keep away the thought of his wife. Annoyed by his forgetfulness, she hires a psychoanalyst, who diagnoses and cures the case according to Freud. After a tedious beginning *The Judge* (1922) gets down to the Œdipus complex. Because of his fixation upon his mother and their common hatred of his father, poor Richard is unable, try as he may, to fall in love with Ellen. She sees what is wrong, and so does the mother, who commits suicide in the vain attempt to free her son. Though less mediocre than *The Return of the Soldier, The Judge* also suffers from unassimilated theory. By 1928, however, novelists could play with the familiar stuff of Freud. Mary Butts in *Armed with Madness* tells of a week-end party at which all the guests have read Freud and Frazer. With a symbolic spear they fish a cup from the well. Clarence, who dreams and tells, shoots symbolic arrows at Scylla. Others of inter-

[7] *Life and Death of Harriett Frean* (1922), brief, swift, and excellent, is the tragedy of a repressed girl, prevented by her parents from becoming adult. For May Sinclair see Dorothy Brewster and Angus Burrell: *Modern Fiction* (1934).

mediate sex pursue their doxies through the trees. This exciting book, of interest to the historian, cannot detain the critic.

Katherine Mansfield's employment of the Œdipus complex in "*Je ne parle pas français*" is more successful than any of these. Treating it indirectly, she makes it the center of a small tragedy. It is likely, however, that the idea for this story came from her friend D. H. Lawrence, not directly from Freud. And Virginia Woolf, publisher of Freud, may owe him much. What is the meaning of the waves and what of the lighthouse? Many of her stories occupy a region midway between reverie and dream, but Virginia Woolf seems to have been less attracted to theories of the unconscious than to those of conscious duration.

Never a confirmed Freudian, Aldous Huxley treated Freud facetiously at first, then casually, before rejecting him. "The Farcical History of Richard Greenow," a grotesque story in *Limbo* (1920), follows the case of Richard from split personality to madhouse. Mary, the advanced young person of *Crome Yellow* (1921) knows her Freud. Having dreamed of ladders and wells, she seeks love as cure for her repressions. She is a figure of fun. But Spandrell, the diabolist of *Point Counter Point* (1928), is almost tragical. His life, based on Baudelaire's, is a splendid case history of the Œdipus complex.

While Mann, Proust, and Gide were following the possibilities of perversion, English novelists, lagging as usual a little behind, were not altogether indifferent. In *The Well of Loneliness* (1928) Radclyffe Hall lavished sentiment on her Lesbians; and Compton Mackenzie in *Extraordinary Women* (1928) smiled at his. These unimportant studies of abnormality prepared the way for better ones. Christopher Isherwood's excellent novels of pre-Nazi Berlin, *Mr. Norris Changes Trains* (1935) and *Goodbye to Berlin* (1939), less narratives than character sketches, deal in the prose of Hemingway with people whose sexual aberrations complicate their social complexity. Sally Bowles is a nymphomaniac of the most abandoned sort, and Mr. Norris, like Proust's Charlus, is a masochist whose perversion is dispassionately presented as an element of a many-sided personality. These eccentrics also serve as symbols of the decadent society that produced the Nazis. In *Prater Violet* (1945), a slighter novel on a similar theme, while Isherwood's constant hero (called Isherwood, but not necessarily to be identified with him) reveals his amours, the sex of that hero's lovers is elaborately concealed. In *Maiden Voyage* (1943) and *In Youth Is Pleasure* (1945) Denton Welch's hero (called Denton Welch, but not necessarily to be identified with him) invites Krafft-Ebing. After dreaming of lying in open wounds, this adolescent lashes himself, shuts himself in closets, or chains himself to lawn-rollers.[8]

Liam O'Flaherty and Graham Greene, Isherwood's cousin, entered the field of the psychoanalysts and pathologists in those powerful accounts of tortured souls which seem compounded of equal parts of Freud, Dostoyevsky, the thriller, and the movies. *The Black Soul* (1924), *Mr. Gilhooley* (1926), and *The Assassin* (1928), by O'Flaherty, depict violent souls, possibly mad, certainly neurotic. The black soul in the novel of that name is a returned soldier, tortured by convictions of futility, pursued by delusions, who finally composes his psychic chaos through the love of a woman and the murder of her lunatic husband. The elementary violence of this story of the Aran Islands is repeated in the story of Mr. Gilhooley, an equally neurotic Dubliner. And in *The Assassin* Mc-

[8] In the stories in *Burning Cactus* (1936) Stephen Spender deals with neurotics and perverts. In *Earl Lavender* (1895) John Davidson had used masochism and sadism for theme according to a romantic pattern. Hugh Walpole's *Mr. Perrin and Mr. Traill* (1911) is a good non-Freudian study of morbid psychology.

Dara's anarchistic ideal reflects the anarchy within his split, maniacal personality.

The atmosphere of the thriller, strong in O'Flaherty, is stronger in Graham Greene. *Brighton Rock* (1938) and *The Power and the Glory* (1940)[9] are first-rate studies of morbid psychology. A Catholic, Greene specializes in the minds of bad Catholics. As the Mexican priest of *The Power and the Glory* flees political persecution through the hallucinatory forests, his fatigued, haunted mind is the theater of a sickness at once mental and spiritual. But at last, becoming priest again and victim, he experiences something of the passion of Christ. The character of Pinkie, the adolescent gangster of *Brighton Rock,* owes more to Freud. While but a lad in his native slum, he observed on Saturday nights the loves of his parents. The consequent trauma makes him incapable of love or of any human feeling except fear and the desire to inflict pain. The little monster, abandoning church and slum and all that reminds him of the past, in which he is fixed, becomes the leader of a small gang "protecting" bookies. He murders, and endures for a time the disgust of marriage to close the mouth of a witness. Plotting the death of his wife, he is apprehended in the nick of time by relentless Ida, the amateur sleuth. It is to hell, constantly in his bad Catholic thought together with fragments of remembered liturgy, that his soul descends. This mixture of detective story, melodrama, case history, and moral theology, one of the impressive novels of recent times, rebukes their disorder.

From D. H. Lawrence, a greater writer than these, we get a more immediate sense of the unconscious. As the achievement of Virginia Woolf is the feeling of immersion in conscious flow, so an achievement of Lawrence is the feeling of immersion in the unconscious. But before

[9] In the United States entitled *The Labyrinthine Ways.*

he began these mysterious descents he devoted a novel to the conscious symptoms of the unconscious. *Sons and Lovers* (1913) is the best novel about the Œdipus complex. Unlike the ladies who studied it in the works of Freud, Lawrence, like the authors of *Hamlet* and *Œdipus Rex* before him, looked into his heart and wrote. Escaping case history for this reason among others, Lawrence wrote a novel of all but first importance, a novel that if inferior to *Ulysses,* is comparable in value to *Jude the Obscure.*

Sons and Lovers reveals the partly conscious enslavement of Paul Morel to his mother. Thrown into her embrace by her hatred of his father and by the death or departure of his brothers, Paul is incapable of other love. Not even the death of his mother can set him free. This subject, treated with the passion that Lawrence brings to it, is of universal appeal, for it is something that, in less exaggerated form, is part of every man's unconscious. Although written in a plain, adequate, and sometimes rhapsodic style, though filled with honest observation and a Hardyesque feeling for suburban nature, and though the father and some other characters maintain intense, separate lives, the book is nevertheless a little morbid because Lawrence was unable to detach himself from the mother whom he celebrates as heroine or to achieve the impersonality that the most personal art requires. He wrote the book in order, by expressing his trouble, to understand and cure it. But the reader, like the reader of *Jude the Obscure,* moved by pity alone, is half appeased.

This great disturbing book was written in 1911 and 1912. Lawrence did not know of Freud until April 1912, when, at his first meeting with Frieda, who was filled with the new theories, the conversation turned to the Œdipus complex. It is possible that Frieda helped Lawrence to point up the second draft of the book and to shape experience by theory. But such assistance was unnecessary;

for, as E. T., the real Miriam, assures us in her memoir, he had been able to determine the nature of his love. Later, after Frieda had more or less released him from his mother, Lawrence read Freud with considerable horror.

In *Psychoanalysis and the Unconscious* (1921) and *Fantasia of the Unconscious* (1922) Lawrence blames Freud for exaggerating sex, especially incest, and making it the sole inhabitant of the unconscious. Freud is immoral, intellectual, scientific, and, what is worse, ignorant of "the flux of sap-consciousness." Lawrence will attend to that. Claiming direct intuition, a faculty denied to Freud, he announces that the true unconscious, unlike Freud's nasty repository of repressed incest, is the soul or life itself. Fulfillment comes from responsiveness to the unconscious, evil from its repression. The great repressive devices, like Freud's, are intellect and civilization. The problem therefore is how to suspend intellect and destroy civilization that the unconscious may make us whole, relating us to others and the universe. Consigning Jung to Freud's limbo, Lawrence considers the relationship of mother and child, lover and lover. With Theosophy and yoga as his guides, he was in a better position than Freud or Jung to understand the unconscious.

Lawrence disliked Freud and Jung, who taught him much, because he disliked his teachers. He read Dostoyevsky, admitted some indebtedness, and condemned him as too mental. He read and dismissed Proust and Gide. And Joyce, whose *Work in Progress* Lawrence looked at in 1928, seemed "putrid." Even the anthropologists, who more or less confirmed Jung's ideas about the unconscious of primitive man, seemed intellectual. Lawrence alone was the master of the unconscious.

It is time, Lawrence announced in 1913, for a revolt against Shaw and Galsworthy, "the rule and measure mathematical folk." These intellectuals, ignorant of the unconscious, seemed worse than Freud or Dostoyevsky, who misunderstood it. It is true of course that Shaw's creatures or most of them are destitute of bowels. Sometimes, however, their disembodied minds become aware of darker regions. Aubrey in *Too True to Be Good,* for example, speaking of the higher centers, from which all great literature and all conversation come, admits that there are also lower centers, "a sort of guilty secret with every one of us." When these centers begin to speak, the shock is terrible. Pursuing conversation and the literature of the higher centers, Shaw commonly repressed these terrible shocks. He took for his province everything from the neck up. Lawrence, declaring his revolt, took for his everything from the neck down.

His settled opinion, Lawrence continued, was that the body, blood, soul, and all the dark centers of the unconscious are wiser than intellect and will. After finishing *Sons and Lovers* he devoted his novels to illustrating this point. His villains are intellectuals or men of goodwill, his heroes and heroines unconscious lovers. He intended his novels to improve the relationship between man and man, man and woman, and to explore upon the æsthetic plane the fulfillment that was denied him. As much of a preacher as Shaw, he devoted his antithetical arts to the salvation of mankind.

Since Birkin, the hero of *Women in Love* (1920), is always around, recommending the irrational, the novel, like Shaw's plays, is too rational to be good. But Lawrence's intention is clear. And when Birkin becomes silent, the unconscious shows itself in irrational conduct, in trances, paroxysms, and transports to which all continually succumb, and in sudden intuitions of the darkness under their necks. Ursula, "that strange, unconscious bud of powerful womanhood," swooning over the little red pistils of the flowers, is almost immediately "gone into the ultimate darkness of her own soul." Gudrun dances, for no reason, before cows. They understand. Even Hermione, that intellectual, has her moments. In voluptuous consummation with violence, she hits Birkin on the head with her paperweight. He goes off to lie among the flowers and, on returning to full consciousness, approves of her momentary triumph over repression. Flowers and paperweights will do the trick, but the easiest way to enter the unconscious is making love. As Birkin and Ursula make love, and they are always making it, "deeper, further in mystery than the phallic source, came the floods of ineffable darkness and ineffable riches."

In *Lady Chatterley's Lover* (1928), another sermon against civilization and intellect, Lady Chatterley is rescued from these impediments by her lover. The plot is simple: they make love. It is unfortunately easy to make fun of this novel, for if it is taken as a realistic account of love, the reader, after some natural awe, must laugh. But that is not the way to take it. Lawrence is not showing what love is or ever was, but what it ought to be. The love of Lady Chatterley is the extravagance of a disappointed man. Its value lies in those beautiful, pathetic descriptions of making love, which have the unnatural brilliance of superior fantasy.[10]

Lawrence chose a gamekeeper for hero because gamekeepers are closer to nature in these civilized times than other Englishmen. Since they would not be gamekeepers if nature had not deprived them of intellect, they are suitable vehicles of the unconscious. In his other books Lawrence used peasants, gypsies, and redskins for the same purpose. The Indian groom who is the hero of *St.*

[10] An early version found among Lawrence's effects was published in 1944 as *The First Lady Chatterley.*

Mawr (1925), that fine *exemplum,* conducts the civilized heroine through horses to mindlessness. These dark, small, horse-loving men rarely emerge above their collars.

The Mexican heroes of *The Plumed Serpent* (1926) discover, like Yeats before them, the value of ritual, myth, and symbol. Through the myth of Quetzalcoatl and the symbols of rain, bird, serpent, star, sun, fish, and tree, which anthropologists assure us were employed by primitive man and which, according to the psychoanalysts, reappear in the unconscious of modern man, Don Ramon and Don Cipriano enter the aboriginal darkness. "Give me the mystery," cries Kate, their disciple, "and let the world live again for me!" The only mystery left in civilized America is the unconscious where one may feel "the velvety dark flux from the earth, the delicate yet supreme life-breath in the inner air." Don Ramon's cult is a device for escaping intellect and civilization, which repress the life-breath, and for descending, through rapture, to the collective unconscious. Restored by their descent, the heroes make love to the heroines and redescend. Even their most responsible acts, leading a revolution or reforming a church, have the character of dream.

In 1914 Lawrence said in a letter that he was using "true instinctive or dream symbolism" in his poems. This statement, which probably marks his first reading of Freud, may refer to the apples, flames, doors, houses, ships, and seas that occur in the poems he wrote at this time.[11] There is no doubt, however, about the Freudian character of *Birds, Beasts and Flowers* (1923). The symbols of "Peach" and "Figs," for example, give these poems universality and a richness absent from the earlier verses.

[11] In "Virgin Youth," an early poem, he uses valley, tower, and fruit for his sexual theme. In one of the poems to his mother he says: "I am a naked candle burning on your grave," as fine an example of double talk as anything in Dylan Thomas.

The novels, too, abound in symbols: Gerald and the horse in *Women in Love,* Aaron's rod in *Aaron's Rod* (1922), and here and elsewhere all the flowers.

In 1925 Lawrence complained: "Those unconscious things of mine hardly sell at all." The prosperity of their author was prevented, perhaps, by the oddness of his characters, who are of two principal kinds. A desire to improve the world led him to the creation of characters with hard outlines and clear labels like those of allegories. The bad people—intellectuals, mineowners, or horse-haters—are generally of this kind. On the other hand a desire to descend into the unconscious led him to characters of such extreme fluidity that they have no outlines at all and no qualities whereby one may be distinguished from another. When they are unconscious, even the labeled characters are undifferentiated; for in the unconscious all men are similar. On his deeper level he achieved the death of character that Virginia Woolf and Dorothy Richardson achieved on theirs. "One can never know," he said, "and never-never understand. One can but swim, like a trout in a quick stream."

The technique that Lawrence used to convey a sense of immersion in the unconscious belongs more to poetry than to prose. By a kind of incantation, using rhythm and hypnotically repeating the words "dark" and "deep," Lawrence suggests what, because it is unconscious, cannot be felt or expressed. In *The Plumed Serpent,* for instance, Don Ramon passes out:

> And tense like the gush of a soundless fountain, he thrust up and reached down in the invisible dark, convulsed with passion. Till the black waves began to wash over his memory, over his being, like an incoming tide, till at last in the darkness, he stood soft and relaxed, staring with wide eyes at the dark, and feeling the dark fecundity of the inner tide washing over his heart, over his

> belly, his mind dissolved away in the greater, dark mind, which is undisturbed by thoughts.
>
> He covered his face with his hands, and stood still, in pure unconsciousness, neither hearing nor feeling nor knowing, like a dark sea-weed deep in the sea. With no Time and no World, in the deeps that are timeless and worldless.
>
> Then when his heart and his belly were restored, his mind began to flicker again softly, like a soft flame flowing without departing.

This incantatory prose, as indirect as the poetry of symbolism, is called upon in every novel for all characters alike to intimate, while they are making love or worshipping the gods, their absence of mind.

Of Lawrence's fiction, *The Plumed Serpent* is the most brilliant. This novel, evoking the landscape of dream or hallucination, burns with a strange inner fire. In exotic splendor it is unlike anything else in English literature, and in the literature of other lands comparable only to *Salammbô*. *Sons and Lovers*, also excellent, is preferred by many for pathos and British solidity. Although *The Rainbow*, *Women in Love*, *Kangaroo*, and *Lady Chatterley* have moments of great beauty and more than feminine penetration, they are not first-rate novels, for their beauties are lost among the sermons. Lawrence's fault in these novels is the intellectuality he always abhorred. The short and longer stories, from "Love among the Haystacks" to "The Man Who Died," show Lawrence at his best, and he was at his best when most unconscious. "I am almost a lunatic," he once remarked. This condition assured him of richness and depth and, along with Blake, Lautréamont, and Rimbaud, of a place in our hearts.

James Joyce, too intellectual for Lawrence and Virginia Woolf, first descended into the regions of the unconscious in the Circe episode of *Ulysses* (1922). This chapter, the most powerful of the book, presents the minds of Stephen and Bloom when, disturbed by drink and fatigue, they are no longer able to distinguish between inner and outer reality. Under the spell of Bella Cohen they turn into swine on the Homeric level as on the psychological level their unconscious minds assume control. It is difficult to tell what is hallucination, unconscious phantasmagoria dream or objective reality. Is Edy Boardmann there like the button from Mr. Bloom's trousers or is she, like the Morning Hours, Virag, and the eight male yellow and white children with valuable metallic faces, something previously dropped into the unconscious and now permitted by abdication of intellect to emerge? Mr. Bloom's unconscious produces most of the objects, fears, hopes, and desires of his day, sometimes personified or distorted, in a typical dream of guilt. His hidden abnormalities, mostly masochistic, appear.[12] Condemned by a jury of experts, he is compelled to prostrate himself before the cruelty of Mrs. Cohen, who may not be there. The ancestors who people his unconscious accuse him and disappear or change to someone else. Everything shifts, changes, blurs.

This dream fantasy is not presented as a stream of consciousness but in dramatic form, with speech tags, stage directions, and occasional descriptions in the manner of Shaw. The dramatization of the unconscious mind was not new when Joyce adopted it. Under the name of expressionism it had appeared on the Continent in the theater, the novel, and painting.[13] Although he may have been encouraged by Flaubert's *Temptation of St. Anthony* or even *Faust*, the likeliest suggestion came

[12] Joyce had dealt with sadism in "An Encounter," *Dubliners* (1914).

[13] Two Irish dramatists, probably influenced by Joyce, turned to expressionism: Denis Johnston and the Earl of Longford: *Yahoo* (1933). On the English stage J. B. Priestley is the chief expressionist: *Johnson over Jordan* (1939), and *Music at Night* (in *Four Plays,* 1944).

from Strindberg's *Dream Play* (1902). It was his aim, says Strindberg:

> to imitate the disconnected but seemingly logical form of the dream. Anything may happen; everything is possible and probable. Time and space do not exist. On an insignificant background of reality, imagination designs and embroiders novel patterns: a medley of memories, experiences, free fancies, absurdities, and improvisations. The characters split, double, multiply, vanish, solidify, blur, clarify. But one consciousness reigns above them all—that of the dreamer; and before it there are no secrets, no incongruities, no scruples, no laws.

Strindberg was pre-Freudian. Joyce's position is less clear. Having lived in Zurich during the stormy years of psychoanalysis, Joyce was aware of it. He makes Stephen, discussing Hamlet, refer in passing to the "new Viennese school." And he makes the relationship of Stephen to father and mother central in his book. Although Stephen seems to have the symptoms of Freud's favorite complex, it is probable that Joyce, like Lawrence in *Sons and Lovers,* unassisted by theory, had himself in mind. Dream in the Circe episode proceeds without the intervention of censorship. Mr. Bloom, of course, may be uninhibited, but it is more likely that his dream is innocent of Freud. For the abnormalities of his hero Joyce had read not only the pathologists but, while in Zurich, a collection of letters from sexual eccentrics.

During the seventeen years Joyce worked at his next great work, he called it *Work in Progress.* When in 1939 he got what he was doing done, he called it *Finnegans Wake.* This novel, the principal literary exploration of the unconscious mind, deals with dream.[14]

[14] Joseph Campbell and Henry Morton Robinson: *A Skeleton Key to Finnegans Wake* (1944). Edmund Wilson: *The Wound and the Bow* (1941). Samuel Beckett, Frank Budgen, Stuart Gilbert, Eugene Jolas,

From the beginning of the book to the end, 628 pages distant, and then to the beginning again, the reader, like an earwig, inhabits the sleeping consciousness of H. C. Earwicker, who is an earwig in the reader's consciousness. Earwicker's sleep, unbroken except for a restless interval in the sixteenth chapter, is light, heavy, profound, and light again, and correspondingly easy or difficult to follow, as his night wears on. To furnish the mind of his sleeper and express it, Joyce used the theories of Freud, Jung, Bruno, and Vico. By their aid and that of many others he created a dream to suit his individual hero, yet so ideal, general, and long that it would do very nicely for the Seven Sleepers.

As in all dreams, according to Freud, the censor is at work in Earwicker's dream, disguising things, condensing, combining, and distorting them, and making symbols. His wife, Maggie, and his daughter, Isabel, become at times the river Liffey, a cloud, and the sea. Earwicker himself becomes the hill of Howth. His twin sons become Shem and Shaun, projections of his own selves, and all conflicting opposites, the fox and the grapes, Napoleon and Wellington, Mutt and Jeff. During the night one of those subtle changes in family relationships that fascinated Joyce occurs, and Earwicker's interest is transferred from wife to children. To disguise this hint of incest from itself, the censor makes Isabel a niece, Iseult, and other women. Earwicker's sleep is troubled by some sin or misdemeanor he has committed in the park, but censorship disguises this so well that we never know what it is. Disguised, it appears as a harmless encounter with a cad who asks the time or an encounter with soldiers. Like Mr.

Thomas McGreevy, *et al.*: *Our Exagmination Round His Factification for Incamination of Work in Progress* (1929). Frank Budgen: "Joyce's Chapters of Going Forth by Day," *Horizon,* IV (September 1941). Eugene Jolas: "My Friend James Joyce," *Partisan Review,* VIII (March-April 1941). Harry Levin: *James Joyce* (1941).

Bloom, Earwicker suffers from guilt, is tried by a jury (the customers in his pub),[15] and is plagued by gossip, especially that of the two washerwomen who wash his dirty linen in public. During the course of his dream the images are those identified by Freud: the ascent of the ladder and the fall, the Tower of Babel, Lipoleum's hat, the ride in a jaunting-car, and all the rest. Even the letter, disinterred from the dump, is given a psychoanalytic interpretation by a professor who cites *Studium Sexophonologistic Schizophrenesis.* Referring in another place to the softnosed peruser of the letter, who "might mayhem take it up erogenously" if a girl should somersault off her "bisexycle," the voice of sleep cheerfully continues: "but we grisly old Sykos have done our unsmiling bit on 'alices, when they were yung and easily freudened."

From Jung, who became a friend, Joyce took many things, especially the theory of the collective unconscious. Following Freud, Jung held that dreams are regressions to the infantile and primitive, that ancient myths and modern dreams are identical and common to the sleeping consciousness of all men. Jung's theory of myth and dream accords with the theory of Giambattista Vico, who held that myths and heroes are projections of man's deepest life and that through them we may discover the nature of their projectors. Joyce combined Jung and Vico, making *Finnegans Wake* a compendium of all the myths, heroes, and fables of the world, and Earwicker's consciousness not only that of an individual, but that of all men at all times. Since his dream is everyman's, Earwicker dreams of much that he does not know in languages he has never heard. But almost always the universal has a personal application. He dreams of Tristan and Iseult because he lives in Chapelizod, where Iseult was born, because his

[15] The jury and the four old men represent Earwicker's superego or conscience. H. C. E. suffers from a castration complex.

daughter is Isabel, and because Tristan is tree-stone, the tree and stone beside the Liffey. Earwicker dreams of Adam because his room has an Adam fireplace, of Vico because Dublin has a Vico Road, of death and resurrection because of Dublin's Phoenix Park and the Irish-American ballad of Finnegan's Wake, sung in pubs. He dreams of Swift, Goldsmith, and Wellington because they were Irish, of the conflict of opposites because his twin sons are rivals. "And so wider."

The language of this dream is a dream language based upon the theories of Freud and upon the explication by Humpty Dumpty of "Jabberwocky." There are as many references to Lewis Carroll in *Finnegans Wake* as to Freud. The portmanteau word into which several meanings are telescoped is efficient, amusing, and witty. In his essay on wit Freud makes it plain that wit is the product of the unconscious, and in his book of dreams he gives many examples of verbal distortions, puns, and double talk. The puns and distortions of Freud's exemplary dreams occur singly, often one to a dream. But the pun is mightier than the word; knowing this, Joyce took the hint from Freud and Dodgson, elaborated it, and made of double talk, if one may take these words literally, his vehicle. This rich language, sometimes melting like Dali's watch, sometimes combining four or five levels of meaning in a word, is at once beautiful and complicated. "Distorted mirage, aloofliest of the plain," mutters the voice of sleep, echoing Goldsmith, or, falling asleep in sleep: "him jawr war hoo hleepy hor halk urthing hurther," or, remembering glory: "be British . . . to your bellybone and chuck a chum a chance." Often the language is distorted by the Freudian censor into the familiar symbols, "sexcaliber hrosspower," for example, an ingenious combination of gun, sword, car, and horse.

It cannot be disguised from the reader that, however light and gay, this book is difficult. Its subject is what is most important: man, woman, love, and children, death and resurrection, sin and repentance, sleeping and waking, and the preoccupations of modern man, time, space, relativity, flux, and the unconscious. The subject, though important, does not, of course, guarantee the importance of the book. But if read aloud as it should be read, it becomes a triumph of rhythm, sound, image, suggestion, of poetry in fact; and it is plain that here is one of the most amusing of novels. It is not realistic; for, as Freud assures us, dreams are not elaborate but condensed. Upon an intellectual frame Joyce composed an ersatz dream. Not quite dream, but summarizing all dreams, it leads through man's recesses.

Yeats, as we have seen, had preceded Joyce into these recesses. Ignorant of Freud, and ascribing all to the occult, which permitted suspension of intellect, Yeats seems, even in the nineties, to have guessed the meaning of what he brought to the surface. Later he discovered that what he had called Anima Mundi is what doctors of medicine were beginning to call "the subconscious," and that dream is but our unfulfilled desire, distorted by the conscience.[16] In the preface to *Fighting the Waves* he remarked that a German psychoanalyst had traced the "'mother complex' back to our mother the sea."[17] The holidays from intellect that he had so carefully managed, the dreams he had provoked, enjoyed, and used as materials for poetry, had led him, he was now aware, to his deepest self. Undiscouraged by this discovery, he continued to use the materials from

[16] See *Per Amica Silentia Lunæ* (1917).

[17] In *Wheels and Butterflies* (1934). Yeats's most obviously Freudian fantasies are *The King of the Great Clock Tower* (1934) and *A Full Moon in March,* a later version of the same play. It is not accidental that in 1928 he adapted *Œdipus Rex* to the modern stage.

Anima Mundi under the new name or the old, content that the symbols he employed were rich and many-leveled.

Part of what we call excellence in poetry is the response by our unconscious to the unconscious of the poet, and part our unconscious response to his conscious art. More than any other poet of our time Yeats drew upon his hidden self, and above all others had power to control and shape his dark materials. When his friend A. E. said in *The Living Torch* (1937) that poetry comes from man's sleeping consciousness, he had his own poetry in mind. Its failure is the failure of his waking consciousness to use what it received.

Walter de la Mare, fixing dreams by craft, is closer to Yeats. In *Behold, This Dreamer!* (1939), where he discusses imagination and dream, de la Mare tells of dreams he has had of climbing stairs, opening doors, or flying. All poetry of any value, he says, is based upon such materials. As for Freud's interpretation, he rejects it vehemently, saying that if Freud is right, it is better to ignore him and enjoy the dream. De la Mare's best poetry, so haunting and mysterious, is the manifest content of his dreams. Critics have called him an escapist, but a poet who, however careless of Freud and the world of politics, confronts his unconscious cannot be said to escape reality.

Although Eliot the critic was careless of Freud, Eliot the poet gave to the central parts of *Ash Wednesday* the air of a surrealist hallucination, and to *Family Reunion* a psychoanalytic complexion. Like Lawrence, Robert Graves and W. J. Turner sometimes used dream symbols in their poems.[18] In general, however, the poets of Eliot's genera-

[18] E.g., Graves: "A Child's Nightmare," *Fairies and Fusiliers* (1917), and Turner: *Landscape of Cytherea* (1923).

tion were as reluctant to profit by Freud's discoveries as later poets were eager.

The climate of Auden was heavy with Freud, Lawrence, and Marx. To these incompatibles the poet added Georg Groddeck, an authority on the unconscious, and Homer Lane, a kind of Mary Baker Eddy, who laid the blame for disease on mind and undertook the cure of neural itches. Undertaking in his turn the diagnosis and cure of social neurosis, Auden tried to heal the split between ego and id, individual and society, by poetry, politics, and religion. At their worst his poems are case-books and at their best integrating myths. Two of the most interesting poems, the first and thirtieth of *Poems* (1930), the one an exhortation, the other a prayer, are based on Homer Lane. But the effect of Freud, whom Auden in his Marxist moments condemned for private solutions, is more pervasive. In the Prologue to *The Orators* (1932), that queer mixture of oratory and journal, of Freudian regressions and political fantasy, Freud's symbols and the Œdipus complex acquire poetic and social values. The social plays Auden wrote with Isherwood are more Freudian than Marxist. Few of these plays and poems are quite successful, for, dealing consciously with the unconscious, Auden generally wrote from the top of his head. Social purpose and a good education made him deliberate, didactic, and allegorical. But sometimes, evading intellect, he descended for a holiday to the unconscious he so often had in mind.[19]

[19] "In Memory of Sigmund Freud," *Collected Poetry* (1945). In "Let me tell you a little story," an excellent ballad, Miss Gee has a Freudian dream. Her case history, based also upon Homer Lane and Marx, is a commentary upon our world. In *The Destructive Element* (1935) Spender discusses the "clinical" and sexual imagery Auden took from Freud and fused with Marx to present the problem of the individual in society. Cf. Francis Scarfe: *Auden and After* (1942).

C. Day Lewis, who was driven by a political purpose more orthodox than Auden's to produce verse in greater quantities, admits in *Revolution in Writing* (1935) that poetry has power of survival only when it talks to the "deep unconscious levels within us" as fables do and myths. Although recognizing Freud's importance in this domain, Day Lewis felt compelled to reject him and his domain as individualistic and liberal. Our times, says Day Lewis, force upon every writer a hard decision, whether to serve the revolutionary masses or man's individual unconscious. Literature must follow the way of Marx or the way of Freud: toward satire, allegory, and semireligious drama on one hand, or on the other toward music, subtlety, complex association, and the deeper levels of man. This dilemma, so excellently stated, was that which confronted his generation, and the verses, allegorical plays, and satires that followed their choice show what it was. Spender, a better poet than Day Lewis, allowed himself as he walked beside the party line an occasional deviation. But it was left for other younger men to deviate into nonsense.

With the aid of surrealism the young explored Freud's underworld of dream and madness. Breaking the barriers between dream and reality, between the mad and the sane, surrealism is the climax of the romantic movement or its final decay. More specifically it is the climax of the symbolist tradition of Rimbaud, who, with Freud to help him, became again an agreeable ancestor. Surrealism is a product of France, and, though increasingly international in its development, it retains in other lands the character of an import.

The immediate ancestors of the surrealists were Jarry, Apollinaire, who gave it its name, and the Dadaists. Dada, a nihilistic group expressing the futility of the war, was founded by Tristan Tzara in Zurich on February 8, 1916, at six p.m.[20] Convinced of the uselessness of literature and of all things, the Dadaists illustrated the uselessness of all things by their conduct and their art. They issued foolish poems, painted outrageous pictures, held exhibits, and at their public meetings in Paris threw tomatoes, which the audience returned. At the Dada exhibition of paintings in Cologne the public was supplied with hatchets to destroy the exhibits. Louis Aragon's poem "*Suicide*" consists of the letters of the alphabet in their normal order. Pasting bus tickets on paper, Tzara called the arrangement "*Douleur en cage.*" To compose a poem, said Tzara, one should cut words from a newspaper, shake them carefully in a bag, draw out the words. "The poem will be like you." Achieving what Verlaine had dreamed, Dada destroyed literature. At this point, André Breton observed: "The only way for Dada to continue is for it to cease to exist." Therefore he founded surrealism.

Breton was a disciple of Freud, from whom he had learned the importance of the unconscious and the technique of analysis by uncritical monologue. Impressed by the destruction of literature, he decided to rebuild it from the depths of the mind, to avoid the errors of realism and logic, and to affirm the mysterious and the wonderful. One night while he was falling asleep, the image of a man vertically cut in two by a window emerged from his unconscious. This image could be used, he thought, in a poem he was composing. To get other images he tried the technique of rapid monologue, by which the patients of psychoanalysts are persuaded to expose themselves. With Philippe Soupault, Breton commenced automatic writing. The results were destitute of structure, but full of buffoonery and useful images. Naming the results surrealism in honor of Apollinaire, they published their automatic texts as *Les Champs magnétiques* in 1921, and in 1924

[20] See Wilson, *Axel's Castle,* for Tzara's "Memoirs of Dadaism."

Breton issued the first surrealist manifesto. Here he defined surrealism as psychic automatism by which, in the absence of rational control and of all æsthetic or moral preoccupations, reality is expressed. We believe, he announced, in the superior reality of dream and in childhood recaptured. As predecessors he named Lautréamont, Rimbaud, St.-J. Perse, Monk Lewis, the Delphic oracle, and many others. As addicts of "the new vice," which affects them like opium, he named Aragon, Crevel, Desnos, Péret, and Éluard. To this manifesto he added as exemplary text his own "*Poisson soluble.*" "The flora and fauna of surrealism," he observed, "are shameful."

Éluard quickly emerged as the best poet of the group. Max Ernst, Picasso, Chirico, Yves Tanguy, and later, Salvador Dali became its painters. Magazines, *La Révolution surréaliste* and *Le Surréalisme au service de la révolution,* spread the new faith and announced in 1925 the conversion of the surrealists to dialectical materialism. While other reds improved the outer man, they would improve the inner. But their refusal to write proletarian literature or propaganda or to abandon Freud caused the orthodox to regard them as little better than bourgeois anarchists. Aragon left his friends for the Communist Party. Breton's second manifesto (1930), reaffirming Freud, insists upon Marx. The other major development of surrealism was provided in 1929 by Dali, who, inventing the technique of paranoia, began to find in the external world corroboration of his obsessions. "The only difference between myself and a madman," he said, "is that I am not mad."

The dreams recorded in pictures, poems, narratives, and texts by the surrealists differ from *Finnegans Wake,* which Joyce was composing in Paris during the development of surrealism. Although Joyce's intricate arrangement presents the unconscious, it is conscious. The surrealists, however, half-approving of Joyce, published him in *transi-*

tion together with photographs of some "objects" that, to display his paranoia, he had discovered near his home.

In England, as we have seen, the thirties were divided into two overlapping times, the first the time of Auden, the second that of Dylan Thomas. Auden's generation, inclining toward Marx, more or less accepted Freud. Thomas's, inclining toward Freud, accepted Marx less and less. Both generations were influenced by the surrealists, who had achieved a confusion of Marx with Freud. Orthodox surrealism in England was of little value perhaps, but its peripheral effects helped to shape and color some of the best writing of our time—the poems of Dylan Thomas and Lawrence Durrell, for example, and their prose.

Softly penetrating English literature for several years, affecting even T. S. Eliot, surrealism emerged at last in London at the exhibition in the New Burlington Galleries in June 1936. Breton attended the opening with Mme Breton, who had blue hair. Sheila Legge's face was smothered in red roses. The principal address, delivered by Dali from within a diver's helmet, was inaudible.

To improve this occasion, Herbert Read, a member of the committee, edited *Surrealism* (1936), the "definitive manifesto" of the British group. His introduction, dismissing mockery and sneers, hails surrealism as Marxist and romantic. It will liquidate classicism and capitalism alike. The poetry by which this will be accomplished is identical with dream. In 1935, he continues, he had a dream that he made into a poem with as little conscious control as possible. As printed here, this poem, though faithful to its "myth," misses poetry. But as example the poem and its analysis by the author served an excellent cause. To this manifesto André Breton contributed an essay in praise of Freud, Marx, and the Gothic novel. Hugh Sykes Davies announced in his essay that if the surrealists are the tail of romanticism, this tail is prehensile.

David Gascoyne quickly became the leading surrealist. In 1935 he anticipated Read by issuing *A Short Survey of Surrealism,* an excellent historical account, illustrated with reproductions and translations. In 1936 he published *Man's Life Is This Meat,* a collection of poems many of which seem to be imitations in words of surrealistic paintings. Dedicating his poems to Yves Tanguy, Dali, and others, he celebrates "the last head with its fingers plaited in curls," a "tightrope covered with moths," and "perfumed lenses." His prose poems recall Rimbaud's, his images are those of Freudian dreams, but his poems are too consciously contrived to be as overwhelming as he desired. England needed surrealistic poetry. He carefully provided it.

> The face of the precipice is black with lovers,

he sang, and, in another poem:

> An arrow with lips of cheese was caught by a floating hair.

Since logical connections are foreign to the unconscious, and in his poetry other connections are uncommon, single lines will do to illustrate the new world of imagery.[21]

Petron (1935) by Hugh Sykes Davies, a prose narrative with overtones of Monk Lewis, Shelley's *Alastor,* and Salvador Dali, is orthodox surrealism. Setting out on his terrible journey, Petron encounters a man who cuts his

[21] Gascoyne translated Breton's *What is Surrealism?* (1936) and Dali's *Conquest of the Irrational* (1935). In *Hölderlin's Madness* (1938) Gascoyne added some verses of his own to his translations from the mad German. Gascoyne's *Poems 1937–42* (1943) are less surrealistic although many show the influence of Éluard, Supervielle, and Jouve.

In 1936, translations of Éluard's poetry by Samuel Beckett, Denis Devlin, and others were issued as *Thorns of Thunder,* edited by George Reavy. At this time or later there were translations of Lautréamont, Lorca, and Péret.

fingers into hands, then each of the resulting fingers into smaller hands until he has thousands of them. Then, passing a string through his head from ear to ear, he pulls a loop through his nostril, and swallows it. Petron flees, howling, only to meet a man whose jaw hangs between his knees, a crab disemboweling himself, and other marvels. If the reader wonders about the size of these adventures, says Davies, he should hire a cow, tie her at the foot of a cliff, and jump off the cliff, observing the size of the cow as he falls. "That is exactly the scale on which we are working."

That mixture of buffoonery and wonder which Breton prized is also illustrated in the magazine *Contemporary Poetry and Prose*, ten issues of which appeared in 1936 and 1937 under the editorship of Roger Roughton. Although he denied that his magazine was the official organ of the "loosely-constituted" group, it is the nearest approach in England to the French official magazines. About half the contributions are surrealistic.[22]

In this periodical the best and maddest stories are those of Dylan Thomas, who, though not a member of the group, dealt with their materials. Among the strangest of his excursions into hallucination and madness is "The Mouse and the Woman," whose hero dreams in his asylum of men with mouse-nests in their beards. "The Map of Love" explores dream's topography.[23] A Welshman, Thomas came naturally by his manner; but there is little

[22] Translations of Lautréamont, Jarry, Tzara, Rimbaud, Breton, Lorca, Éluard, and Cros by Francis Scarfe, Gascoyne, and others set the tone. Mad in the French manner: "A Myth" by Scarfe, "I Have Done My Best for You" by Sheila Legge, "The Light of the Lion's Mane" by Gascoyne, and "The Journey" by Roughton.

[23] These stories have been reprinted in *The Map of Love* (1939) and (in the United States) in *The World I Breathe* (1939). "The Burning Baby" is a story of incest told in the surrealist manner; "The Holy Six" illustrates the buffoonery of the unconscious; "Prologue to an Adventure," a vision of sin, ends mythically in Noah's Flood.

doubt of his acquaintance with the French, who in these stories add confusion to his gifts.

At first glance Thomas's poems seem mad.[24] The images are those of surrealist texts or, sometimes, of Rimbaud. "The sea-legged deck" is a picture by Dali. But on closer inspection the chaos of images assumes a kind of order and it becomes apparent that under the mad surfaces the poems are deliberate arrangements. What is more, they make sense at last or seem on the edge of making it. Differing in this respect from the surrealists, Thomas resembles them because, inspired by Freud, he also uses the imagery of dream and madness, which, however, he subjects to further distortion according to Welsh poetic usage, the example of Hopkins and Joyce, and his own ingenuity. Led to myth by Freud, he makes the Bible his myth.

The poems of Thomas present the underworld of sex in the familiar symbols.

> When, like a running grave, time tracks you down,
> Your calm and cuddled is a scythe of hairs. . . .

Here the "running grave" and the "scythe of hairs," so baffling at first glance, are Freudian symbols, mixed for the occasion with the idea of death in order to imply that love is death. "Running" in association with "tracks" presents an image of pursuit and, by its immediate context, of liquid corruption. Medieval horror is intensified by the nature of time's scythe, which cuts hairs or, since we are mammals, is itself of hair. By these rich interconnections and suggestions, which may be compared with the tenuity of A. E. Housman, Thomas has expressed in two lines the central preoccupation of every man. In most of his poems he is preoccupied with love, death, the gestation of the

[24] *18 Poems* (1934), *Twenty-Five Poems* (1936), *New Poems* (1943), *Deaths and Entrances* (1946).

fetus, and the four seasons. For these universal themes he created a special language by separating, according to the practice of Mallarmé, ordinary words from ordinary contexts and usages and, by ingeniously combining or displacing them, renewing them for poetry.

Applying Hegelian dialectic to imagery, Thomas pairs incompatibles to create a new synthesis of entrances and deaths. And as if for William Empson, to whom he addressed ironic homage, Thomas arranges ambiguities and startling interconnections. In the poem on the "man aged one hundred" the word "lock" has literal, metaphysical, and sexual levels, and in other poems the word "tree" combines religion and sex. "Man be my metaphor," said Thomas, but he meant parts and functions of man. Man's physiology and his dreams are the metaphor by which Thomas expresses man. The point is not metaphor or theme, however attractive, but the poetry they help create. At its worst exploratory and cathartic, this poetry at its best is almost of the first order.

In answer to questions asked by the editor of *New Verse,*[25] Thomas described his poetry as "a formally watertight compartment of words," and, confessing his debt to Freud, said:

> Poetry, recording the stripping of the individual darkness, must, inevitably, cast light upon what has been hidden for too long, and, by so doing, make clean the naked exposure. Benefiting by the sight of the light and the knowledge of the hidden nakedness, poetry must drag further into the clean nakedness of light more even of the hidden causes than Freud could realise.

The debt to Freud is greater than the debts to Hegel and Empson, for what Thomas does is create by artificial dream-work artificial dreams. Their surfaces are perplexing, their ambiguities and condensations those of censor-

[25] No. XI (October 1934).

ship. These poems can be enjoyed like dreams for manifest wonders, but to be understood they must be subjected not only to æsthetic analysis, but to Freudian as well.

"Where once the waters of your face" is the logical elaboration of a Freudian metaphor. Intricate in design, triumphant in rhythm, it presents the scenery of love, death, and birth again. The "bags of blood," the "bushy jaws," the hair and milk of "When once the twilight locks no longer," convey a dream of birth and a dream of corruption and guilt within this dream. Father, mother, and child at once, the dreamer is freed by dream of his obsessions and, as the air brightens, awakes. The elegy for Ann Jones and "Altarwise by owl-light," the mythical sonnet sequence that mixes Freud and the Bible, though closer to the light of day, are no less wonderful.

In "Ballad of the Long-Legged Bait" strict quatrains deliberately roughened, orderly progression, and organic cross-references appear to carry some great significance. Each part is crowded with meaning, but the whole, although the life-cycle seems intended, remains unclear like some portentous dream. Using bait to catch children, the fisher is man, the whales, and God the Father; but as the tone changes, he himself is caught and his bait, dying in giving birth, becomes Eden and the world. Except for paired opposites and distortions, the images appear spontaneous, although selected with an eye to Freud. Some, like those of dream, seem equally effectual on three or four levels. In its context, for example, "windows of waves," a descriptive image, dissolves into widows of waves and windows of wives. Such ambiguities, composing the substance, not the decoration of the poem, make it too private for general intrusion. But that, like Donne, Thomas can make such conceits express his passion is proved in another poem by his cry "Deliver me . . . from maid and head." Caught by the pun, we may miss the meanings and the anguish, fail to see that in these allusions to birth, love, and intellect he is calling for release from the cycle.

One may ask what happens to a poem when the poet, knowing Freud, consciously uses the unconscious. Does secondary elaboration rob the poem of power? Or can the unconscious, deprived of its common symbols, express itself without them, in new symbols perhaps or by rhythm or tone? If the poem seems magical, as Thomas's poems do, the unconscious has found another way, deviously affecting us while we are occupied with what used to be its symbols.[26]

George Barker[27] and Henry Treece, poets of Thomas's generation who drew images for their early poems from Freud and the Bible, are neo-Thomist. Their lyrics, like those of Thomas, owe some of their strangeness and charm to vestigial traces of surrealism. By 1938, because of its Marxist pretensions perhaps, surrealism, after flashing so bravely in the pan, had lost some of its power to move the imaginations of the young, but its dark light had been so intense that typical images and atmospheres remained to decorate the poems of Charles Madge, Peter Yates, and many others. Even Nicholas Moore, that copious singer of married love, lapses upon occasion into Dali's unconscious.[28]

[26] For Thomas: Marshall W. Stearns: "Unsex the Skeleton," *Sewanee Review, LII* (July-September 1944); Henry Treece: "Corkscrew or Footrule," *Poetry (London)*, May-June 1941; Francis Scarfe: *Auden and After* (1942); Elizabeth Drew and John Sweeney: *Directions in Modern Poetry* (1940).

[27] One of the most brilliant poets of the Thomas generation, Barker is distinguished by extravagance of imagery and technical dexterity. *Poems* (1935); *Calamiterror* (1937), his closest approach to Thomas and surrealism; *Lament and Triumph* (1940); *Selected Poems* (1941); *Sacred and Secular Elegies* (1943); *Eros in Dogma* (1944).

[28] E.g., Francis Scarfe: "The Merry Window" and "Defence of Gothic," *Inscapes* (1940); Charles Madge: "The Waltz" and "Flight of

As surrealism declined, a group known as the New Apocalypse, midway between surrealism and sanity, emerged. In *The New Apocalypse* (1939) and *The White Horseman* (1941), manifestoes and anthologies, G. F. Hendry and G. S. Fraser, the spokesmen and, to some extent, poets of the group, made principles of Thomas's practice, paid their respects to Freud and Lawrence, and dissociated themselves from Auden and the surrealists alike. Auden was too external and social. The surrealists were too mad. The Apocalyptics, new romantics, proposed, like their romantic predecessors, dream, myth, fantasy, and "obscure terrible desires," controlled, however, by sanity so that the complete man and not his depths alone might be expressed. Uniting the conscious with the unconscious, they proposed to penetrate by selected images the "psychic landscape." One might expect in Apocalyptic poetry something like that union of Housman and Thomas achieved by Henry Treece, who was, as a matter of fact, the principal poet of the group.[29] In the best of his myths and ballads he approximates the Apocalyptic ideal of poems "clear and mysterious as glass."

> But on the eleventh day the dead
> Looked from their priest-holes, seeing only sea,
> And the green shark-cradles with their swift
> Cruel fingers setting the ocean's curls.

In their manifestoes the Apocalyptics praised Franz Kafka, that strange genius whose works were being translated into English during the thirties.[30] Exactly suited to

the Margarine," *The Father Found* (1941); Nicholas Moore: *The Island and the Cattle* (1941); Roy Fuller: *Poems* (1939). *Arson* (1942) is the magazine of the belated English surrealists.

29 *Invitation and Warning* (1942), *The Black Seasons* (1945), *Collected Poems* (1946). Treece edits *Transformation* (1942), an annual.

30 *The Castle* (1930), *The Great Wall of China* (1933), *The Trial* (1937), *The Metamorphosis* (1937). Edwin and Willa Muir are the chief translators.

the anxieties, guilt, and horror of this period, his stories helped reinforce the effect of the surrealists, of whom he may be regarded as a predecessor. But while they dealt in madness, he dealt in dream.

Kafka's stories of the neurotic mole, of the clerk who awakens one morning to find himself an enormous bedbug, of the clerk who is arrested and tried on an incomprehensible charge, of the surveyor who attempts, with two curious assistants, to penetrate the unknowable castle —these stories are bad dreams. Their effect of grotesque humor depends upon the attitude of the heroes, who, attempting to adjust themselves to the circumstances of nightmare, display the common sense of Alice and the sweet reasonableness of Spinoza. It is true that these stories, reflecting the position of the European Jew, are parables of social and religious adjustment, but it is less painful to enjoy their manifest content as a dreamer, innocent of Freud, may enjoy his dream. This, however, was not the way of Kafka's English admirers.

Auden and Isherwood, their tendency toward fantastic social allegory increased by their admiration of Kafka, owe him the dreamlike quality of *The Ascent of F6*. Spender praised him.[31] But the member of the Auden group whose admiration produced the most significant results is Rex Warner, whose anti-Nazi parables, deriving their character from Auden and Kafka, more nearly approach the latter.[32] That scene in *The Professor* (1938) where a crowd of people tries to move about a small room already crowded with furniture has the oppressive quality of the scene in Kafka's *Trial* where spectators in the courtroom occupy a balcony whose ceiling is too low for them

[31] In *The Destructive Element*. Among English adaptations: Edward Upward: *Journey to the Border* (1938); C. S. Lewis: *That Hideous Strength* (1945), Anna Kavan: *Asylum Piece* (1946).

[32] *The Wild Goose Chase* (1937), *The Aerodrome* (1941).

to raise their heads. Despite these interludes of authentic dream, the passages of grotesque humor, and the beautiful prose at Warner's command, his novels are burdened with significant conversation and debate to the point of tediousness. If one is tempted, however, to compare Kafka and Warner to the latter's disadvantage, it may be recalled that the political situation confronting Kafka was not yet ominous enough to make him indifferent to the reader's claims.

The social and political allegories of Ruthven Todd, though bearing a family resemblance to Warner's, are more like Kafka's. With four or five exceptions the poems of *Until Now* (1941) are untouched by surrealism, but Todd's connection with the English surrealists seems to have given his novels a madder atmosphere than rational Warner could evoke. In *Over the Mountain* (1939), another anti-totalitarian fantasy, the mountain resembles Auden's F6 and Kafka's castle. The childish police might have been Kafka's invention. Christopher Aukland of *The Lost Traveller* (1943), wandering through his nightmare, tries to invoke the rights of the British subject in situations infinitely foreign to them. Like Kafka's hero he transgresses unknown laws, is tried before mysterious tribunals, and, condemned for his nameless transgression to secure the extinct Great Auk, discovers himself to be that bird. The political implications are nicely subordinated to dream.

The short stories of William Sansom, *Fireman Flower* (1944), are the closest approximations to Kafka. These delirious visions of firemen in the intricate warehouse, of maze, potting-shed, and their occupants, and of the leg-roasting beauty seem portentous allegories but, like dreams, remain unclear. Fear is the principal emotion, the machinery is Freud's, and the manner is persuasively matter-of-fact.

Two novels of the thirties also occupy a region somewhat this side the frontiers of surrealism. *The Black Book* (1938) by Lawrence Durrell is nihilistic. Part prose-poem, part nightmare, and published, of course, in Paris, it recalls the horrors and manners of Henry Miller, who is enjoying the favor of young Englishmen.[33] *The Amaranthers* (1936) by Jack B. Yeats, as inconsequential and significant as a dream, concerns railroading, both model and full-scale, in a nameless country. The plot is stupid and hilarious, the style elaborately Irish in rhythm and syntax. It is not surprising that Jack Yeats is the brother of the poet who noted his dreams and took for his own a poem from the surrealistic oracle of Delphi.

[33] Durrell was associated with Henry Miller on the staff of the *Booster*, a magazine published in Paris, 1937–8. Dylan Thomas was a contributor. See Nicholas Moore: *Henry Miller* (1943).

CHAPTER X

Myth and the Natural Man

CIVILIZATION, to Freud in one sense, to Marx in another, the cause of all our ills, showed other curers other cures. Sometimes, however, these cures appear less cure than flight. Victorian ideas of progress had generally yielded to the conviction that we are not progressing, and that if we were, it would be bad. Although some, like Wells, remained progressive, others sought to improve themselves by return to flowers, peasants, and savages. Some lost and found themselves in myths, and some, in Joycean circles, mounted their bisexycles and were off. Such improvements or escapes had helped compose romantics from the start. Under the influence of anthropology, improvement or escape took old directions and a fresh disguise.

Peasants and primroses of Wordsworth, myths of Blake and Shelley, and noble savages provided a natural background for anthropologists, archæologists, and Mme Blavatsky. Under their direction the noble savage of earlier romantics became ignoble though no less instructive. Darwin had proved Wordsworth's nature cruel. But cruel indifferent primroses offered fiercer delight and, compared with vacant lots, were lovable.

Among the first of modern anthropologists, Sir Edward Tylor, using the comparative method, devoted *Primitive Culture* (1871) to the study of animism. Sir James Frazer followed with *The Golden Bough,* published in 1890 and expanded to its present dimensions between 1911 and 1915. He pleased no less by matter than by style. Enamored of structure, he tried to unify his learned chaos by a central theme, the mystery of the priest of Nemi, which he dramatically employed for his opening. To beguile the common reader he devised a florid prelude in the manner of Ruskin, a period piece today, suggesting by its decorations and questions a Gothical chalet of 1870. With this ornament the severity of the footnote maintains a curious warfare. But tiring fortunately of difficult splendor, he lapsed into simplicity, lightened by irony, at times, and grace. However crowded with facts, the tremendous book is readable. It is to this that Frazer owes part of his appeal to the literate mind, but part he owes to disclosures for which that mind was waiting. The recurring tragedy of the priest of Nemi led Frazer to seek explanatory parallels in taboo, magic, and the dying and resurrected god. Returning to Nemi, his convenient center, with this freight, he hung it on the Golden Bough. His own piety seemed proof against disclosures that made religion myth and myth a clue to modern minds, peasant, savage, and civilized alike. The accumulation of facts begun by Frazer was increased by Bronislaw Malinowski, whose researches into savage customs appeared in the twenties, and by others, American, German or, like Malinowski, British. Inflamed by Frazer, the literary mind was ready for these, who seemed, like Freud and Jung, providers for romantic needs.

For many readers Freud, Jung, and Frazer were the most congenial people in the world. Nor was this odd, for Freud, following Frazer on taboo, found among savages the substance of childhood and our dreams. The primitive mind, he found, determines modern neurosis. Following his master, Jung discovered the identity of neurosis and myth, of which the collective unconscious is the present repository. The waking mind of primitive man is the unconscious mind of modern man, who is at once far more and no less primitive than he dreams.

These disclosures were accompanied by those of the archæologists. Following Schliemann of Mycenæ, Sir William Petrie dug up Egypt and Sir Arthur Evans Crete. Their excavations provided furniture for dreams of a fabulous past. The Palace of Minos with its elegant plumbing and intricate corridors called to mind an occupant who, obsessing Joyce, Picasso, and all surrealists, has become our favorite animal.

Such a symbol, though proper to that time and to ours, may seem a little precious. The Minoan verses and the amphitheater of Aldous Huxley's story "Eupompus Gave Splendour to Art by Numbers" cannot altogether escape this reproach. But others used the new learning more soberly. Christopher Caudwell used anthropology to establish the communal character of poetry, Gerald Heard used it to establish the trouble with man, and even Shaw, who refers to Frazer in the preface to *Androcles* (1913), appears to have used him to interpret Christianity in that extravagant play. Others, innocent of Frazer and Jung, or with their help, returned to peasant, soil, and child. Some were simple Wordsworthians (too long in city pent), some romantic primitivists of other varieties, and some explorers exploring with new instruments. The only one who had everything was D. H. Lawrence.

Lawrence was Wordsworthian, but there was nothing simple about him. He loved nature and saw in it the remedy for what ails us, but having read Darwin, he loved something hostile or indifferent with which he had to struggle for success. The heroine of *St. Mawr* (1925) finds peace in nature's malevolence as she establishes polarity with tree, flower, earth, and horse. To these she has been led by a horse-rubber, a man, like the gamekeepers, gypsies, and redskins of Lawrence's other stories, close to nature. The hero of *Kangaroo* (1923) finds consolation in a farmer of Cornwall, and Lawrence himself in *Sea and Sardinia* (1921), one of the best of his glowing travel books, pursues peasants. The function of these natural men was to save him and his heroines from civilization. This is primitivism. It is only when civilization is overripe, as in Augustan Rome, Gibbon's England, or the age of Mr. Bloom, that men attempt to cure the time by past or peasant.

Frazer had found the past vestigial in peasant and barbarian. Lawrence turned from peasants to men of Ceylon, Australia, and Tahiti, but, disappointed, found the closest approximation to the noble savage in the Indians of New Mexico. Degenerate perhaps, they nevertheless retained in their drums and dances something of the noble past. Lawrence described their dances in the bright hypnotic prose of *Mornings in Mexico* (1927) and told their meaning in *Reflections on the Death of a Porcupine* (1925) and the other essays of this period. What he wanted, not to be found in practice, must be created again from such vestiges. What he wanted, however, was to be found in books. Among anthropologists he had read Frazer, Tylor, Jane Harrison, and Frobenius, among archæologists Petrie. Some of these he loved, some, like Frazer, he despised as intellectual and corrected by intuition, but all were useful, supplying him with hints upon which to improve. His heroes are always speaking of Egyptians, Chaldeans, or darkest Africans. Birkin of *Women in Love* (1920) adores the mystic sensualism of African sculpture, and the hero of "The Ladybird" adores the scarab. Lawrence looked at Indian dances through Tylor's eyes and Jane Harrison's spectacles. These authorities showed him how to interpret vestiges and through them to recapture man's ancient relationship with earth, trees, cows, and serpents. And Mme Blavatsky, of course, showed him how to interpret these authorities.

In *The Plumed Serpent* (1926) they conspire with Mexican archæologists like Zelia Nuttall and Lawrence's genius to produce one of the most wonderful novels of our time. Its theme is the recovery by myth and symbol not only of Mme Blavatsky's Atlantis, but of Tylor's animistic past. Through the myth of Quetzalcoatl the antediluvian is recovered and civilization destroyed. There is compulsory dancing in the streets. Inspired by one myth, this novel creates another. Its intensity comes from archetypal patterns of rebirth that Lawrence, pursuing the childish, the primitive, and the unconscious, improved by his hypnotic arts. In the preface to *Fantasia of the Unconscious* (1922) he had recognized the value of myth and symbol for recapturing the past; and elsewhere he found them lying "too deep in the blood and soul" for intellect to follow. The frames of other novels come from myth, that of *The Trespasser* (1912) from Wagner's *Ring*, that of *The Boy in the Bush* (1924) from Genesis. Part of their attractiveness comes from these frames and part from that evocation of place for which he is famous.[1]

Back in Italy, Lawrence exhumed with the help of archæologists the lost Etruscans. Their meaning for the modern world, as presented in *Etruscan Places* (1932), is that of Egyptians or Indians. And in his last illness he turned to Christian mythology. That fine new myth of

[1] Memoirs of Lawrence: Catherine Carswell: *The Savage Pilgrimage* (1932); Mabel Dodge Luhan: *Lorenzo in Taos* (1932); Dorothy Brett: *Lawrence and Brett* (1933); Frieda Lawrence: "*Not I, but the Wind . . .*" (1934); Knud Merrild: *A Poet and Two Painters* (1938).

Jesus *The Man Who Died* is based upon Frazer's pattern of dying and resurrected gods. Lawrence's Jesus is converted to primitive animism. By *Apocalypse* (1931), exposing symbolic dragon, horses, and numbers to the lights of anthropology and Theosophy, Lawrence saved what Jesus saves.

At first blush E. M. Forster might be taken for a lesser Lawrence. In each of Forster's novels an oaf is used as a foil to the civilized. The animal vitality of Carella in *Where Angels Fear to Tread* (1905) quarrels with the deadness of the British suburb. The "rustic strength" of Wonham in *The Longest Journey* (1907) counteracts the unreality of the public scholars. The Indians and low-caste Englishmen of the other novels are similar. But unlike those of Lawrence, these oafs are not ideal. Carella is the son of a village dentist, and, what is worse, he is conventional and cruel. Wonham is less the natural man than what man has made of natural man. Although these imperfect instruments uncover the nature of society by contrast and resemblance, they are no better, on the whole, than the society they uncover. Far from the regions of good and evil where Lawrence ran rapidly from black to white, Forster, remaining in England, straddled.

This posture is conspicuous even in "The Story of a Panic," the most Laurentian of all Forster's stories. The respectable Englishmen, of course, are immune to Pan, but Gennaro, the Italian primitive of whom one expects much, is untrue to him for gold. This defection is compensated for, however, by the conduct of Eustace, an oaf, who, inflamed by Pan, picks flowers and goes shouting down the valleys in his nightie. Miss Beaumont of "Other Kingdom," another child of nature, is discouraged by her Philistine lover who fences-in the sacred wood. Dressed in green, she either climbs the fence or, what is more likely, becomes a tree. The uncertainty is typical.[2]

The savages of W. H. Hudson are nobler. Like Hudson himself they succumb to "strange rushes or bursts of feeling" at the sight of bird or flower. As a lad on the pampas, drawn to nature by nature, he increased its pull by reading Wordsworth's poems and Gilbert White's *Natural History of Selborne.* Hudson's subsequent work as a field naturalist, consisting in descriptions of plants and beasts, together with anecdotes of their behavior, is amateur. In his opinion scientific biologists were too sedentary, too intent upon reasons and causes. To Darwin, whose natural selection seemed mechanical and cruel, Hudson preferred Lamarck and Samuel Butler, who were on familiar terms with the life force. Nature, like Wordsworth's primrose, was not only natural but something more. Like Wordsworth and Thoreau, Hudson became a mystical pantheist, thrilling to the noise of birds or the look of plants. A scientist would classify bird and plant; a rationalist might think it rational to eat them; but Hudson felt wonder alone as he botanized on Wordsworth's grave.

In *The Naturalist in La Plata* (1892) Hudson recorded his loving observations of flora and fauna, imperiled, and for this more dear, by encroaching civilization. In *A Shepherd's Life* (1910) and *A Hind in Richmond Park* (1922) he looked through England for what was still unspoilt by fences and motor cars. Lamenting the natural past before their incursions, he chose from what was left the smaller and gentler "beasties," leaving the bolder animals to Darwin. Gentle nature and her people were antidotes to cities and theirs.

Although barbarous, the gauchos of the pampas were "nature's noblemen," and in England farmers and shepherds were their more perfect, because British, equiva-

[2] *The Celestial Omnibus* (1911) and *The Eternal Moment* (1928) contain other faunish and Laurentian stories.

lents. Hudson differed from Lawrence, whom he abhorred, in disliking gamekeepers. He differed from Lawrence in making little use of anthropologists. Although Hudson had read them and was sufficiently impressed to refer to his own religion as animism, he saw little use in their studies of remote peoples when Salisbury Plain afforded such exemplary specimens of natural man.

The hero of *Green Mansions* (1904) flees the city and his artificial lady for the jungle. This Venezuelan refuge is to be compared only to that jungle of improbable apes devouring improbable blossoms under improbable trees which Henri Rousseau arranged. A man of the pampas who had never seen a jungle, Hudson allowed his fancy to decree a place where natural beauty is unimpaired by nature. Sheltered by the superior foliage of this Utopia lives Rima, an ambiguous thing, half woman and half bird. This child of this nature is a creation not of Hudson the naturalist but of Hudson the transcendentalist. The real children of nature, the Indians who inhabit the edge of Hudson's jungle, throwing poisoned darts as if they had been reading Darwin, are too natural to please. Although supernatural nature is successfully created in this romance, the loves of Rima and her refugee are incredible.

Hudson's memorable works are those in which his feelings were centered upon the actual, his field observations, where sentimentality is less intrusive, some of the less imaginative sketches of *El Ombú* (1902), and his autobiography, *Far Away and Long Ago* (1918), which, in its degree, is as enchanting as Proust's recovery of times past. The style of these nostalgic works is perfect for its purpose. The words, placing no barrier between reader and writer, are lucid and fastidiously chosen, the rhythms easy and natural. It is a style so perfect that it cannot be thought of apart from his matter, the youth of a continent and the age of a countryside.

The dying countryside, victim of Darwin and civilization, was Hardy's concern and the background for tragedy or melodrama. *The Poor Man and the Lady,* his first novel, written in 1868, shows Hardy a nature-lover. His first poems show him a Darwinist. In the later novels the pastoral descriptions and the rustics are the result of a quarrel between Wordsworth and Darwin, the first knowing nature beneficent, the second knowing it malign. Landscapes and rustics, not decorations but parts of the story, provide source, parallel, or relief for the protagonists whose earthy drama needs chorus and setting. But this quarreling accompaniment is so intense that often, as in *The Woodlanders* (1887), it remains alone in memory. Uneasy in cities, Hardy found imperfect refuge in re-creating the past, for the countryside of which he wrote was at its best vestigial. This knowledge, the cause of intensity, was another cause of gloom.[3]

Writers of Hardy's school, apportioning the counties among them, endlessly described the landscapes in which they set their melodramas. These middle-class refugees from what their class had done to nature found or created vestiges of a more natural past. Torn like their master between Wordsworth and Darwin, and almost aware that in turning their backs upon cities they were rejecting the important reality of their class, they became morbid. And so did their peasants, trees, and flowers.

The province of Eden Phillpotts is Devonshire, of Sheila Kaye-Smith Sussex, of D. H. Lawrence Nottinghamshire. Phillpotts begins *The Secret Woman* (1905) with a long description of Dartmoor, its flora, its contours, and a farm or two. After a while he notices the heroine and says: "it may be said concerning the girl that the possibility of pas-

[3] The substance of *The Poor Man and the Lady* is to be found in *An Indiscretion in the Life of an Heiress* (1935), edited by Carl Weber. *Far from the Madding Crowd* (1874) set the pattern for Hardy's followers.

sion was manifest in the atmosphere of her." After being described, she says: "We'll have to be sold up, I reckon." She is right. The villainous money-lender, however, is merely one element of a melodrama of marital infidelity, murder, and conscience. Jesse, who shares Hardy's philosophy, interrupts devotions to nature by thoughts of her mechanical indifference. In *Joanna Godden* (1921) Sheila Kaye-Smith, a better novelist, presents the marshes, their farmers, and Joanna. Though somewhat larger than life, this bouncing girl is victim, like Tess, to character and place. *Sussex Gorse* (1916) is earthier, grimmer, and farther from the madding crowd. Young Lawrence was a more eminent disciple. *The White Peacock* (1911), *Sons and Lovers* (1913), *The Rainbow* (1915), and "Love among the Haystacks," written in 1912, are filled with Hardyesque descriptions of the woods and pastures near Nottingham and of haymakers, milkmen, and gamekeepers. It was Hardy who turned Lawrence's eyes from the mines and towns, which constituted his reality, to pastures. As the attractive repulsiveness of these vestiges became with Mme Blavatsky's help the positive and negative polarity of his later novels, Lawrence abandoned Hardy's rural primitivism for a more exotic kind. But he returned to Hardy's countryside in *Lady Chatterley's Lover.*[4]

The novels of Mary Webb, attractive to ministers of state, are well-made melodramas. Stating her theme, the title of *Gone to Earth* (1917) refers specifically to death and foxes. Hazel, the fox-loving heroine, is a child of nature. When she keens, her keening is "the grief of rainy forests" and their joy. She has so deep a fellowship with trees and flowers that her blood is a kind of sap, and her love of suffering rabbits is infinite. Falling from conventional virtue, this innocent is so earthy that she remains

[4] For Lawrence's essay on Hardy see *Phoenix* (1936). *Rings on Her Fingers* (1930) by Rhys Davies is imitation Lawrence.

unsoiled. Although enjoyed by the squire, married to a Presbyterian, and nagged by his mother—representatives of the cruelty and morality of civilization—she retains her nature. External nature, though a little dismal, is a refuge from cities and unnatural man. But, as in Hardy, doom broods over the forests. Natural forces, as in *Jude*, and man's cruelty send Hazel to earth among her symbols. It is unfortunate that Mary Webb made of her symbolic novel a tract against fox-hunting, but however tractarian and melodramatic, it is elevated above its kinds by lyrical description and solidity. Most notable among her stories of the Welsh marches (Shropshire is her province) is *Precious Bane* (1924). This romance of long ago, told by the hare-shotten heroine, who possesses the beauties of language, reveals her love and the fatal ambition of her farming brother. The rustic hero, kind to sufferers, rescues Prue from bull-baiting rustics in the nick of time and carries her off on a horse. There are magicians about, but the magic of harvest and country winters is a greater magic than theirs.[5]

John Cowper Powys, who calls himself Wordsworthian in his Rousseauistic *Autobiography* (1934), became Hardy's friend and disciple. His most ambitious novel is *Wolf Solent* (1929). Although the neurotic hero has ecstasies over the natural beauties of Dorset, for which he has abandoned the city, he is aware that the "blowflies of dissolution" are at work. He turns up stones to find hidden abominations or visits neighbors. Most of them are corrupt,

[5] *The House in Dormer Forest* (1920). Stella Gibbons: *Cold Comfort Farm* (1932) is a pleasing burlesque of the Hardy tradition.

Many of the short stories of H. E. Bates, although they owe their method to Joyce and Mansfield, belong to the rural tradition: *Cut and Come Again* (1935); *Day's End* (1928); *Country Tales* (1940), collected stories. See Bates's *The Modern Short Story*, a critical survey. *The Poacher* (1935), a novel, shows the conflict between vestigial nature and the encroaching city.

sinister, or daft. Adoring bodies apart from souls and souls apart from bodies, Wolf learns to endure horrors less horrible than those of machine or town.

Meanwhile dramatists and poets had been returning to the countryside and its people. The peasant plays of Synge, Lady Gregory, Colum, Lennox Robinson, George Shiels, and other Irishmen seem less unreal than their English counterparts because Ireland is more pastoral than England, but even these Irish plays represent the nostalgia of the sophisticated. The Aran Islands and the farms of Limerick or Cork, dear to Irish novelists as well, were rapidly assuming the character of the Land of Youth. In England dramatists were less rustic, but two of the best plays of the higher drama belong to this tradition. The well-born heroine of Granville-Barker's *Marrying of Ann Leete* (1901) runs off with her father's gardener as if she were Lady Chatterley herself. "We've all been in too great a hurry getting civilised," says Ann. "I mean to go back." Although still unhappy, she is happier. John Masefield's *Tragedy of Nan,* produced by Granville-Barker in 1908, is the best English tragedy of our time. Although dealing with farmers, this Gloucestershire tragedy is less primitivistic than elemental. The symbolic tide, the many-sidedness of Nan, and that "delighted brooding on excessive, terrible things" that Masefield commends in his preface make the play, despite austerity of dialect, comparable to the work of Synge, his friend and undoubtedly his model.

Masefield's *Everlasting Mercy* (1911), a long narrative poem in colloquial diction and doggerel octosyllabics, uncovers the excesses of a village. His other verse was inspired in part by A. E. Housman's Shropshire ballads, which, representing the frustrations of the civilized by plowmen, trees, and lads hanging around, did as much as Hardy's verse to countrify the Georgian muse. Departing at last with laurels from the general view, Masefield devoted his sonnets to the worship of Beauty with a Platonic B. More elegant, T. Sturge Moore revived the idyll of Theocritus, himself a refugee from civilization. W. H. Davies at his best is somewhat more natural. Having read Wordsworth, Davies became a hobo as he confesses in *The Autobiography of a Super-Tramp* (1908), a work of astonishing simplicity, and in the latter stages of his wandering carried Wordsworth with him. The lyrics of this artful innocent have a childlike quality and at their best freshness and charm. At first he used inversions, archaic diction, and the banalities of a dead tradition to praise the country and to damn the town. But later he acquired directness for his simplicity. "The Soul's Destroyer," "Nature's Friend," and "A Happy Life" celebrate the beauties and ignore the horrors of the Wordsworthian landscape, its daffodils, cows, and feathered friends. In "Return to Nature" Davies tells how he flies the city "to green things, like a bird." His escape from urban reality, he admits, is a kind of cowardice, but peace at any cost is better than contemporary pain.[6] This lyrical Hudson was Hudson's friend and the friend, of course, of Edward Thomas, whose Wordsworthian descriptions excited Robert Frost. Farmers, barns, flowers, the open road attracted Thomas's accurate eye, inspiring quiet verses, better than most in this kind.[7] The technique is as old-fashioned as the accurate eye. But as with the verses of Davies, the rural monotony of these is sometimes redeemed by freshness or by an imaginative turn.

Although less contemptible than recently supposed and less bucolic, the Georgian poets are sometimes contemptible and commonly bucolic. They withdrew from reality, not to an ivory tower, but to an oast-house. Disheartened

[6] *The Poems of W. H. Davies* (1940).
[7] *Collected Poems* (1936).

even in their happy time by its disorder and its noise, they sought peace among loud cattle and neglected gardens. The consequences of this withdrawal are apparent in their verse. It is sterile on the whole, derivative in substance and technique, and at its best suburban.

The Georgians were less a group than an idea in the head of Edward Marsh, by turns secretary to Joseph Chamberlain and to Winston Churchill. In 1911 this gentleman decided to become what Swinnerton called "wet nurse" to the muse. King Edward had died in 1910, the Georgian era had begun, the time looked right for poetry's revival. That this was possible was shown by *The Everlasting Mercy,* a fitting expression of new times. Calling for poets, Marsh conferred. The result was *Georgian Poetry,* a biennial anthology to create or advertise a poetic renaissance. The first volume appeared in 1912, the last of five volumes in 1922. Edward Marsh was editor, Harold Monro publisher. Georgian poetry, or what they published, is that part of contemporary poetry which appealed to the taste of Edward Marsh. As might be supposed, this taste was conservative. Interesting poets, thought radical, were carefully excluded as those were who, face to face with reality, found rhythms for it and suitable metaphors. Intended to mean up-to-date, "Georgian" came to mean reactionary.

Being up-to-date meant accepting the frames of Wordsworth and Tennyson and the rhetoric of Keats, purged of richness and strength, however, in order to achieve the condition of Housman. The purge was sometimes incomplete, as in the verses of John Drinkwater, Robert Nichols, or Francis Brett Young, which seem composed of the words of Keats, and sometimes too complete, as in J. C. Squire's "To a Bull Dog," bare and flat to the point of banality. The more bucolic Georgians were these, together with Gordon Bottomley, Edmund Blunden, John Freeman, and D. H. Lawrence. Most were trying to achieve not only the condition of Housman but the condition of Joyce Kilmer at the moment of "Trees." D. H. Lawrence was included because of his pastoral interests, but his growing tendency toward free verse and exotic imagery must have caused uneasiness. From the ranks of older nature-lovers Marsh picked Davies, Masefield, de la Mare, and T. Sturge Moore. These gave the anthology its reputation.[8]

But the leading Georgians were far less botanical. Lascelles Abercrombie contributed quantities of academic blank verse. Before contributing his nature poems, W. W. Gibson had written *Daily Bread* (1910), short blank-verse dialogues on the poor submitting to operations, dying in mines, or falling into furnaces. But the rhythms and images are too antiquated for these modern occasions. Rupert Brooke was more effectual. Instead of following the lead of these belated Victorians, he turned for the technique of some of his best poems to Webster, Marvell, and Donne. "Heaven" is witty, odd, and elaborately conceited in the manner of the seventeenth century. Even "Grantchester" is partly redeemed from its Georgian heritage by the brightness of that century. Brooke was the most talented of the Georgians, and had he lived he might have developed along the lines of T. S. Eliot, finding in the wit of Donne a vehicle suited to our divided times.[9]

D. H. Lawrence was also one of the imagists. These poets, otherwise barred from *Georgian Poetry* by their

[8] Sir Edward Marsh: *A Number of People* (1939). James Elroy Flecker: "The New Poetry and Mr. Housman's 'Shropshire Lad,'" *Collected Prose* (1922). Harold Monro: *Some Contemporary Poets* (1920).

Among the better works of the Georgians: Masefield: *Reynard the Fox* (1919); Harold Monro: *Collected Poems* (1933); Edmund Blunden: *Poems* (1930). "The Bull" by Ralph Hodgson was generally admired.

[9] *Poems* (1932) (with memoir by Marsh); *John Webster and the Elizabethan Drama* (1916).

free verse, their clear images, their hatred of diffuse description and shop-worn rhetoric, were little less botanical than the Georgians, and Lawrence could feel as much at home with them as they with him. It took T. S. Eliot with his dead geraniums to change all that. Emerging from among the imagists, he finished them and the Georgians too, and lost himself in the unnatural past.

Others seeking the past lost themselves in childhood and history. With the aid of psychoanalysts the meaning of Wordsworth, Rimbaud, and Proust became evident, and childhood was recaptured. History, that preoccupation of romantics, was recaptured with the aid of archæologists and anthropologists. Unlike the Georgians, who sought the past in nature, some of those who sought it in childhood and history were explorers. Their intention was not to escape the present but to enrich it.

In spite of Wordsworth's "Ode," Victorians commonly thought children small adults who differed from large adults in providing better opportunities for sentiment or escape. Peter Pan's refusal of adult responsibility, though reflecting a social pattern, owes its undeniable vividness to symbols provided by Barrie's unconscious. The maternal cave, the lagoon, and the intruders, whether pirate, crocodile, or ticking clock, give the fantasy a richness beyond intention. Making these symbols conscious, Freud also changed the child from small adult to child, without always improving, however, the literary result. *The Green Child* (1935) by romantic Herbert Read is another *Peter and Wendy.* Rejecting responsibility, Olivero, the hero of this romance, returns to the scene of his infancy in order to recapture it, meets a sexless child (green because like Rima close to nature), and with her, sinking into a pool, re-enters the maternal cave. Read's knowledge of what his hero was about does not make him different from Barrie's or better.

But "The Innocent Eye," a part of *Annals of Innocence and Experience* (1940), is not escapist but exploratory. In this autobiography Read recovers childhood by the method of Proust. Smelling smells, hearing the notes of violins, Read follows associations through widening circles of memory until the forgotten past is there again, the sights and sounds of a "virgin sensibility" and the pulsing of its "green heart." These sensations are confused with dream. Did he see or dream the monstrous steam-roller and the sausage clouds? He does not know, but he does know the value of the innocence that the writer, if a poet, must employ. To Read, childhood is the unconscious, imagination, ecstasy, and nature itself, and art the recovery of the childish eye. These Wordsworthian and Freudian musings may owe something to Rimbaud, with whom Read was familiar. For to Rimbaud the memory of childhood was equivalent to vision and madness, as to psychoanalysts it is the equivalent of the unconscious and the primitive. Dylan Thomas, invoking in one of his inverted sonnets a memory of "the black stairs," shared these convictions.

A High Wind in Jamaica (1929) by Richard Hughes is the best novel of the infant consciousness. The little victims of pirates, who are somewhat ineffectual and *démodé,* live in a world of decorum and taboo whose interpenetration of adult reality, domestic, piratical, or legal, is his theme. An adult, he says, has no more chance of "intellectual sympathy" with these animals than with an octopus, for their consciousness, differing in kind, occupies another plane. Emily's values are peculiar because like other children Emily is mad. Amnesia protects her innocence, as misunderstanding ours. Neatness, humor, and benign aloofness increase the horror of the charming story.

Since Hughes's excellent book deals with the 1860's, it is historical, but Hughes did not use history for romantic escape as Maurice Hewlett had. In recent times the historical novel and poem, less common in England than in America, have been used in the research of lost times, a research various in kind and purpose. Some is patriotic, some amusing, and some instructive.

Once in Sussex, Rudyard Kipling sent out roots to establish himself in the present by means of the past. Some of his stories, such as "Friendly Brook" and "My Son's Wife," praise the soil, not as Hardy's followers did—because it is natural—but because it is English. The nostalgic Americans of these stories, who, like Mr. Eliot of Mayfair and East Coker, are trying to do what cannot be done, are symbols of himself. Undiscouraged, however, Kipling exhumed the county's past, using history and happy intuition for shovels, and Puck to unify the separate mounds. For this reason Puck of *Puck of Pook's Hill* (1906), though related to Forster's Pan, is less impractical. Puck discloses Saxons, Normans, and Romans of the Thirtieth Legion. These disclosures are filled with tenderness for England's age-old soil, older than other soils and richer. The three levels of meaning to which Kipling refers in his autobiography are designed perhaps for boys, patriots, and imperialists.

The intention of Charles M. Doughty was similar, but his audience is more doubtful. *The Dawn in Britain* (1906), an epic in six volumes, is composed in blank verse as uncouth as his prose, but less attractive. Archaic diction, neologisms, inversions, astonishing ellipses, do what they can to suit and to conceal the doughty deeds of "what antique wights dwelled ere in this sweet soil." Asked to recover this matter from the "vast abysm of buried ages," the Muse comes up with Samoth, Brennus, and Britomart. Hardy readers, unaware that this ersatz epic is unreadable, have compared Doughty to Hopkins. But the Germanic oddities of Hopkins are poetry.

The British past also obsessed Arthur Machen, who, walking Welsh forests or rummaging *grimoires*, had taken "all obsolescence to be his province." Lucian, the hero of *The Hill of Dreams* (1907), of whom Machen spoke these words, exaggerates the concerns and feelings of his creator. As he walks the forests, Lucian feels that awe of nature which seems to have been the primitive emotion. Recapturing it like Lawrence, he centers it in the ruins of a Roman fort, where, like Forster's people, he submits to panic. This faunal experience, fixing his awe, unlocks the past. Lucian spends his time in fantasies of the Celtic-Roman period, a time of mingled horror and exquisiteness, of Pan and Walter Pater. This refuge, somewhat over-furnished by drugs, enables Lucian to forget the Philistines and the suburb. What their enemy feels, Machen felt, and in the jeweled, cadenced, and elaborate prose that he learned from Stevenson, he kept our time at a distance. In *Far Off Things* (1922), the first part of his autobiography, Machen confesses that in his effort to translate natural awe into words it became horror. But the glamour of *The Hill of Dreams* is located between these feelings.

The best historical novelists of recent years are Naomi Mitchison and Robert Graves. *Cloud Cuckoo Land* (1925), Miss Mitchison's first important work, is a study of Athens, Sparta, and their colonies during the Peloponnesian War. Although representative of time and place, the characters talk like our contemporaries and face domestic problems like our own. The portrait of Athens, created with the help of Jane Harrison and the historians, is the novel's justification.[10] *I, Claudius* (1934), Graves's first important novel, is a finer reconstruction of the past. This fictive autobiography of the least astonishing of the twelve Cæsars is notable for his character and for the portraits of

[10] *The Conquered* (1923), *When the Bough Breaks* (1924), *Black Sparta* (1928), *Vienna Diary* (1934).

his abominable contemporaries, Livia, Tiberius, Caligula, and all the monsters, poisoners, and unnatural mothers of natural children. Their time, worse if possible than ours, is of use in making ours more bearable. The temperate tone of Claudius is a conceit.[11]

After these successes both Graves and Mitchison turned to anthropologists and archæologists for help in further explorations. For *The Corn King and the Spring Queen* (1931) she had help from E. M. Forster and Gerald Heard as well as from the works of Frazer, Petrie, and many others. This novel (too long) concerns the fertility festivals of barbarians on the Black Sea between 228 and 187 B.C. Forgetting her duty to the crops, the Spring Queen visits Sparta and Petrie's Egypt, where Isis, her cousin, observes the annual rebirth of Frazer's Osiris. These anthropological delights are tempered by Naomi Mitchison's socialistic concern with the rich and the poor. With Frazer's help, Graves retold the story of the Argonauts in *The Golden Fleece* (1944) and made myth history. Centaurs are not monsters but glyphs of a totemistic fraternity, the apples of the Hesperides are oranges, the harpies birds. As for the Symplegades, they are not there. Voyaging soberly among facts, Jason and his crew illustrate the war between the partisans of the Great Mother and of patriarchal Zeus. Hercules, a dim-witted buffoon, and timid Jason, serving both, piously fertilize the crops. Sometimes tedious, this academic adventure is often of interest, but making myth commonplace may seem a pity on the whole to those for whom myth's value is unconscious or magical.

Explaining myth away had little place in the romantic plan. While euhemeristic Graves found actual bulls in the palace of Evans, others led by Freud, Jung, and Frazer,

[11] *Claudius the God* (1934); *King Jesus* (1946). Somerset Maugham's *Then and Now* (1946) is a pleasant historical fabliau, based upon Machiavelli's *Prince* and *Mandragola*.

threaded a labyrinth to find at its center man's nature and its past. The clue of Ariadne led to dream. As intense and strange, the metaphors of myth proved suitable for poems. Preserving mystery while threading it, the clue allowed pursuit of reason, if not to an *altitudo,* to that central place. Such considerations led Lawrence to Quetzalcoatl and the beasts of Revelation, led Dylan Thomas to make the Testaments, New and Old, his myth, led Henry Treece and the Apocalyptics to praise, invent, or use the fabulous. For their art these matters provided theme, structure, and symbol, for their readers a meaning plainly there, but never plain.

Sometimes enlarged from a philosophical or historical core, sometimes from a personal quandary, myth is an integrating device fulfilling the wish of a people or of an artist. To psychoanalysts myth, a product of the primitive imagination, is identical with dream. To recent anthropologists myth is art. Because it preserves the magical view of things, myth recommends itself not only as an antidote to positivism, but in times like these as a way of making literature possible. Seeking to achieve the condition of myth, poets use old myths or construct new ones upon old patterns. By reconciling opposites or giving them the appearance, at least, of singleness, myths, old or new, can keep the world from falling apart or, arranging our confusion, postpone the signs of it.[12]

Minor instances are innumerable. In "The Road from Colonus," E. M. Forster gave value and richness to his

[12] Richard Chase's forthcoming book, *The Quest for Myth,* an excellent survey of ideas of myth, approaches the use of myth in contemporary literature. Analyses of Yeats's "Among School Children" and Auden's "In Sickness and in Health" show how the poets used myth and mythical method to center their feelings. As Chase says, a mythological work in our time is one that out of present emotional necessity adopts the method of the ancient myth-maker and sometimes fuses itself with an old myth.

usual theme of dead respectability by imposing the pattern of Œdipus. Obsessed with classical mythology, Forster made the people of his other stories follow its record in the stars and pause before Orion, a symbol of the vitality they want. Using the Apocrypha for *Tobit Transplanted* (1931) [13] as Lawrence had used Genesis, Stella Benson gave to her story of modern Manchuria a magical air and to Wilfred Chew angelic significance. By ancient magic, earth and its full-bodied creatures become intenser than they are and by the gaiety more ambiguous. To enrich the present by the fabulous past Denis Johnston used the adventure of the Golden Fleece as frame for *A Bride for the Unicorn* (1933).

Myth as frame may cure confusion or give it meaning, but every cure became a fresh disease. Joyce, Yeats, and Eliot, the three important writers of the twenties, employed this frame. To it some of their richness and hypnotic power may be attributed and some of their elegance of shape. But rich, shapely, and familiar though it is, the myth departs from common sense, and whatever departs from it perplexes the common reader, and all the meanings pass him by.

Joyce, who named his creature Dedalus and built him a maze, used myth as plan. The Homeric parallel of *Ulysses* and *Dubliners,* imposing past order upon present con-

[13] In the United States entitled *The Far-away Bride.* In *Tobias and the Angel* (1930) James Bridie dramatized the same myth. Cf. his *Jonah and the Whale* (1932). *Susannah and the Elders* (1937), a fine play, is a reinterpretation of the myth. *What Say They?* (published 1940) uses the frame of Esther for a modern comedy. *The Cathedral* (1922) by Hugh Walpole owes what strength it has to the frame of Job. Cf. Louis Golding's *Miracle Boy* (1927), a novel on the creation of a modern myth upon an ancient pattern. Among the poets who use mythical method are Norman Nicholson: *Five Rivers* (1944), Vernon Watkins: *Ballad of the Mari Lwyd* (1941), Lynette Roberts: *Poems* (1944), Kathleen Raine: *Stone and Flower* (1943), W. S. Graham: *The Seven Journeys* (1944).

fusion, may complicate the narrative it supports, but as Eliot says in "Ulysses, Order and Myth,"[14] the value exceeds the cost. In a time so shapeless as our own, something, he continues, must be imported, preferably from the past, to give our matter shape. But there were other reasons than this for myth. Joyce's trick of imposing Homer's speed upon static situation is intentionally grotesque, as when, emerging from the verbal trance, the Cyclops-Citizen rises at last to throw his biscuit tin. Joyce's purpose was also ironic. His vision of unheroic Bloom in heroic posture is Swiftian, and Homer, like Gulliver's giant, pygmy, or horse, becomes an instrument for man's dissection. Since Bloom is also everyman, Odysseus, his symbol, gives Bloom a stature greater than his own. Victor Bérard's theory of the Semitic origins of the *Odyssey* provides connections with Bloom's other mythical counterparts, Jesus, Sinbad the Sailor, and the Wandering Jew. As Graves made myth modern, so Joyce with Homer's aid made the modern mythical, gave permanence to the impermanent, value and meaning to the trivial, and to the trivial the intensity of dream.

Although *Finnegans Wake* takes its frame from philosophy rather than from myth, the work is filled, as we have noticed, with fabulous matters.[15] According to Vico and Jung, Joyce's guides, these matters, filling the collective unconscious, are its expression. Joyce found his furniture among anthropologists and archæologists as well. With Jung's aid, they gave him primitive man, vestigial in our sleep. The first section of *Finnegan,* with its giants,

[14] *Dial,* November 1923. For the Homeric parallel of *Dubliners* see Richard Levin and Charles Shattuck: "First Flight to Ithaca: a New Reading of Joyce's *Dubliners," Accent,* Winter 1944.

[15] For *Finnegan* Joyce took his basic symbols from the modern myth of Finnegan (a ballad) and from the ancient myths of Finn MacCool, the Phœnix, and the dying and resurrected god. Anna Livia and the Prankquean are myths based upon old patterns.

barrows, and middens, is "antediluvious" on the whole, as "he who runes may rede." Mutt and Jute, who talk of Clontarf, are not only local historians, Irishman and Dane, and creatures of modern myth, but creatures "astoneaged," less articulate contemporaries of that other ancient Mrs. Bloom, the Great Mother. Responsive to period, Earwicker becomes Uru-Wukru, which, because of the syllable "Ur" sounds "arboriginal." References in later chapters to remote periods such as the Aurignacian bring archæology to mind, and the voice of sleep, introducing the Mookse and the Gripes, feels he need not "anthropologize" for quarreling with Lévy-Bruhl.

Commending myth, T. S. Eliot used it for *The Waste Land,* which appeared in the year of *Ulysses.* The notes, which serve the intention of felt thought (for each who read them felt he thought), express indebtedness to Frazer's *Golden Bough,* which has "influenced our generation profoundly," especially the volume on Attis, Osiris, and Adonis, and to Jessie Weston's *From Ritual to Romance* (1920), an application to medieval legend of Frazer and Harrison.[16] From these Eliot took a frame on which to hang the dubious present and show it up, not a narrative frame as of *Ulysses* but a thematic and symbolic frame. Impressed with the fertility ceremonies that might have kept a greater or a lesser man from church, and with all the dying and reborn gods, Eliot adopted those symbols (also used by Lawrence) of desert, drought, and rain which expressed for a generation, as I. A. Richards remarked, its conviction of disillusionment. The Fisher King, the ruined chapel, Parsifal, Tiresias, and Tristan, less universal and hypnotic perhaps, but no less mythical, embody

[16] Jessie Weston gave Eliot his title as well as his images of desert and water. She explains her symbols as Christian adaptations of ancient fertility symbols. In *Family Reunion* (1939) Eliot uses the myth of the Eumenides to integrate a modern situation.

Eliot's hopes or advance his themes. The brilliance of this poem comes as much from these objective correlatives of catalysis, as Eliot would put it, as from the rhythms and the tone. His later poems, *Ash Wednesday* and *Four Quartets,* which use the myth of the dying and resurrected god for decent worship, pleased another generation.

Adoring peasant and magician, Yeats labored for years to attain their condition. From peasant lips came myths for tale or ballad, and from the written cycles myths for poem and play, that by their virtue could make a man forget the times for better ones. By myth Yeats thought he could arrest that long decline from Homer's day and begin the difficult ascent to simplicity and heroism. He used Cuchulain, Fergus, and the two Cathleens of more recent origin to express country, self, and, more than these, the inexpressible. The myth was weapon, vehicle, and metaphor. It was an instrument of integration. In earlier romantics, Blake and Shelley in particular, he found example and encouragement. The synthetic myths of Blake occupied the intellect and Shelley's *Prometheus* the fancy.

On one level the synthetic myth that Yeats constructed on Blake's design, though far more geometrical than his, was intended as a frame for older myths. To fill the waiting structure of *A Vision* he read the ancients and from Frazer learned the meaning of what he learned. Yeats's Leda receives the Swan without the help of Frazer, but Mary, her parallel in "Two Songs from a Play," acts a part in the myth of dying and resurrected gods. The reference to holy Dionysus in these poems and the substance of *The Resurrection* (1934), the play from which they come, show Frazer's hand.[17] It is not surprising, therefore, that

[17] Yeats was one of the first literary men to use Frazer. In the notes to *The Wind among the Reeds* (1899) he cites *The Golden Bough;* and in the notes to *The King of the Great Clock Tower* (1934) he explains his Freudian fantasy in terms of Frazer's mother goddess and the slain god.

in Byzantium, another myth on this convenient frame, the unnatural bard sat singing on a golden bough.

This frame is circular in shape. By it Yeats intended the cyclical movement of history, each cycle of two thousand years repeating on another plane what went before. Each cycle, as we have seen, begins with a mythical conjunction of flesh and spirit. Leda and the Swan and Dove and Virgin began the cycle before ours and our own, and the next, announced in "The Second Coming," will shortly begin with one knows not what. In each cycle the happiest points are those remotest from the confusions of beginning and end. Byzantium occupied a fortunate position. Seated there on his golden bough, the bard, at once in time and out of it, sang cycling songs.

This comforting system, which explains confusion and prepares for worse before the better comes, is not original. A reference to Magnus Annus in "Two Songs from a Play" shows that Yeats had the Platonic year in mind; he knew his Blake and the works of Vico, Nietzsche, and Blavatsky, all of whom held similar doctrine. But—and this is more relevant—he knew Vergil and Shelley. "Two Songs from a Play" repeats the images and phrases of Shelley's chorus from *Hellas*. But another Argo and another Troy are also to be found in Vergil's Messianic eclogue.[18] Yeats and Shelley, with Dryden too, were employing a common tradition. The point is not the resemblance between Yeats and Shelley, but their difference. Where Shelley is diffuse, Yeats is final and intense, for Yeats, of course, was the better poet.

The doctrine of cycles to which Yeats gave the best expression is suitable for those who, loving the past, reject

[18] A passage on the Argo in the first version of "The Adoration of the Magi," a story written in the nineties, anticipates part of "Two Songs from a Play," and another passage in the same story anticipates "The Second Coming."

all notion of rectilinear progress. That this dream of modern times, dear to some Victorians and some of us, is fading is shown by the appearance among the better romantics, especially those of recent times, of cyclical pattern and of that conflict of opposites which seems to go with it. Joyce, who had learned from Vico that history repeats itself, made *Finnegan* circular. The last sentence meets the first and epicycles intricately revolve upon the Viconian ring to the clashing of Bruno's opposites. As the line of progress turned upon itself to become a circle, Lawrence, familiar with the early Greek philosophers and the Theosophists, thought at times of cycles and always of opposites. And even Eliot, esteeming Heraclitus though preferring fixity to movement, and movement within fixity to fixity, observes in "Burnt Norton" the circling boarhound and the boar, and in "East Coker," like Earwicker and Mary Queen of Scots, confuses his end with his beginning. But Aldous Huxley's Shearwater, peddling and sweating in *Antic Hay* on his stationary bicycle, is perhaps the most hopeless symbol of all.

INDEX

Index

Index

Index

Index

Index

Index

Index

Index

Index

Index